FAIRY TAIL: ICE TRAIL

1

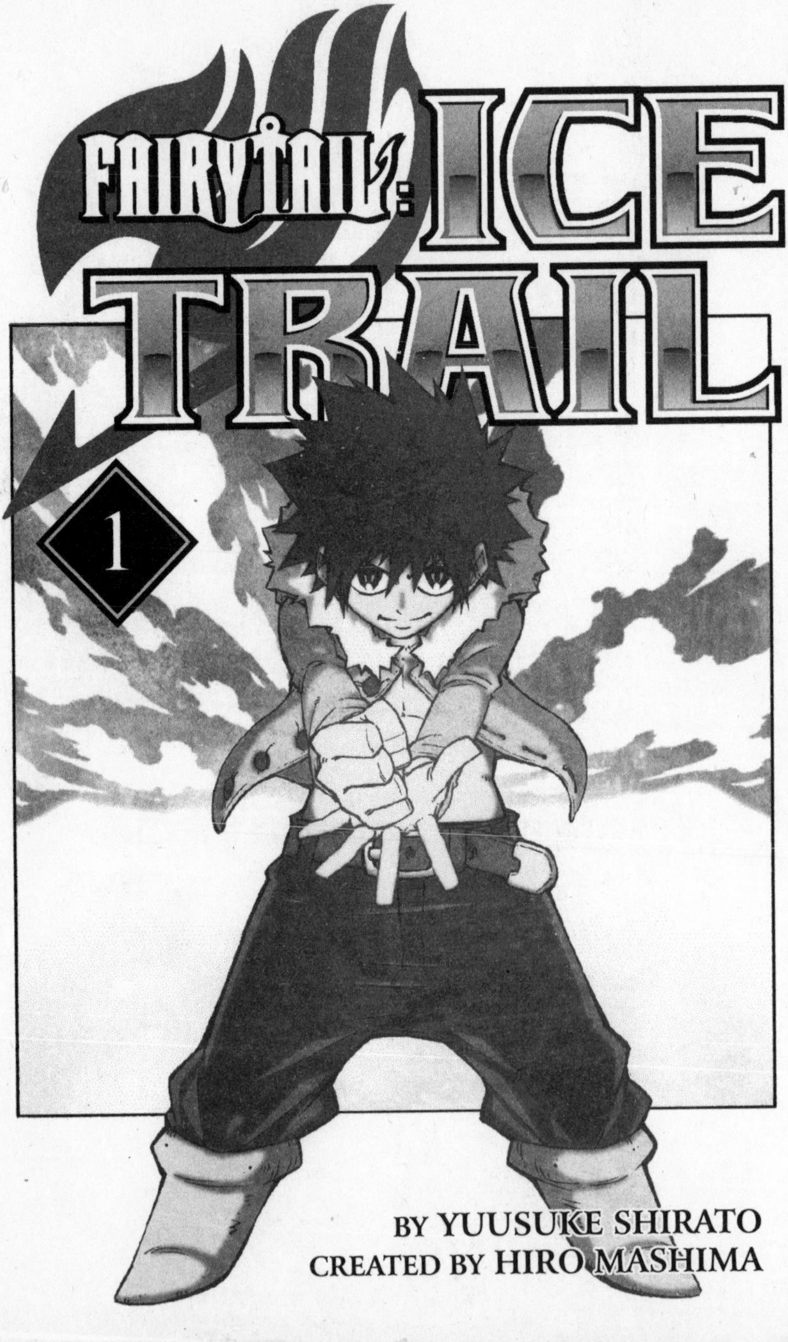

BY YUUSUKE SHIRATO
CREATED BY HIRO MASHIMA

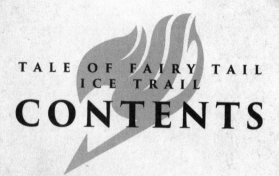

TALE OF FAIRY TAIL
ICE TRAIL
CONTENTS

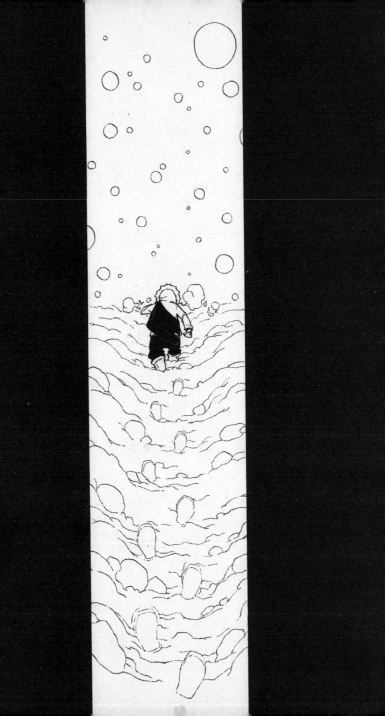

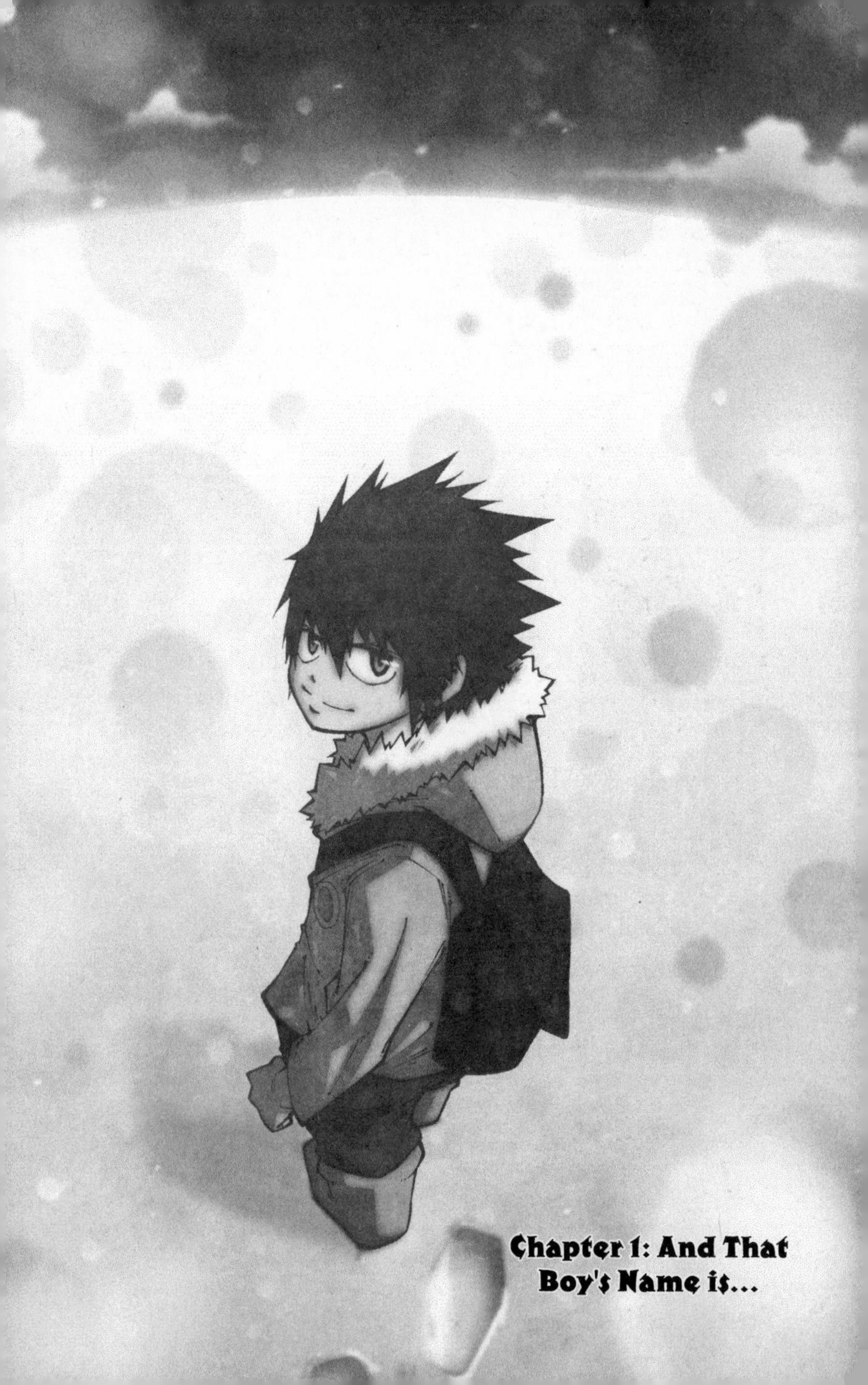

Chapter 1: And That Boy's Name is...

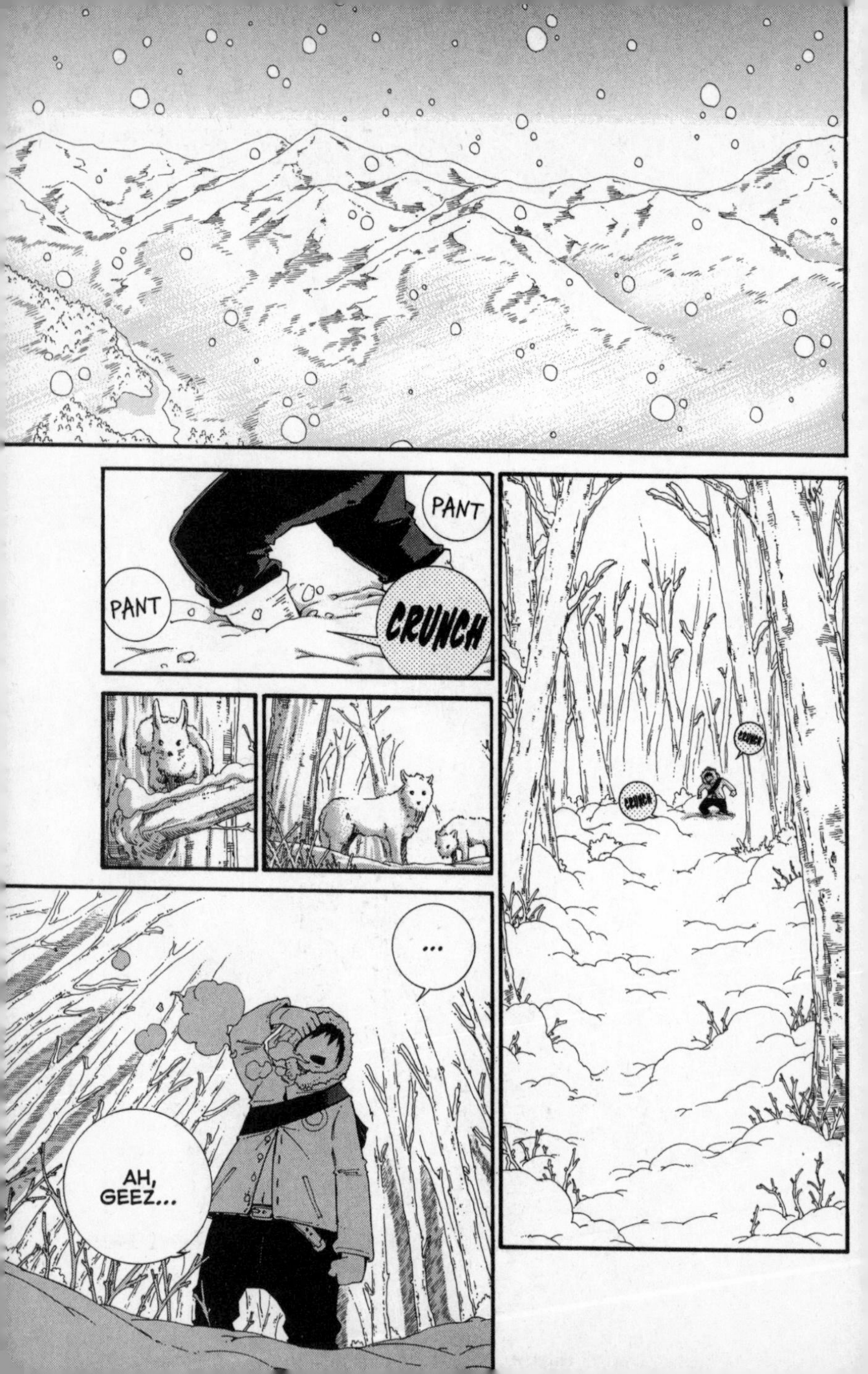
CRUNCH
CRUNCH
PANT
PANT
CRUNCH
...
AH, GEEZ...

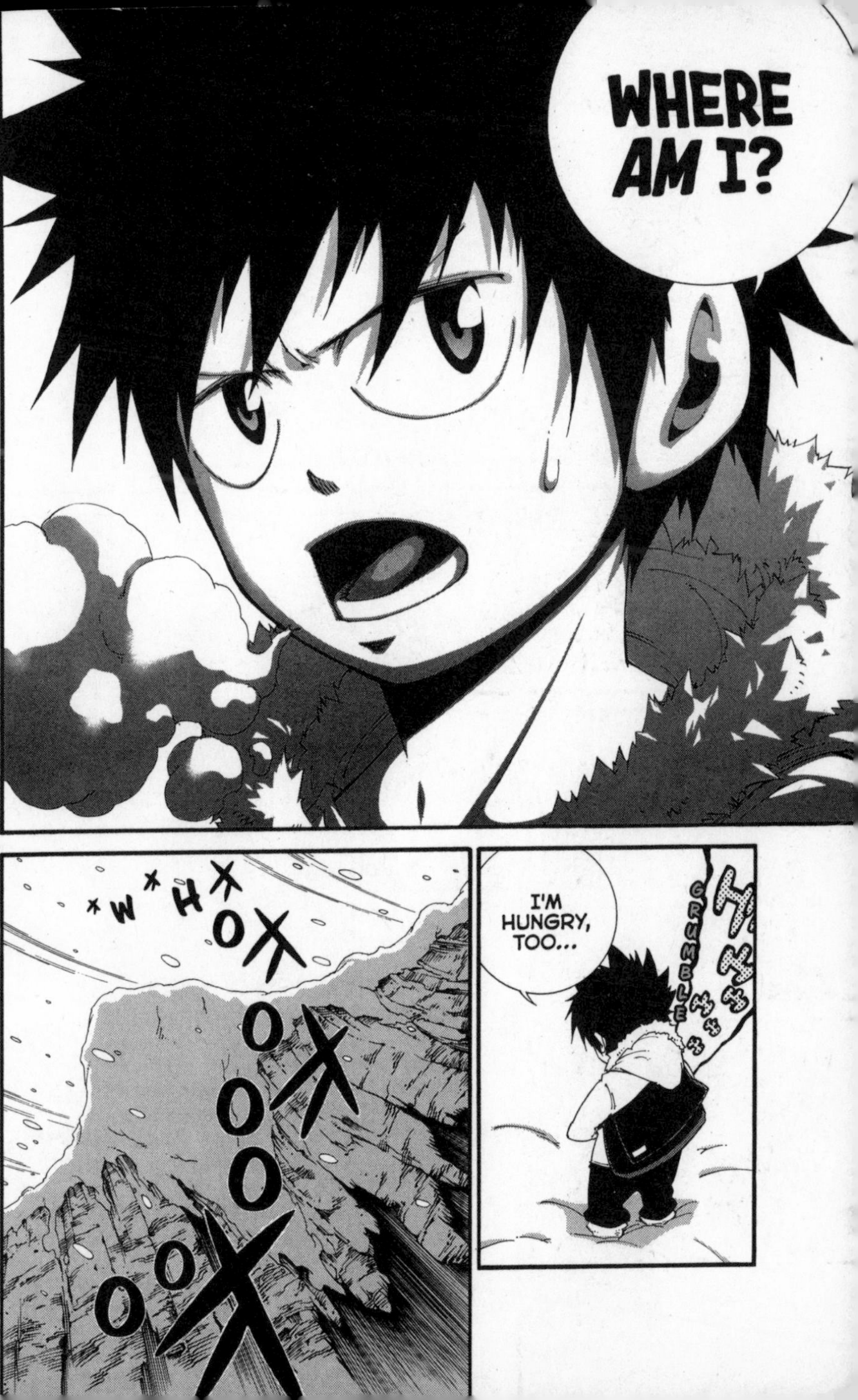
WHERE AM I?
I'M HUNGRY, TOO...
GRUMBLE
WHOOOOOO

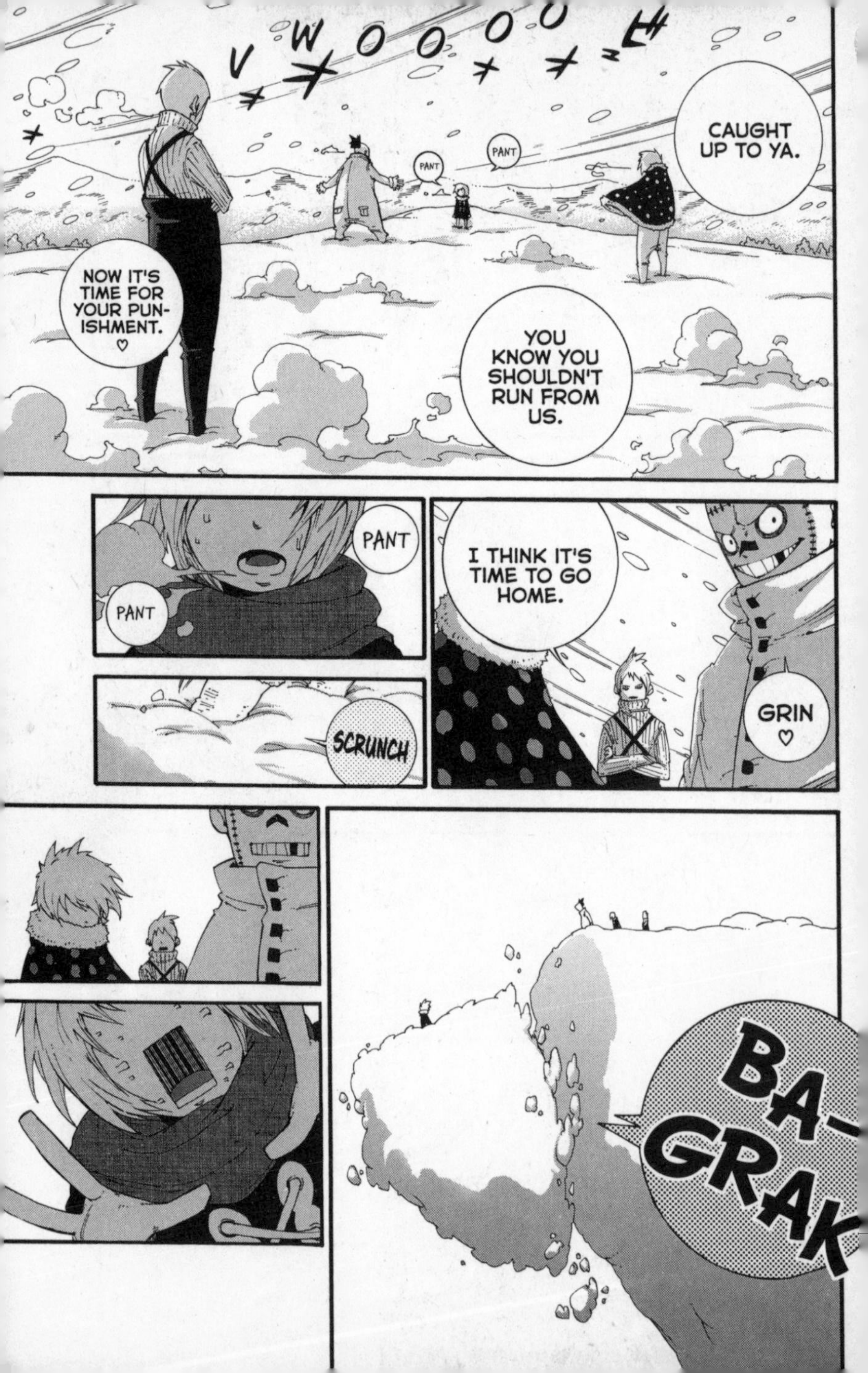
VWOOOOH
CAUGHT UP TO YA.
PANT
PANT
YOU KNOW YOU SHOULDN'T RUN FROM US.
NOW IT'S TIME FOR YOUR PUN-ISHMENT. ♡
I THINK IT'S TIME TO GO HOME.
GRIN ♡
PANT
PANT
SCRUNCH
BA-GRAK

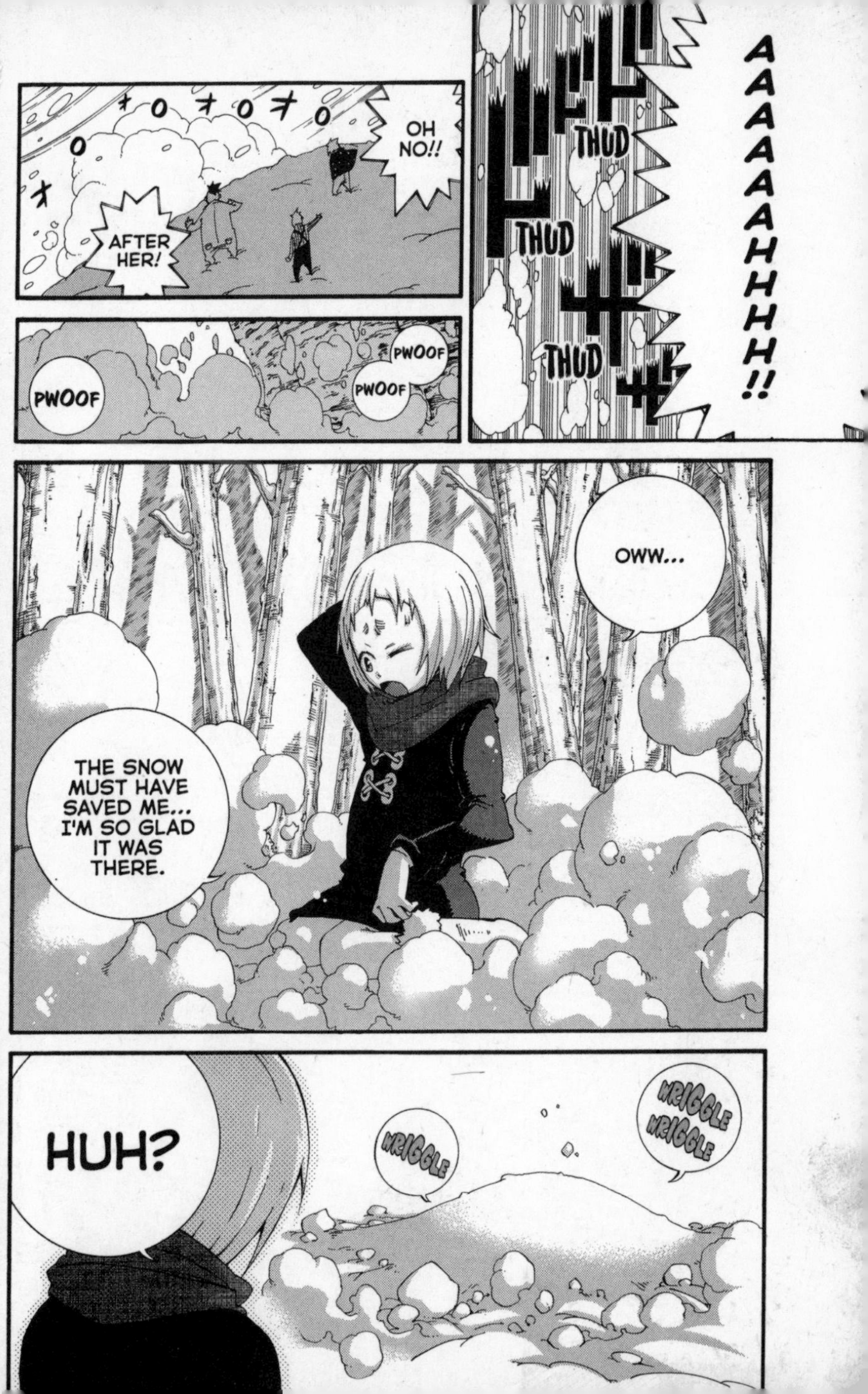
AAAAAAHHHH!!
THUD
THUD
THUD
OH NO!!
AFTER HER!
PWOOF
PWOOF
PWOOF
OWW...
THE SNOW MUST HAVE SAVED ME... I'M SO GLAD IT WAS THERE.
WRIGGLE WRIGGLE
WRIGGLE
HUH?

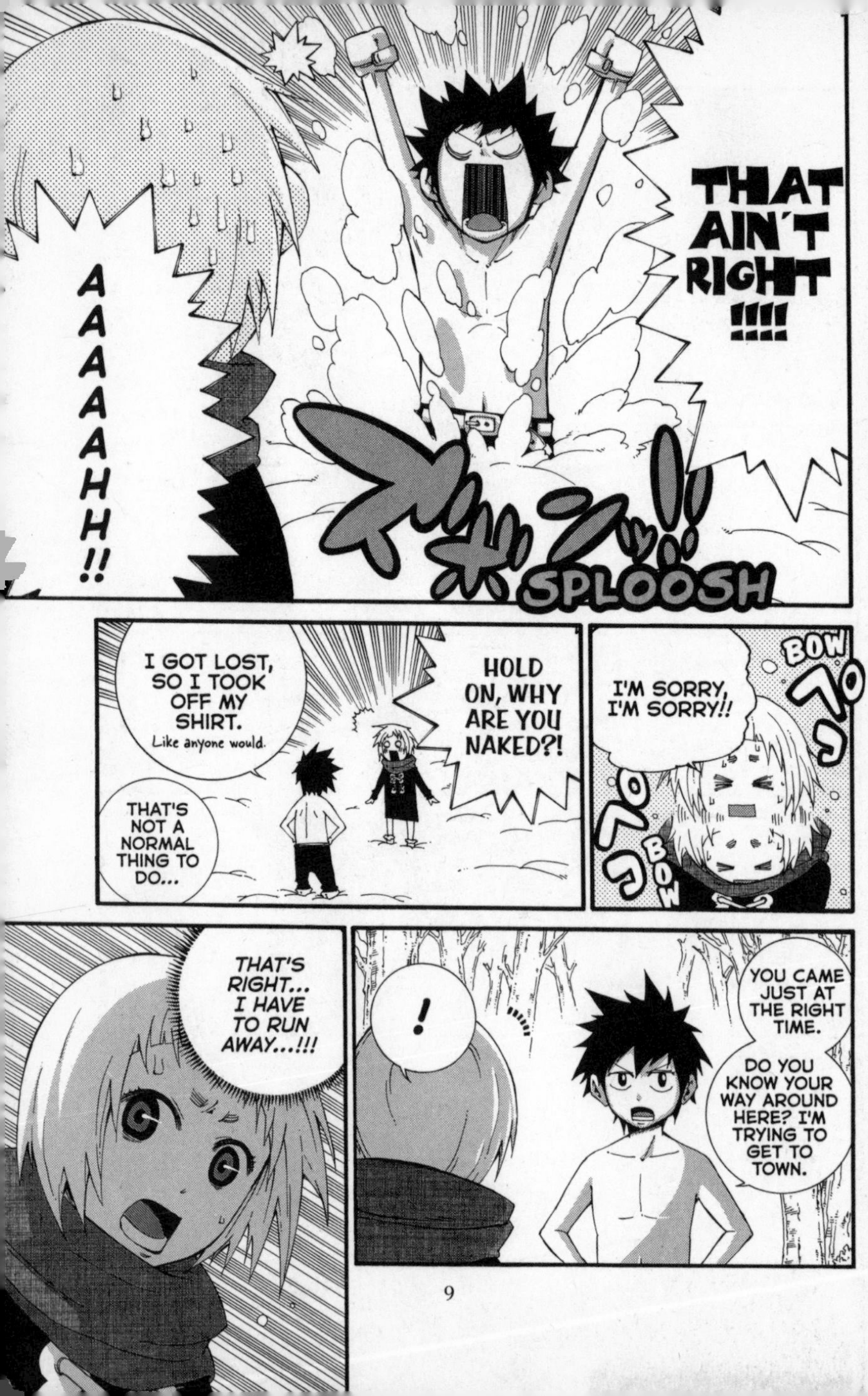
THAT AIN'T RIGHT!!!!
AAAAAAAHH!!
SPLOOSH
I'M SORRY, I'M SORRY!!
BOW
BOW
HOLD ON, WHY ARE YOU NAKED?!
I GOT LOST, SO I TOOK OFF MY SHIRT. Like anyone would.
THAT'S NOT A NORMAL THING TO DO...
YOU CAME JUST AT THE RIGHT TIME.
DO YOU KNOW YOUR WAY AROUND HERE? I'M TRYING TO GET TO TOWN.
!
THAT'S RIGHT... I HAVE TO RUN AWAY...!!!

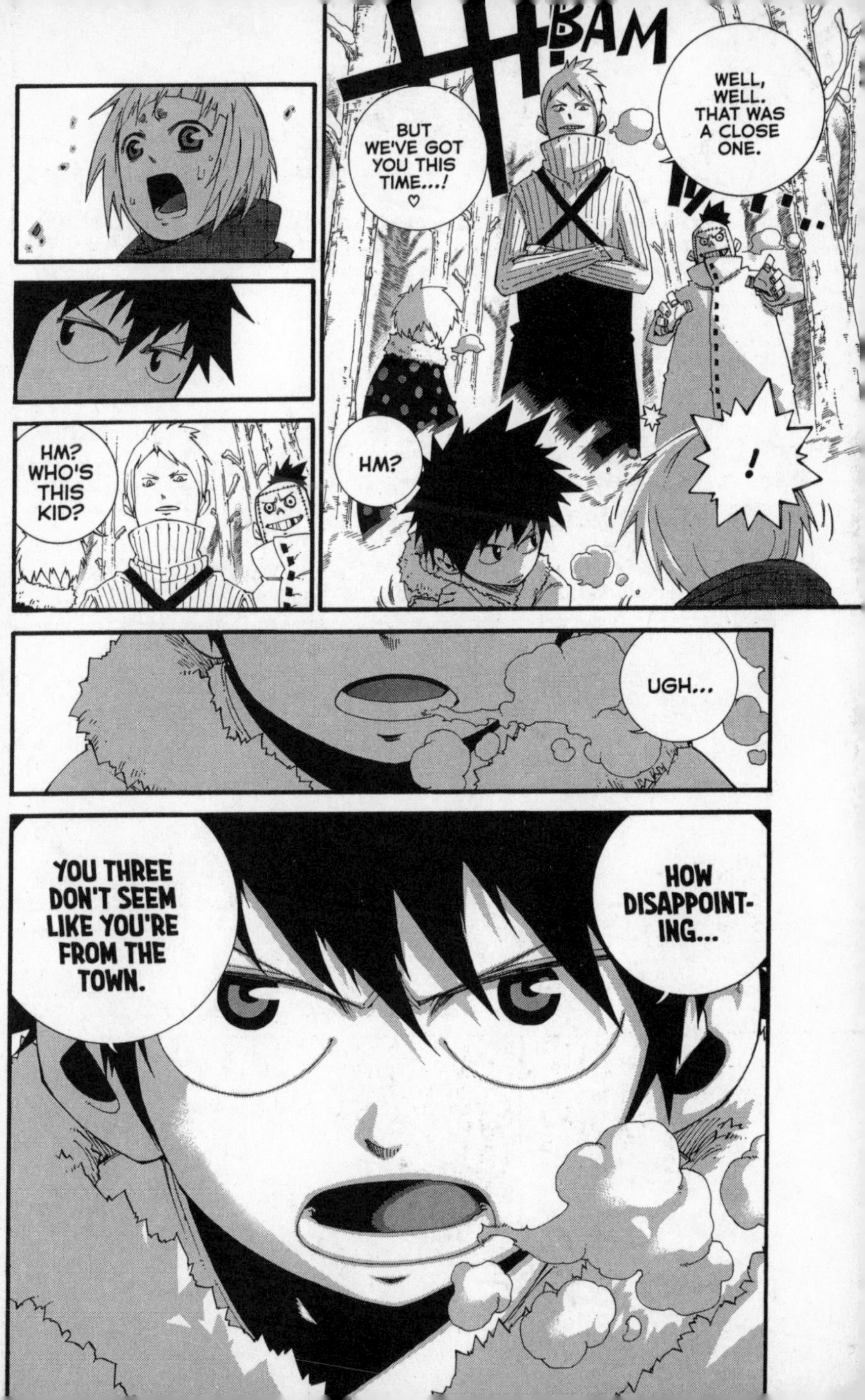
BAM
WELL, WELL. THAT WAS A CLOSE ONE.
BUT WE'VE GOT YOU THIS TIME...! ♡
HM?
!
HM? WHO'S THIS KID?
UGH...
HOW DISAPPOINT-ING...
YOU THREE DON'T SEEM LIKE YOU'RE FROM THE TOWN.

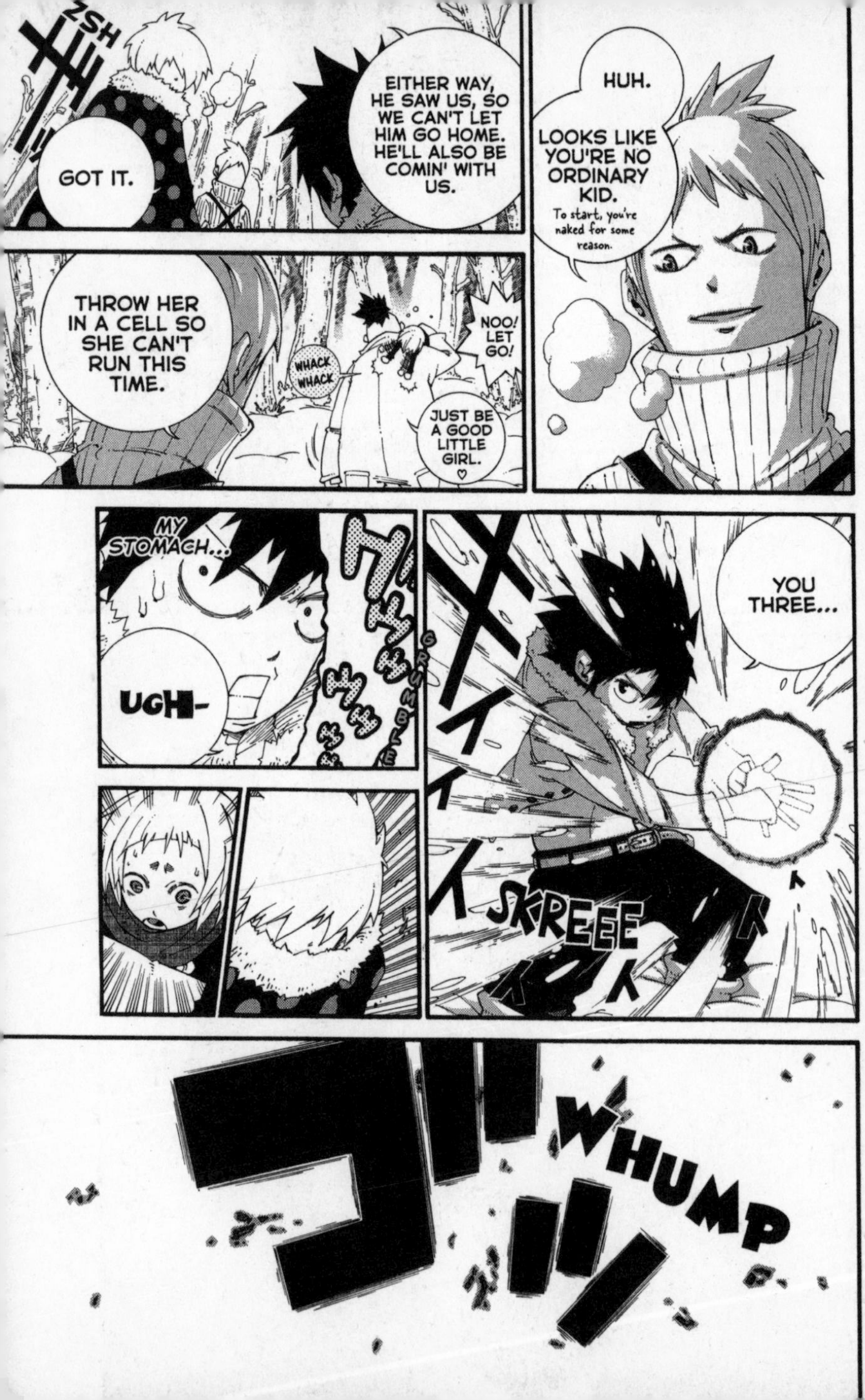
HUH.
LOOKS LIKE YOU'RE NO ORDINARY KID.
To start, you're naked for some reason.
EITHER WAY, HE SAW US, SO WE CAN'T LET HIM GO HOME. HE'LL ALSO BE COMIN' WITH US.
ZSH
GOT IT.
THROW HER IN A CELL SO SHE CAN'T RUN THIS TIME.
NOO! LET GO!
WHACK WHACK
JUST BE A GOOD LITTLE GIRL. ♡
YOU THREE...
SKREEE
MY STOMACH...
UGH-
GRUMBLE
WHUMP

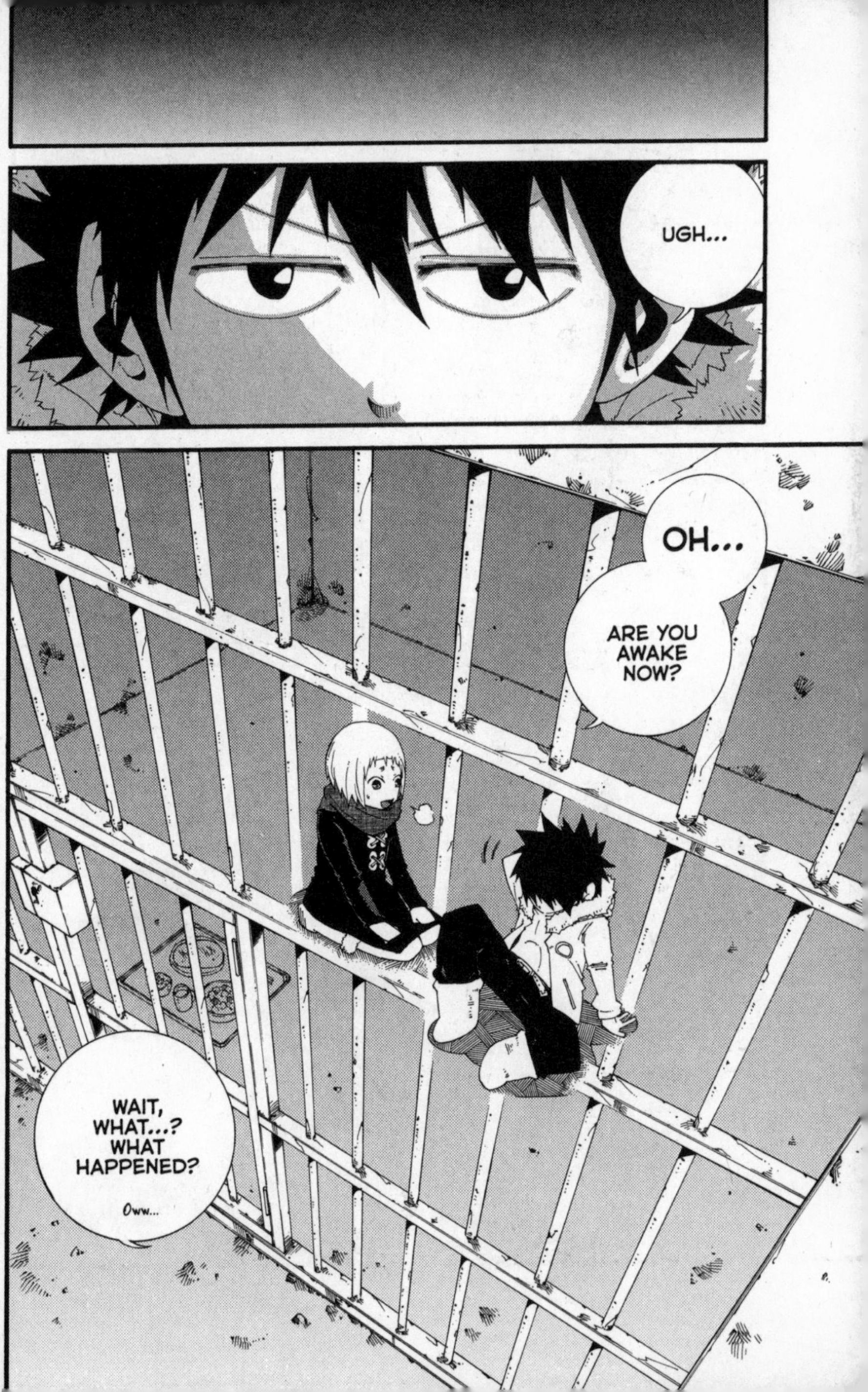
UGH...
OH...
ARE YOU AWAKE NOW?
WAIT, WHAT...? WHAT HAPPENED?
Oww...

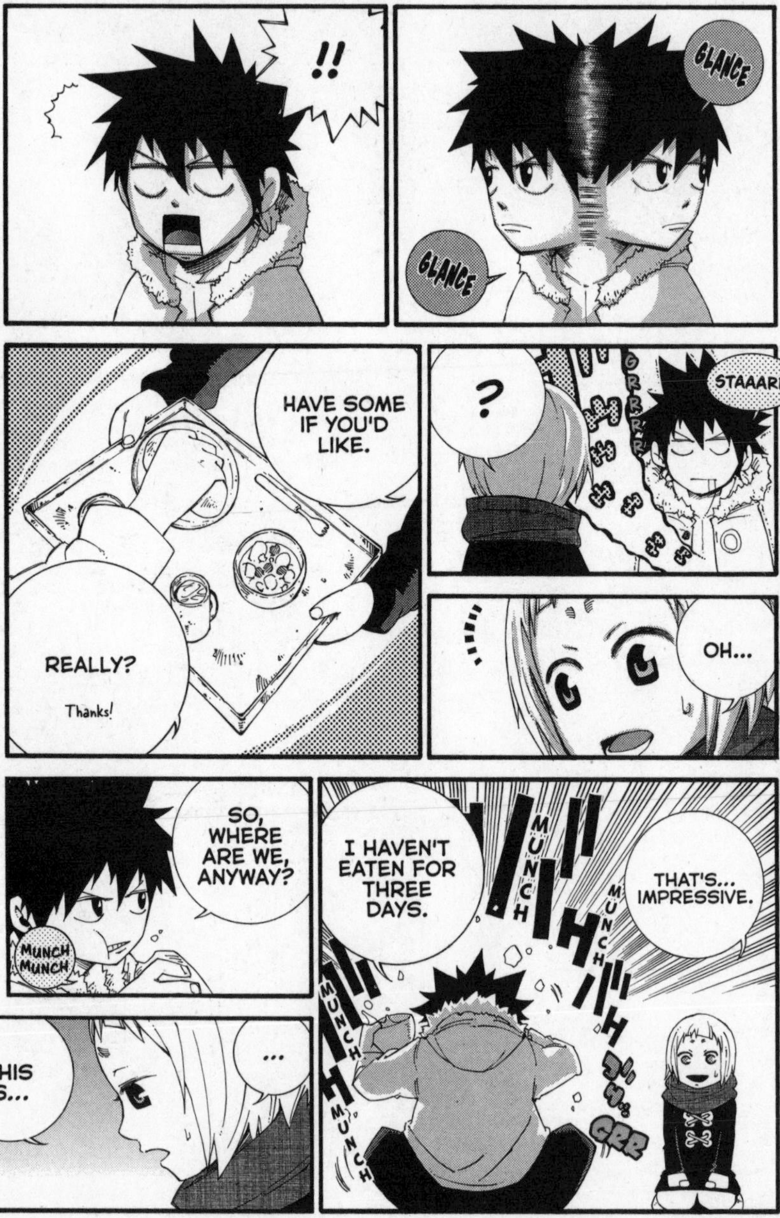
GLANCE
GLANCE
!!
STAAARE
GRRRR
?
OH...
HAVE SOME IF YOU'D LIKE.
REALLY?
Thanks!
I HAVEN'T EATEN FOR THREE DAYS.
THAT'S... IMPRESSIVE.
MUNCH
MUNCH
MUNCH
MUNCH
GRR
SO, WHERE ARE WE, ANYWAY?
MUNCH MUNCH
...
THIS IS...

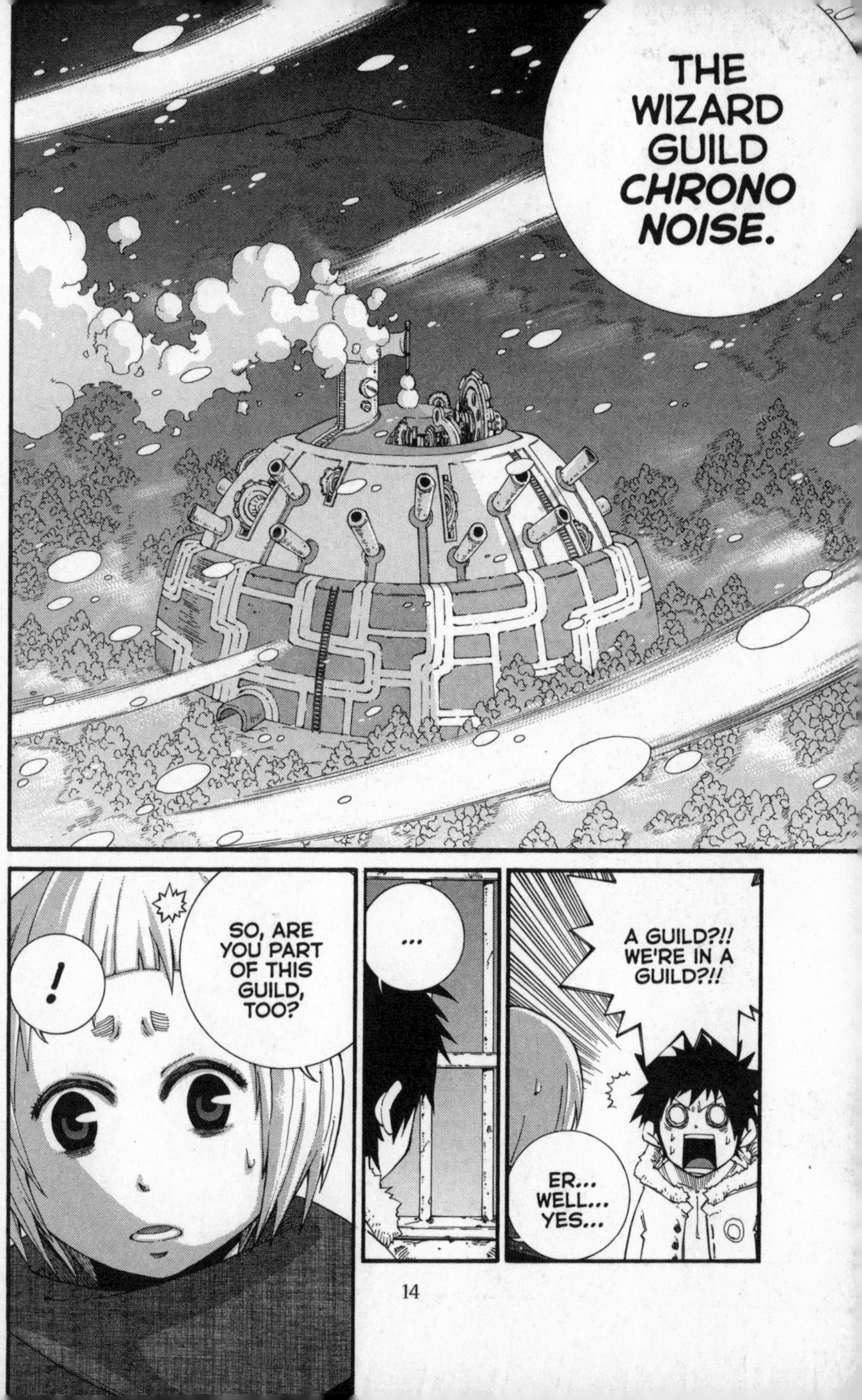
THE WIZARD GUILD CHRONO NOISE.
A GUILD?!! WE'RE IN A GUILD?!!
ER... WELL... YES...
...
SO, ARE YOU PART OF THIS GUILD, TOO?
!

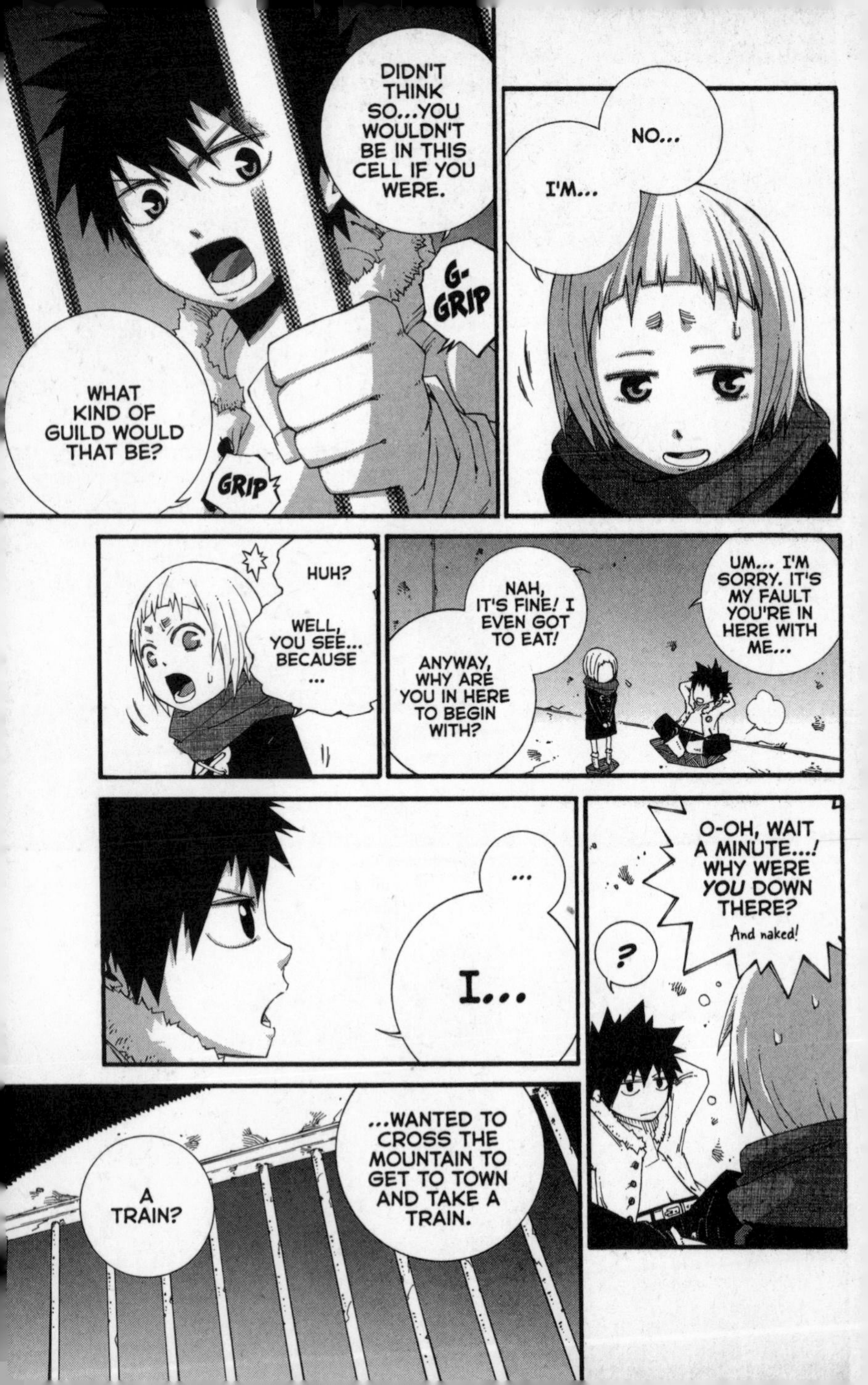
NO...
I'M...
DIDN'T THINK SO...YOU WOULDN'T BE IN THIS CELL IF YOU WERE.
G-GRIP
WHAT KIND OF GUILD WOULD THAT BE?
GRIP
UM... I'M SORRY. IT'S MY FAULT YOU'RE IN HERE WITH ME...
NAH, IT'S FINE! I EVEN GOT TO EAT!
ANYWAY, WHY ARE YOU IN HERE TO BEGIN WITH?
HUH?
WELL, YOU SEE... BECAUSE ...
O-OH, WAIT A MINUTE...! WHY WERE *YOU* DOWN THERE?
And naked!
?
...
I...
...WANTED TO CROSS THE MOUNTAIN TO GET TO TOWN AND TAKE A TRAIN.
A TRAIN?

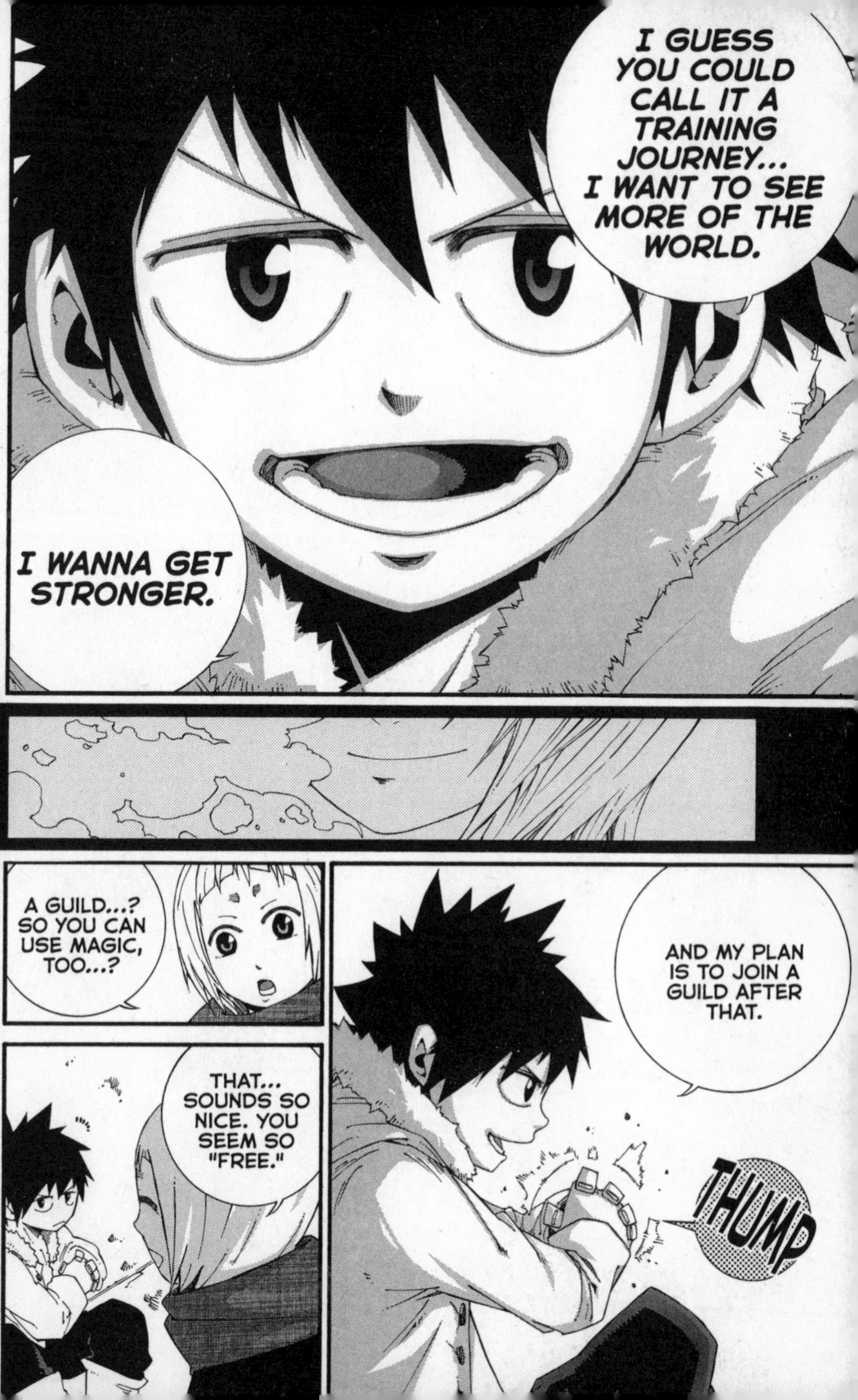
I GUESS YOU COULD CALL IT A TRAINING JOURNEY... I WANT TO SEE MORE OF THE WORLD.
I WANNA GET STRONGER.
AND MY PLAN IS TO JOIN A GUILD AFTER THAT.
THUMP
A GUILD...? SO YOU CAN USE MAGIC, TOO...?
THAT... SOUNDS SO NICE. YOU SEEM SO "FREE."

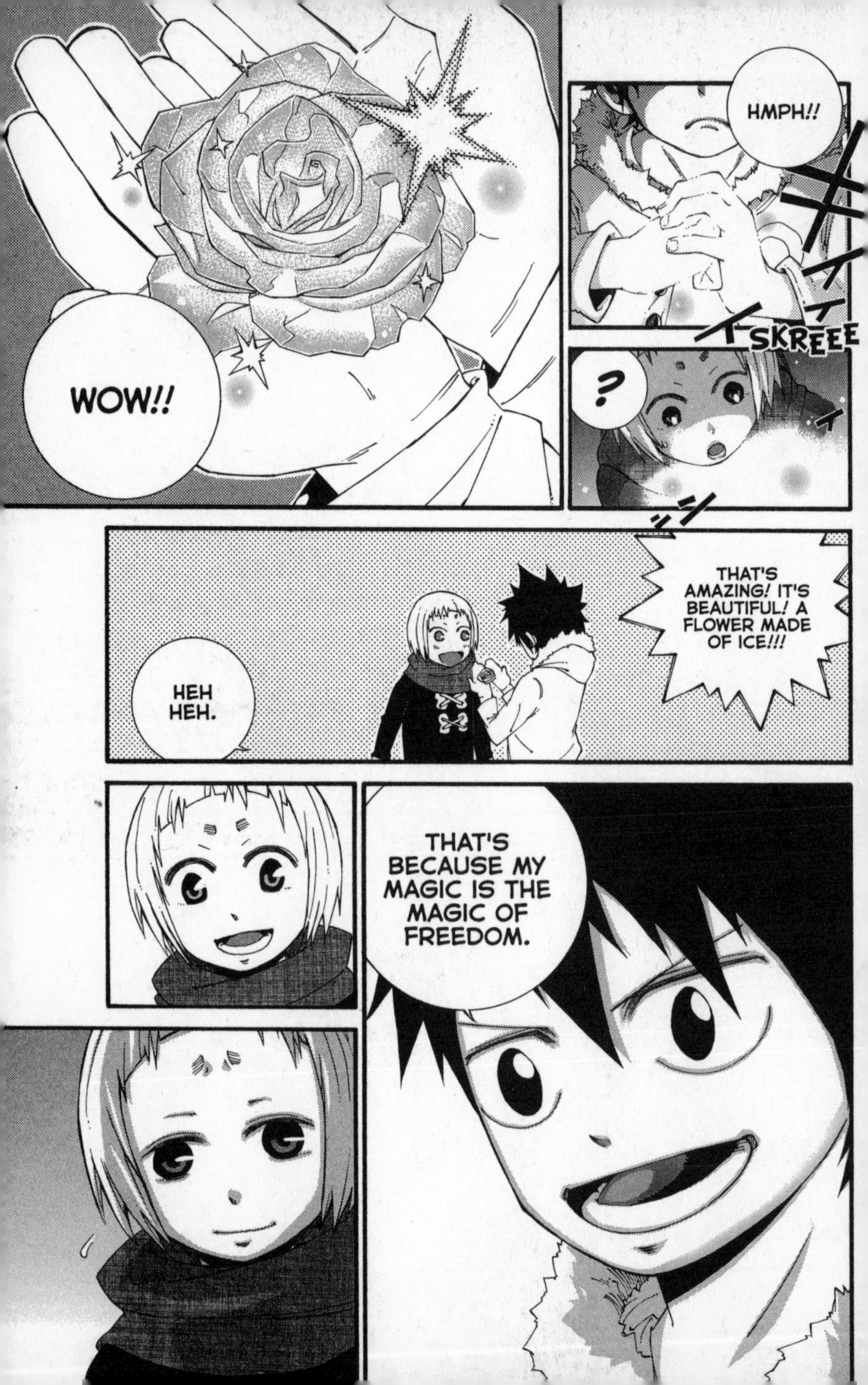
HMPH!!
SKREEE
?
WOW!!
THAT'S AMAZING! IT'S BEAUTIFUL! A FLOWER MADE OF ICE!!!
HEH HEH.
THAT'S BECAUSE MY MAGIC IS THE MAGIC OF FREEDOM.

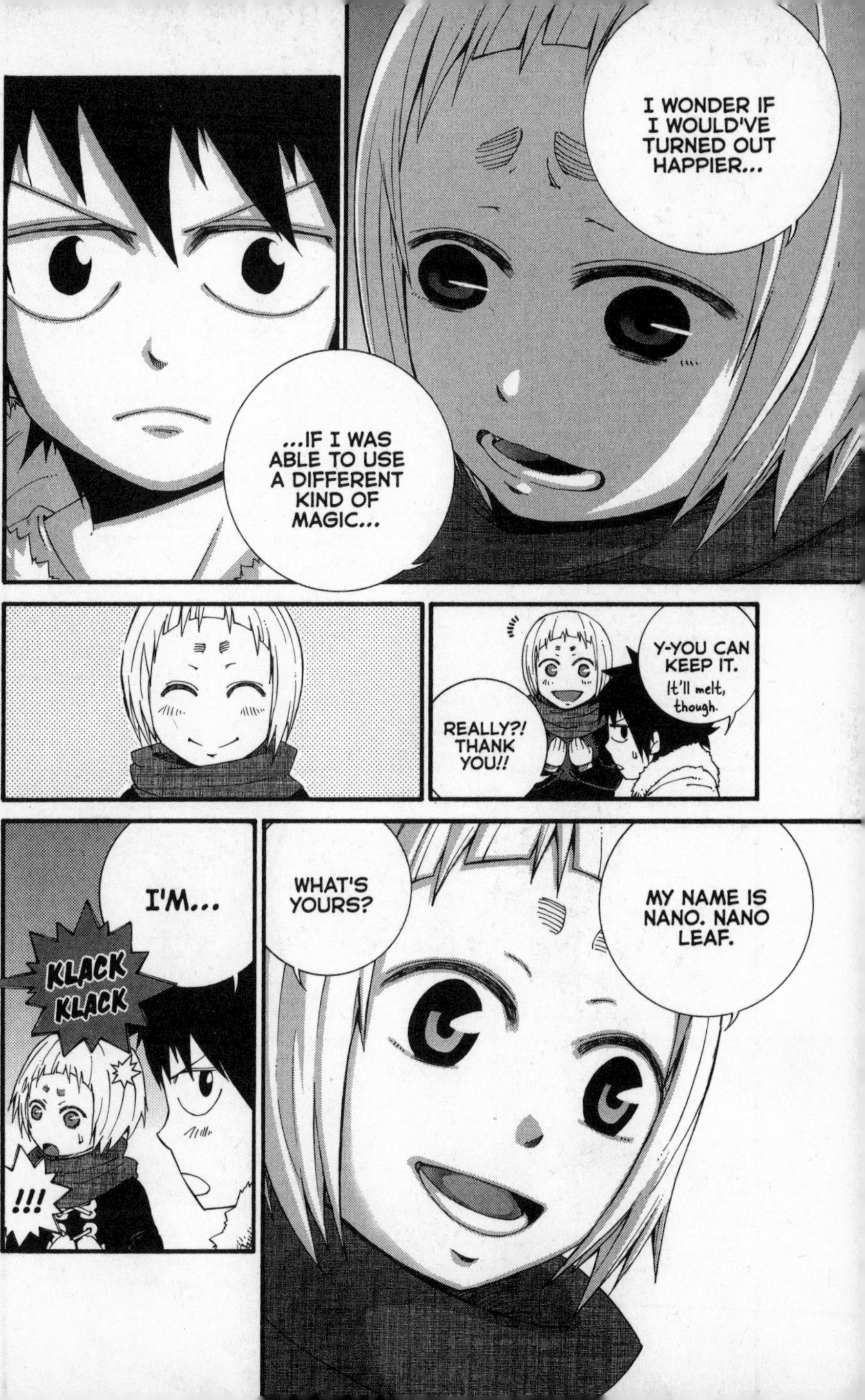
I WONDER IF I WOULD'VE TURNED OUT HAPPIER...
...IF I WAS ABLE TO USE A DIFFERENT KIND OF MAGIC...
Y-YOU CAN KEEP IT. It'll melt, though.
REALLY?! THANK YOU!!
MY NAME IS NANO. NANO LEAF.
WHAT'S YOURS?
I'M...
KLACK KLACK
!!!

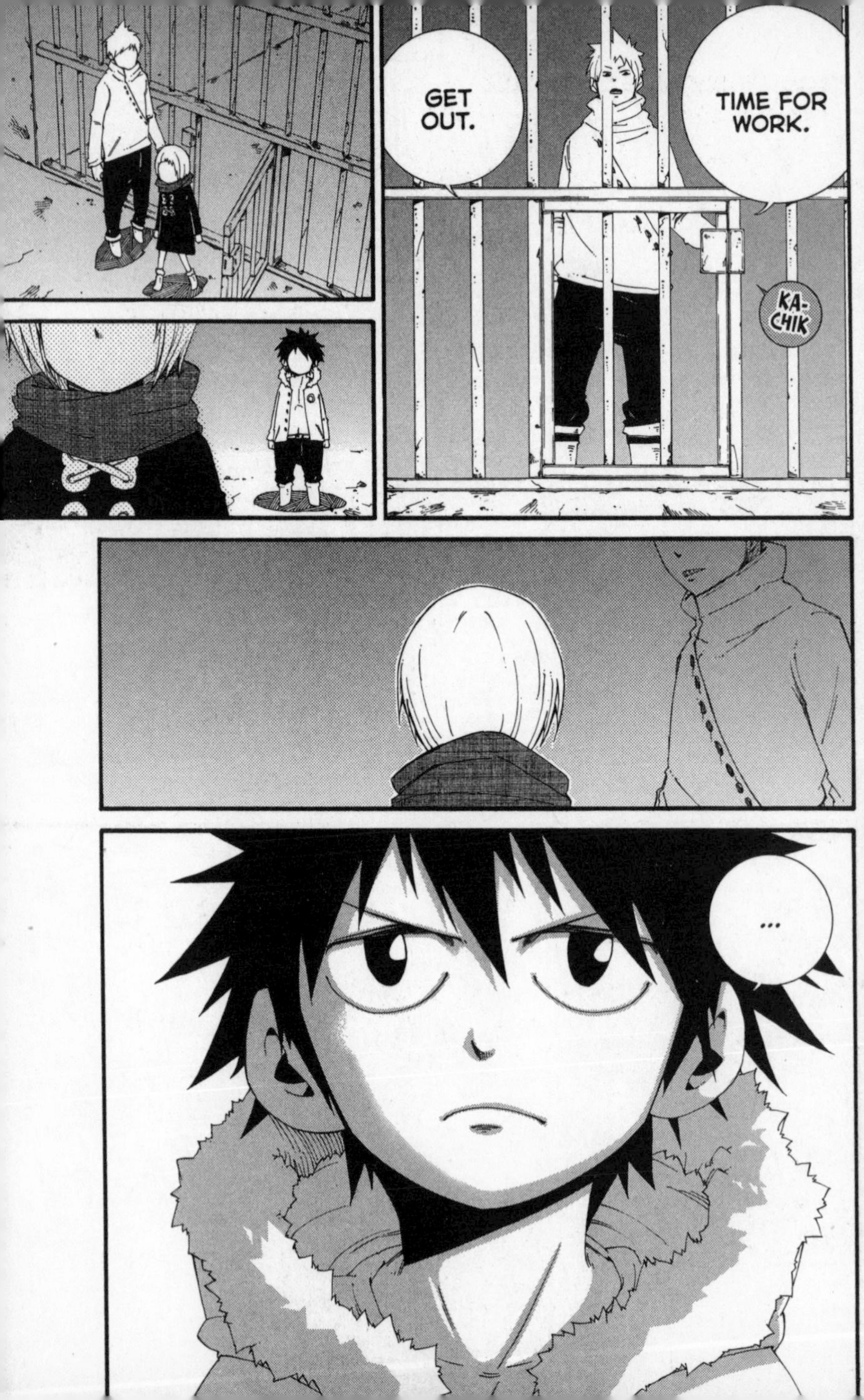
TIME FOR WORK.
GET OUT.
KA-CHIK
...

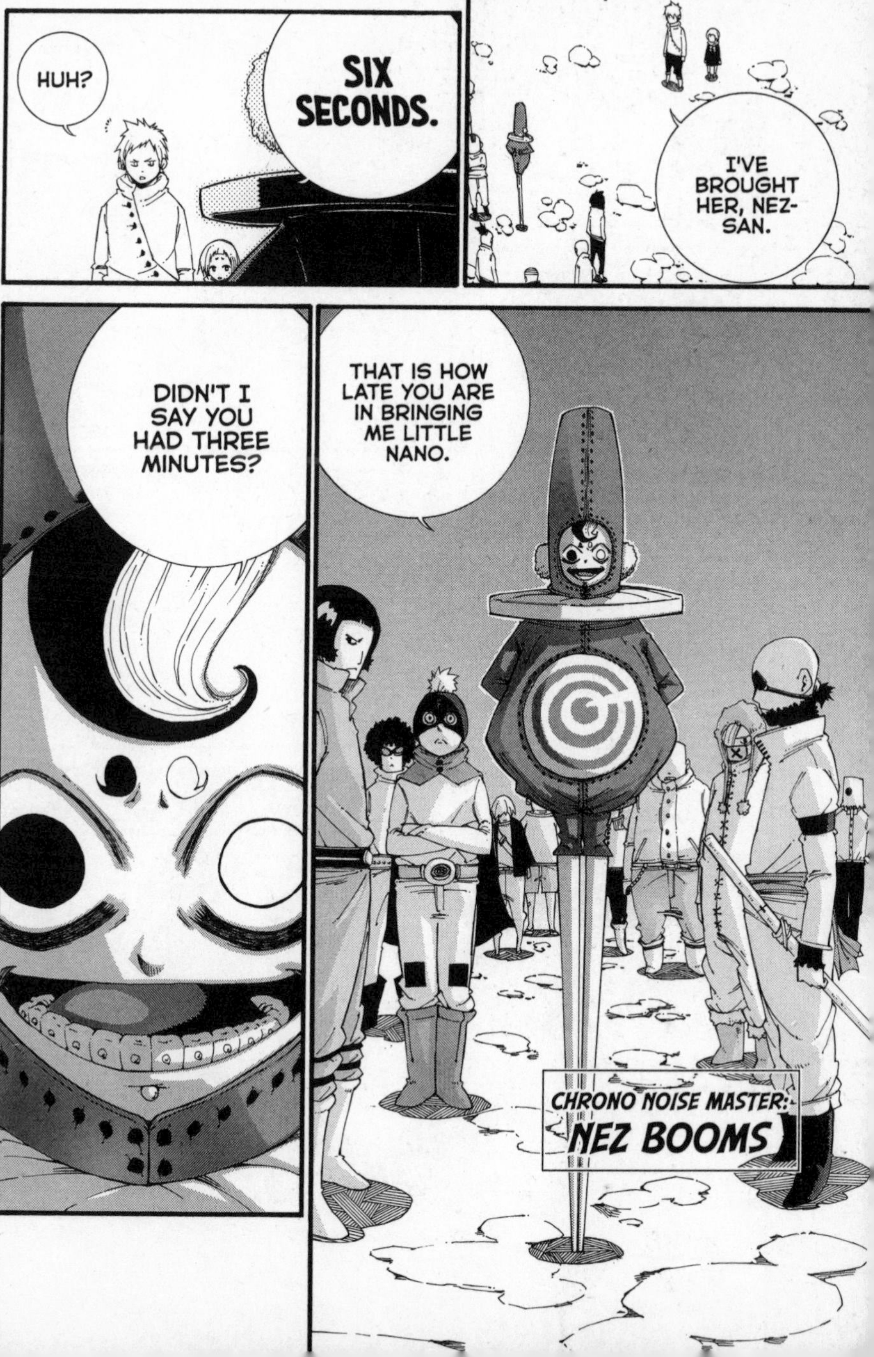
I'VE BROUGHT HER, NEZ-SAN.
SIX SECONDS.
HUH?
THAT IS HOW LATE YOU ARE IN BRINGING ME LITTLE NANO.
CHRONO NOISE MASTER: NEZ BOOMS
DIDN'T I SAY YOU HAD THREE MINUTES?

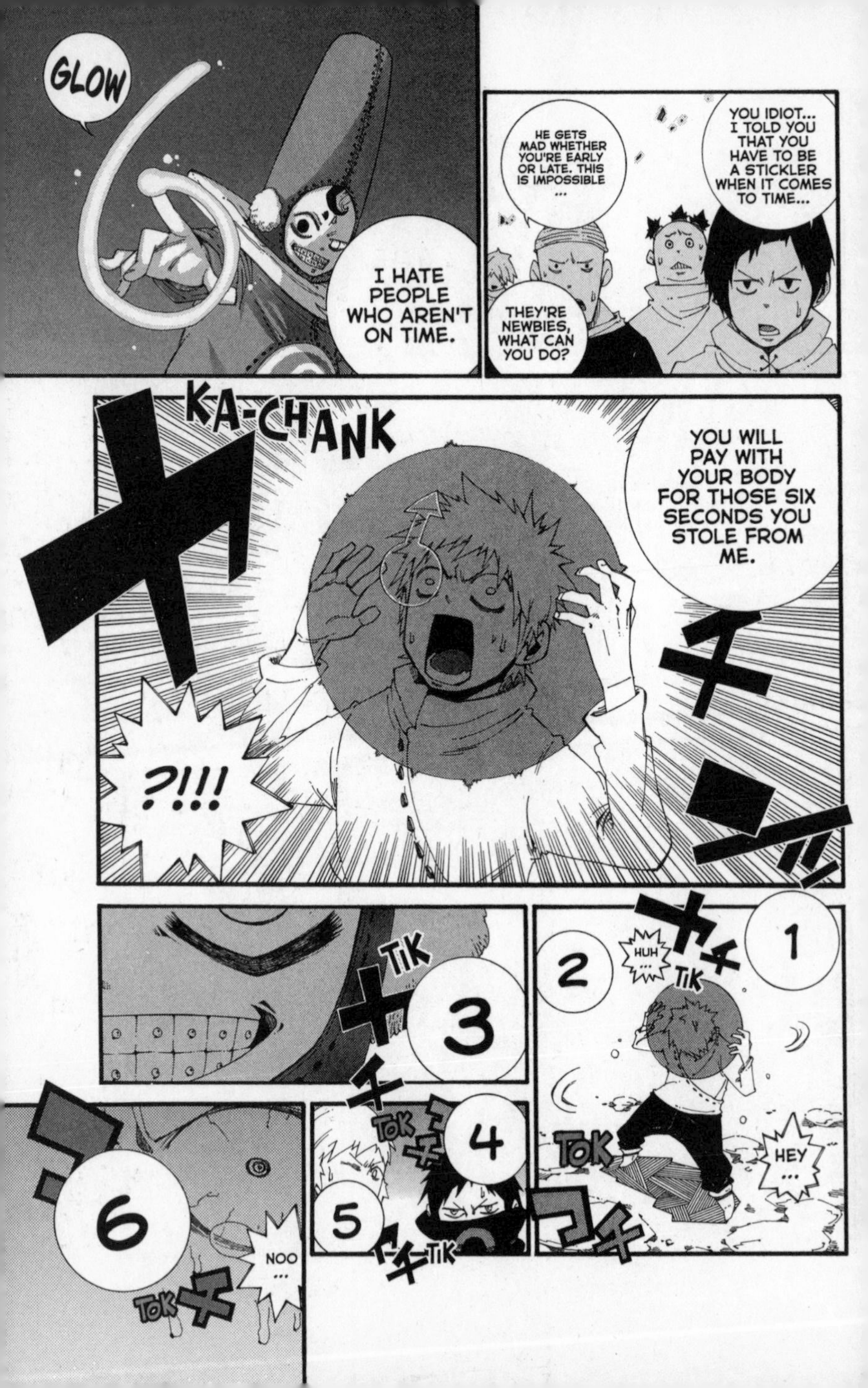
YOU IDIOT... I TOLD YOU THAT YOU HAVE TO BE A STICKLER WHEN IT COMES TO TIME...
HE GETS MAD WHETHER YOU'RE EARLY OR LATE. THIS IS IMPOSSIBLE ...
THEY'RE NEWBIES, WHAT CAN YOU DO?
GLOW
I HATE PEOPLE WHO AREN'T ON TIME.
YOU WILL PAY WITH YOUR BODY FOR THOSE SIX SECONDS YOU STOLE FROM ME.
KA-CHANK
?!!!
1
HUH ...
TIK
2
TOK
HEY ...
TIK
3
TOK
4
5
TIK
6
NOO ...
TOK

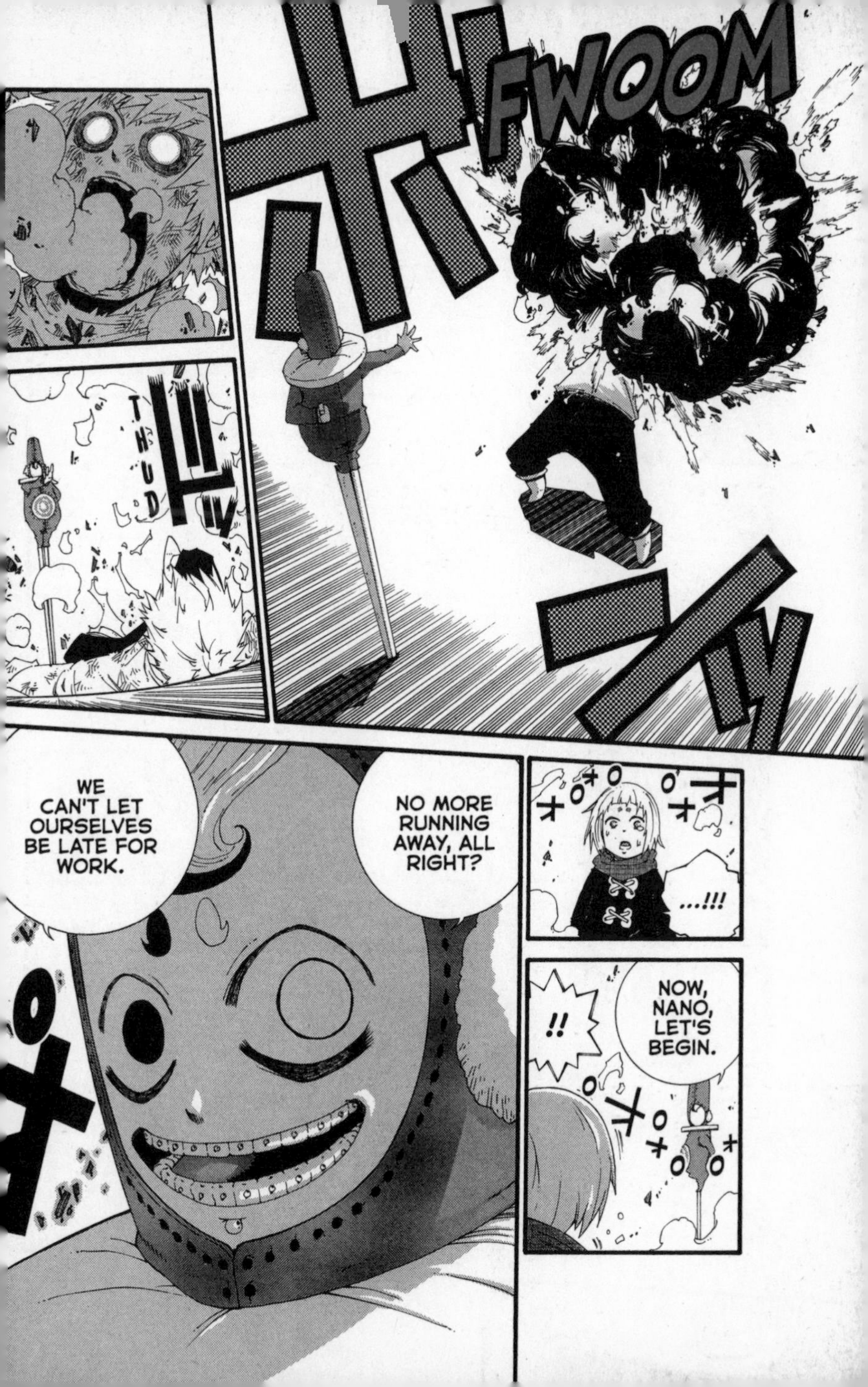
FWOOM
THUD
...!!!
NOW, NANO, LET'S BEGIN.
!!
NO MORE RUNNING AWAY, ALL RIGHT?
WE CAN'T LET OURSELVES BE LATE FOR WORK.

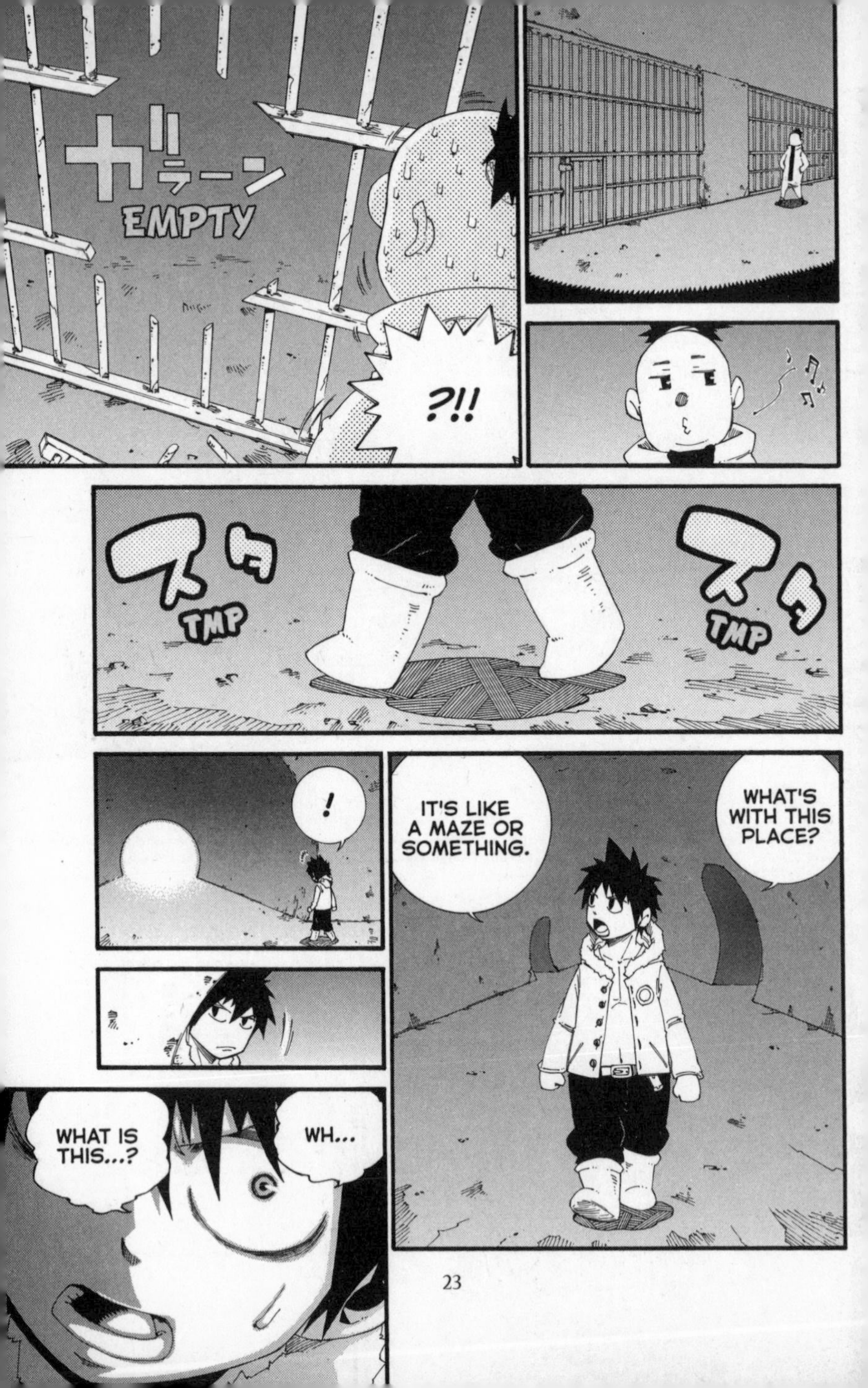
カラーン
EMPTY
?!!
スッ
TMP
スッ
TMP
WHAT'S WITH THIS PLACE?
IT'S LIKE A MAZE OR SOMETHING.
!
WH...
WHAT IS THIS...?

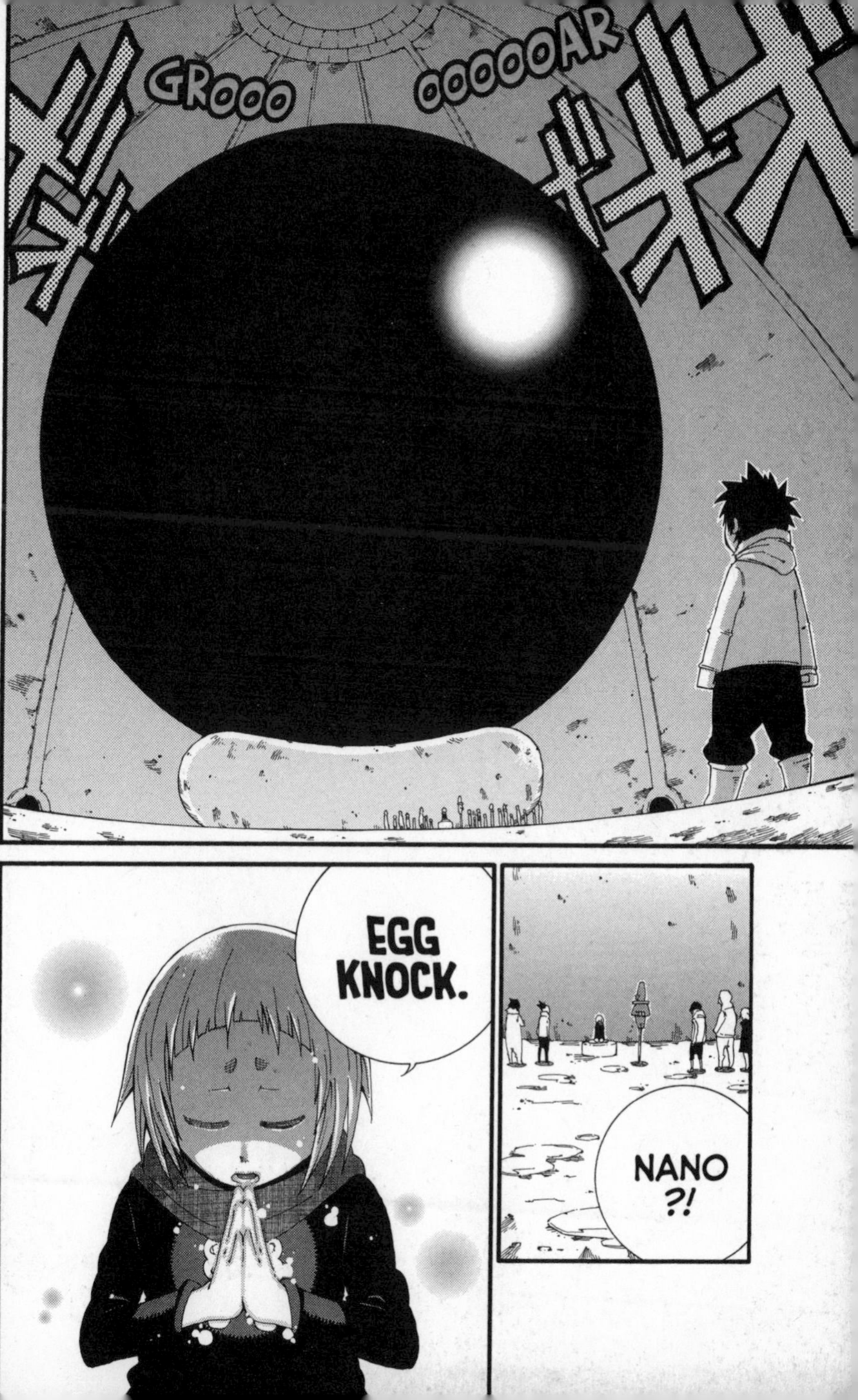
GROOO OOOOOOAR
NANO ?!
EGG KNOCK.

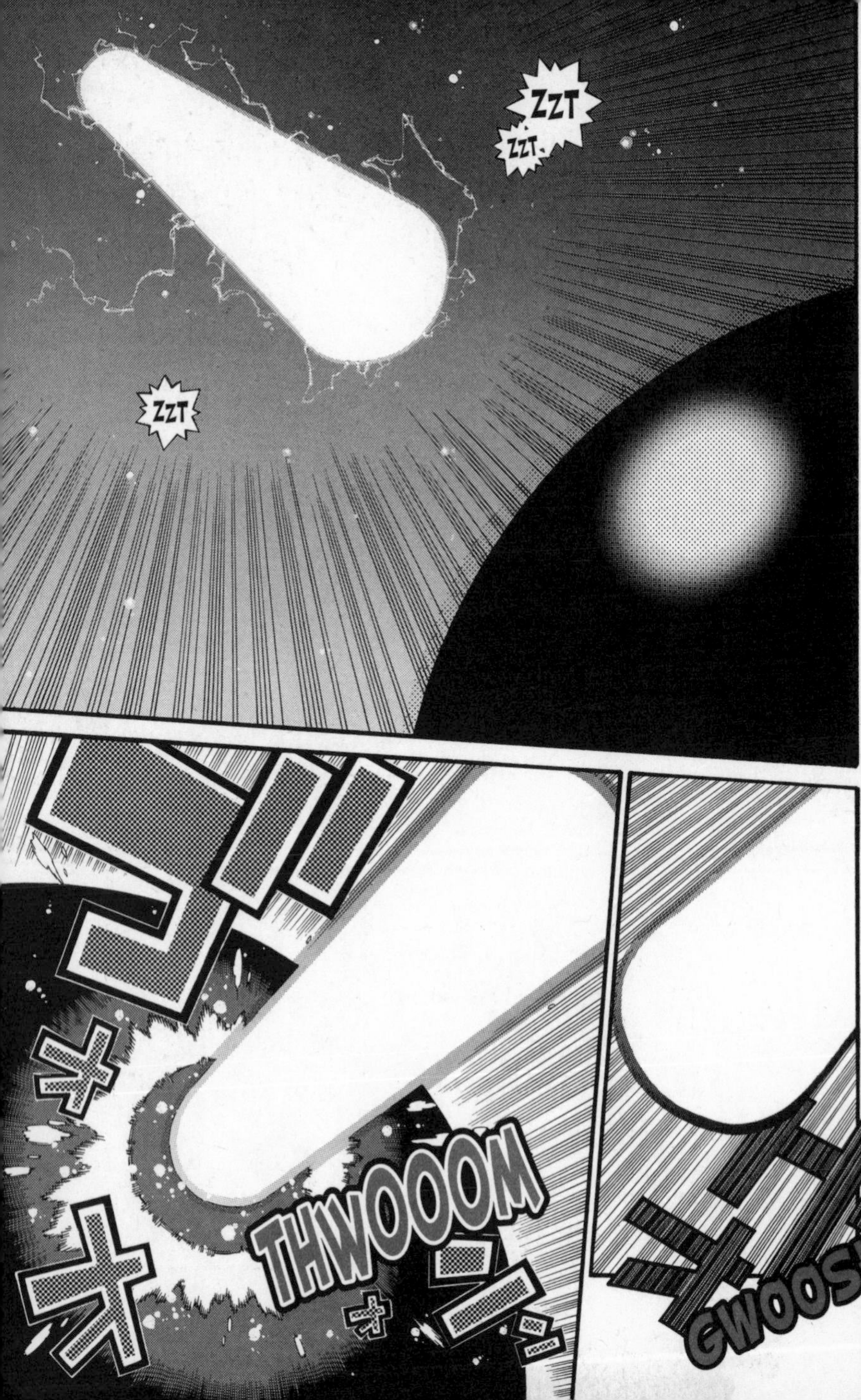
ZZT
ZZT.
ZZT
GWOOS
THWOOOM

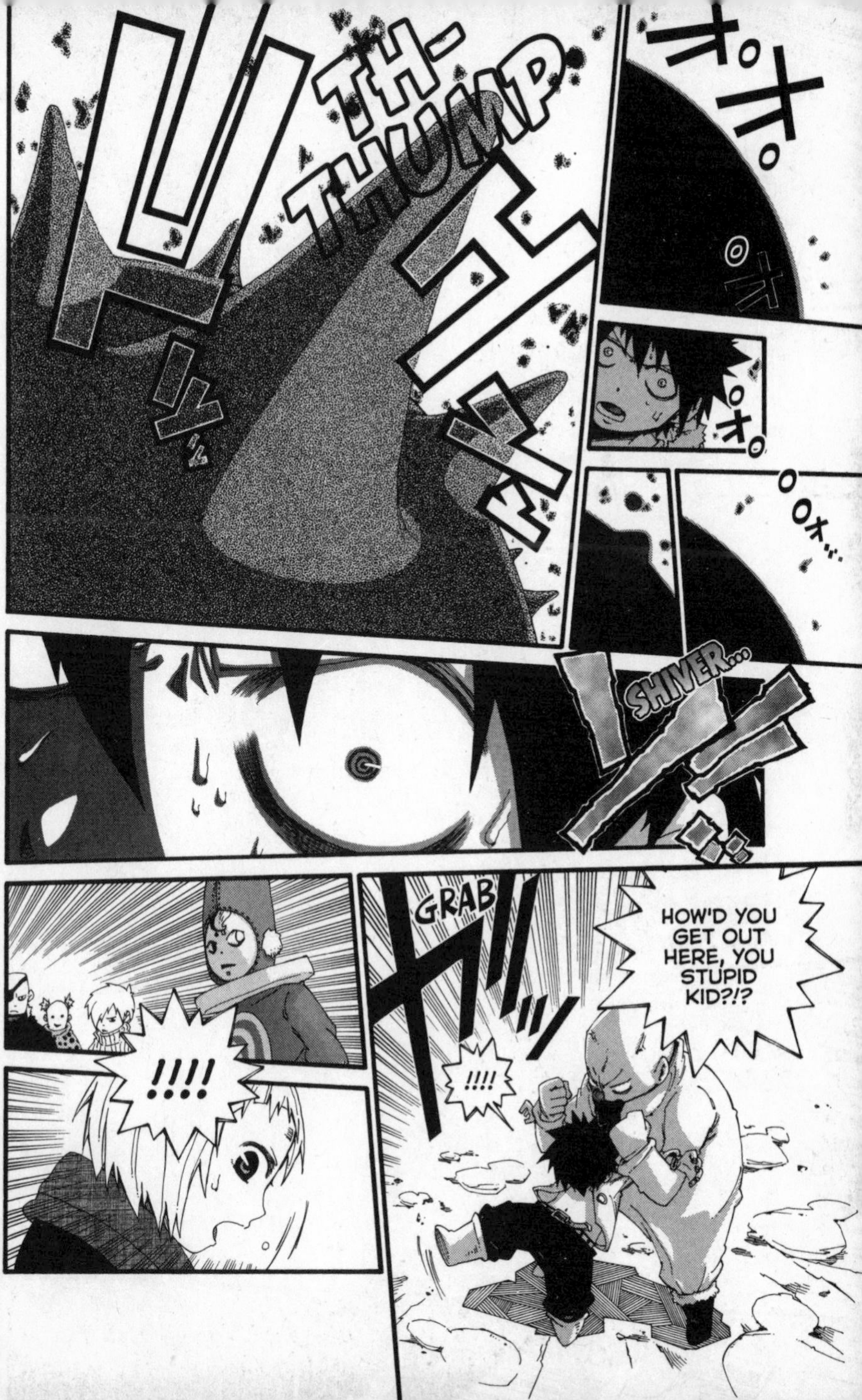
TH-THUMP
SHIVER...
GRAB
HOW'D YOU GET OUT HERE, YOU STUPID KID?!?
!!!!
!!!!

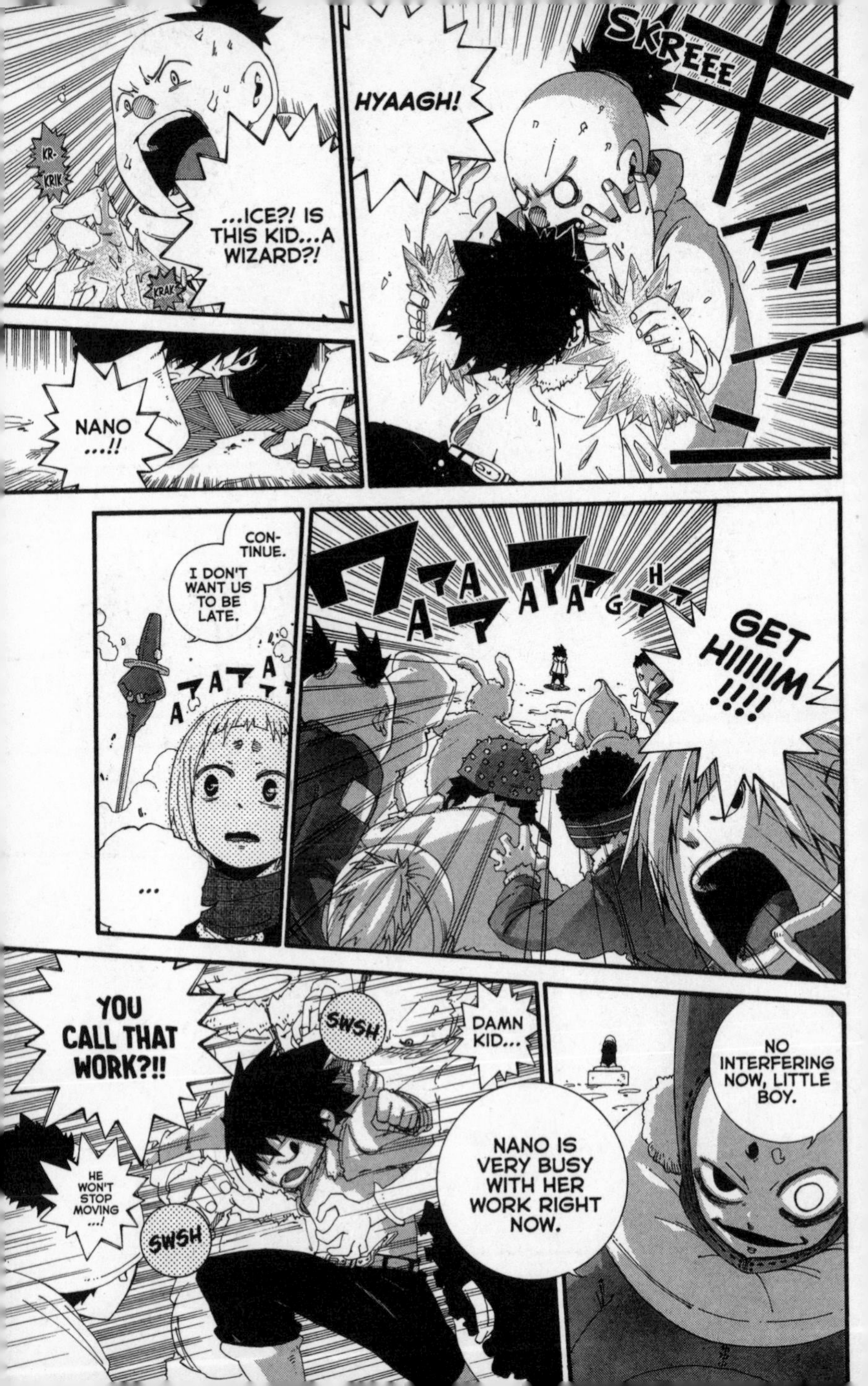
SKREEE
HYAAGH!
KR-KRIK
...ICE?! IS THIS KID...A WIZARD?!
KRAK
NANO ...!!
AAAAAGH
GET HIIIIIM!!!!
CON-TINUE.
I DON'T WANT US TO BE LATE.
AAAA
...
NO INTERFERING NOW, LITTLE BOY.
NANO IS VERY BUSY WITH HER WORK RIGHT NOW.
DAMN KID...
SWSH
YOU CALL THAT WORK?!!
HE WON'T STOP MOVING ...!
SWSH

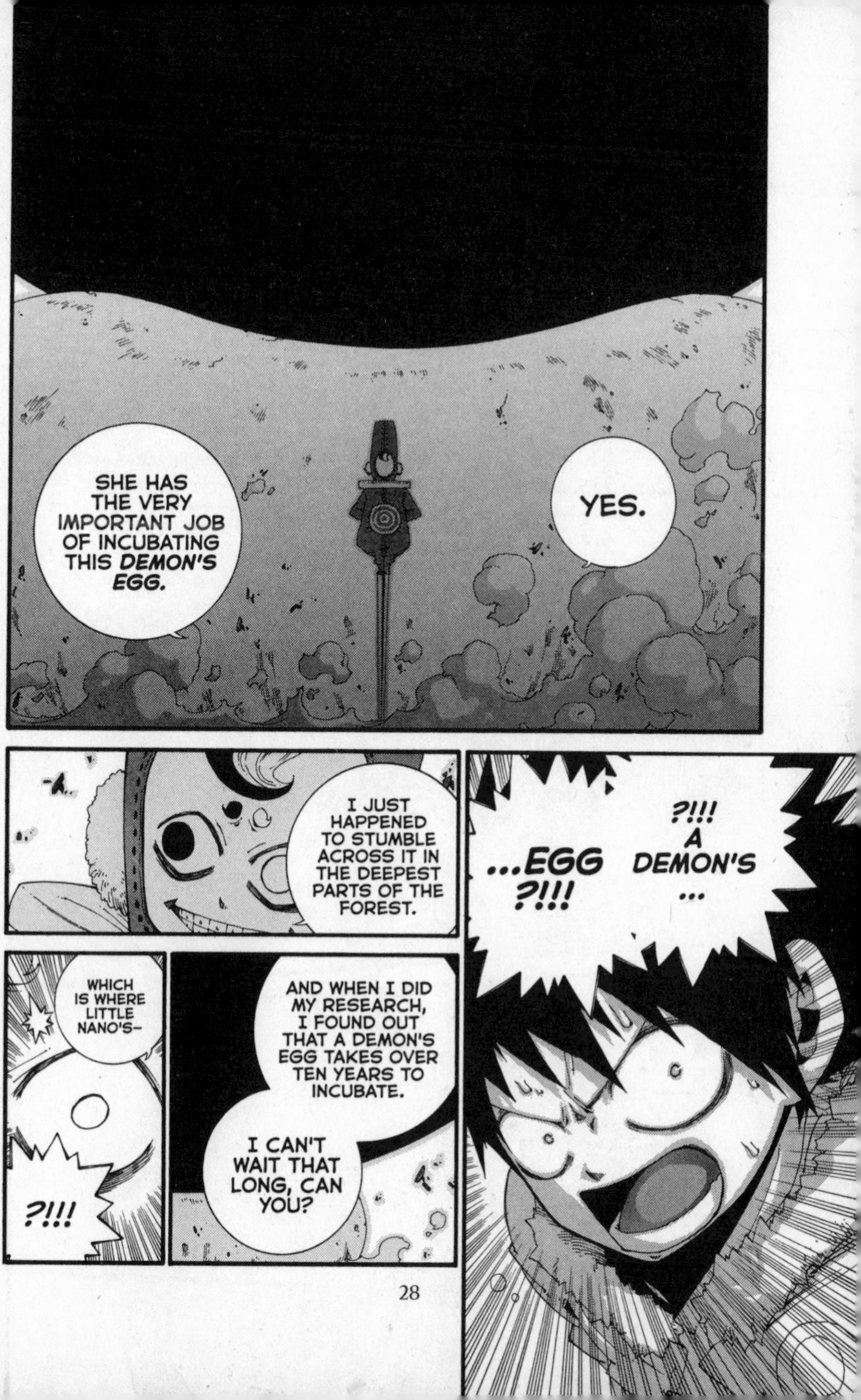
YES.
SHE HAS THE VERY IMPORTANT JOB OF INCUBATING THIS *DEMON'S EGG.*
?!!! A DEMON'S ...
...EGG ?!!!
I JUST HAPPENED TO STUMBLE ACROSS IT IN THE DEEPEST PARTS OF THE FOREST.
AND WHEN I DID MY RESEARCH, I FOUND OUT THAT A DEMON'S EGG TAKES OVER TEN YEARS TO INCUBATE.
I CAN'T WAIT THAT LONG, CAN YOU?
WHICH IS WHERE LITTLE NANO'S–
?!!!

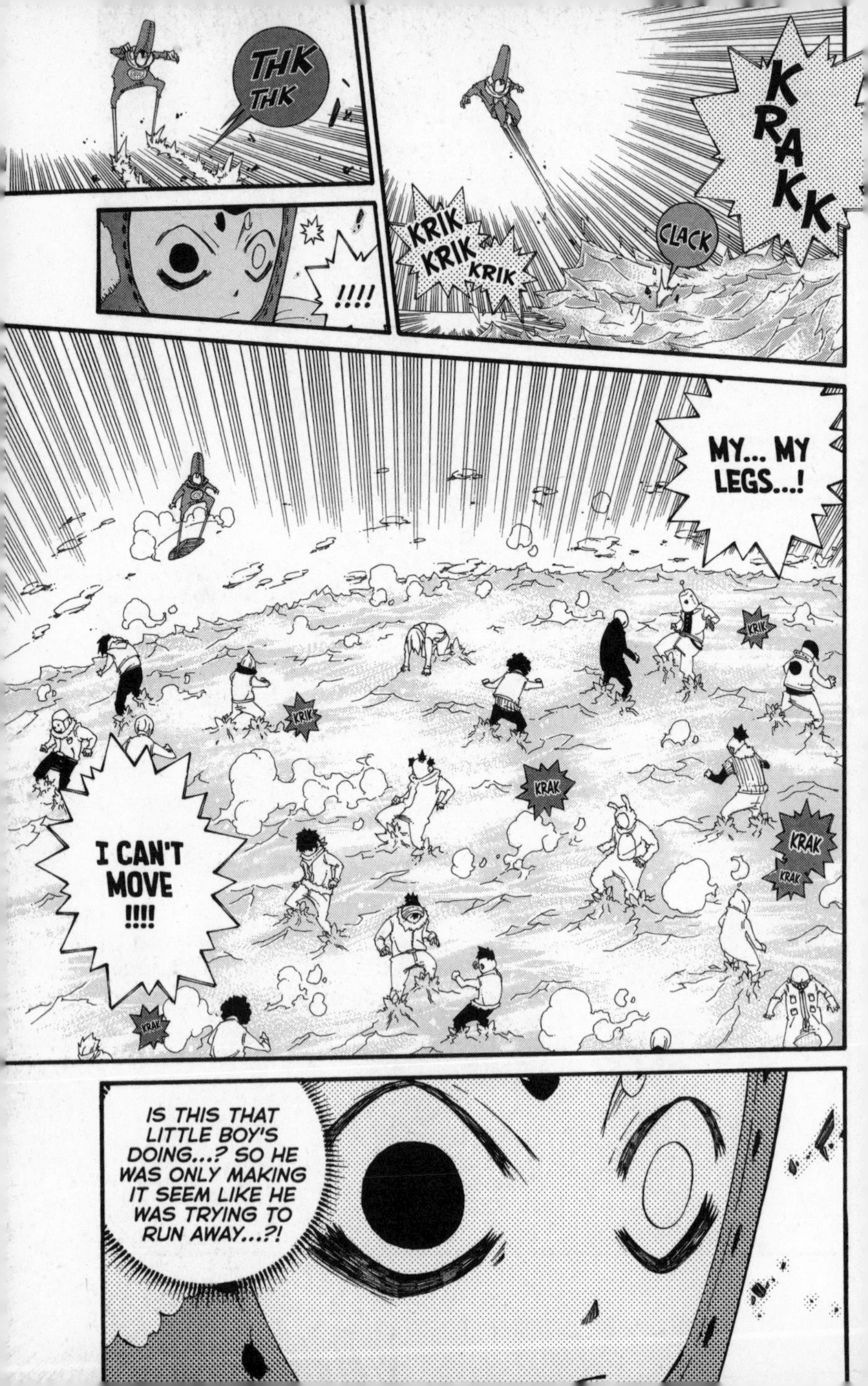
KRAKK
CLACK
KRIK KRIK KRIK
THK THK
!!!!
MY... MY LEGS...!
KRIK
KRIK
KRAK
KRAK
KRAK
I CAN'T MOVE !!!!
KRAK
IS THIS THAT LITTLE BOY'S DOING...? SO HE WAS ONLY MAKING IT SEEM LIKE HE WAS TRYING TO RUN AWAY...?!

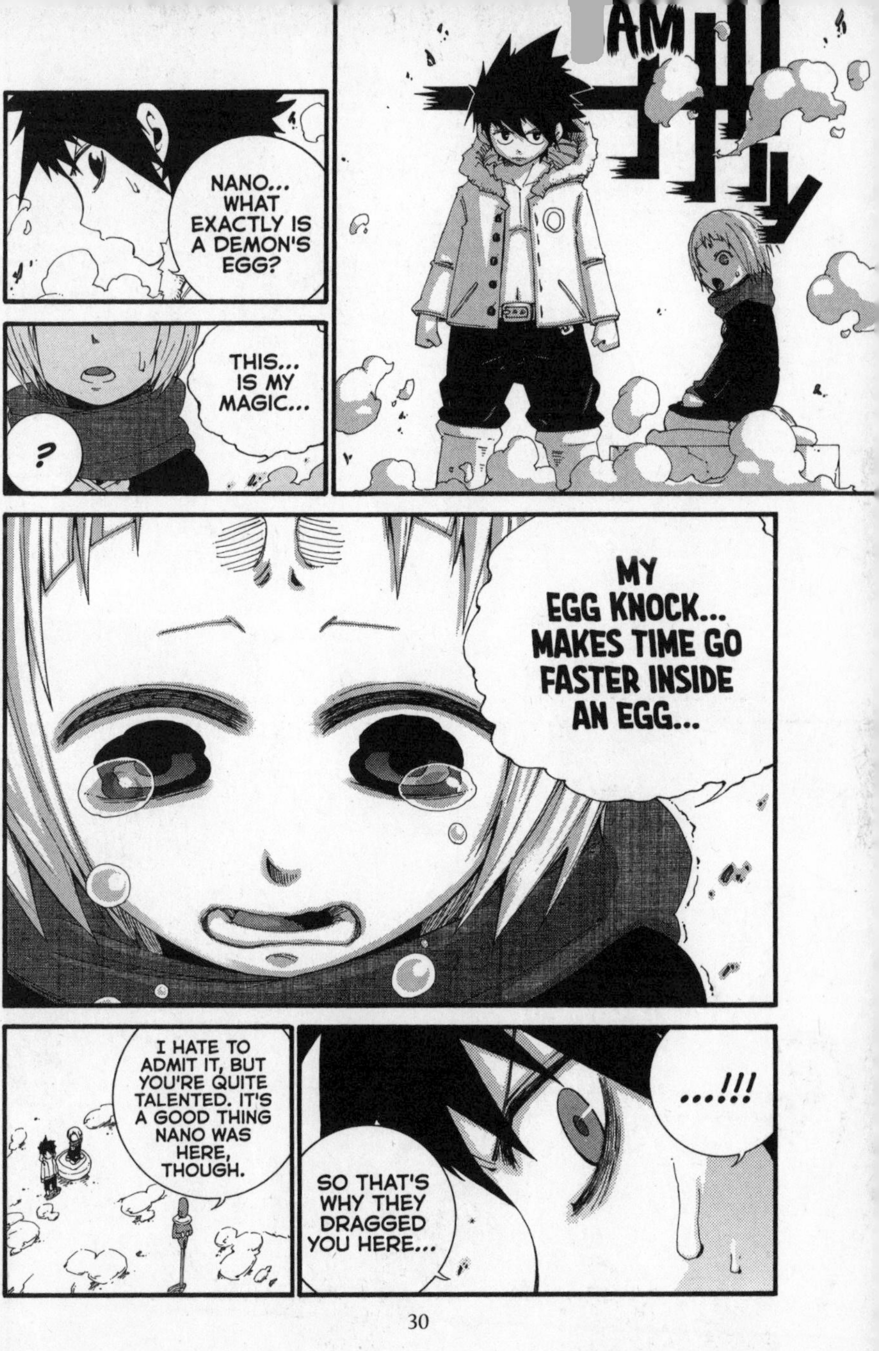

AM
NANO... WHAT EXACTLY IS A DEMON'S EGG?
THIS... IS MY MAGIC...
?
MY EGG KNOCK... MAKES TIME GO FASTER INSIDE AN EGG...
...!!!
SO THAT'S WHY THEY DRAGGED YOU HERE...
I HATE TO ADMIT IT, BUT YOU'RE QUITE TALENTED. IT'S A GOOD THING NANO WAS HERE, THOUGH.

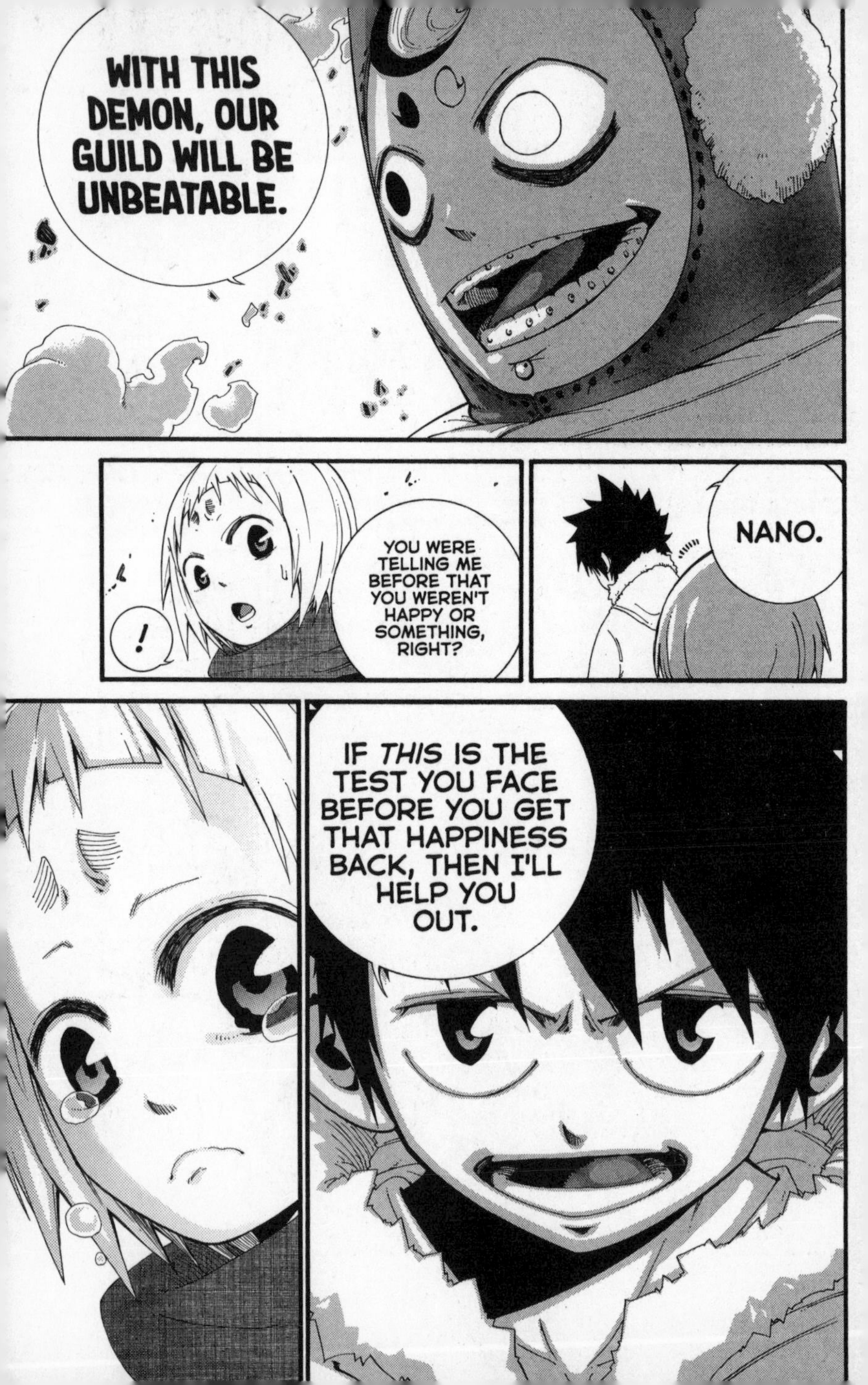
WITH THIS DEMON, OUR GUILD WILL BE UNBEATABLE.
NANO.
YOU WERE TELLING ME BEFORE THAT YOU WEREN'T HAPPY OR SOMETHING, RIGHT?
!
IF *THIS* IS THE TEST YOU FACE BEFORE YOU GET THAT HAPPINESS BACK, THEN I'LL HELP YOU OUT.

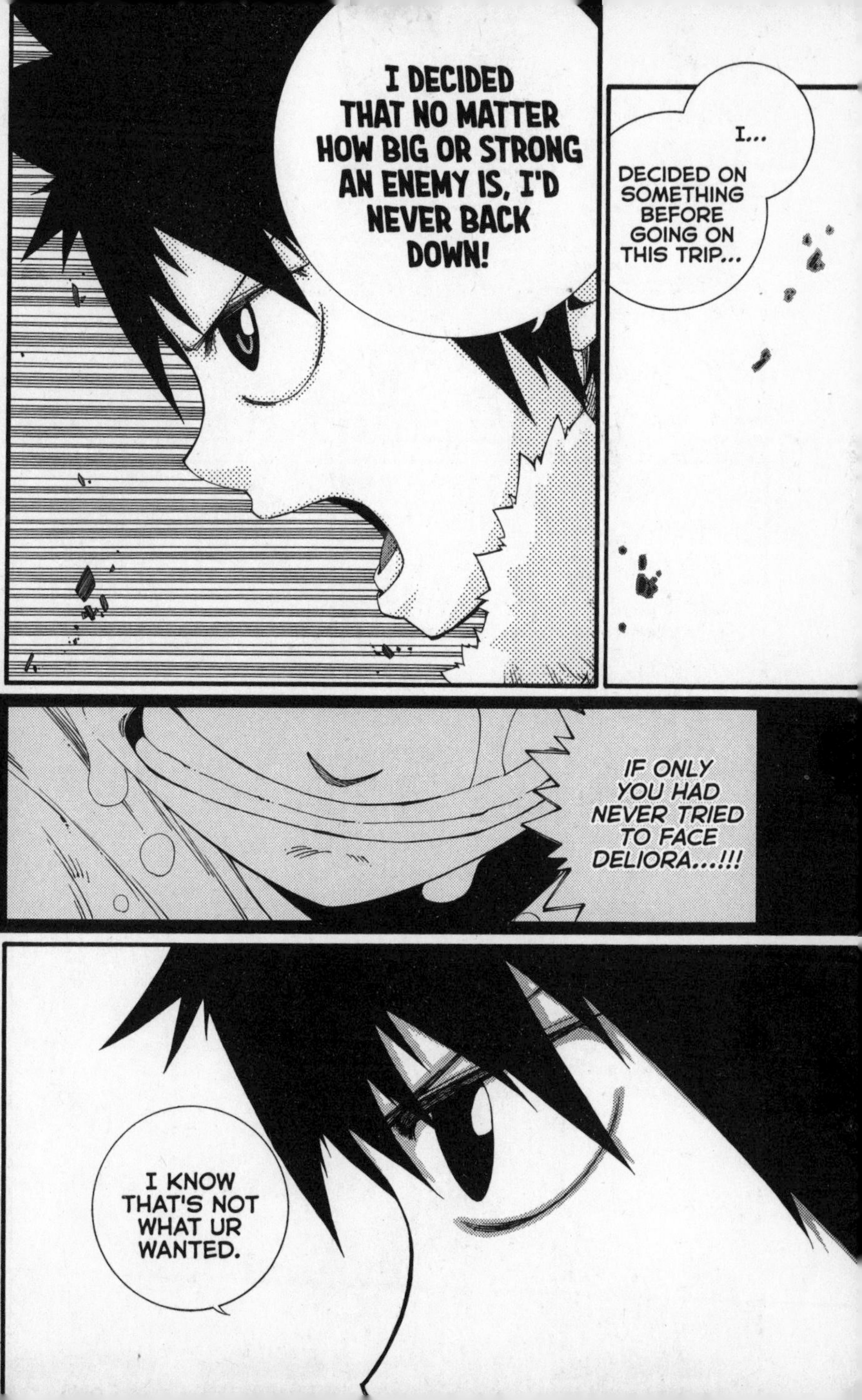
I...
DECIDED ON SOMETHING BEFORE GOING ON THIS TRIP...
I DECIDED THAT NO MATTER HOW BIG OR STRONG AN ENEMY IS, I'D NEVER BACK DOWN!
IF ONLY YOU HAD NEVER TRIED TO FACE DELIORA...!!!
I KNOW THAT'S NOT WHAT UR WANTED.

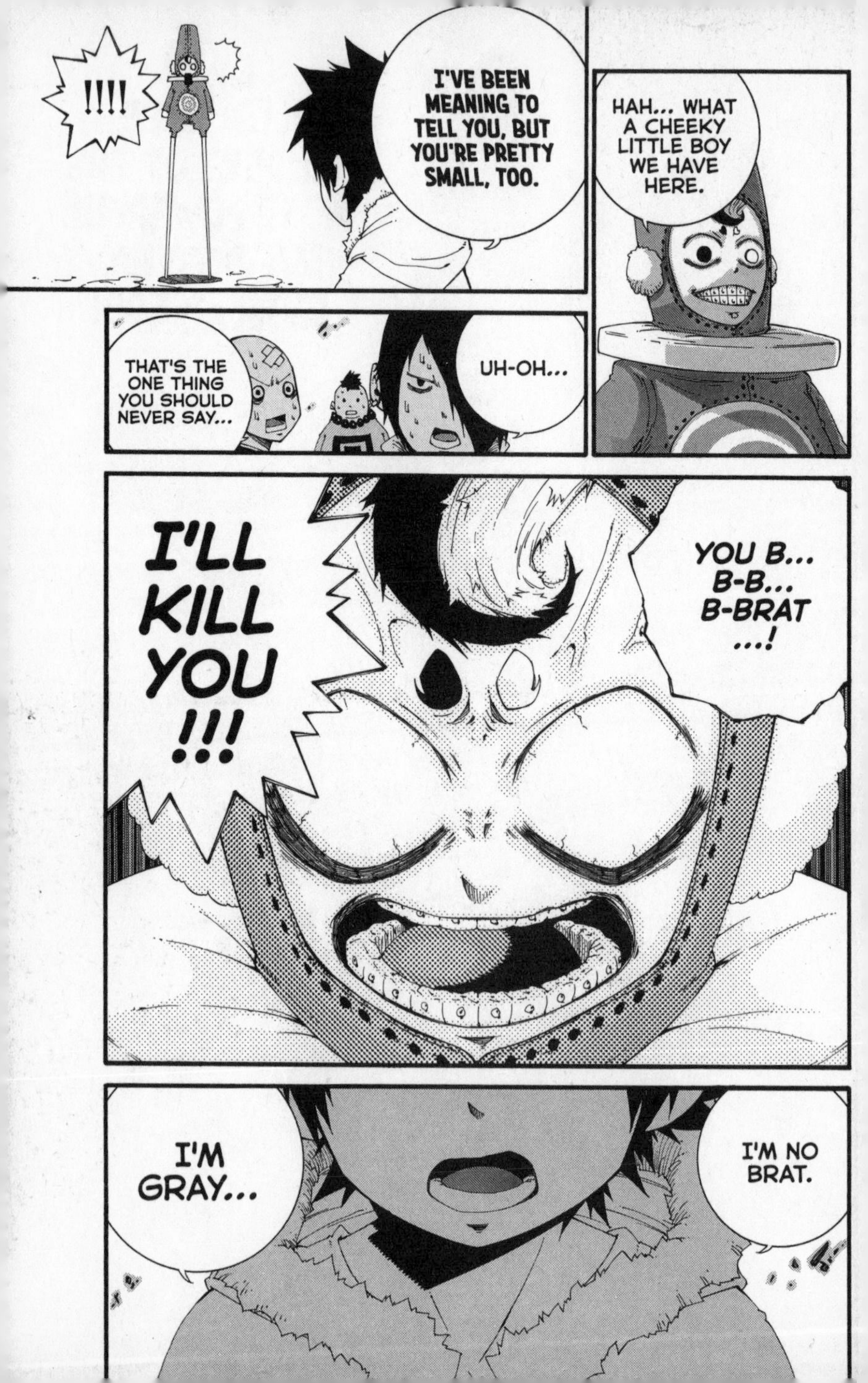
I'VE BEEN MEANING TO TELL YOU, BUT YOU'RE PRETTY SMALL, TOO.
!!!!
HAH... WHAT A CHEEKY LITTLE BOY WE HAVE HERE.
UH-OH...
THAT'S THE ONE THING YOU SHOULD NEVER SAY...
YOU B... B-B... B-BRAT ...!
I'LL KILL YOU !!!
I'M NO BRAT.
I'M GRAY...

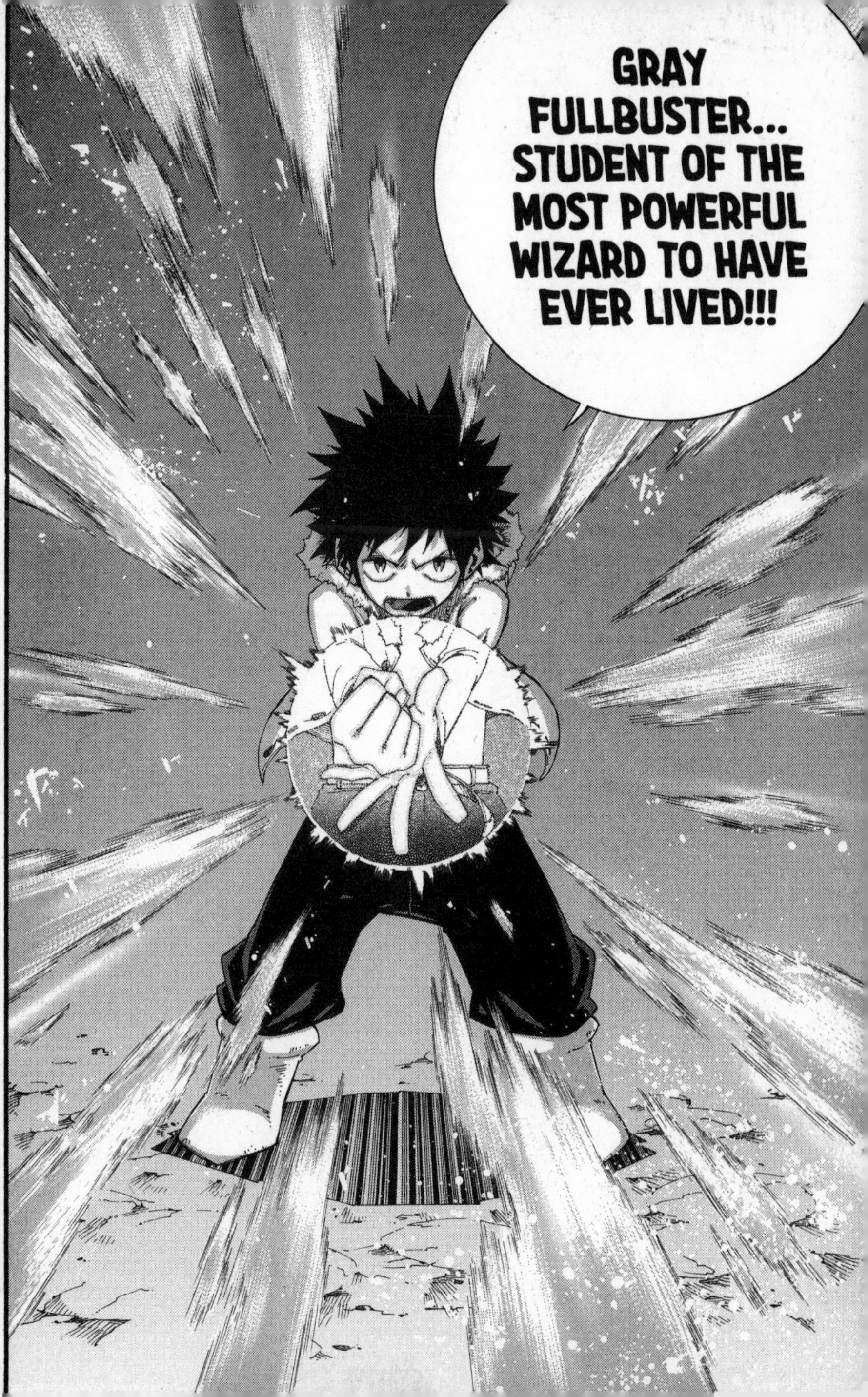
GRAY FULLBUSTER... STUDENT OF THE MOST POWERFUL WIZARD TO HAVE EVER LIVED!!!

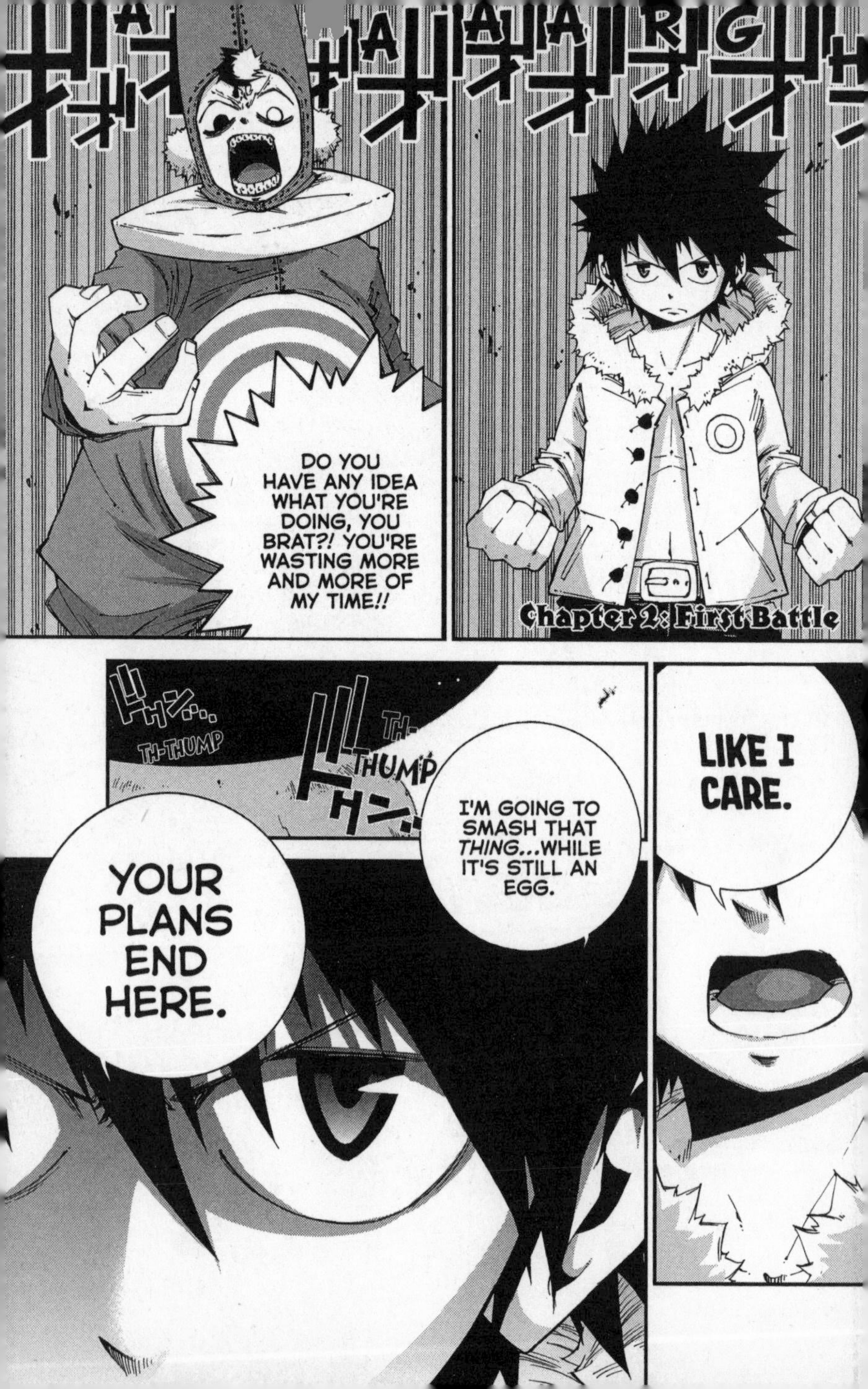
Chapter 2: First Battle
DO YOU HAVE ANY IDEA WHAT YOU'RE DOING, YOU BRAT?! YOU'RE WASTING MORE AND MORE OF MY TIME!!
LIKE I CARE.
TH-THUMP
TH-THUMP
I'M GOING TO SMASH THAT *THING*...WHILE IT'S STILL AN EGG.
YOUR PLANS END HERE.

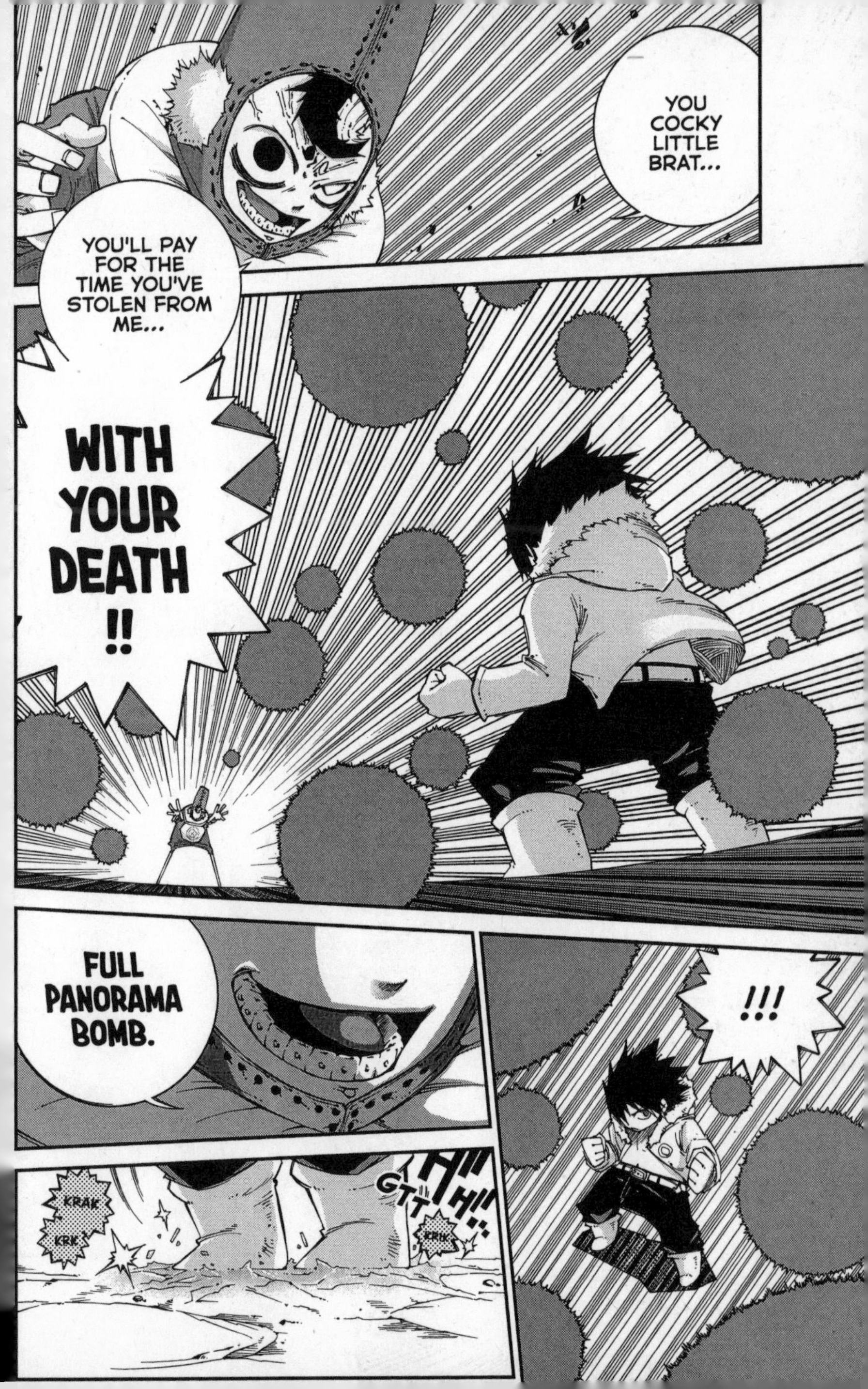
YOU COCKY LITTLE BRAT...
YOU'LL PAY FOR THE TIME YOU'VE STOLEN FROM ME...
WITH YOUR DEATH!!
!!!
FULL PANORAMA BOMB.
GTTHH!!
KRAK
KRK
KRIK

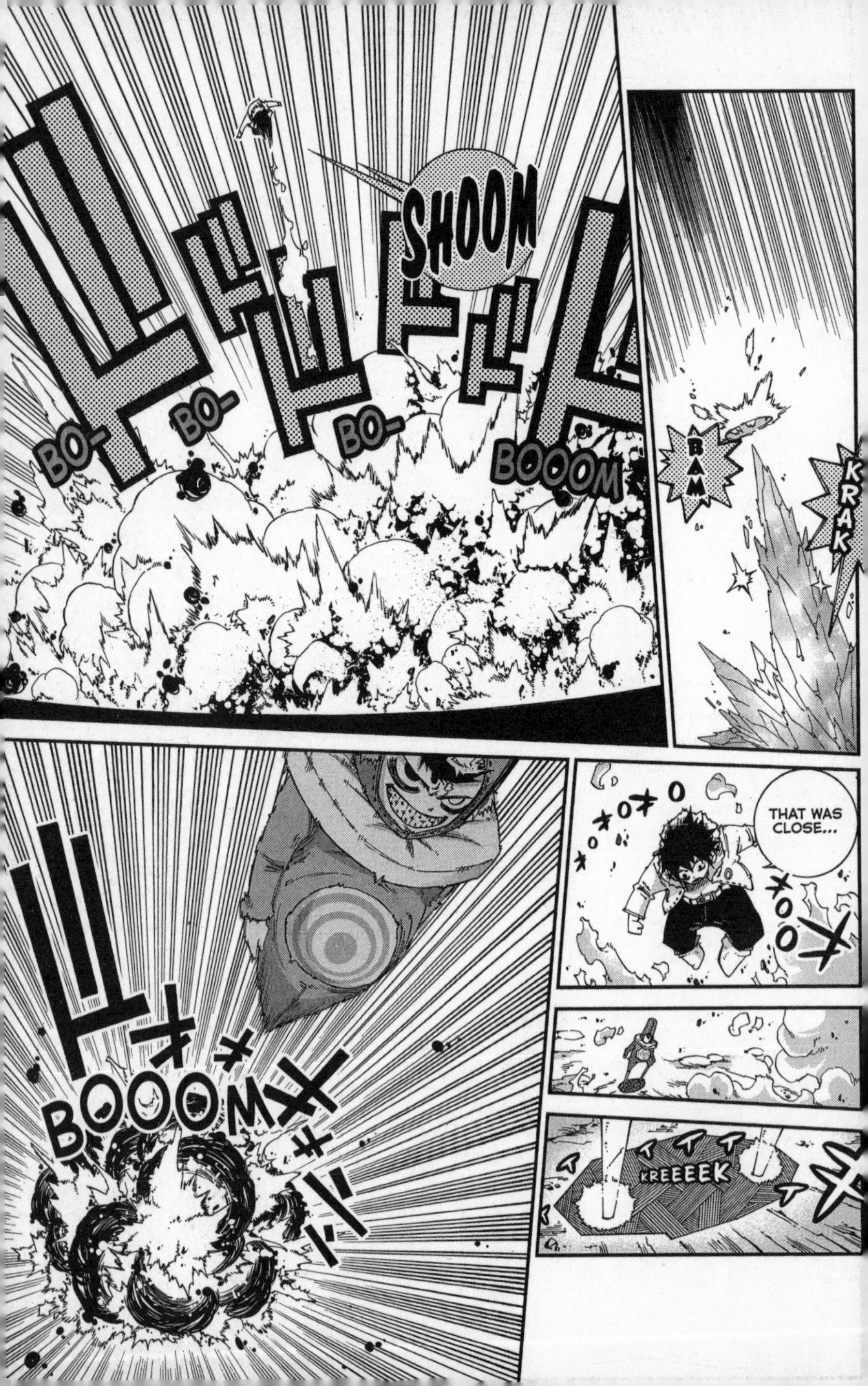
BAM
KRAK
SHOOM
BO-
BO-
BO-
BOOOM
THAT WAS CLOSE...
KREEEK
BOOOM

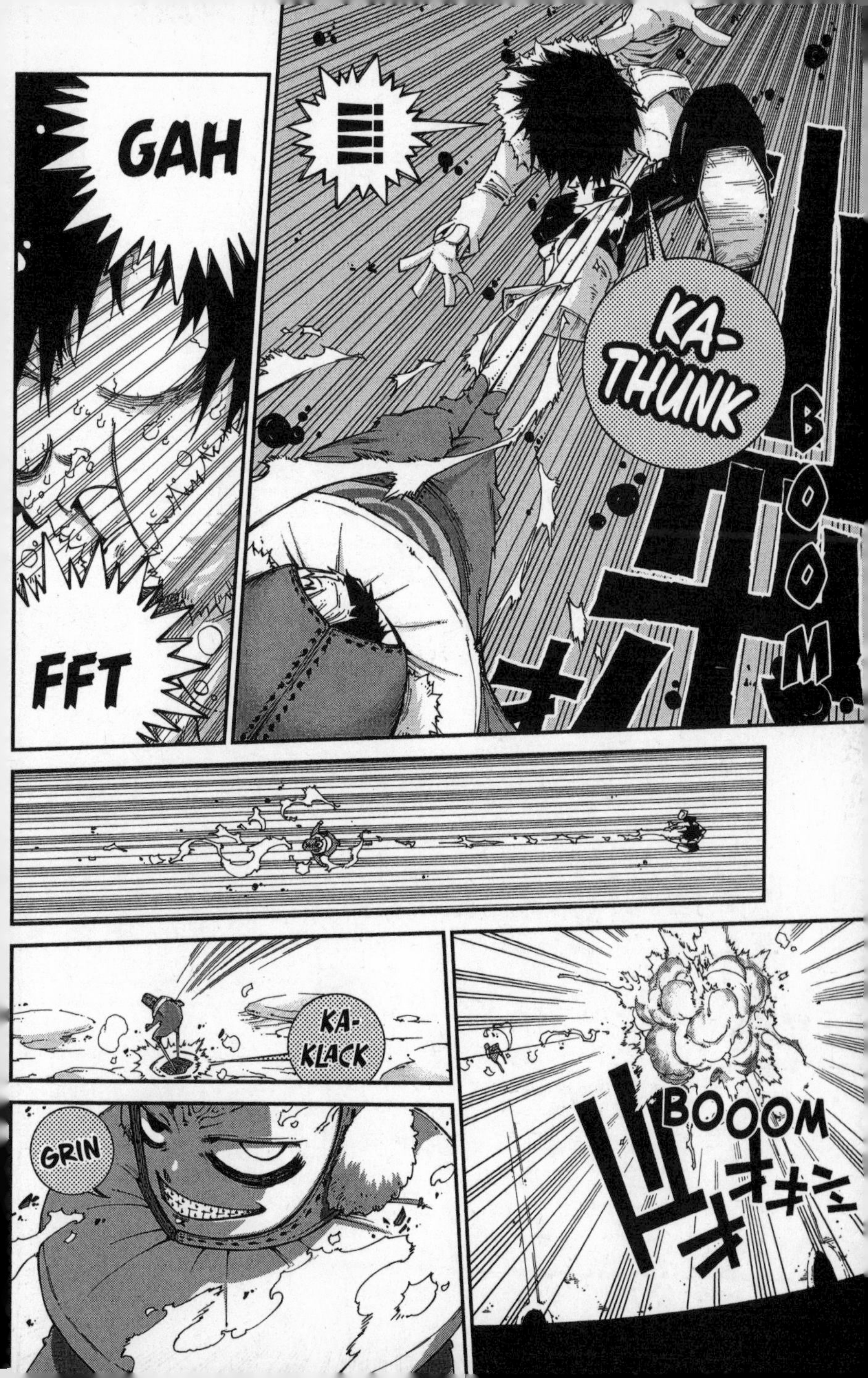
KA-THUNK
BOOOM..
GAH
FFT
BOOOM
KA-KLACK
GRIN

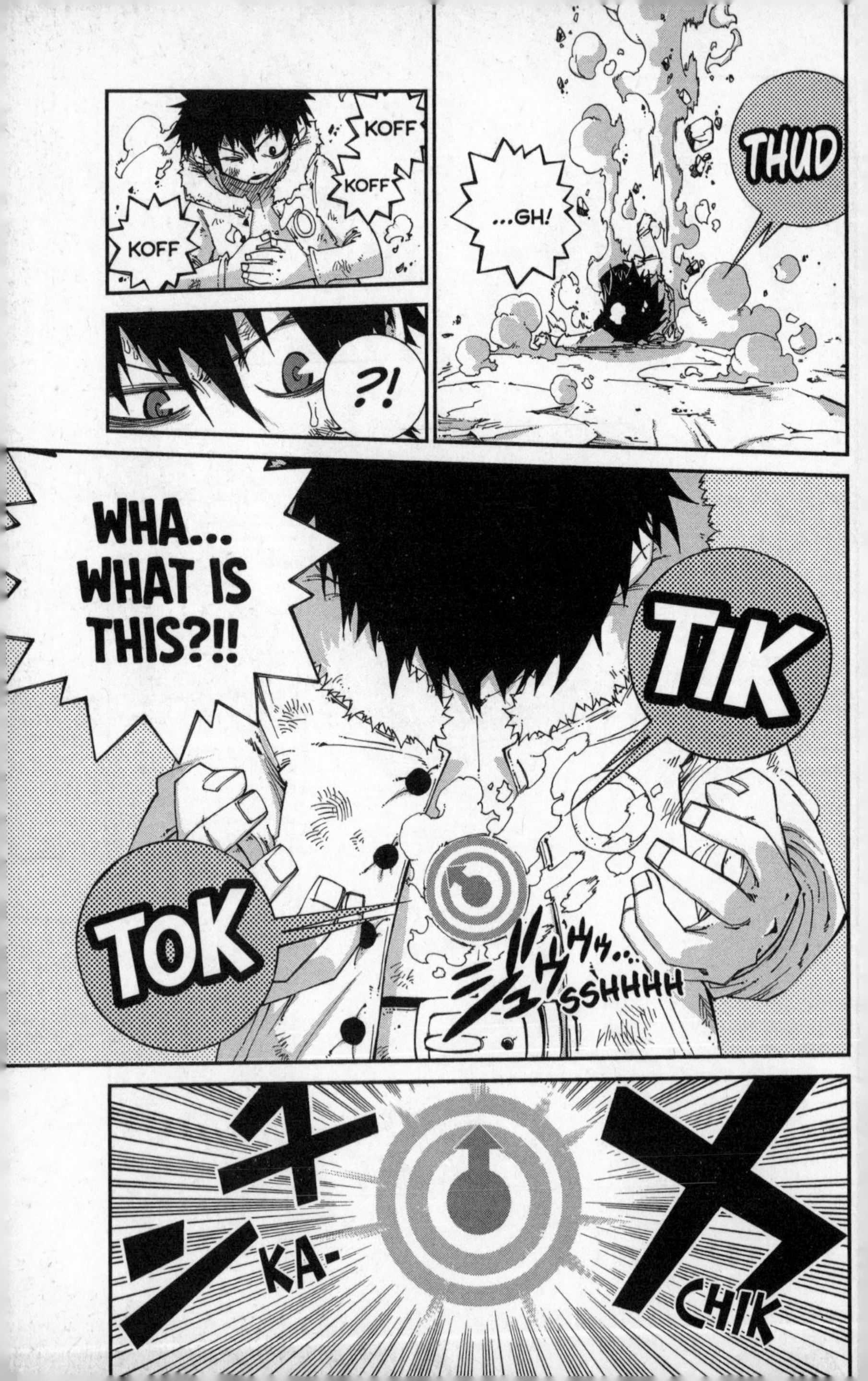
THUD
...GH!
KOFF
KOFF
KOFF
?!
WHA... WHAT IS THIS?!!
TIK
TOK
SSHHHH
KA-
CHIK

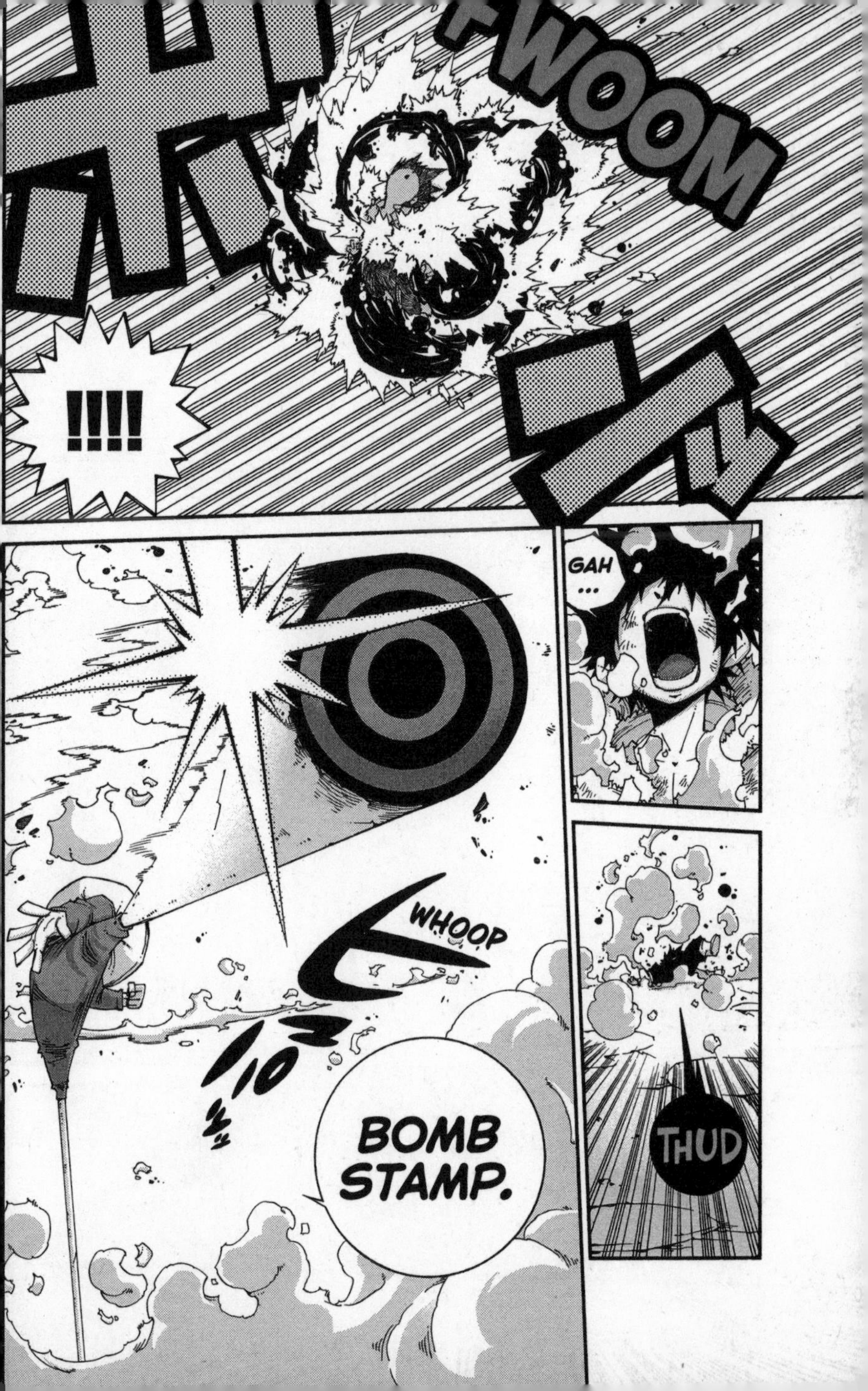
FWOOM
!!!!
GAH ...
THUD
WHOOP
BOMB STAMP.

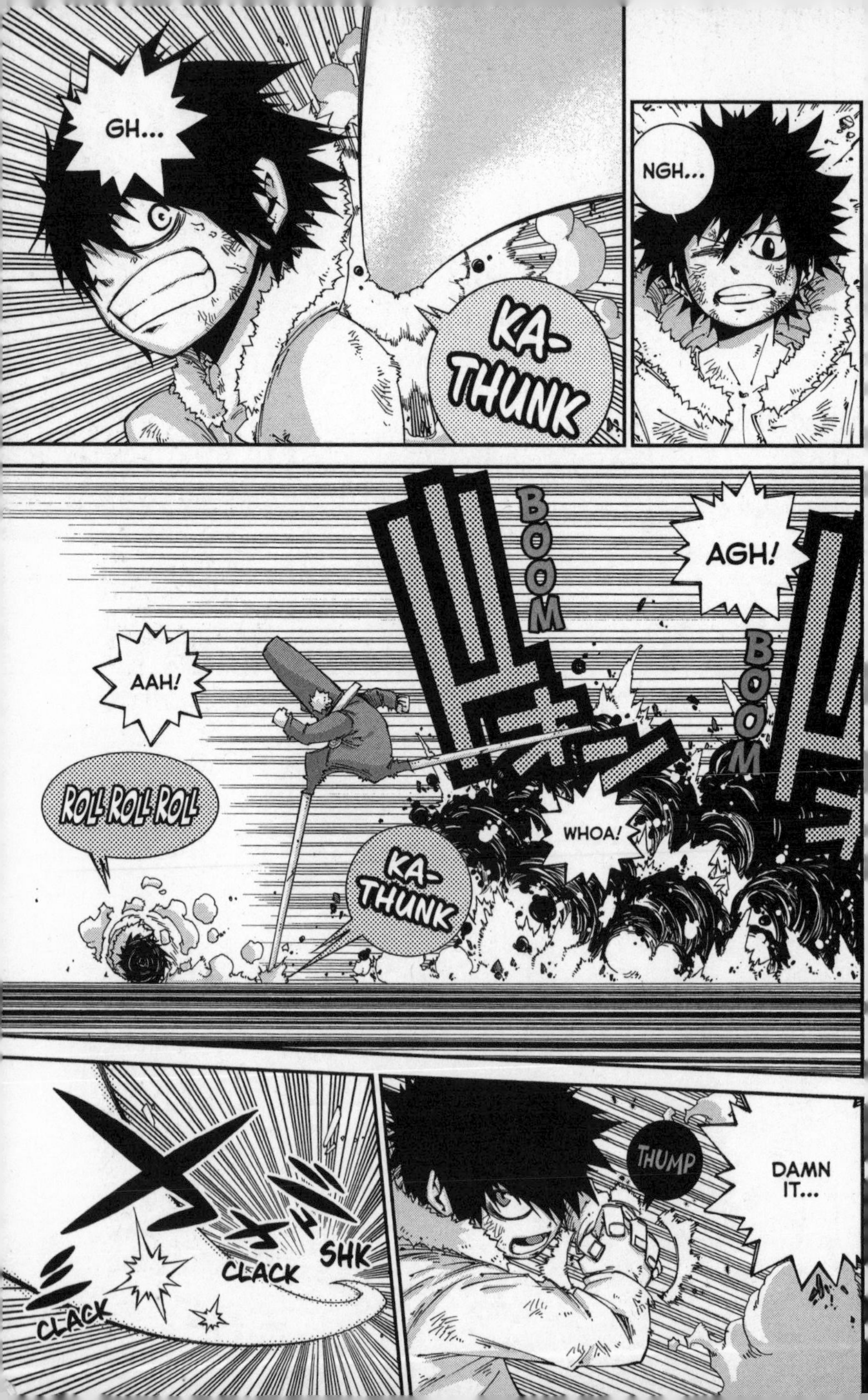
NGH...
GH...
KA-THUNK
AGH!
BOOM
BOOM
AAH!
WHOA!
ROLL ROLL ROLL
KA-THUNK
THUMP
DAMN IT...
SHK
CLACK
CLACK

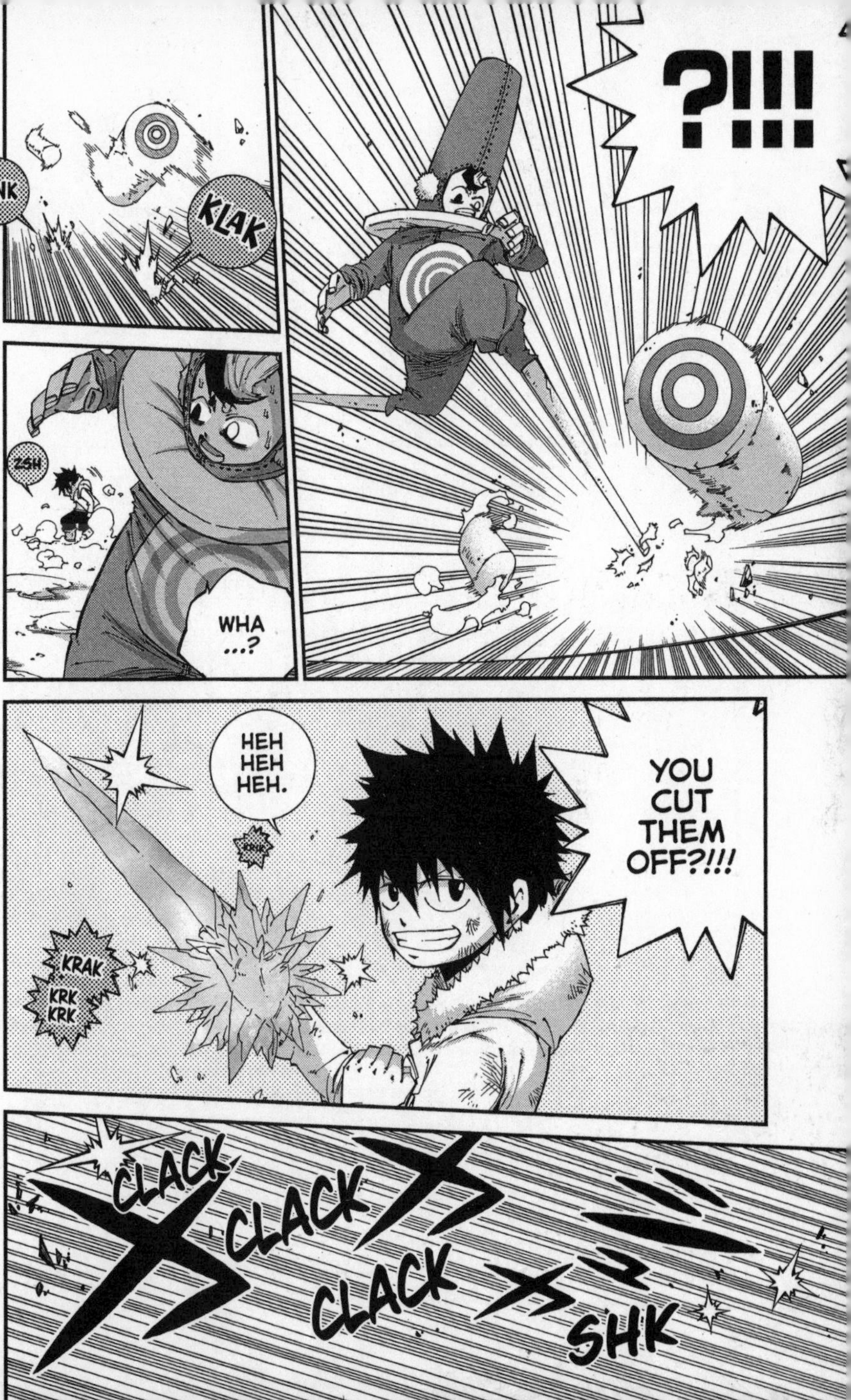
?!!!
KLAK
KONK
ZSH
WHA ...?
YOU CUT THEM OFF?!!!
HEH HEH HEH.
KRK
KRAK
KRK KRK
CLACK
CLACK
CLACK
SHK

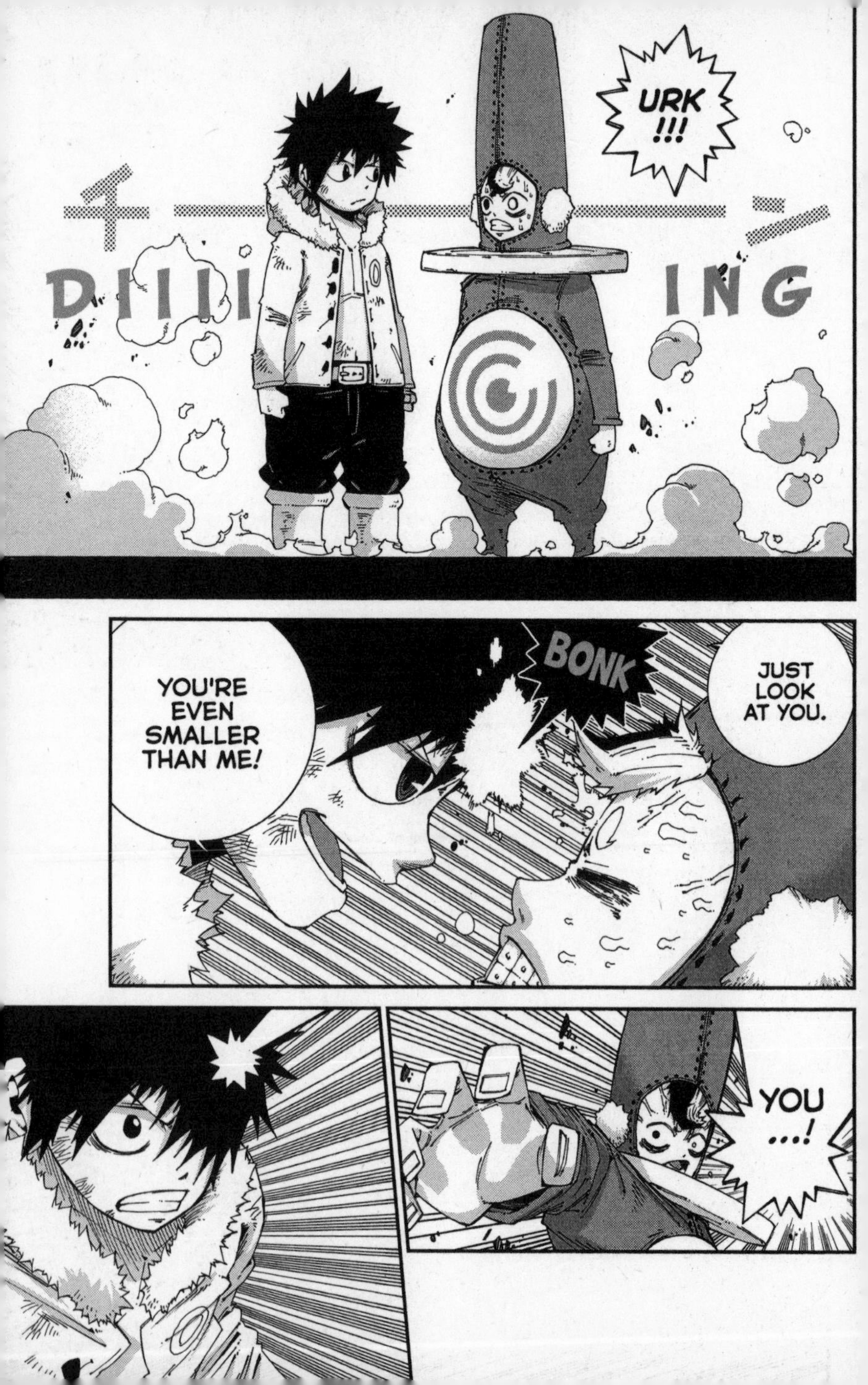
URK !!!
DIIIING
JUST LOOK AT YOU.
BONK
YOU'RE EVEN SMALLER THAN ME!
YOU ...!

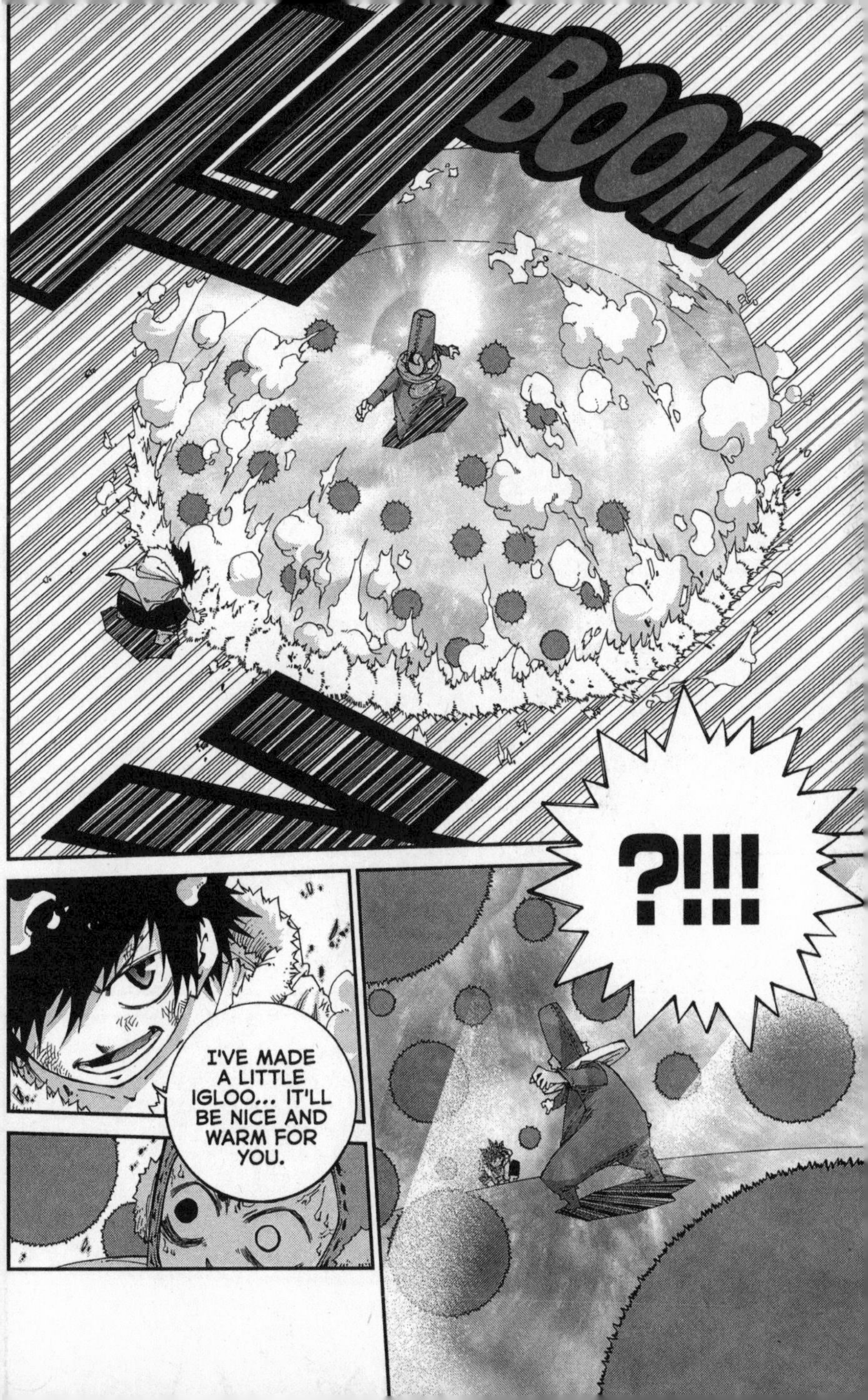
BOOM
?!!!
I'VE MADE A LITTLE IGLOO... IT'LL BE NICE AND WARM FOR YOU.

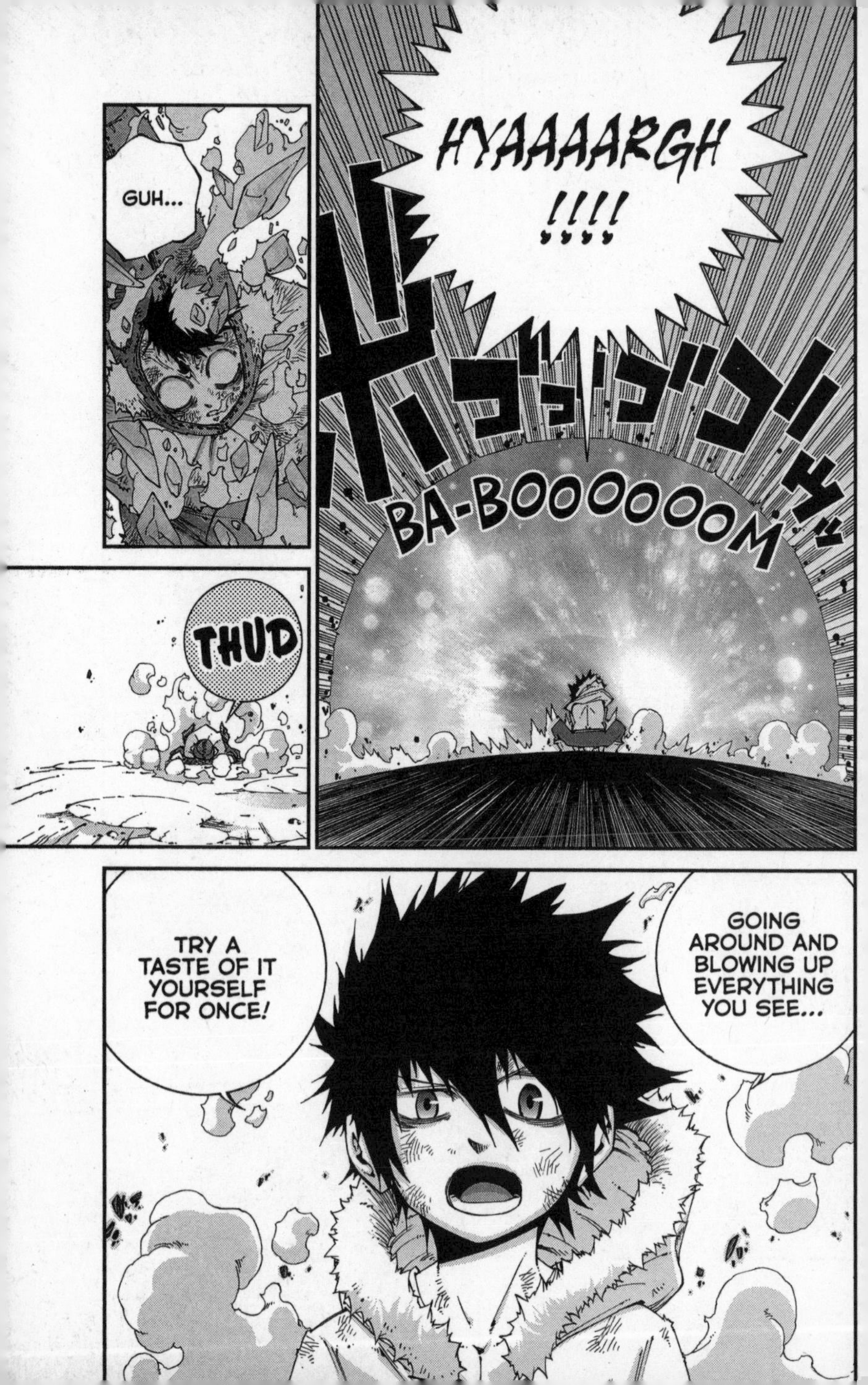
HYAAAARGH !!!!
BA-BOOOOOOM
GUH...
THUD
GOING AROUND AND BLOWING UP EVERYTHING YOU SEE...
TRY A TASTE OF IT YOURSELF FOR ONCE!

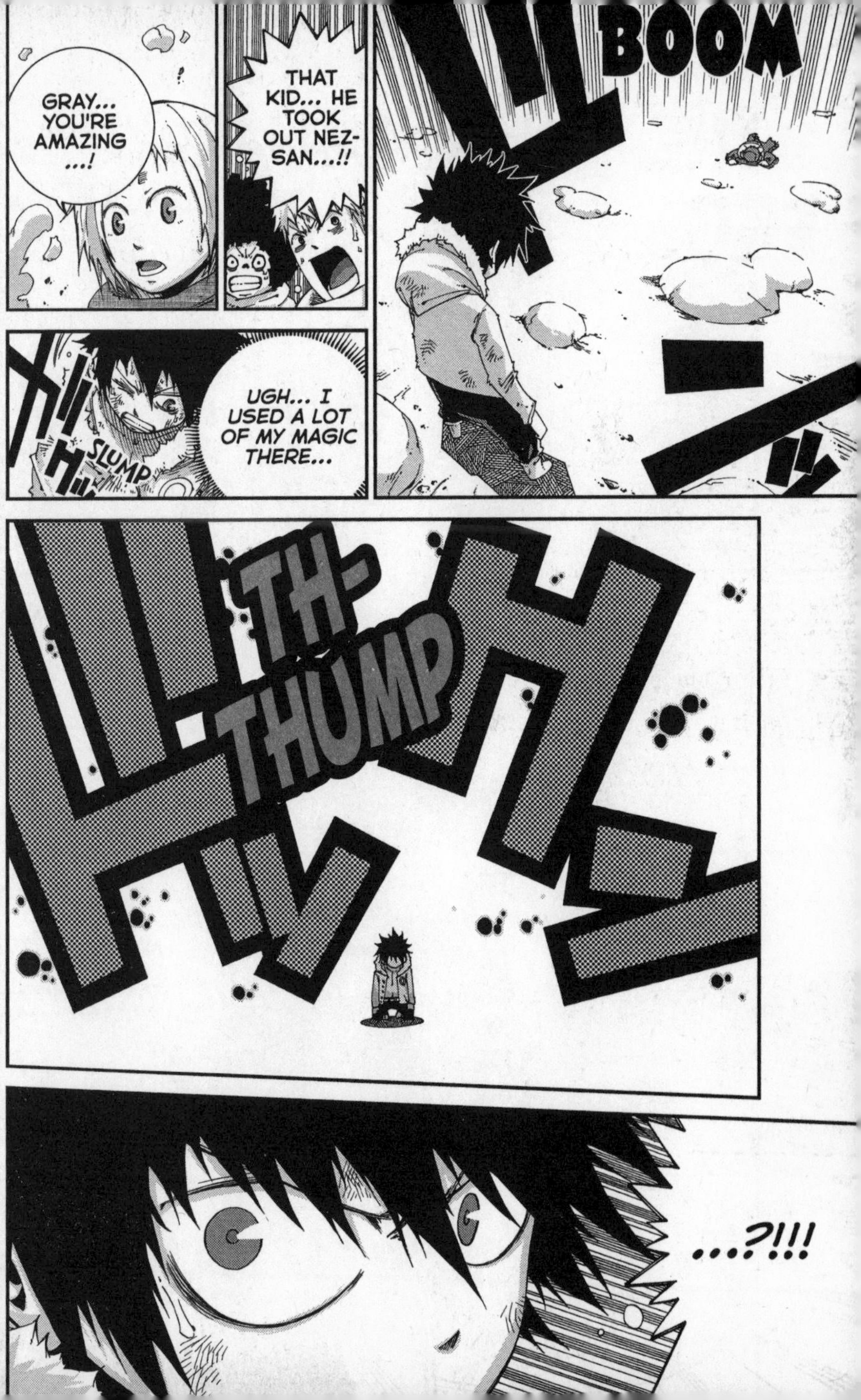
BOOM
THAT KID... HE TOOK OUT NEZ-SAN...!!
GRAY... YOU'RE AMAZING ...!
UGH... I USED A LOT OF MY MAGIC THERE...
SLUMP
TH-THUMP
...?!!!

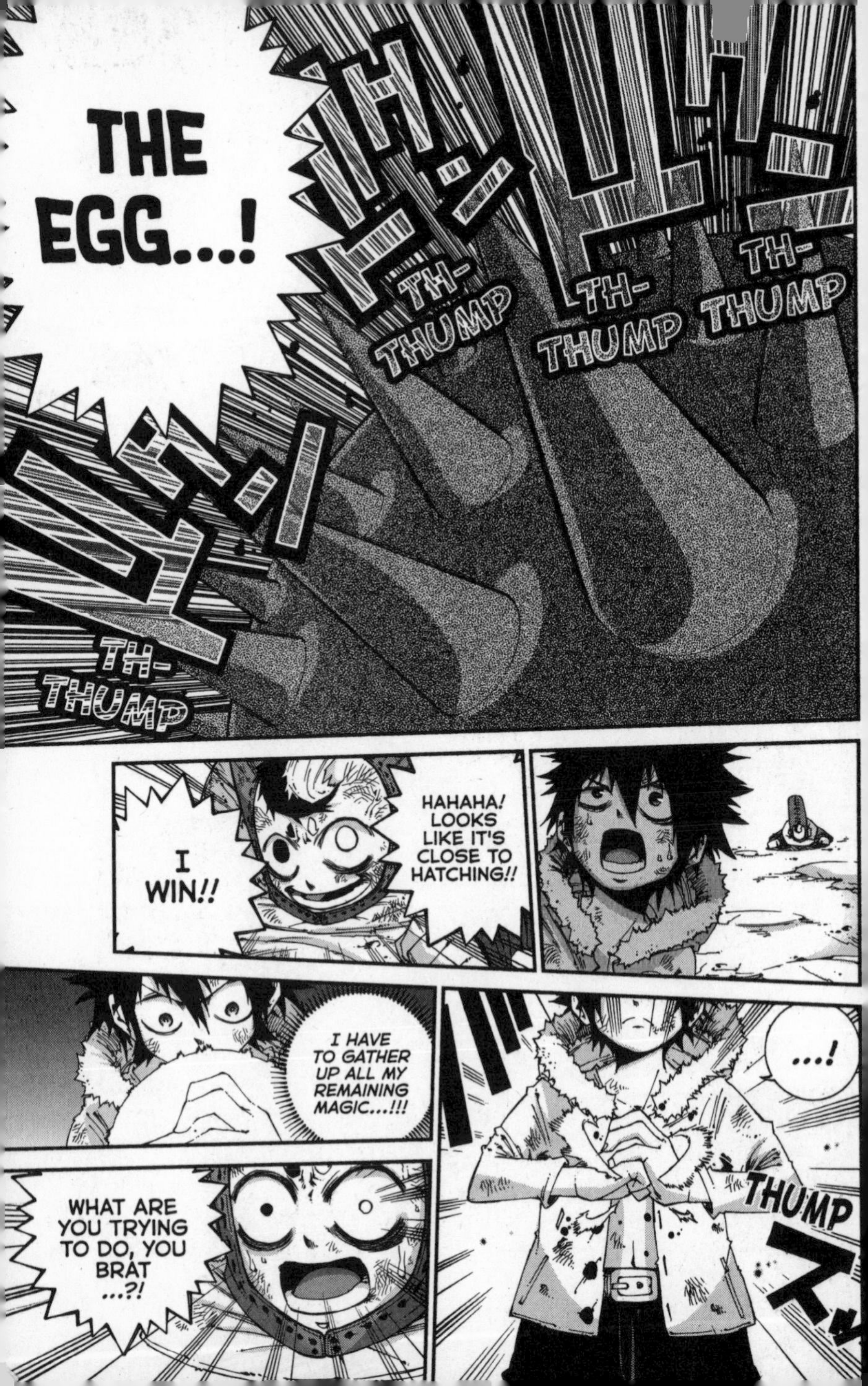
TH-THUMP
TH-THUMP
TH-THUMP
THE EGG...!
TH-THUMP
HAHAHA! LOOKS LIKE IT'S CLOSE TO HATCHING!!
I WIN!!
...!
THUMP
I HAVE TO GATHER UP ALL MY REMAINING MAGIC...!!!
WHAT ARE YOU TRYING TO DO, YOU BRAT ...?!

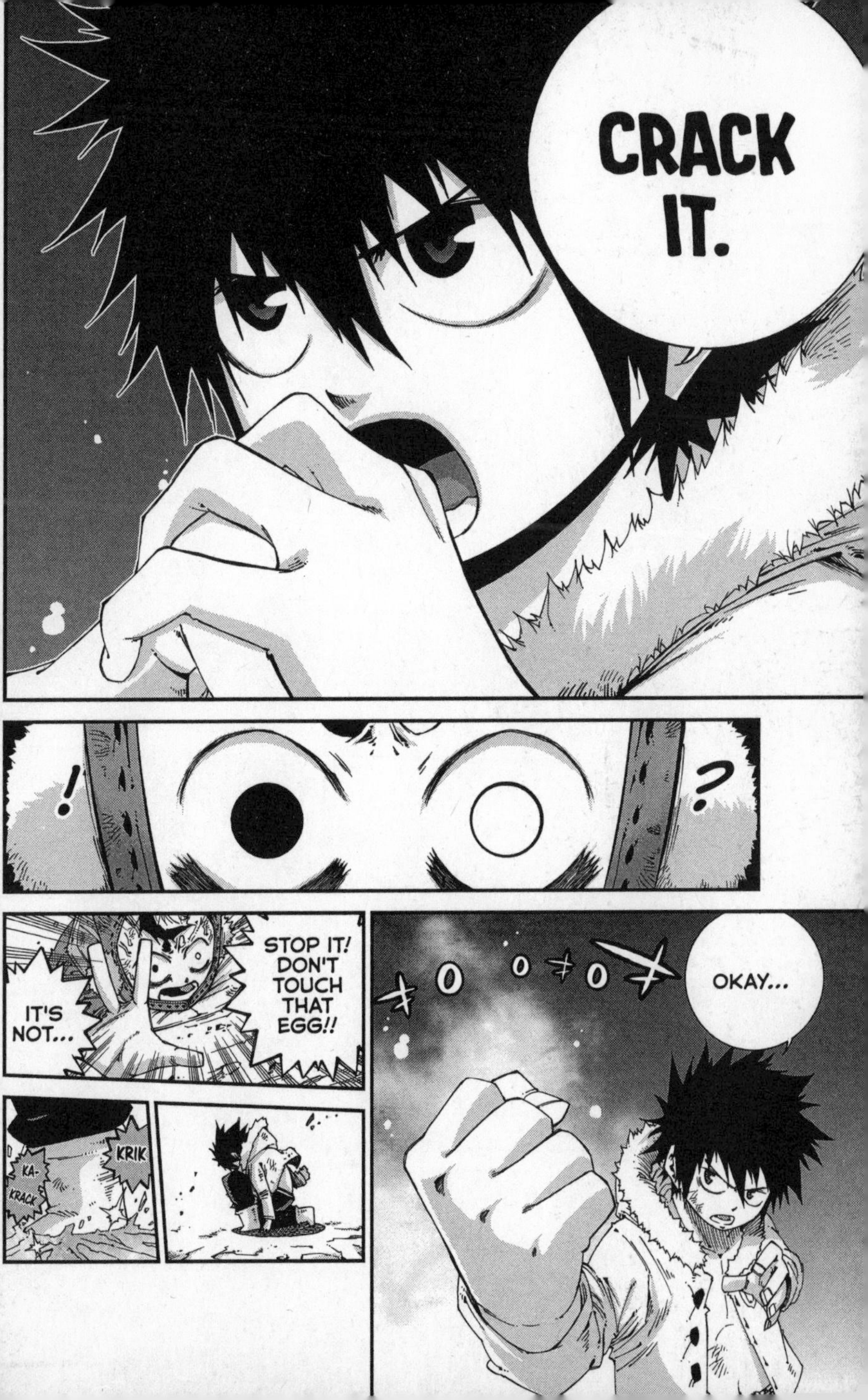
CRACK IT.
!
?
OKAY...
STOP IT! DON'T TOUCH THAT EGG!!
IT'S NOT...
KRIK
KA-KRACK

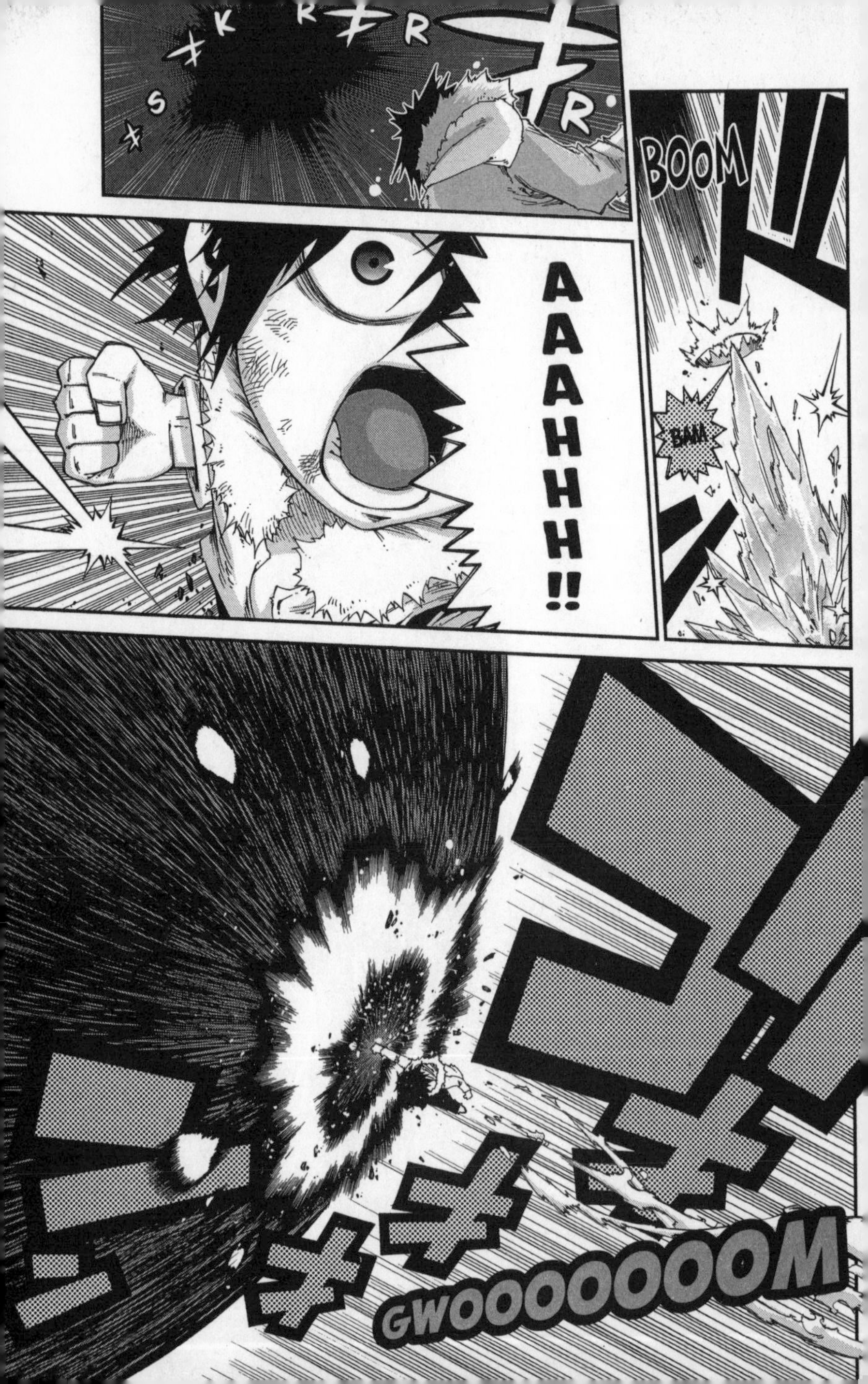
BOOM
BAM
SKRRR
AAAHHH!!
GWOOOOOOOM

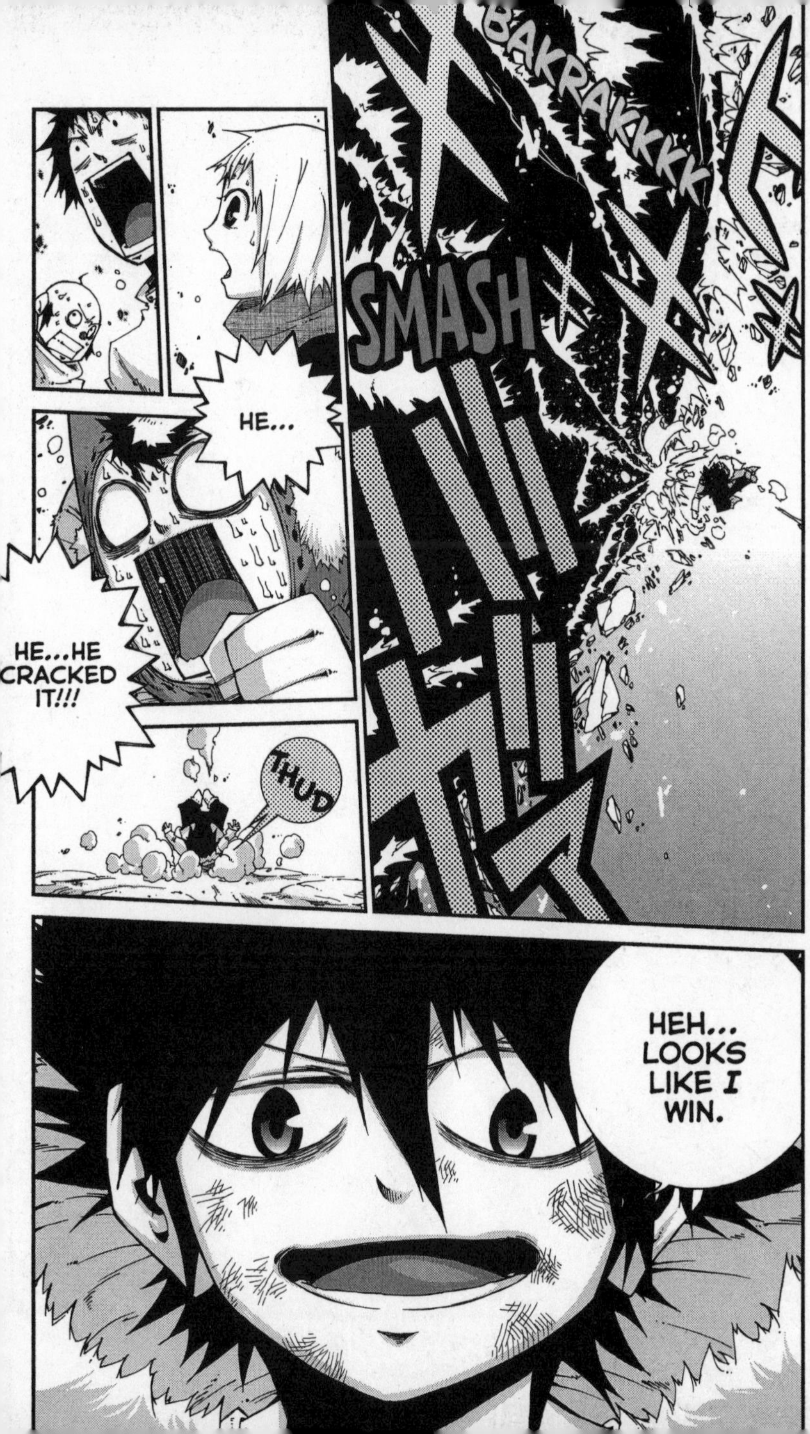
BAKRAKKKK
SMASH
HE...
HE...HE CRACKED IT!!!
THUD
HEH... LOOKS LIKE I WIN.

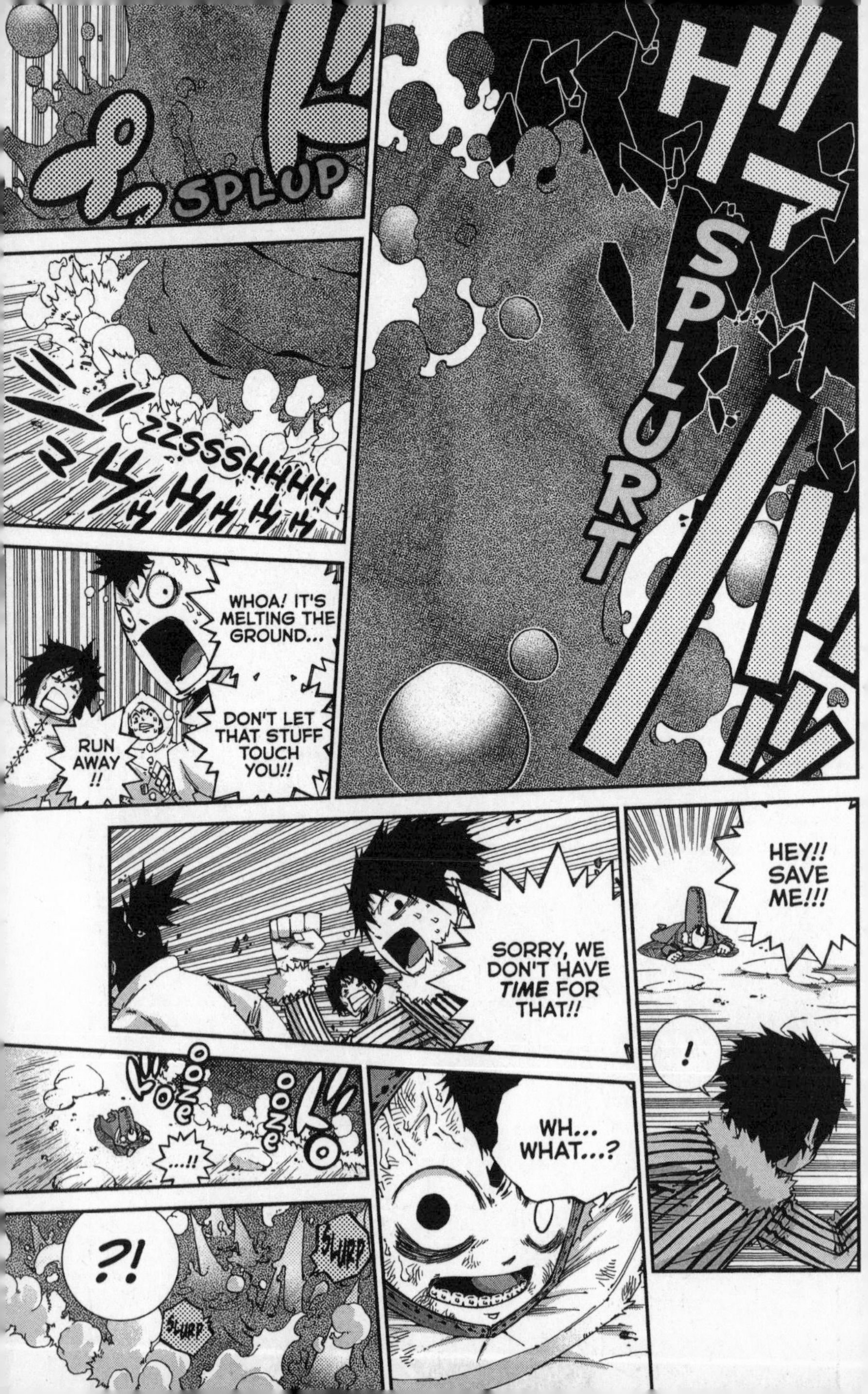
SPLURT
SPLUP
ZZSSSSHHHH
WHOA! IT'S MELTING THE GROUND...
DON'T LET THAT STUFF TOUCH YOU!!
RUN AWAY !!
HEY!! SAVE ME!!!
!
SORRY, WE DON'T HAVE *TIME* FOR THAT!!
WH... WHAT...?
oooze
oooze
...!!
?!
SLURP
SLURP

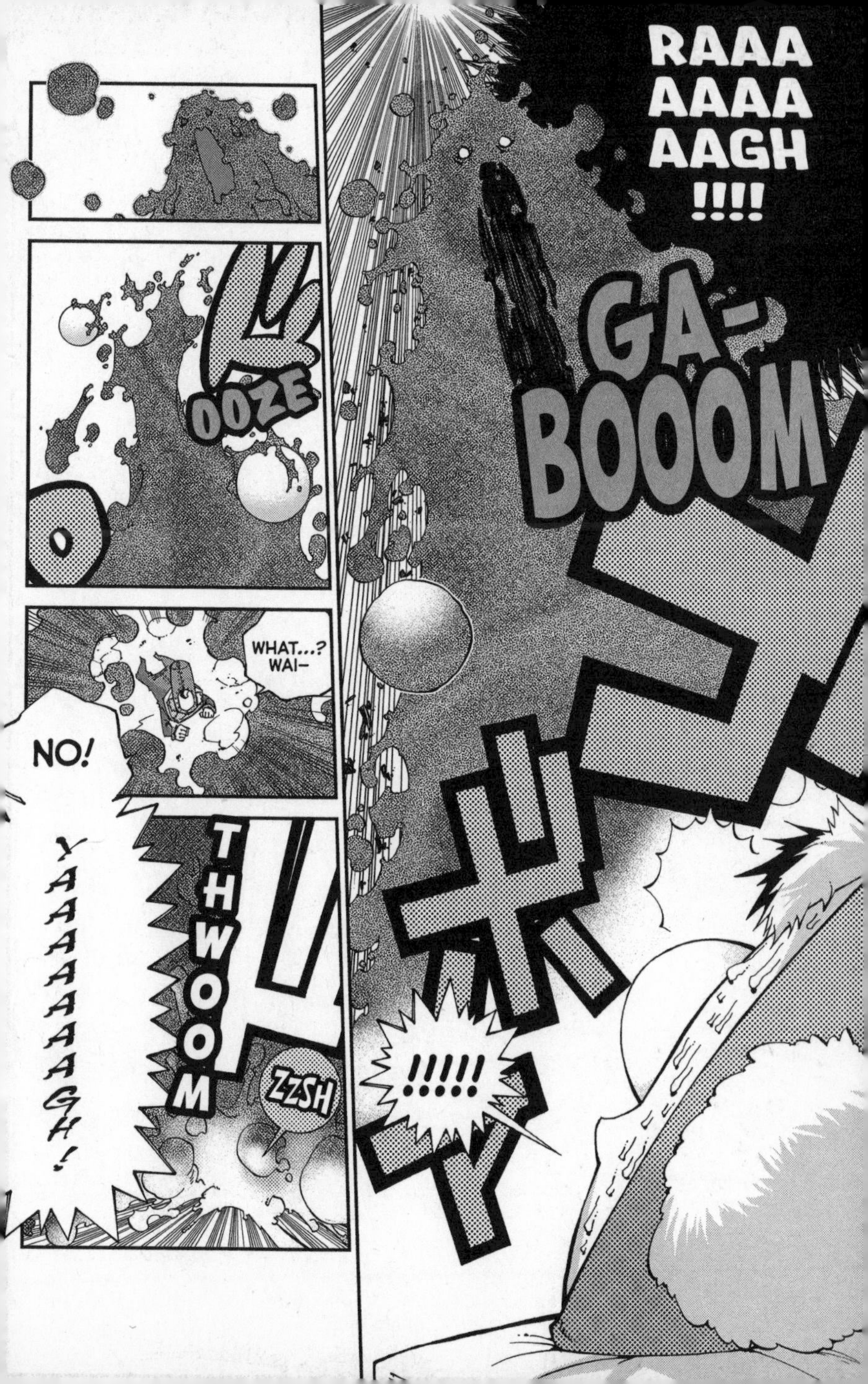
RAAA AAAA AAGH !!!!
GA-BOOOM
!!!!!
OOZE
WHAT...? WAI–
NO!
THWOOM
ZZSH
YAAAAAAAAAGH!

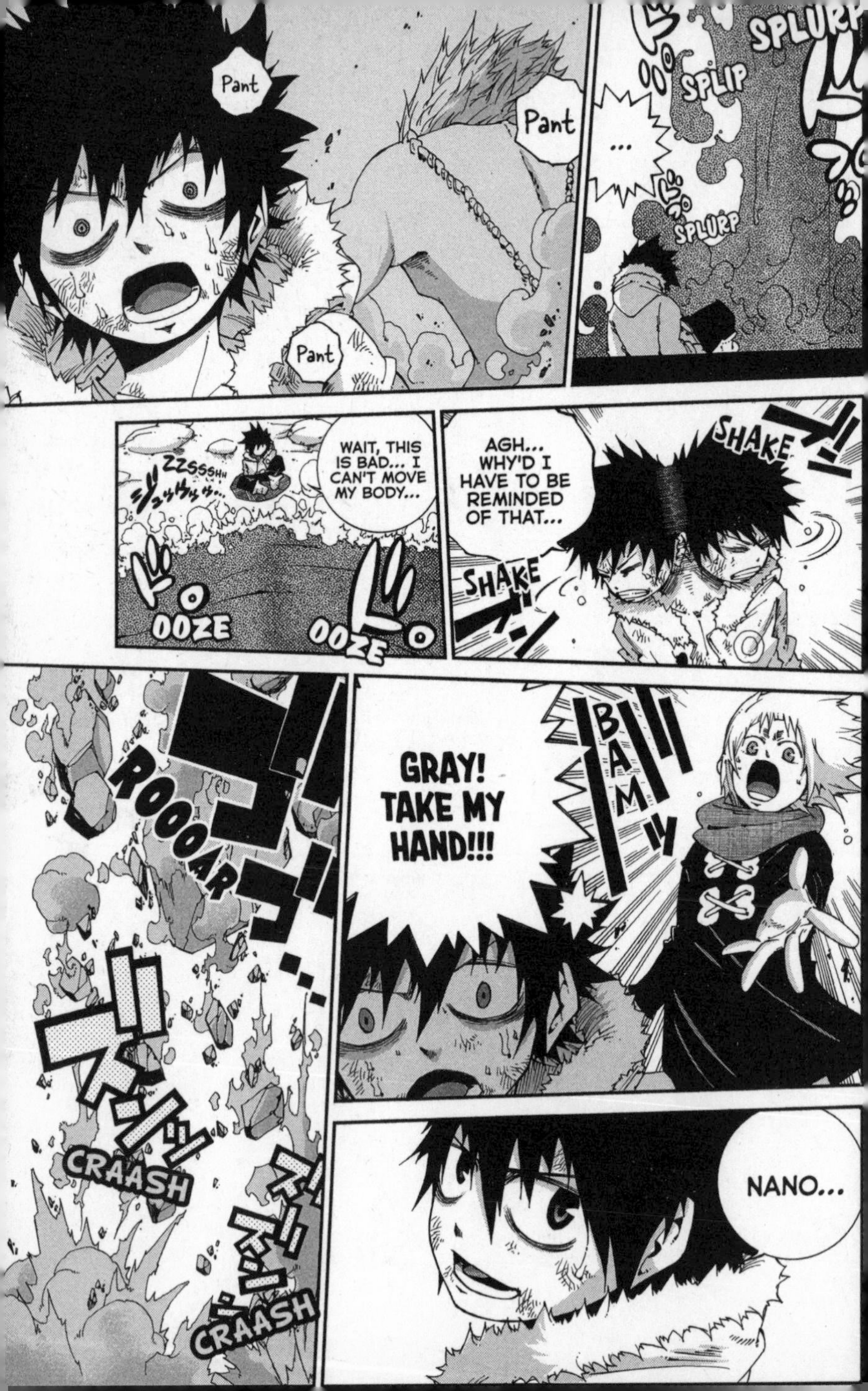
SPLURP
SPLIP
...
SPLURP
Pant
Pant
Pant
SHAKE
AGH... WHY'D I HAVE TO BE REMINDED OF THAT...
SHAKE
WAIT, THIS IS BAD... I CAN'T MOVE MY BODY...
ZZSSSHH
OOZE
OOZE
BAM
GRAY! TAKE MY HAND!!!
NANO...
ROOOOAR
CRAASH
CRAASH

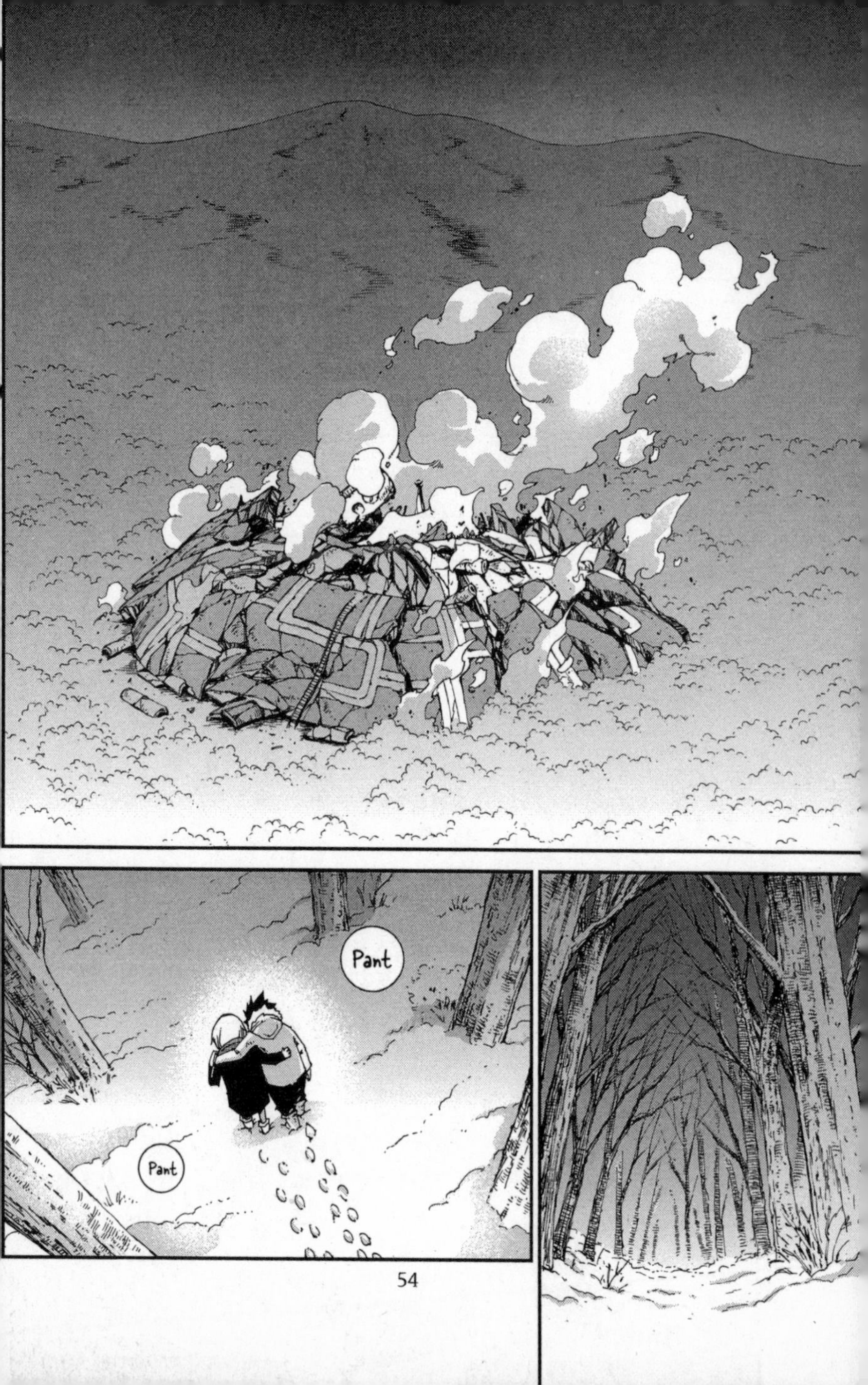
Pant
Pant

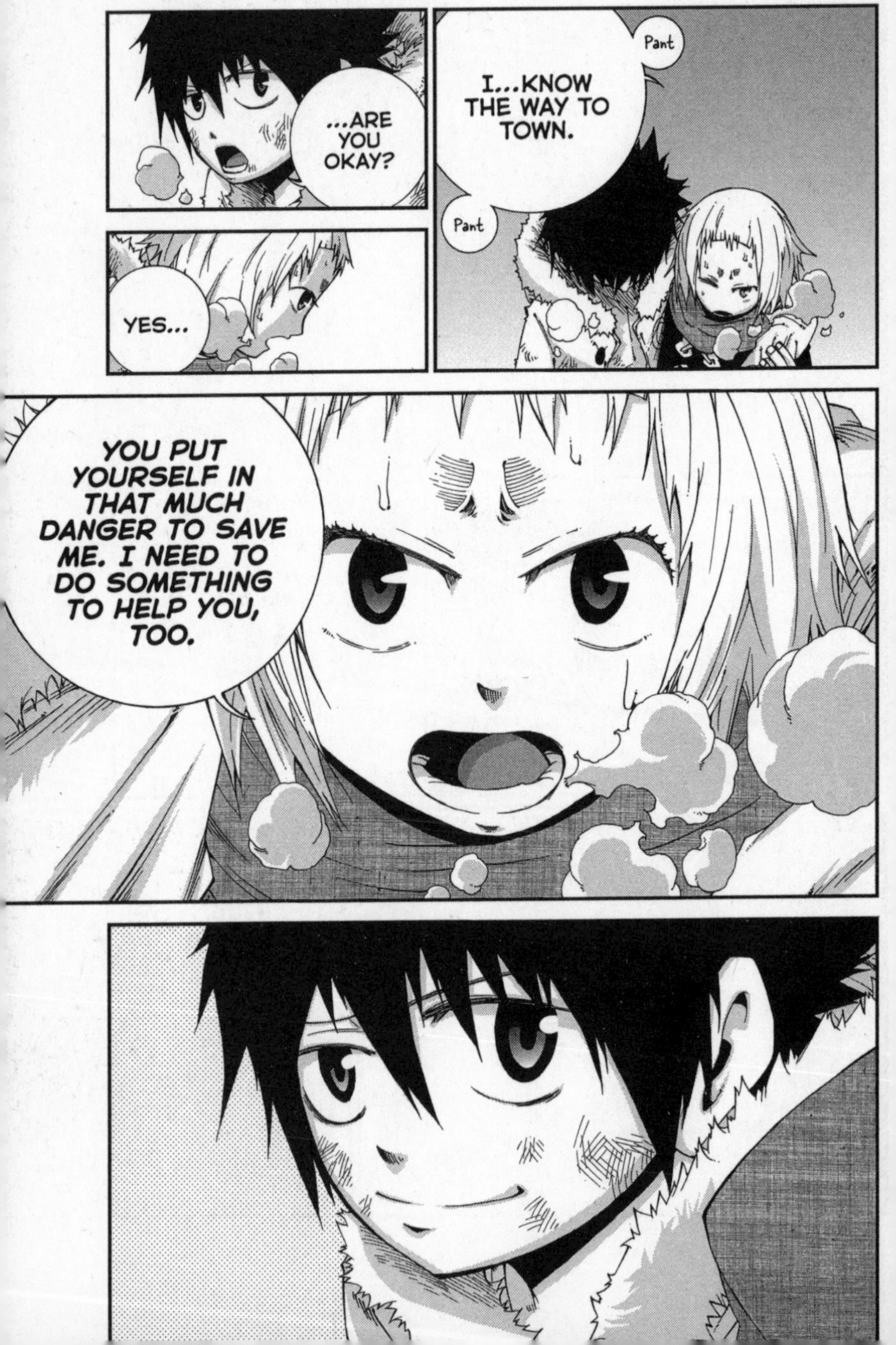
...ARE YOU OKAY?
YES...
Pant
I...KNOW THE WAY TO TOWN.
Pant
YOU PUT YOURSELF IN THAT MUCH DANGER TO SAVE ME. I NEED TO DO SOMETHING TO HELP YOU, TOO.

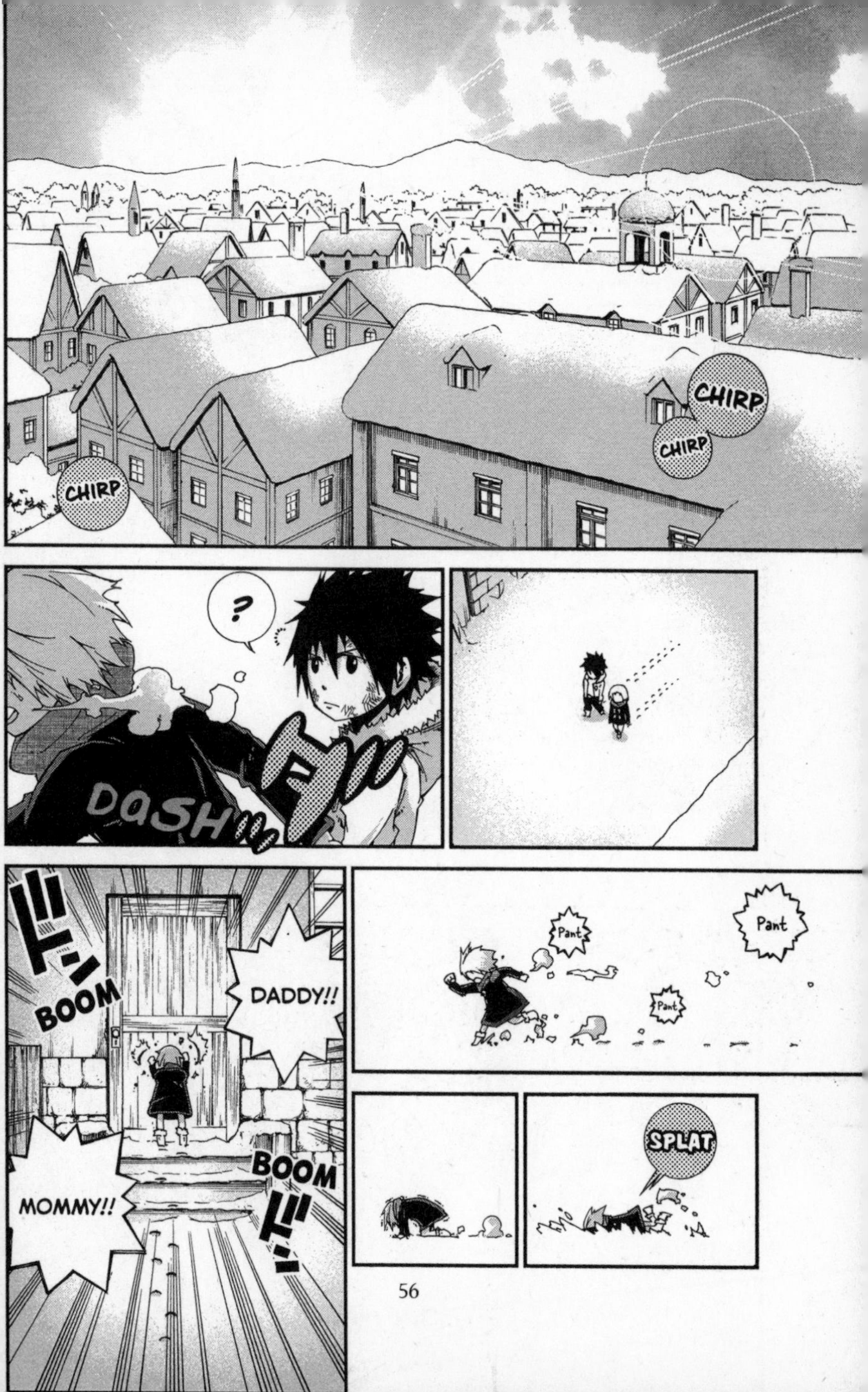
CHIRP
CHIRP
CHIRP
?
DASH
Pant
Pant
Pant
SPLAT
DADDY!!
BOOM
BOOM
MOMMY!!

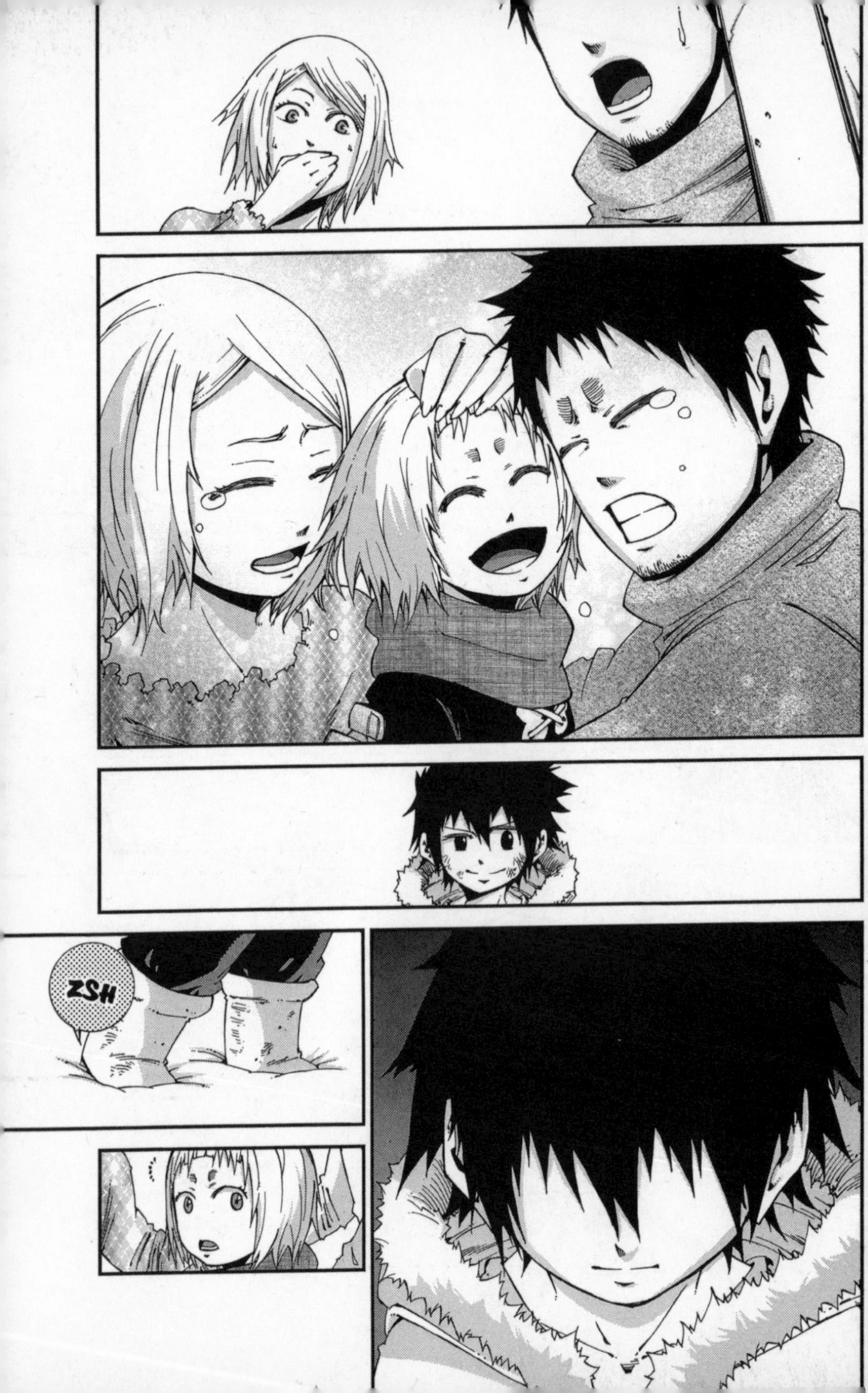
ZSH

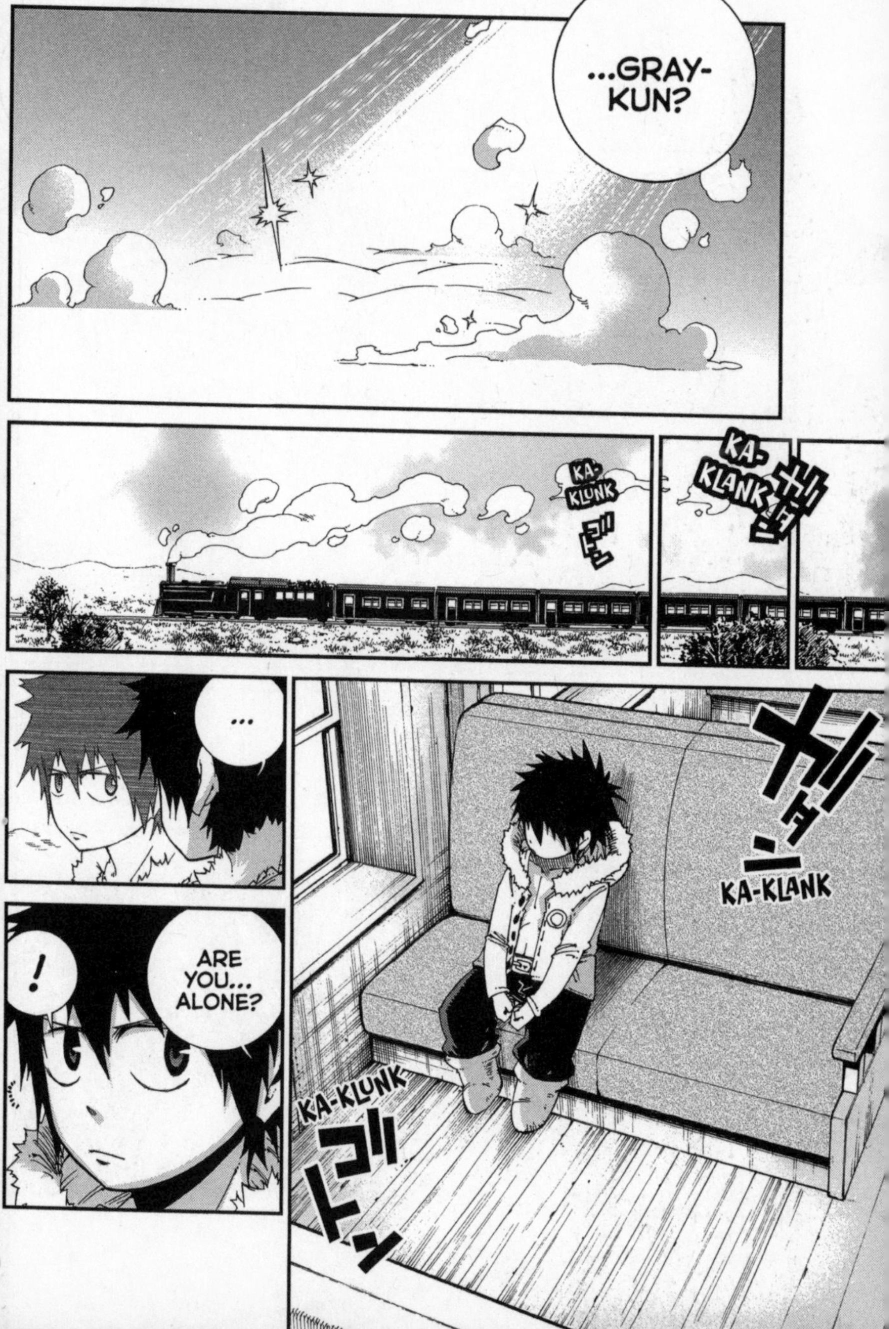
...GRAY-KUN?
KA-KLANK
KA-KLUNK
KA-KLANK
KA-KLUNK
...
!
ARE YOU... ALONE?

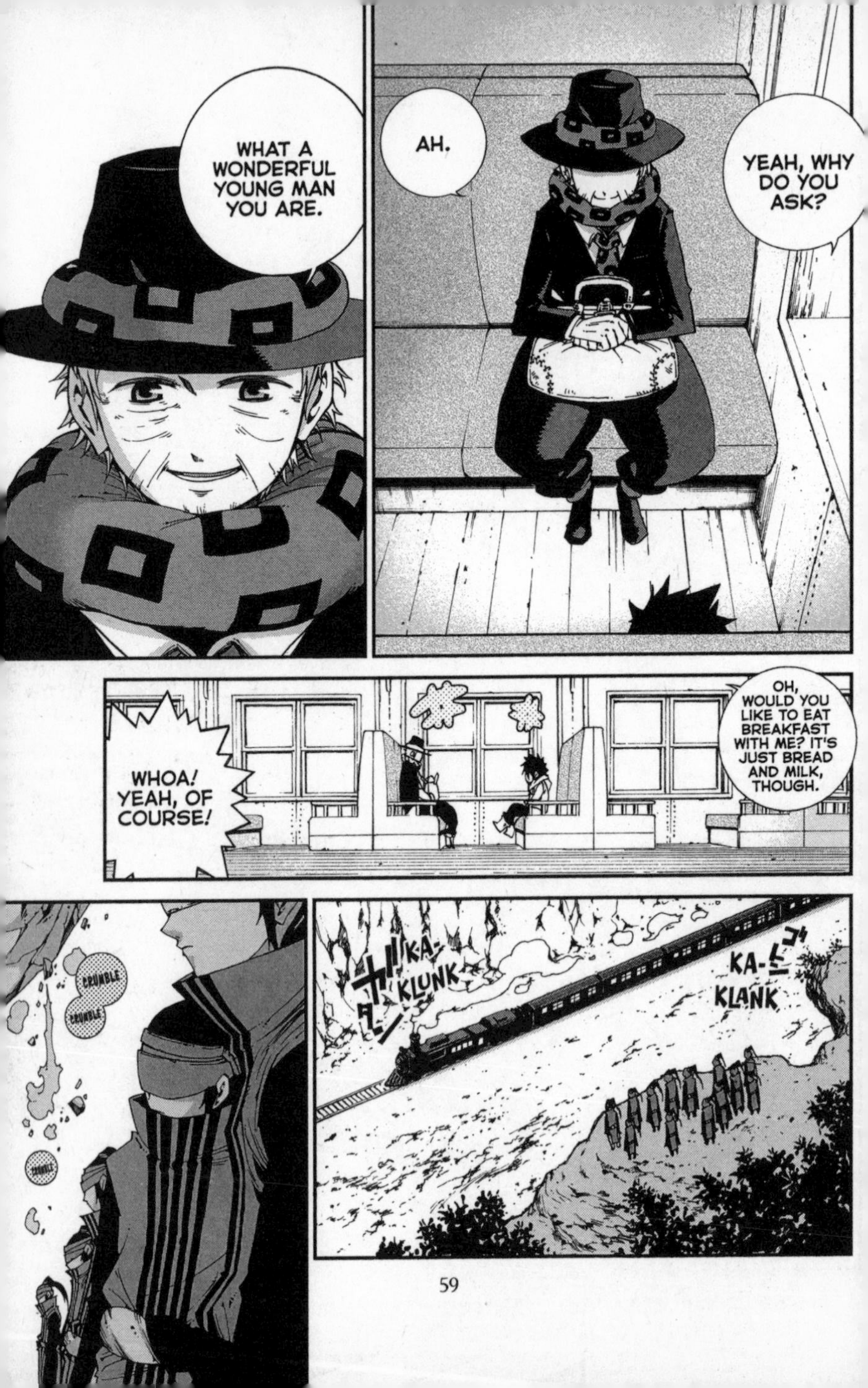
YEAH, WHY DO YOU ASK?
AH.
WHAT A WONDERFUL YOUNG MAN YOU ARE.
OH, WOULD YOU LIKE TO EAT BREAKFAST WITH ME? IT'S JUST BREAD AND MILK, THOUGH.
WHOA! YEAH, OF COURSE!
KA-KLANK
KA-KLUNK
CRUMBLE
CRUMBLE
CRUMBLE

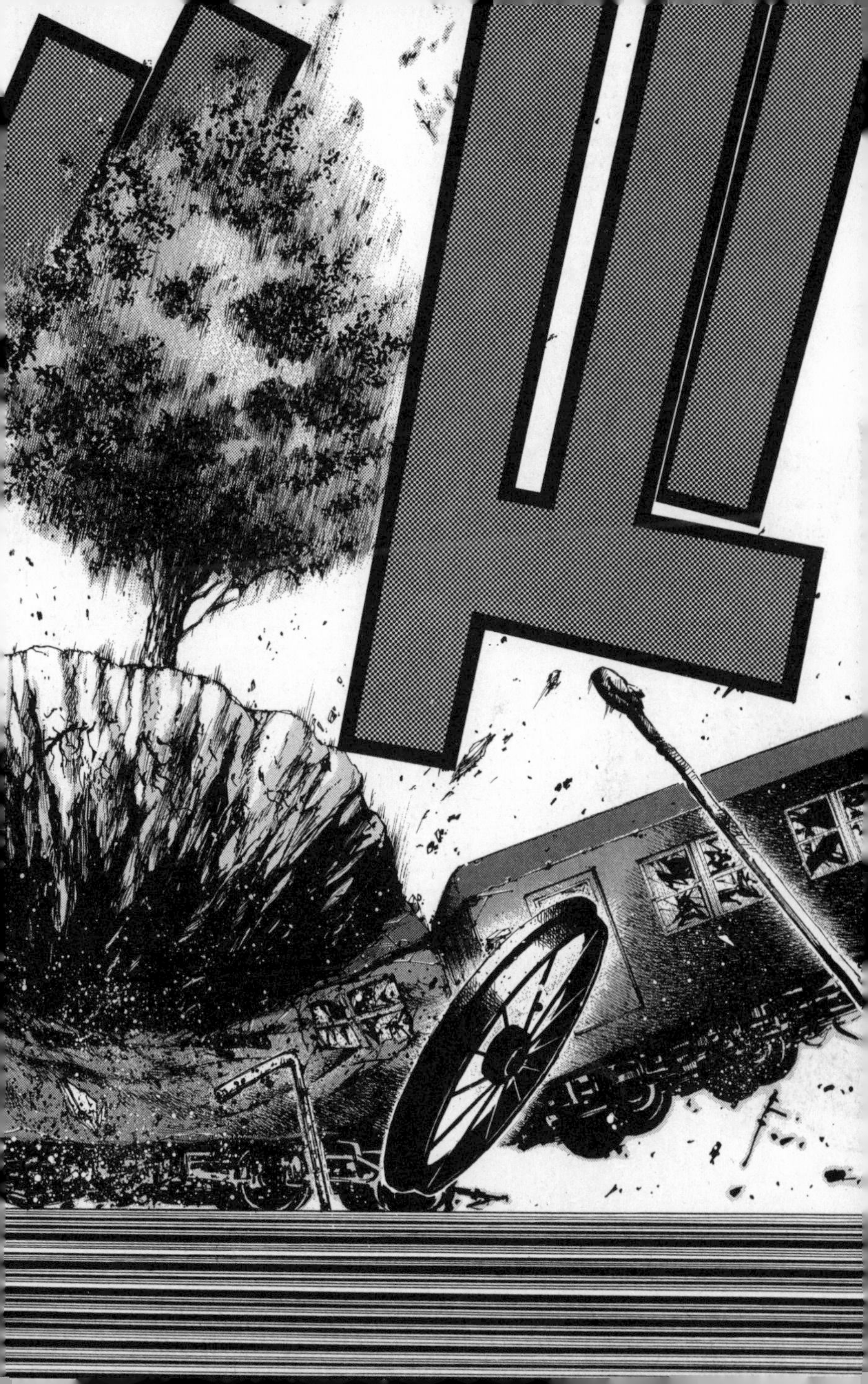

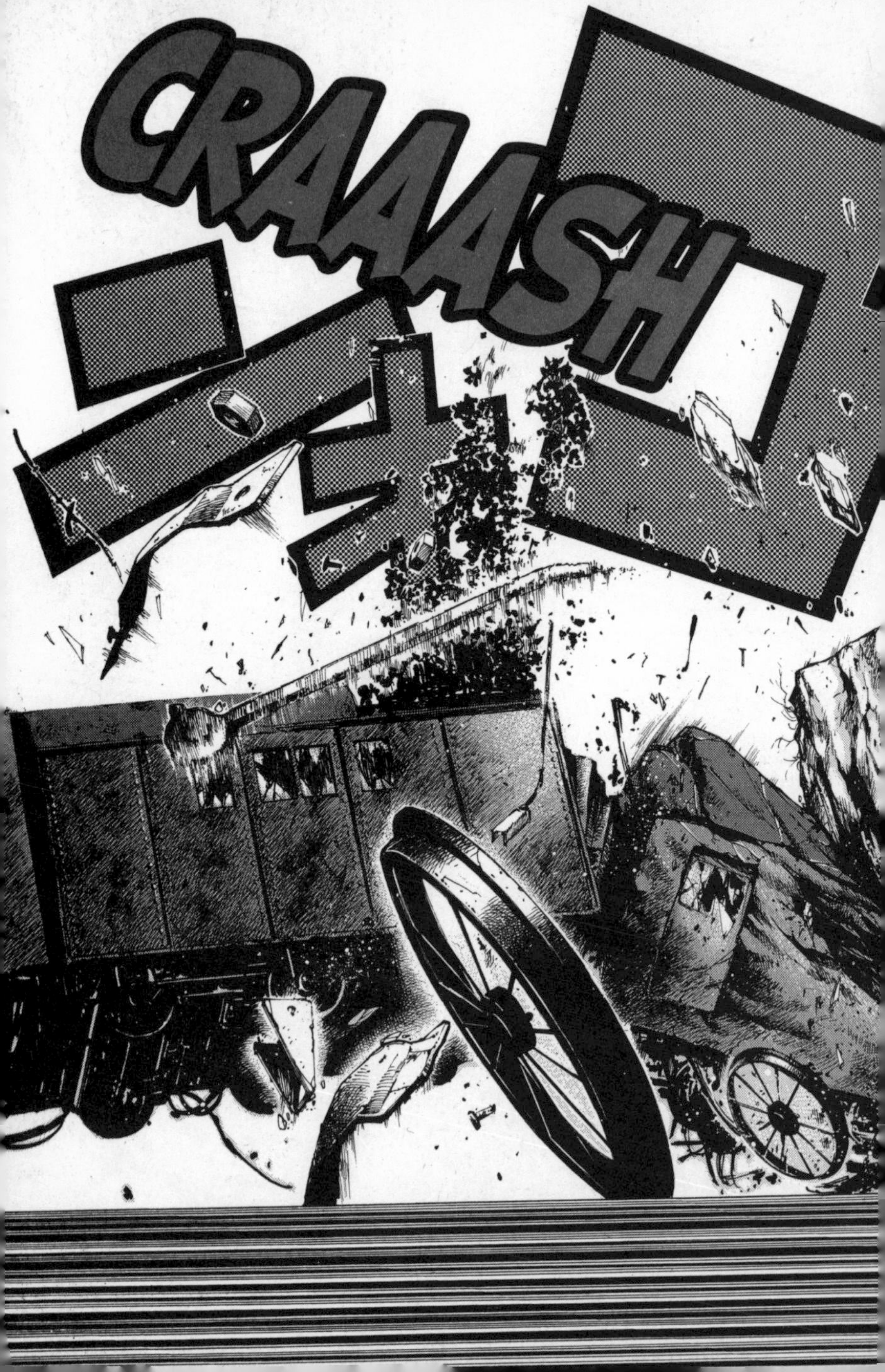
CRAAASH

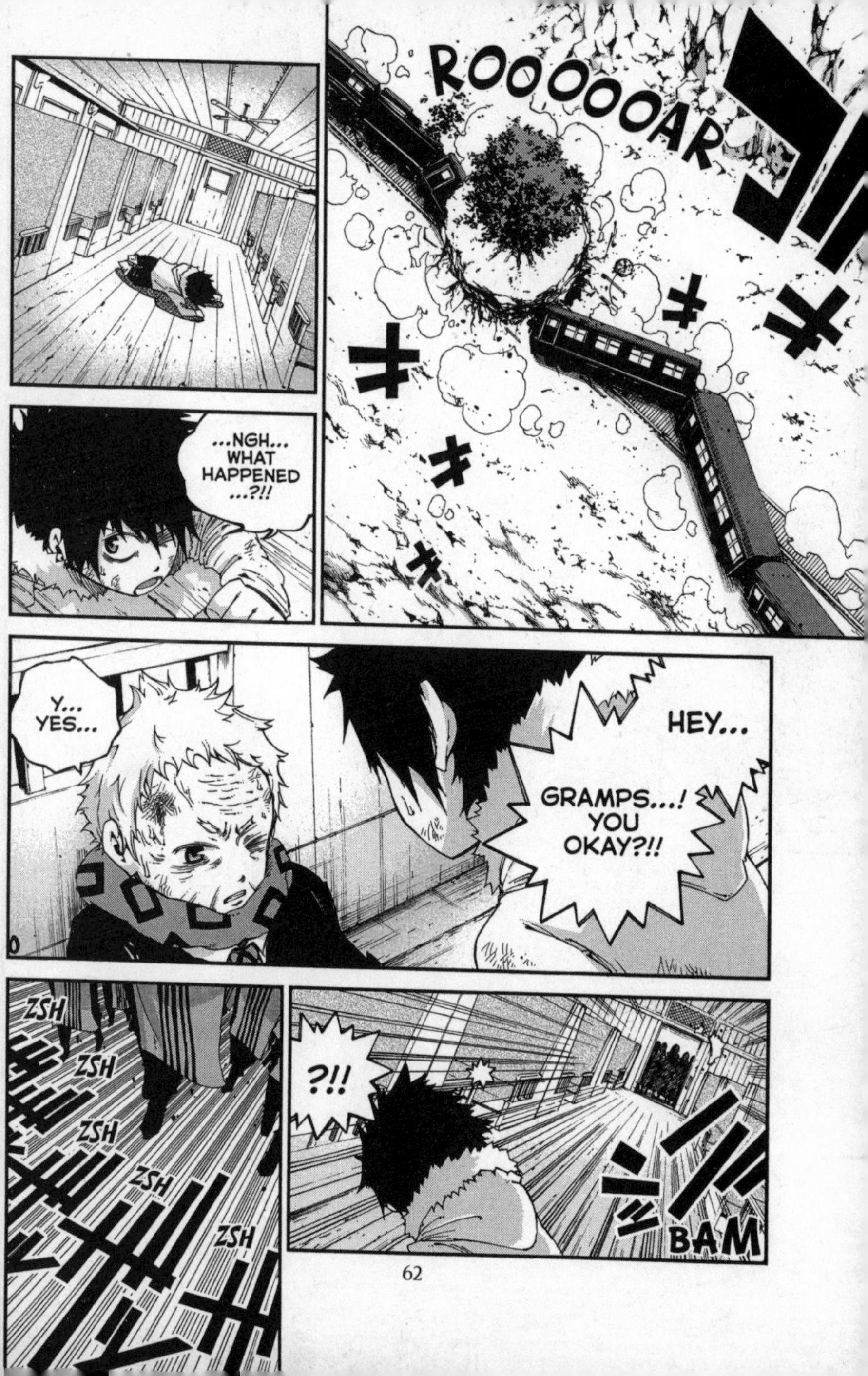
ROOOOOAR
...NGH... WHAT HAPPENED ...?!!
HEY...
GRAMPS...! YOU OKAY?!!
Y... YES...
?!!
BAM
ZSH
ZSH
ZSH
ZSH
ZSH

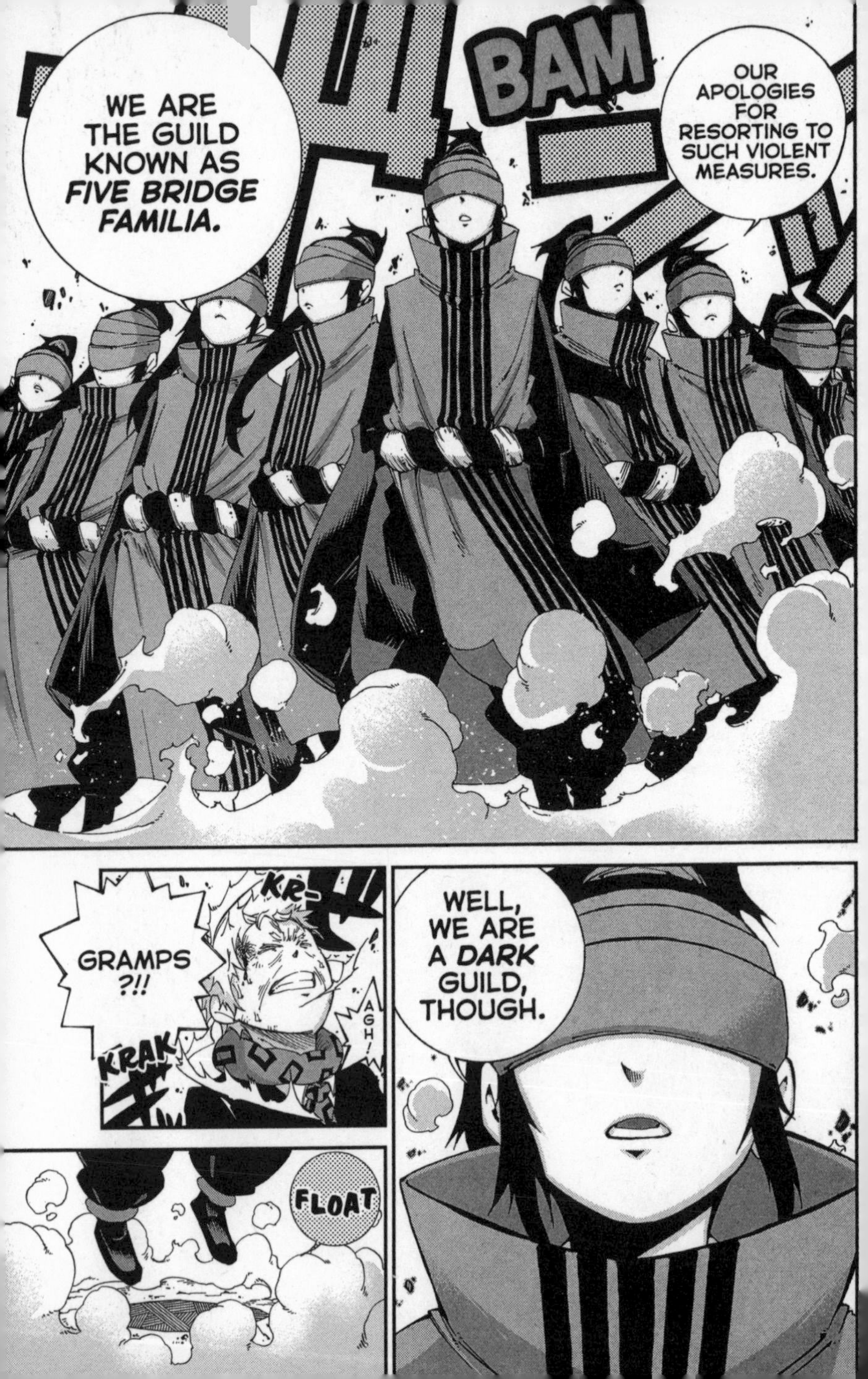
OUR APOLOGIES FOR RESORTING TO SUCH VIOLENT MEASURES.
BAM
WE ARE THE GUILD KNOWN AS *FIVE BRIDGE FAMILIA.*
WELL, WE ARE A *DARK* GUILD, THOUGH.
KR-
GRAMPS ?!!
AGH!
KRAK
FLOAT

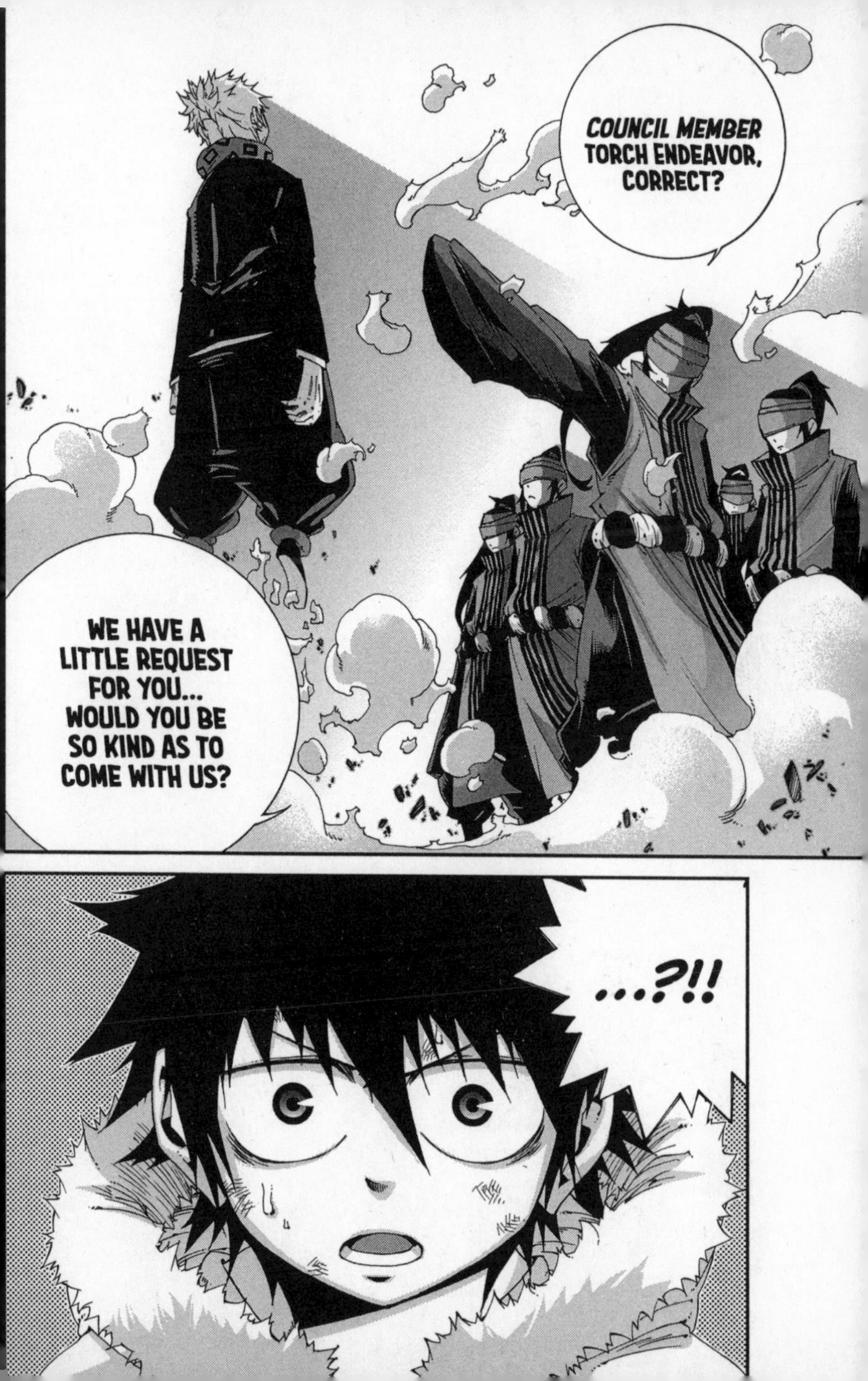
COUNCIL MEMBER TORCH ENDEAVOR, CORRECT?
WE HAVE A LITTLE REQUEST FOR YOU... WOULD YOU BE SO KIND AS TO COME WITH US?
...?!!

Chapter 3: Black Vox

FAIRY TAIL: ICE TRAIL

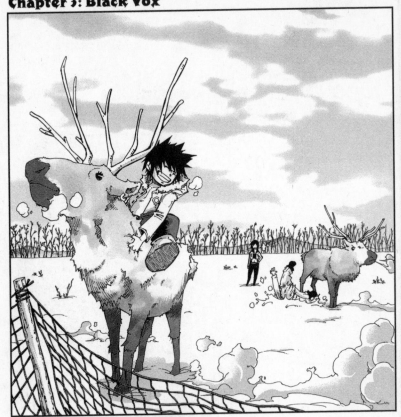

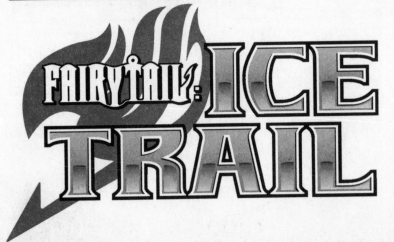

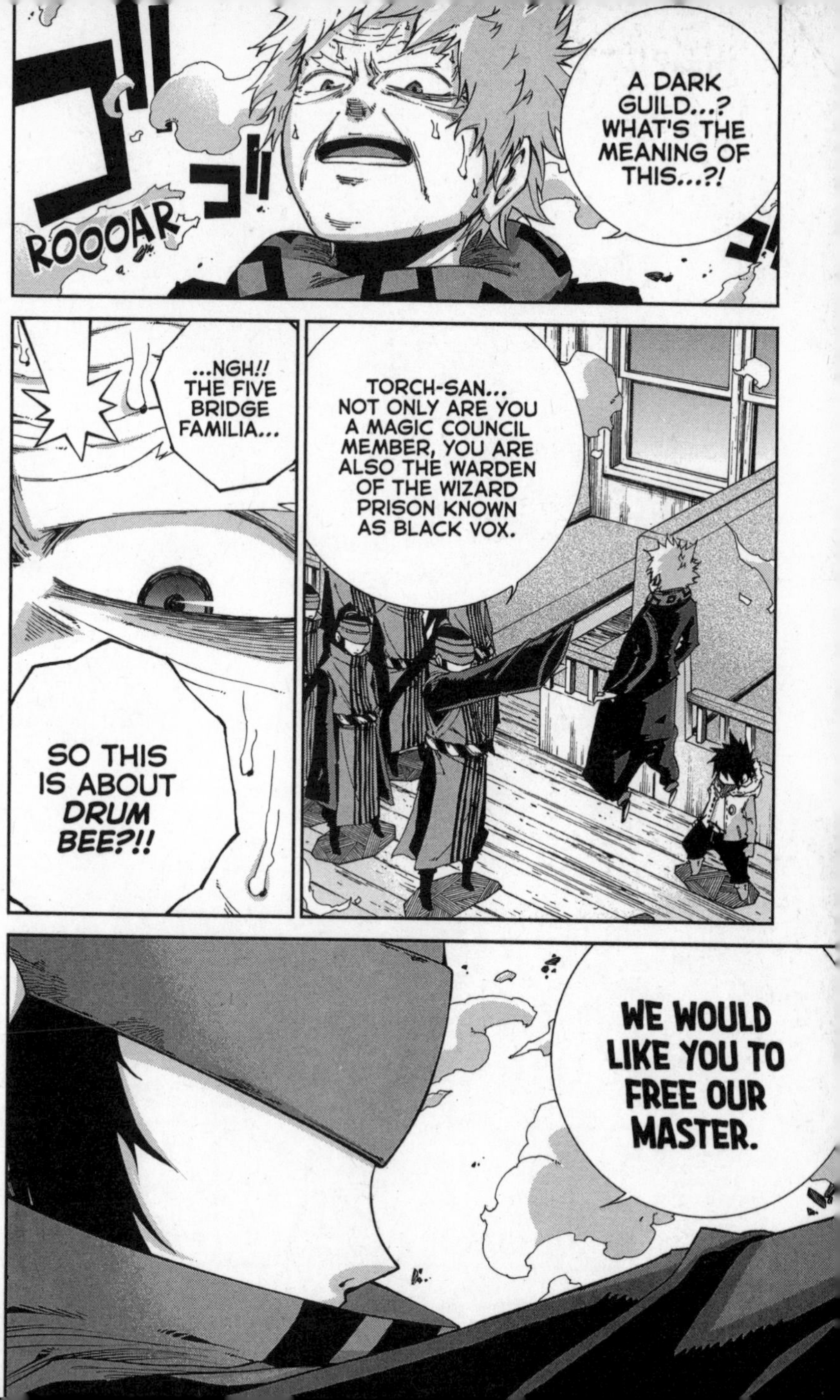
A DARK GUILD...? WHAT'S THE MEANING OF THIS...?!
ROOOAR
TORCH-SAN... NOT ONLY ARE YOU A MAGIC COUNCIL MEMBER, YOU ARE ALSO THE WARDEN OF THE WIZARD PRISON KNOWN AS BLACK VOX.
...NGH!! THE FIVE BRIDGE FAMILIA...
SO THIS IS ABOUT *DRUM BEE*?!!
WE WOULD LIKE YOU TO FREE OUR MASTER.

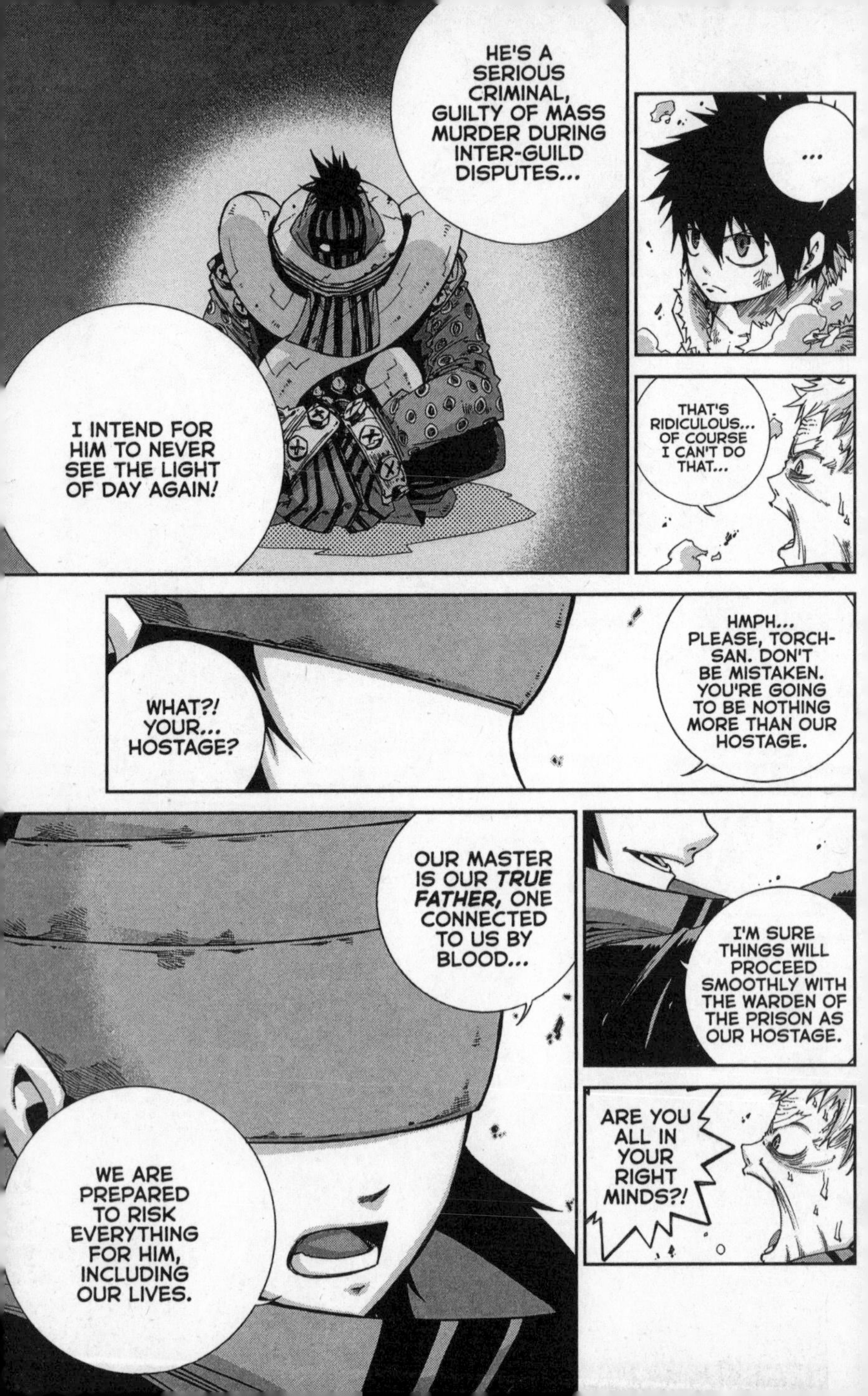
...
THAT'S RIDICULOUS... OF COURSE I CAN'T DO THAT...
HE'S A SERIOUS CRIMINAL, GUILTY OF MASS MURDER DURING INTER-GUILD DISPUTES...
I INTEND FOR HIM TO NEVER SEE THE LIGHT OF DAY AGAIN!
HMPH... PLEASE, TORCH-SAN. DON'T BE MISTAKEN. YOU'RE GOING TO BE NOTHING MORE THAN OUR HOSTAGE.
WHAT?! YOUR... HOSTAGE?
I'M SURE THINGS WILL PROCEED SMOOTHLY WITH THE WARDEN OF THE PRISON AS OUR HOSTAGE.
ARE YOU ALL IN YOUR RIGHT MINDS?!
OUR MASTER IS OUR *TRUE FATHER,* ONE CONNECTED TO US BY BLOOD...
WE ARE PREPARED TO RISK EVERYTHING FOR HIM, INCLUDING OUR LIVES.

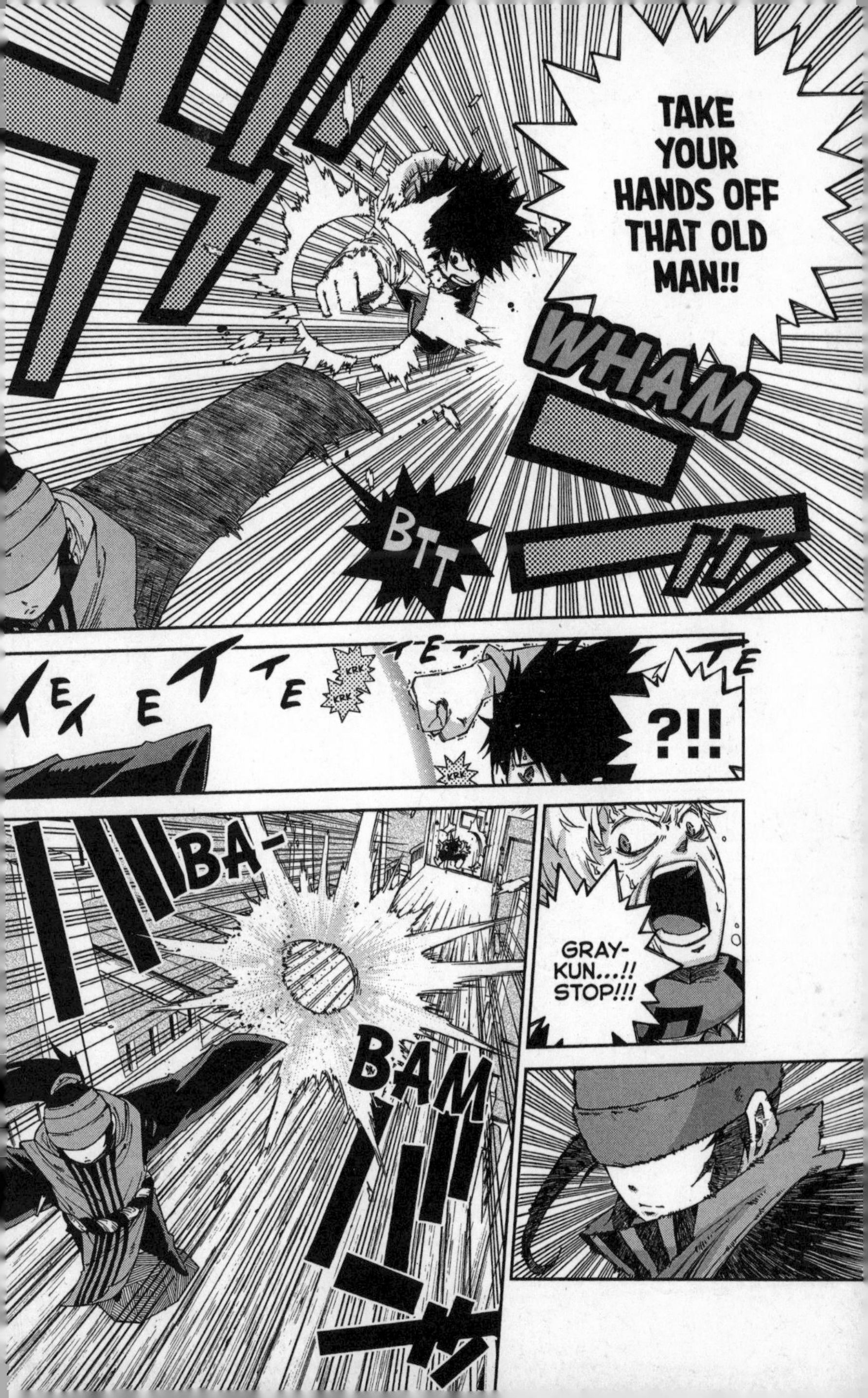
TAKE YOUR HANDS OFF THAT OLD MAN!!
WHAM
BTT
?!!
TE
TE
KRK
KRK
KRK
TE
TE
TE
GRAY-KUN...!! STOP!!!
BA-
BAM

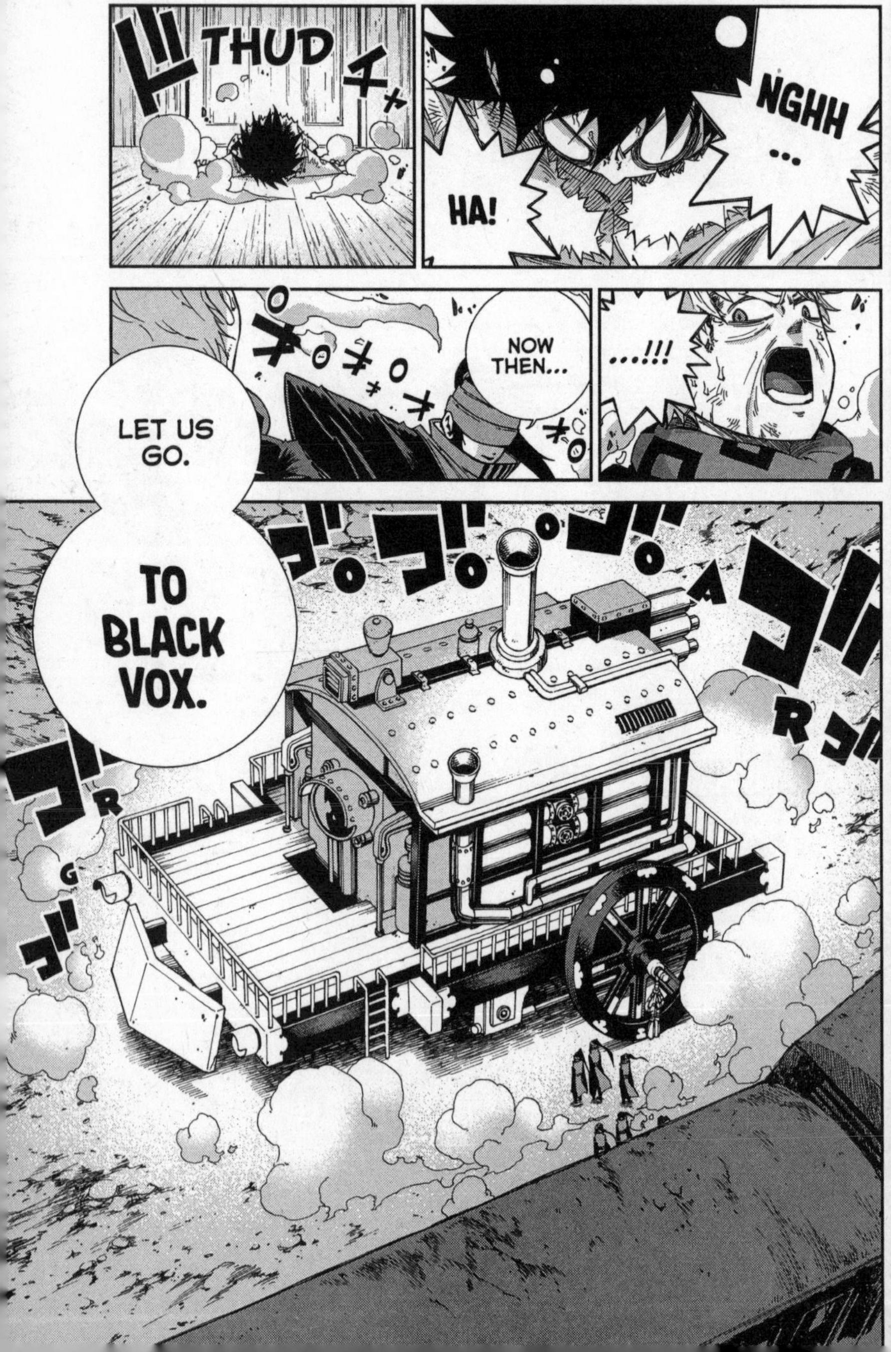
NGHH ...
HA!
THUD
...!!!
NOW THEN...
LET US GO.
TO BLACK VOX.

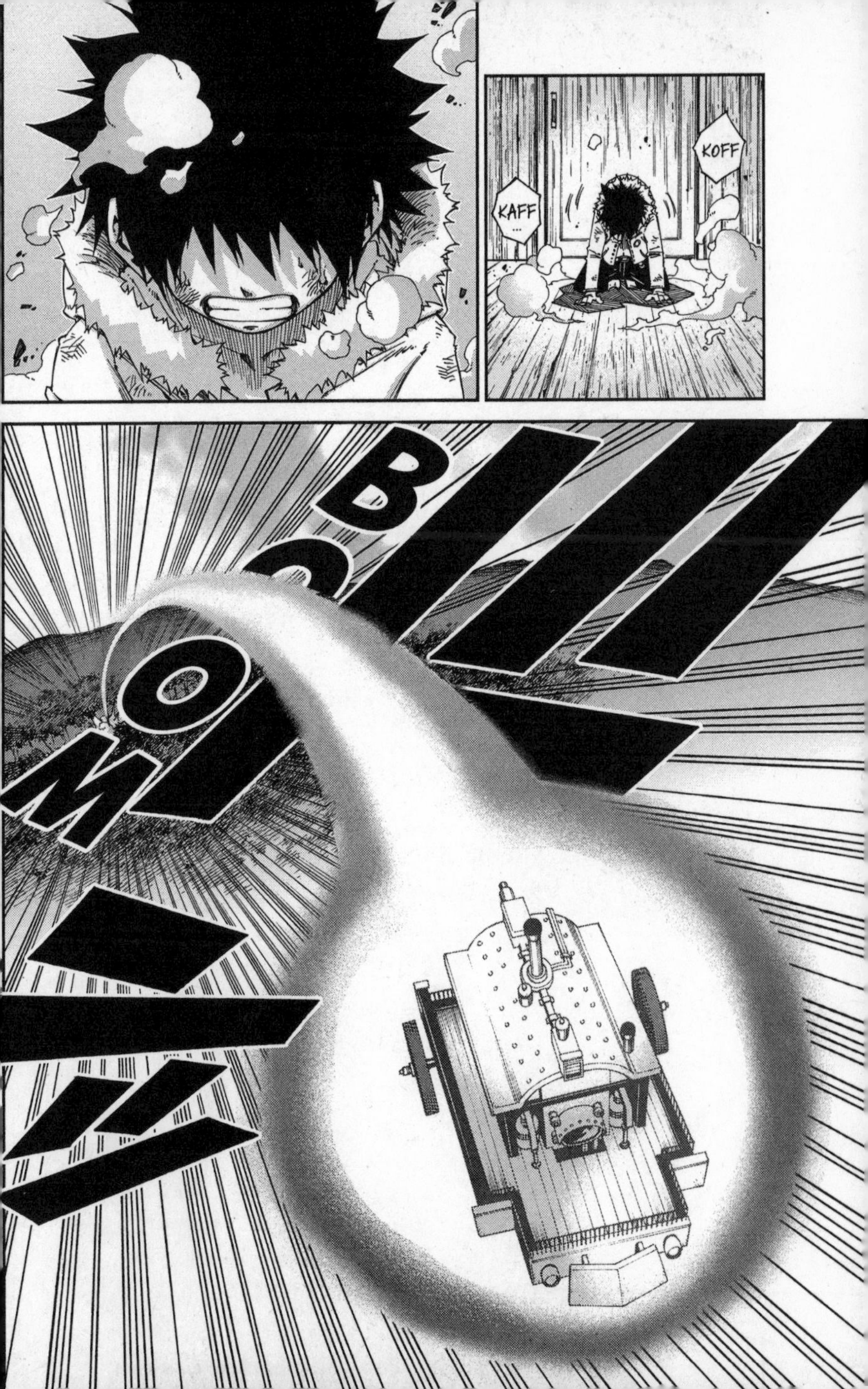
KOFF
KAFF ...
BOOM

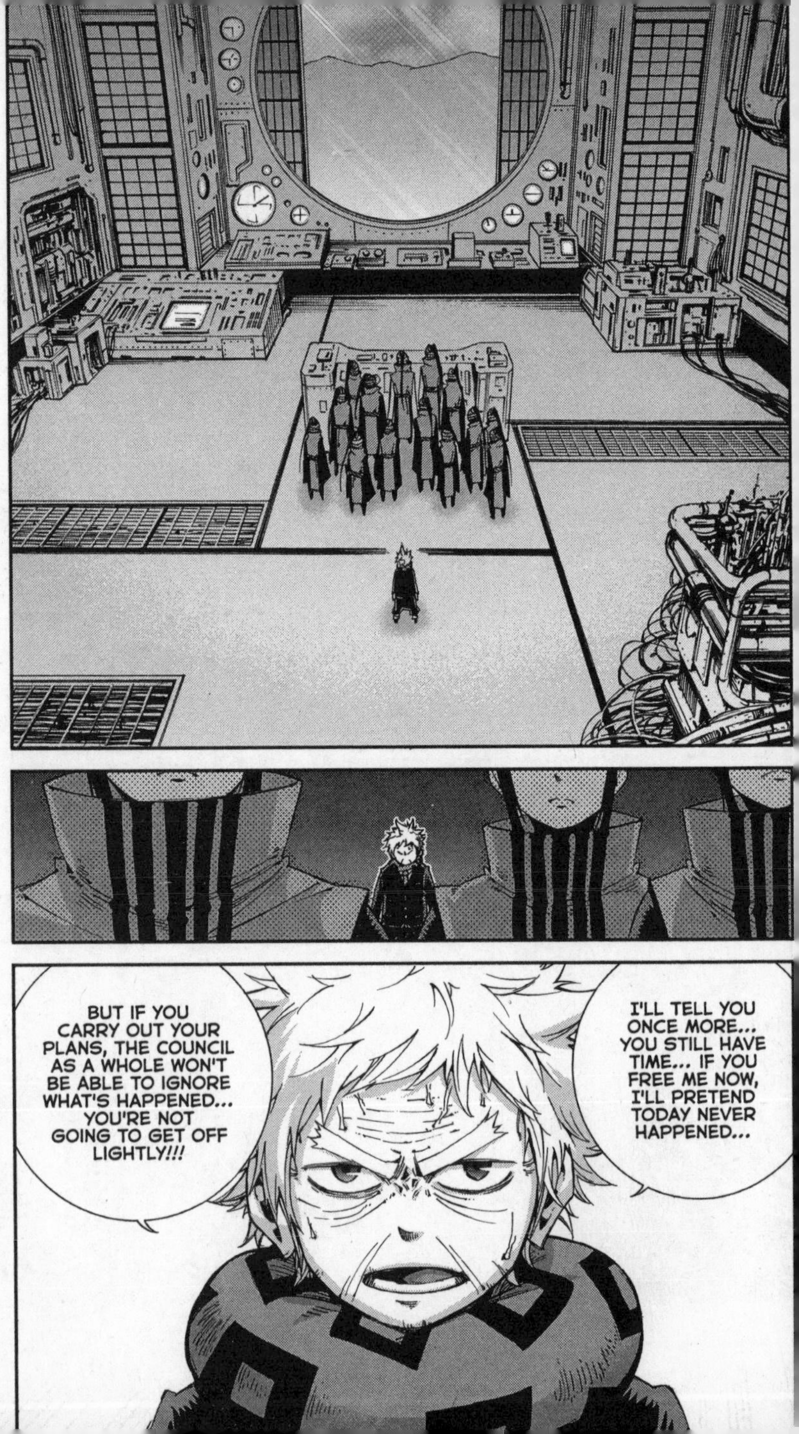
I'LL TELL YOU ONCE MORE... YOU STILL HAVE TIME... IF YOU FREE ME NOW, I'LL PRETEND TODAY NEVER HAPPENED...
BUT IF YOU CARRY OUT YOUR PLANS, THE COUNCIL AS A WHOLE WON'T BE ABLE TO IGNORE WHAT'S HAPPENED... YOU'RE NOT GOING TO GET OFF LIGHTLY!!!

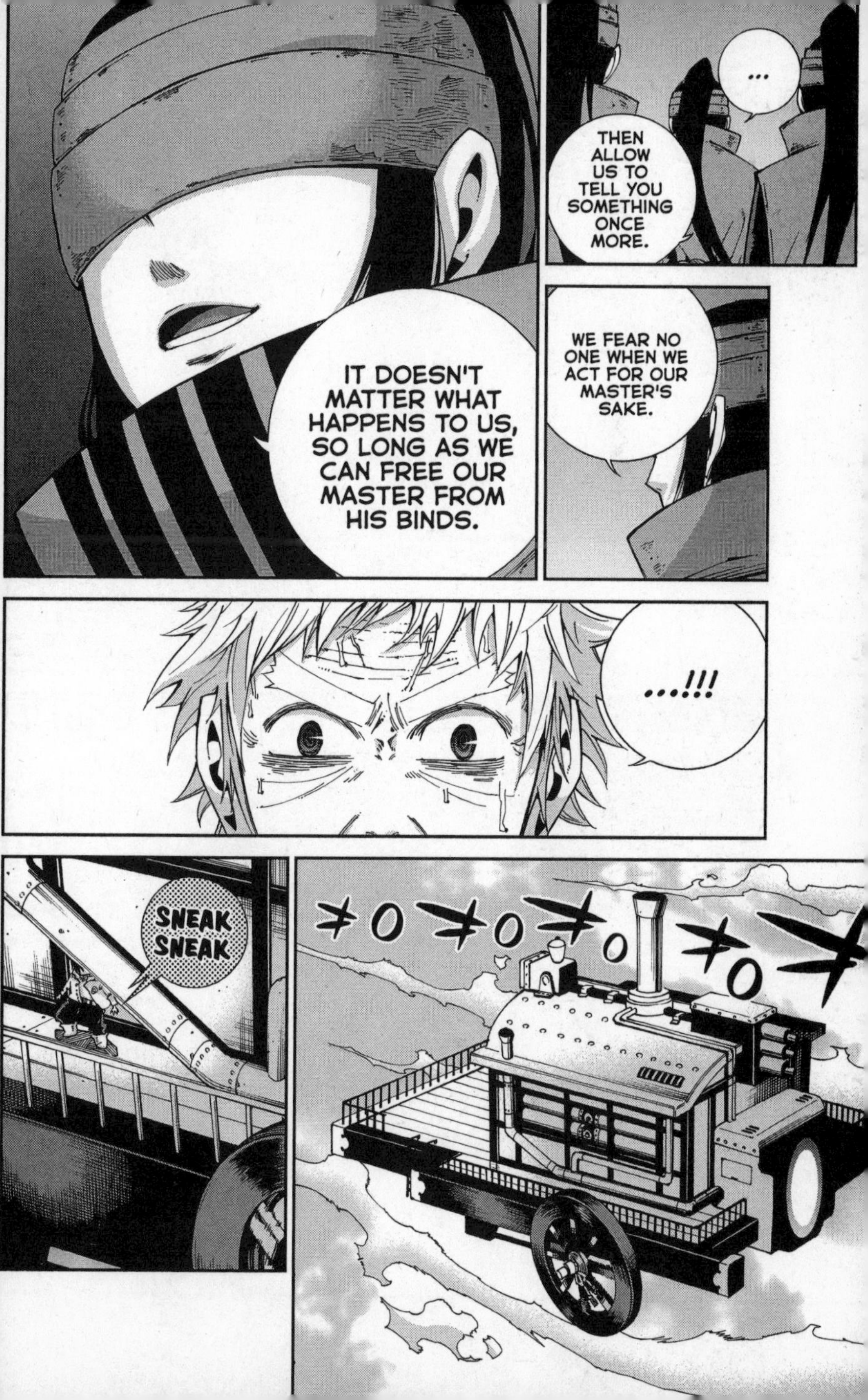
...
THEN ALLOW US TO TELL YOU SOMETHING ONCE MORE.
WE FEAR NO ONE WHEN WE ACT FOR OUR MASTER'S SAKE.
IT DOESN'T MATTER WHAT HAPPENS TO US, SO LONG AS WE CAN FREE OUR MASTER FROM HIS BINDS.
...!!!
SNEAK SNEAK

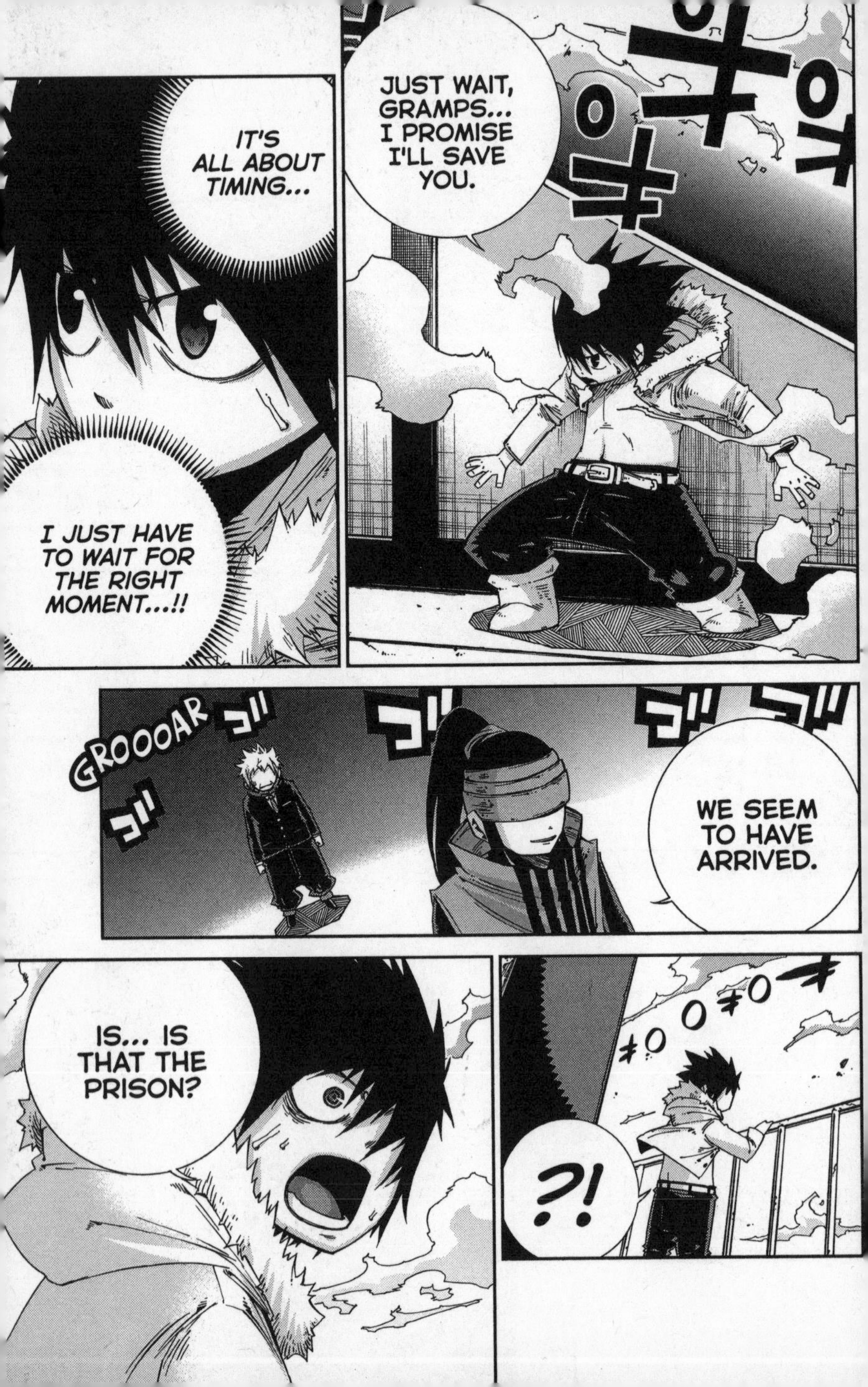

JUST WAIT, GRAMPS... I PROMISE I'LL SAVE YOU.
IT'S ALL ABOUT TIMING...
I JUST HAVE TO WAIT FOR THE RIGHT MOMENT...!!
WE SEEM TO HAVE ARRIVED.
GROOOAR
?!
IS... IS THAT THE PRISON?

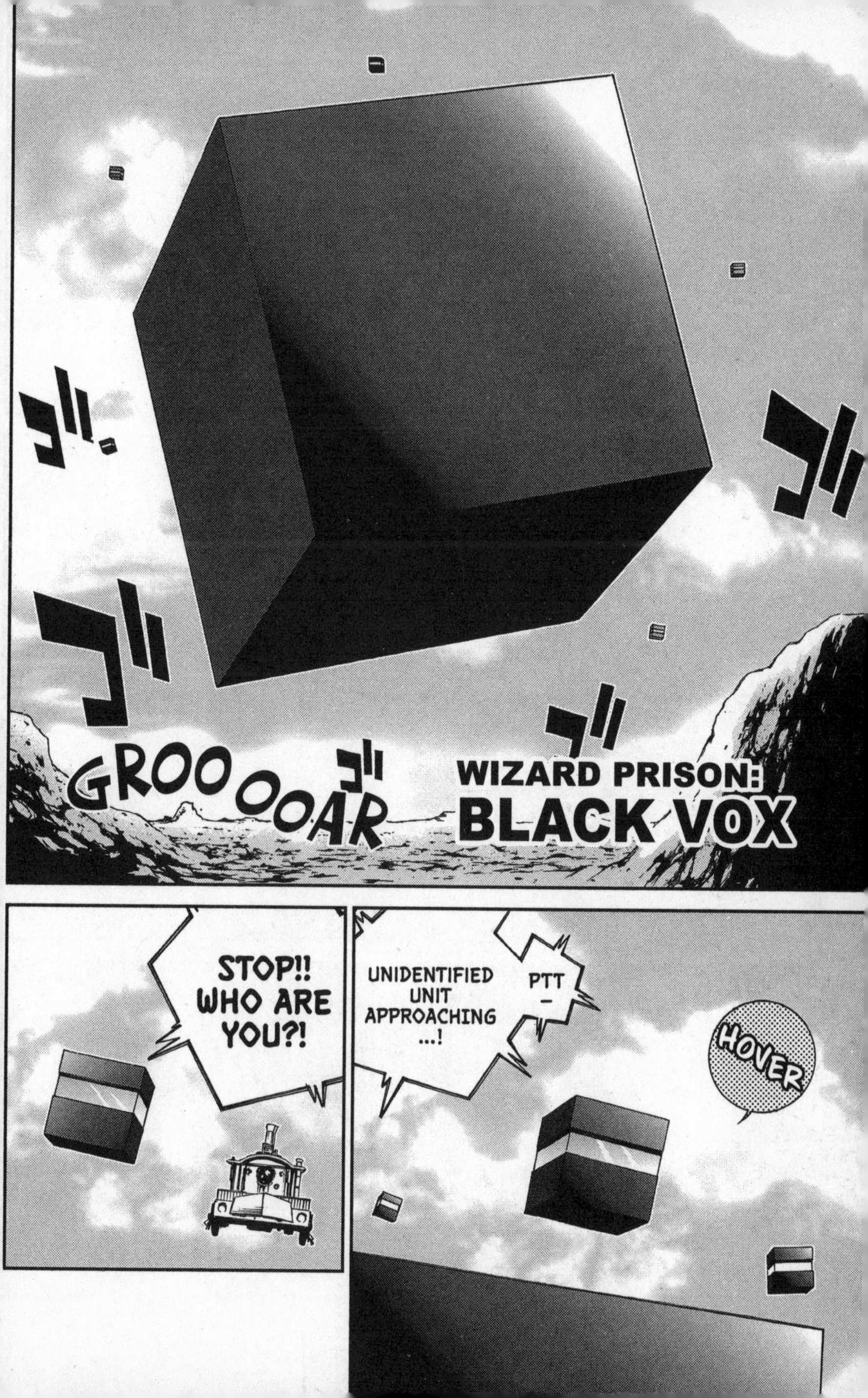
WIZARD PRISON:
BLACK VOX
GROOOOAR
PTT —
HOVER
UNIDENTIFIED UNIT APPROACHING ...!
STOP!! WHO ARE YOU?!

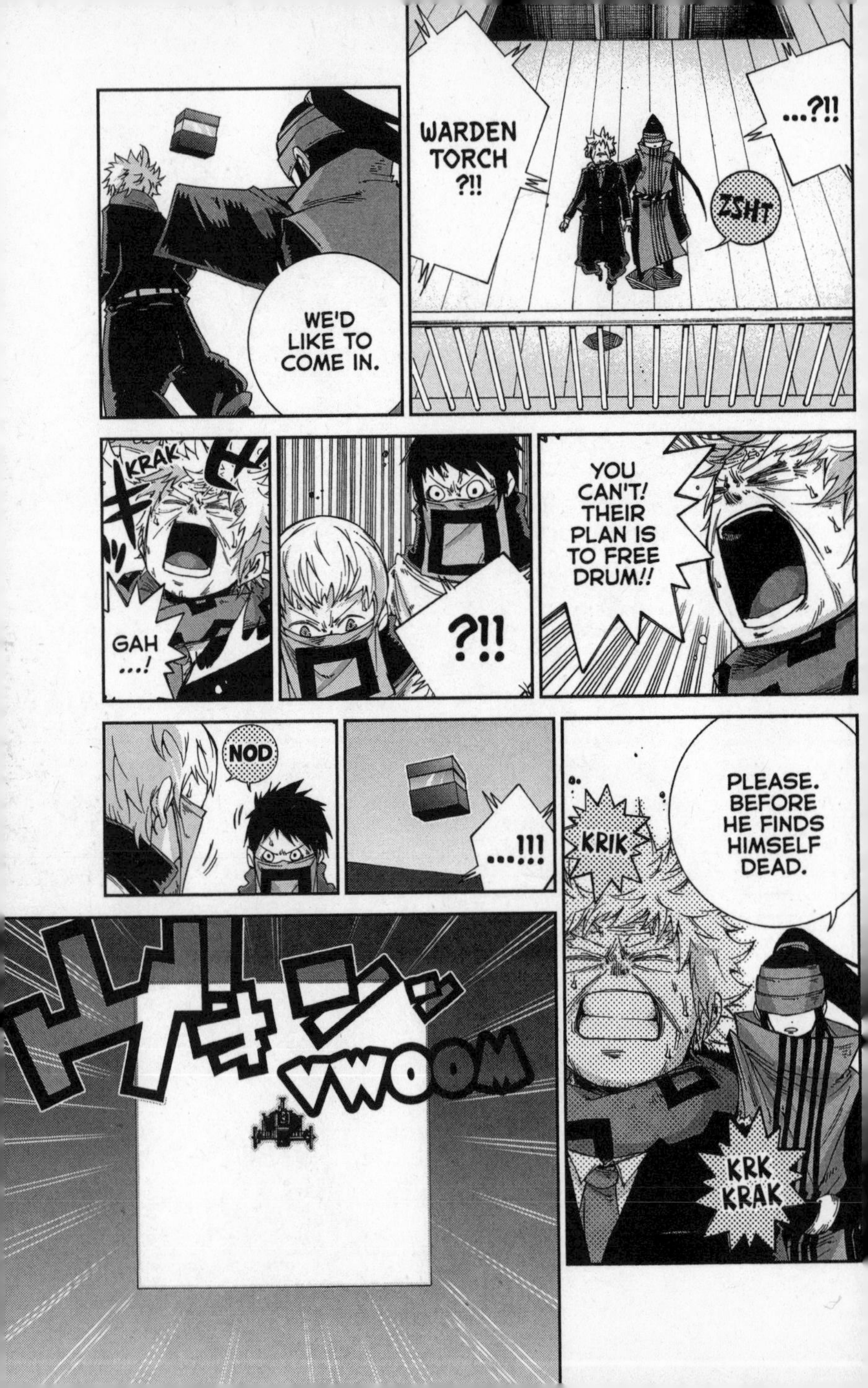
...?!!
WARDEN TORCH ?!!
ZSHT
WE'D LIKE TO COME IN.
YOU CAN'T! THEIR PLAN IS TO FREE DRUM!!
?!!
KRAK
GAH ...!
PLEASE. BEFORE HE FINDS HIMSELF DEAD.
KRIK
KRK KRAK
...!!!
NOD
VWOOM

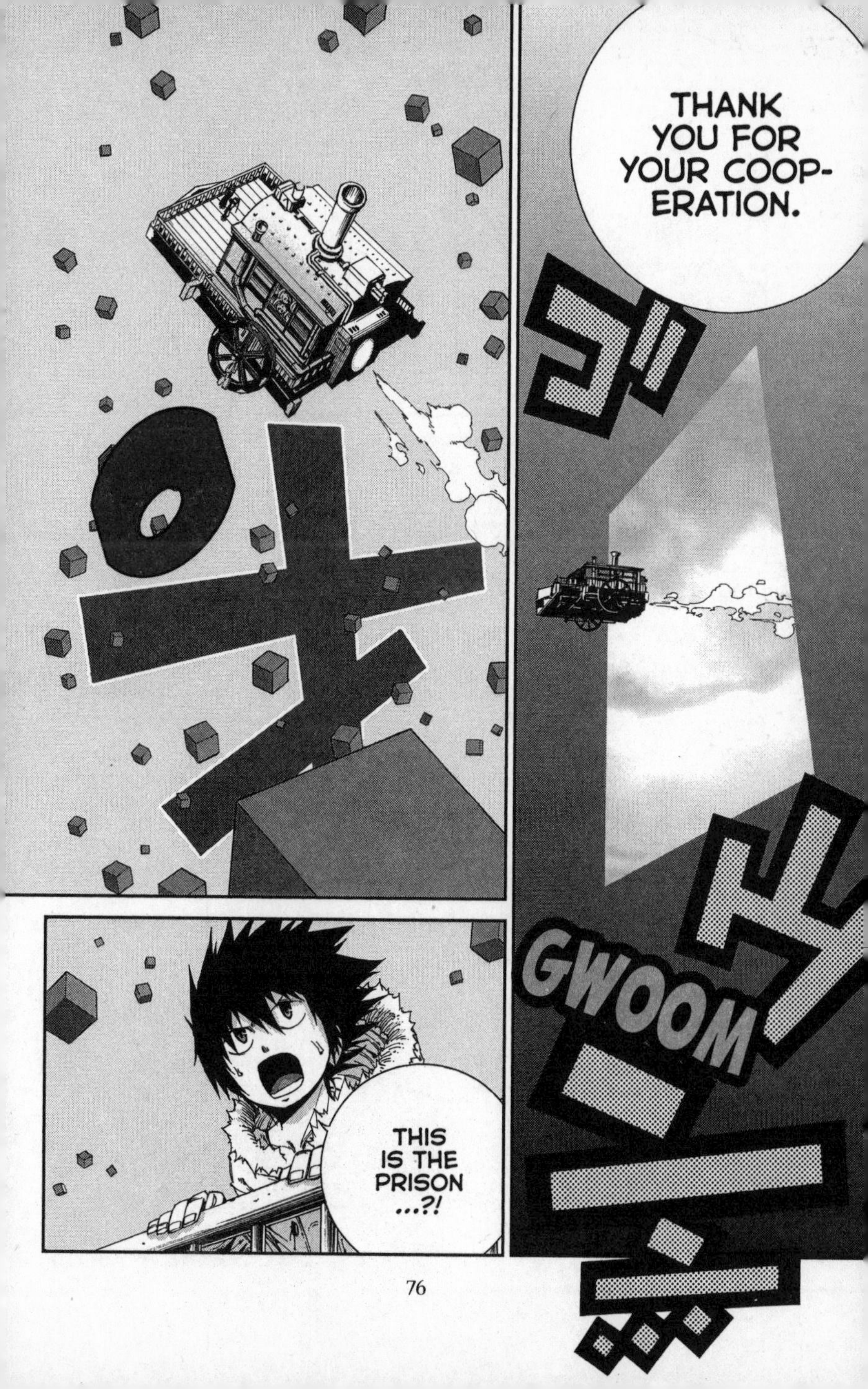
THANK YOU FOR YOUR COOP-ERATION.
GWOOM
THIS IS THE PRISON ...?!

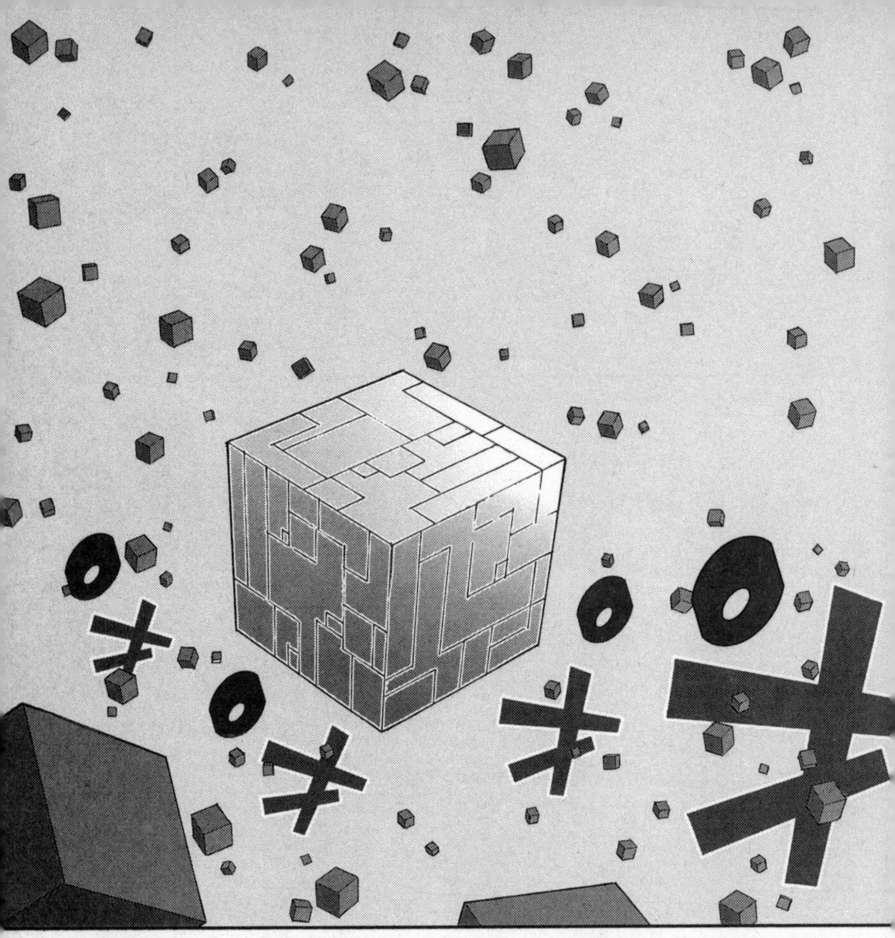

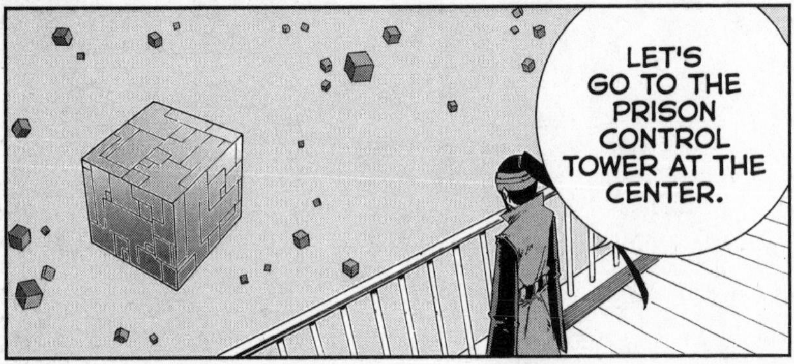
LET'S GO TO THE PRISON CONTROL TOWER AT THE CENTER.

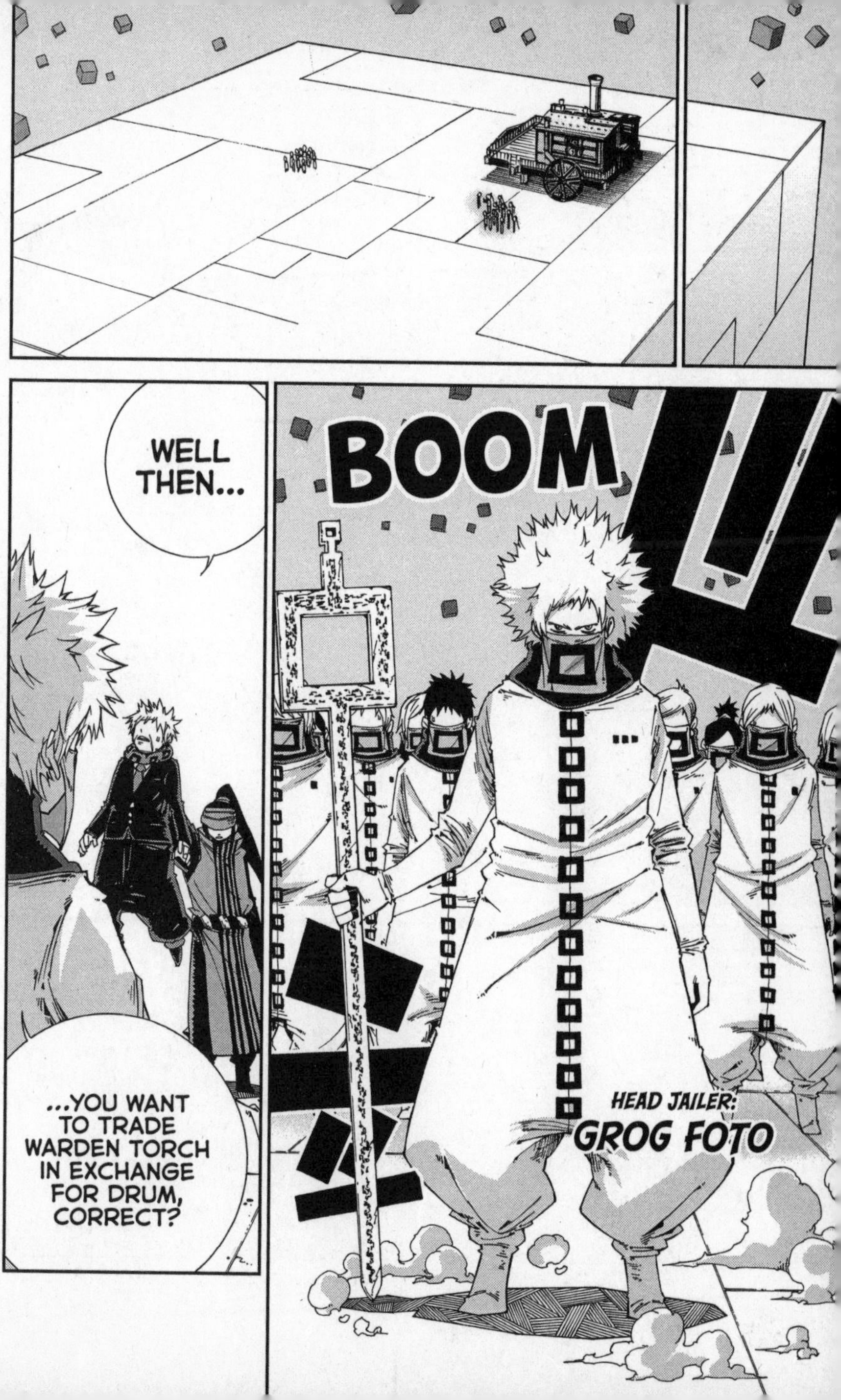
BOOM
HEAD JAILER:
GROG FOTO
WELL THEN...
...YOU WANT TO TRADE WARDEN TORCH IN EXCHANGE FOR DRUM, CORRECT?

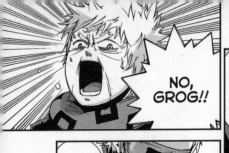

NO, GROG!!

WE WILL KEEP OUR PROMISE.

YES.

...

BUT YOU, WARDEN TORCH, ARE LIKE A FATHER TO ME... SO PLEASE...

I'M SORRY...

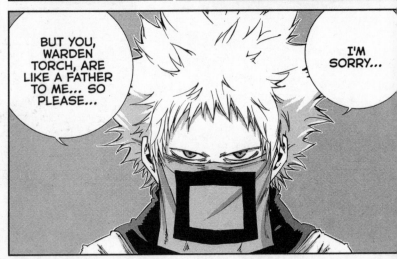

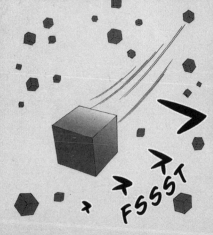

FSSST

...!! GROG!

VVM

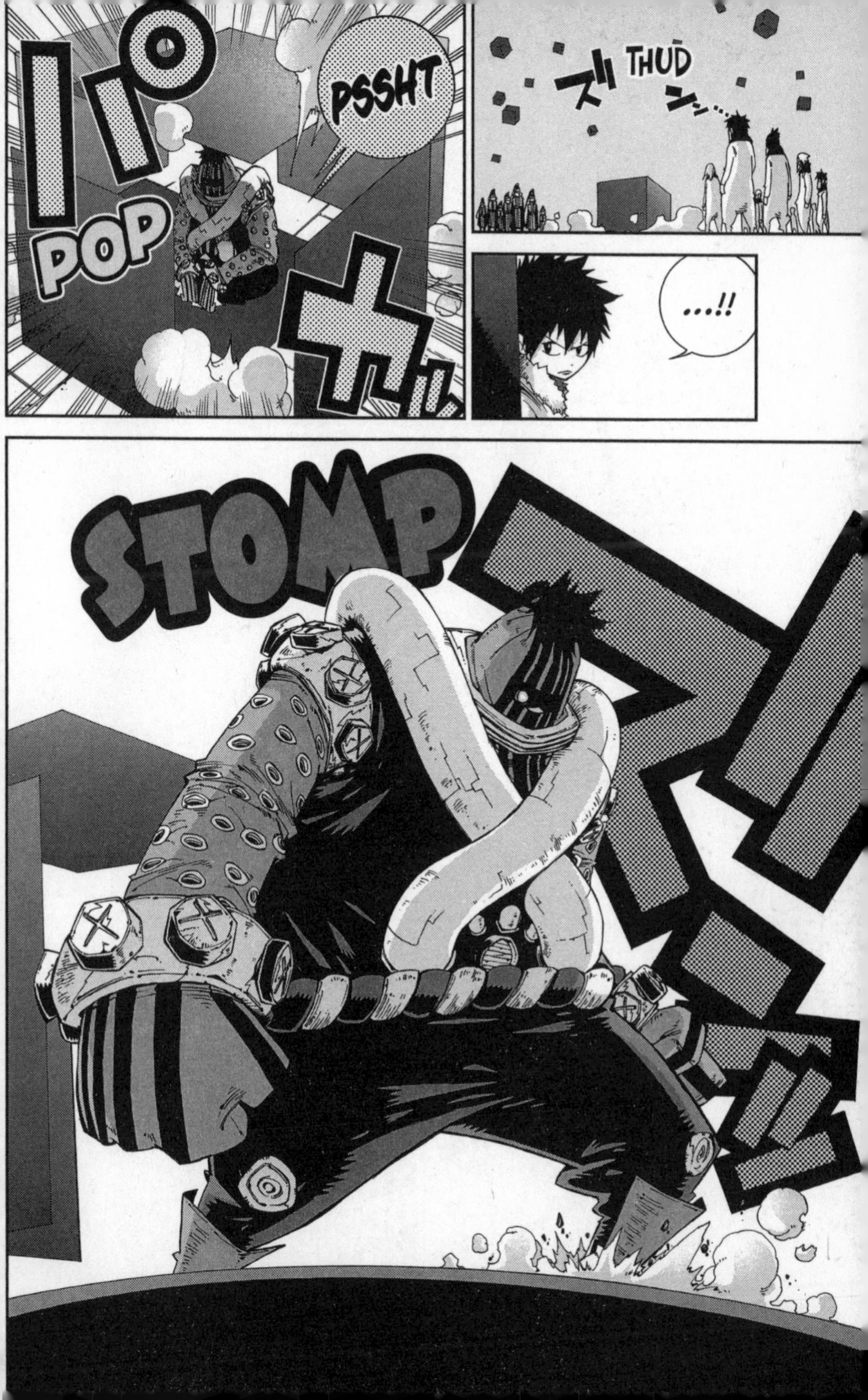
THUD
...!!
PSSHT
POP
STOMP

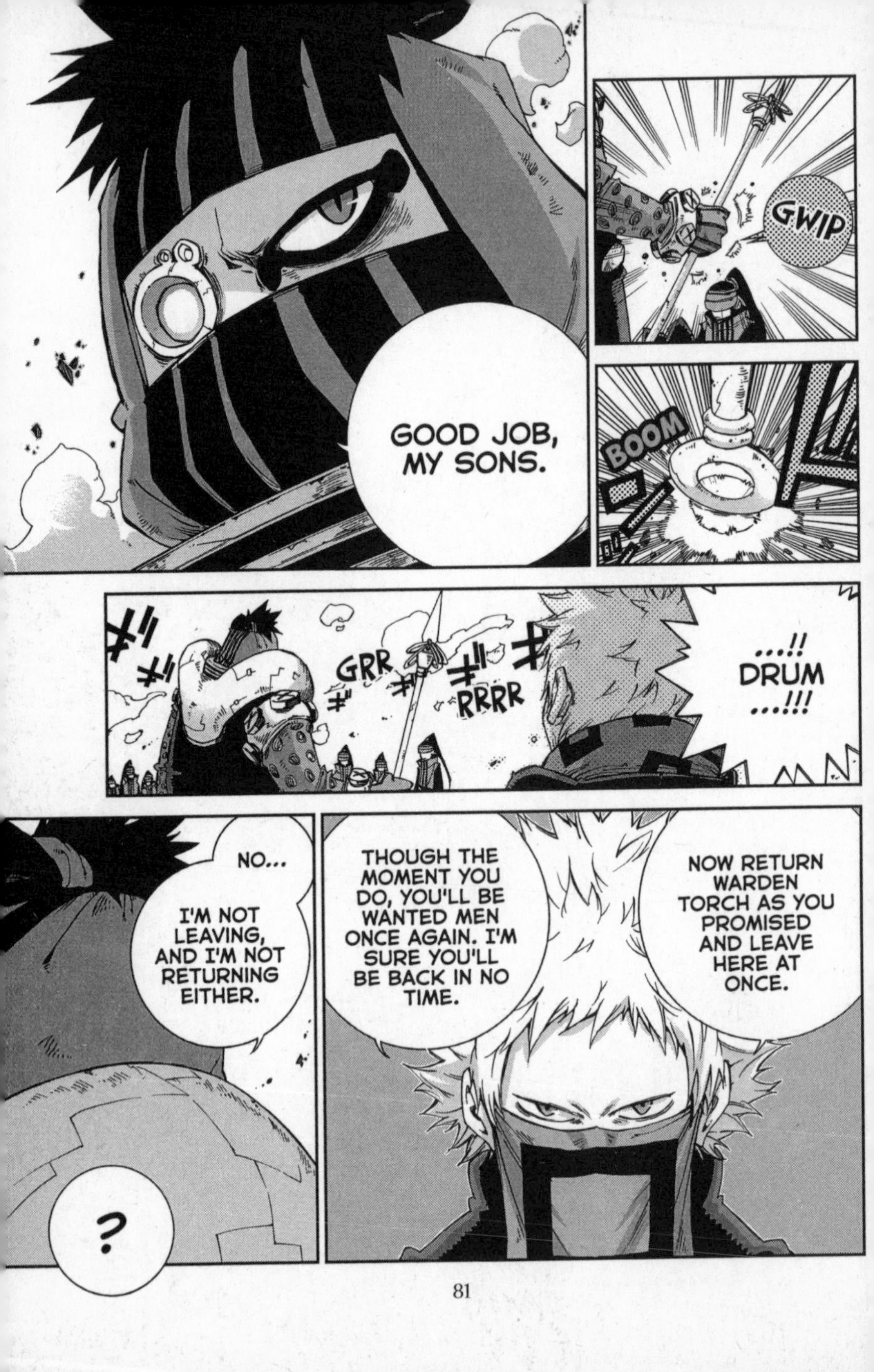
GWIP
BOOM
GOOD JOB, MY SONS.
...!! DRUM ...!!!
GRR
RRRR
NOW RETURN WARDEN TORCH AS YOU PROMISED AND LEAVE HERE AT ONCE.
THOUGH THE MOMENT YOU DO, YOU'LL BE WANTED MEN ONCE AGAIN. I'M SURE YOU'LL BE BACK IN NO TIME.
NO...
I'M NOT LEAVING, AND I'M NOT RETURNING EITHER.
?

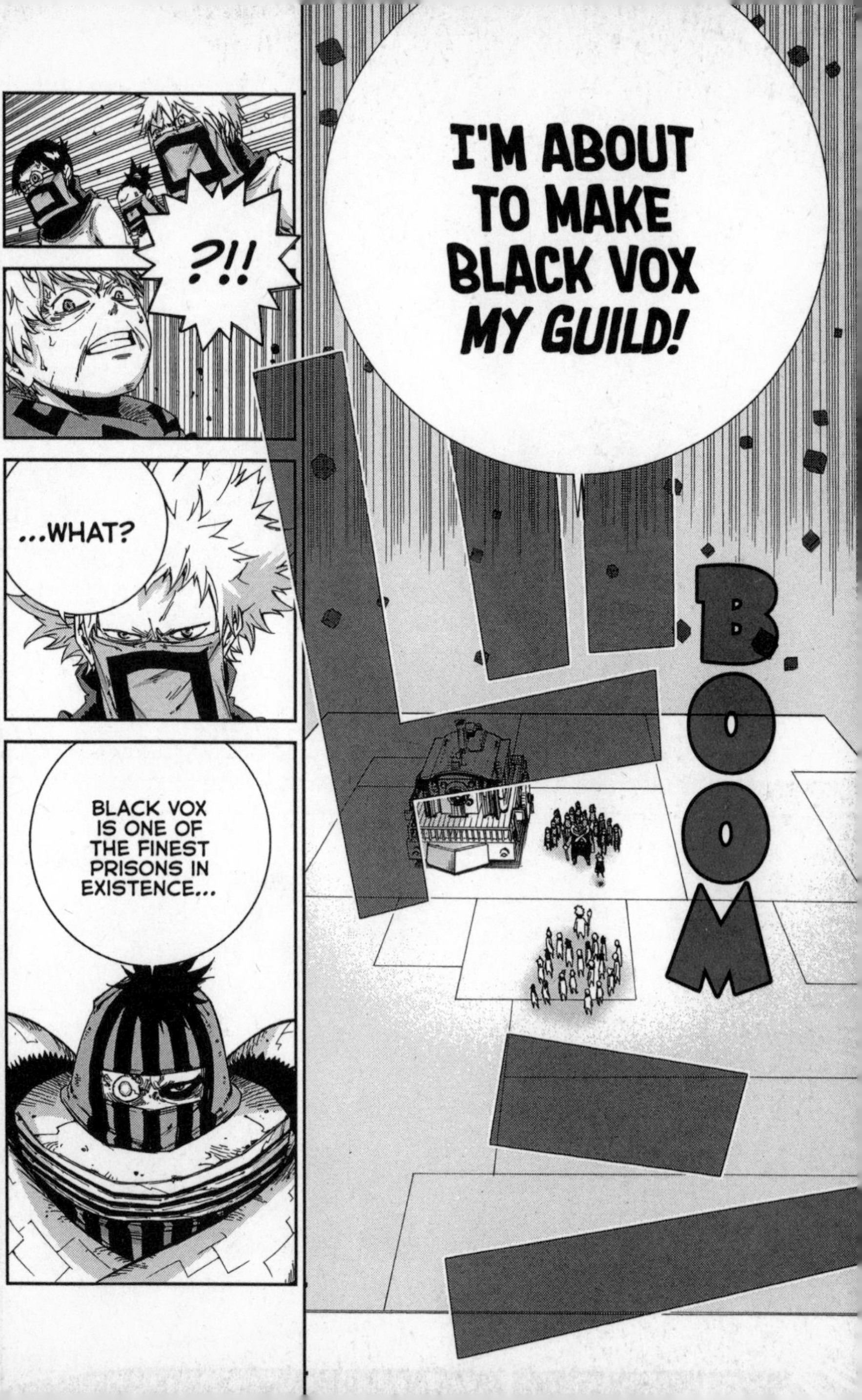
I'M ABOUT TO MAKE BLACK VOX MY GUILD!
BOOM
?!!
...WHAT?
BLACK VOX IS ONE OF THE FINEST PRISONS IN EXISTENCE...

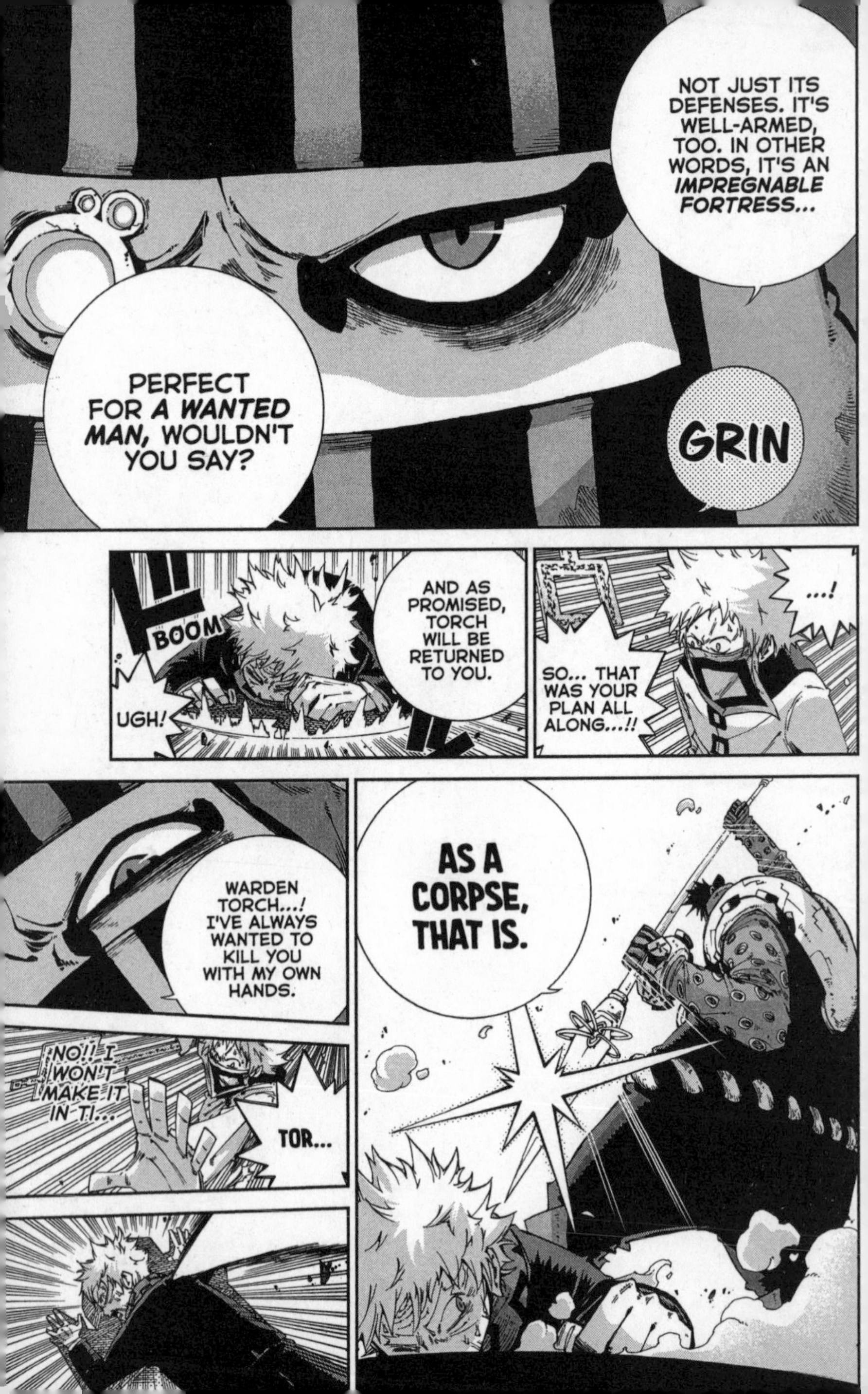
NOT JUST ITS DEFENSES. IT'S WELL-ARMED, TOO. IN OTHER WORDS, IT'S AN *IMPREGNABLE FORTRESS...*
PERFECT FOR *A WANTED MAN,* WOULDN'T YOU SAY?
GRIN
...!
SO... THAT WAS YOUR PLAN ALL ALONG...!!
AND AS PROMISED, TORCH WILL BE RETURNED TO YOU.
BOOM
UGH!
AS A CORPSE, THAT IS.
WARDEN TORCH...! I'VE ALWAYS WANTED TO KILL YOU WITH MY OWN HANDS.
NO!! I WON'T MAKE IT IN TI...
TOR...

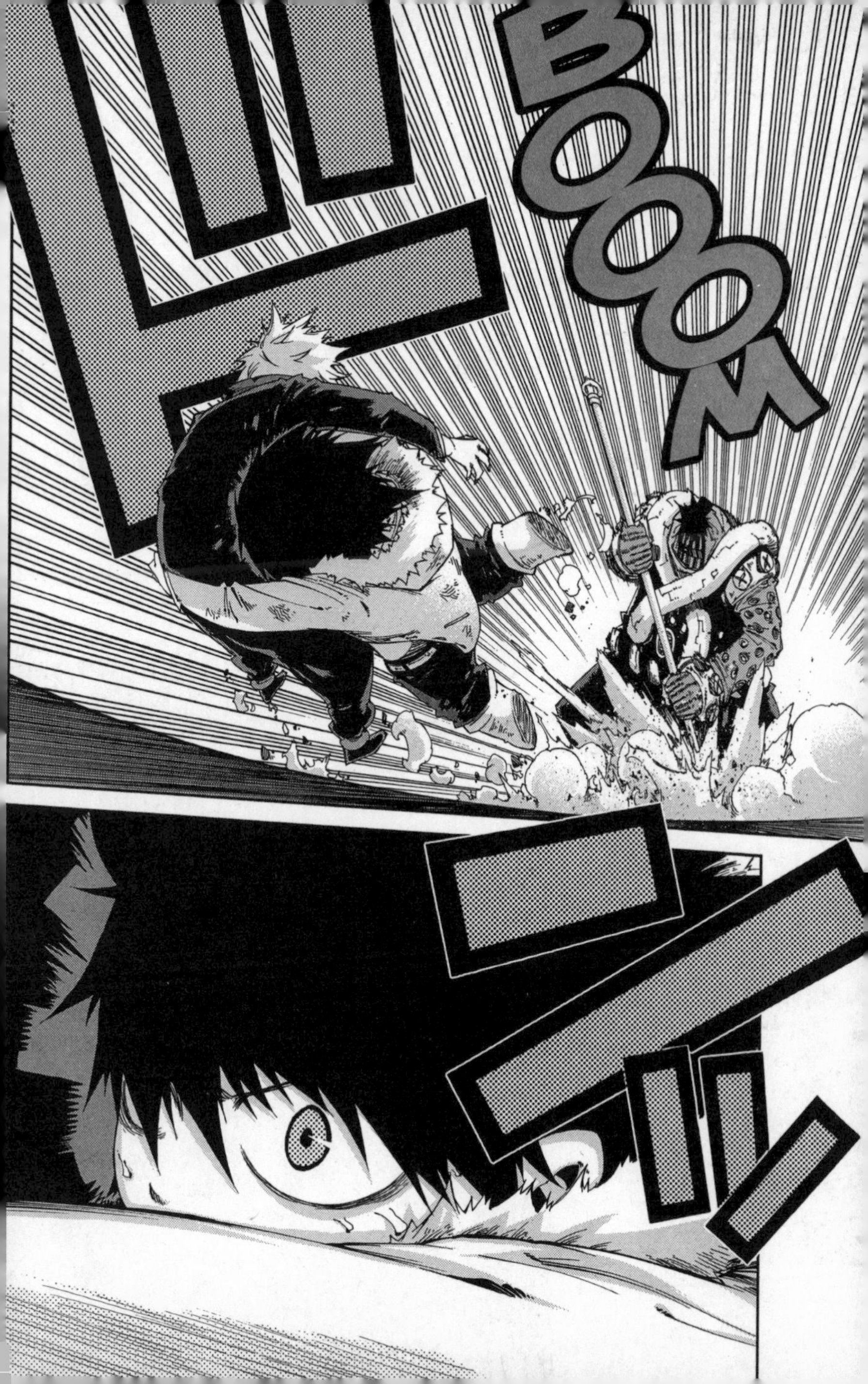
BOOOOM

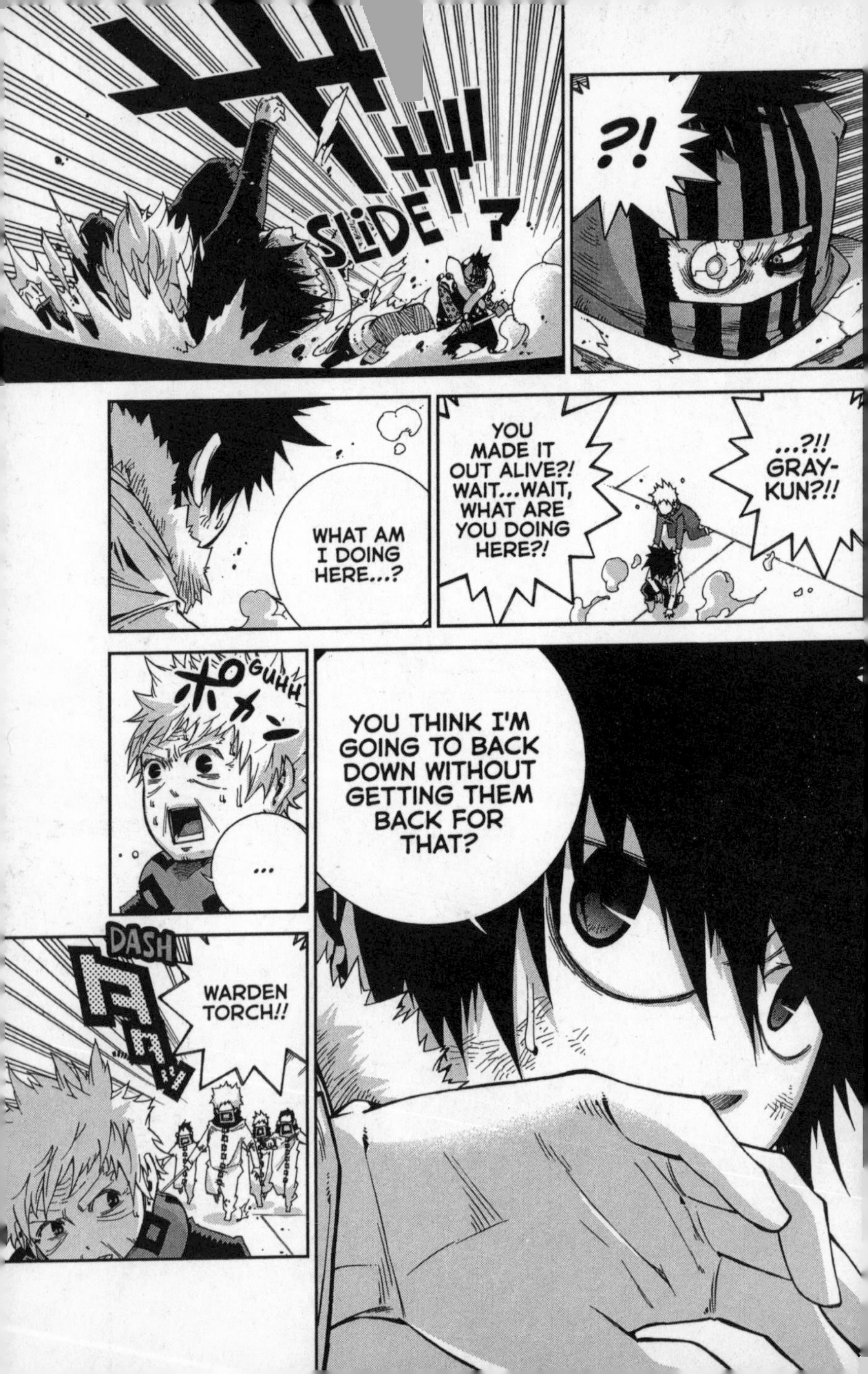
?!
SLIDE
...?!! GRAY-KUN?!!
YOU MADE IT OUT ALIVE?! WAIT...WAIT, WHAT ARE YOU DOING HERE?!
WHAT AM I DOING HERE...?
YOU THINK I'M GOING TO BACK DOWN WITHOUT GETTING THEM BACK FOR THAT?
GUHH
...
DASH
WARDEN TORCH!!

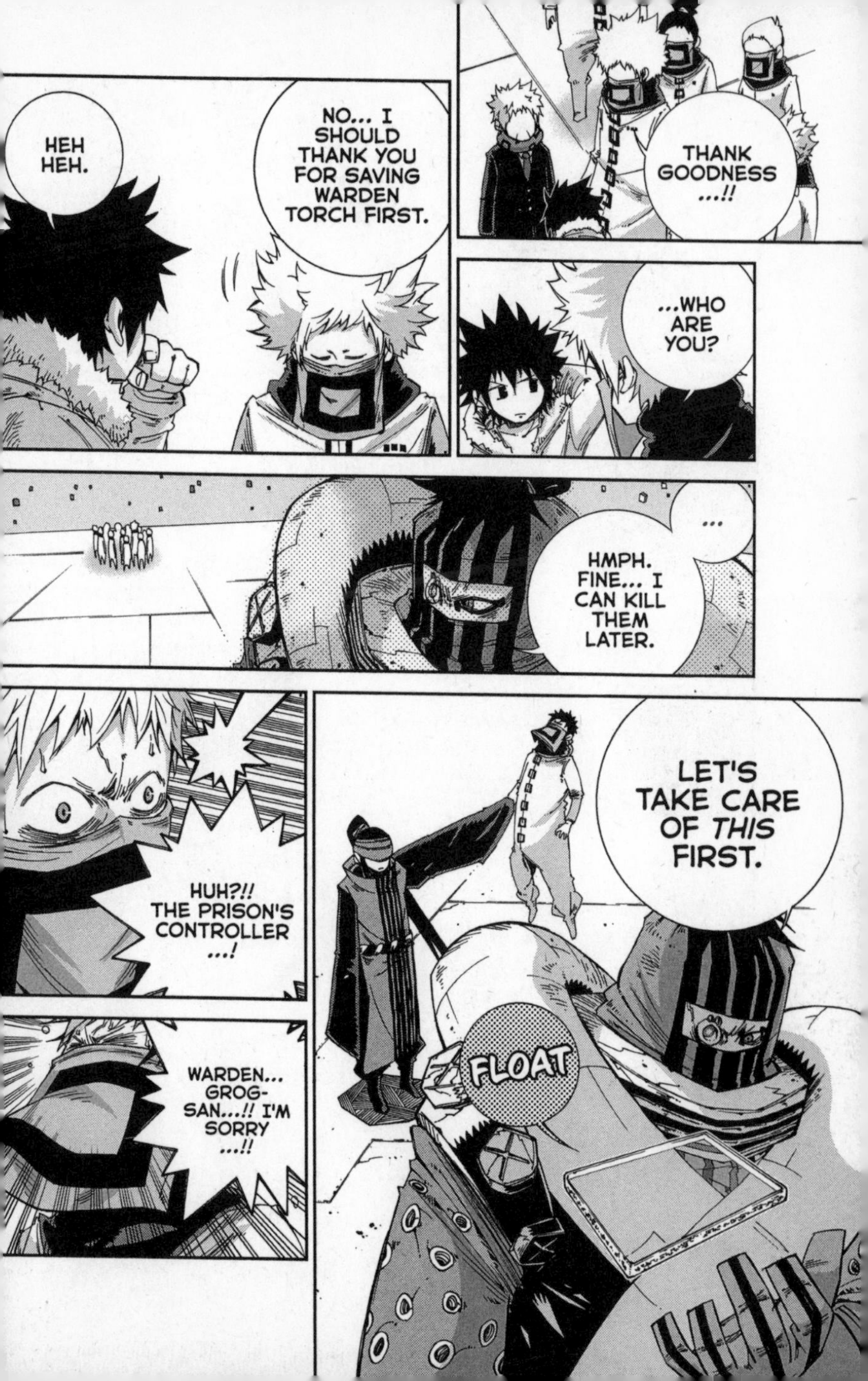
THANK GOODNESS ...!!
...WHO ARE YOU?
NO... I SHOULD THANK YOU FOR SAVING WARDEN TORCH FIRST.
HEH HEH.
...
HMPH. FINE... I CAN KILL THEM LATER.
LET'S TAKE CARE OF *THIS* FIRST.
FLOAT
HUH?!! THE PRISON'S CONTROLLER ...!
WARDEN... GROG-SAN...!! I'M SORRY ...!!

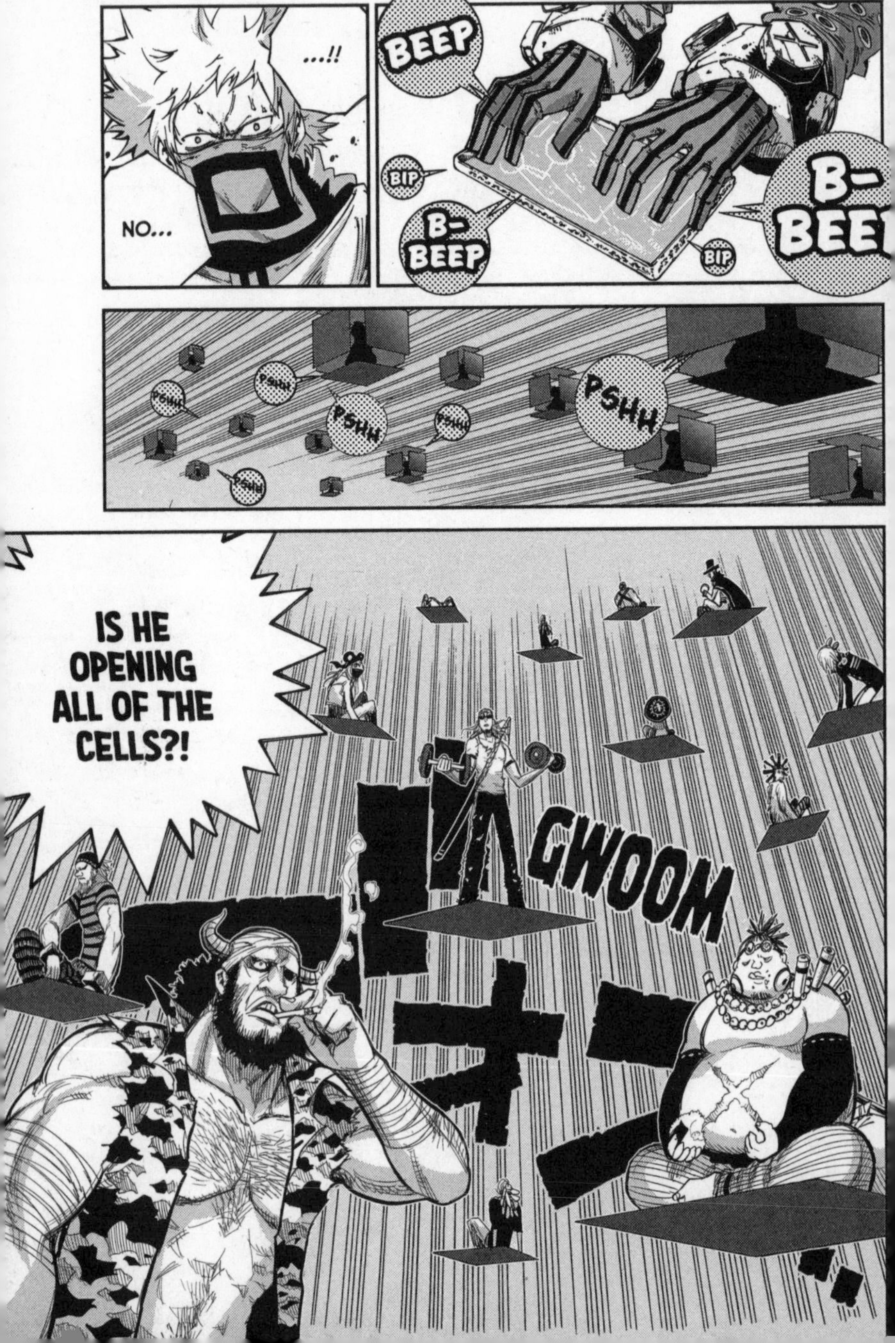
B-
BEE
BEEP
BIP
B-
BEEP
BIP
...!!
NO...
PSHH
PSHH
PSHH
PSHH
PSHH
PSHH
GWOOM
IS HE OPENING ALL OF THE CELLS?!

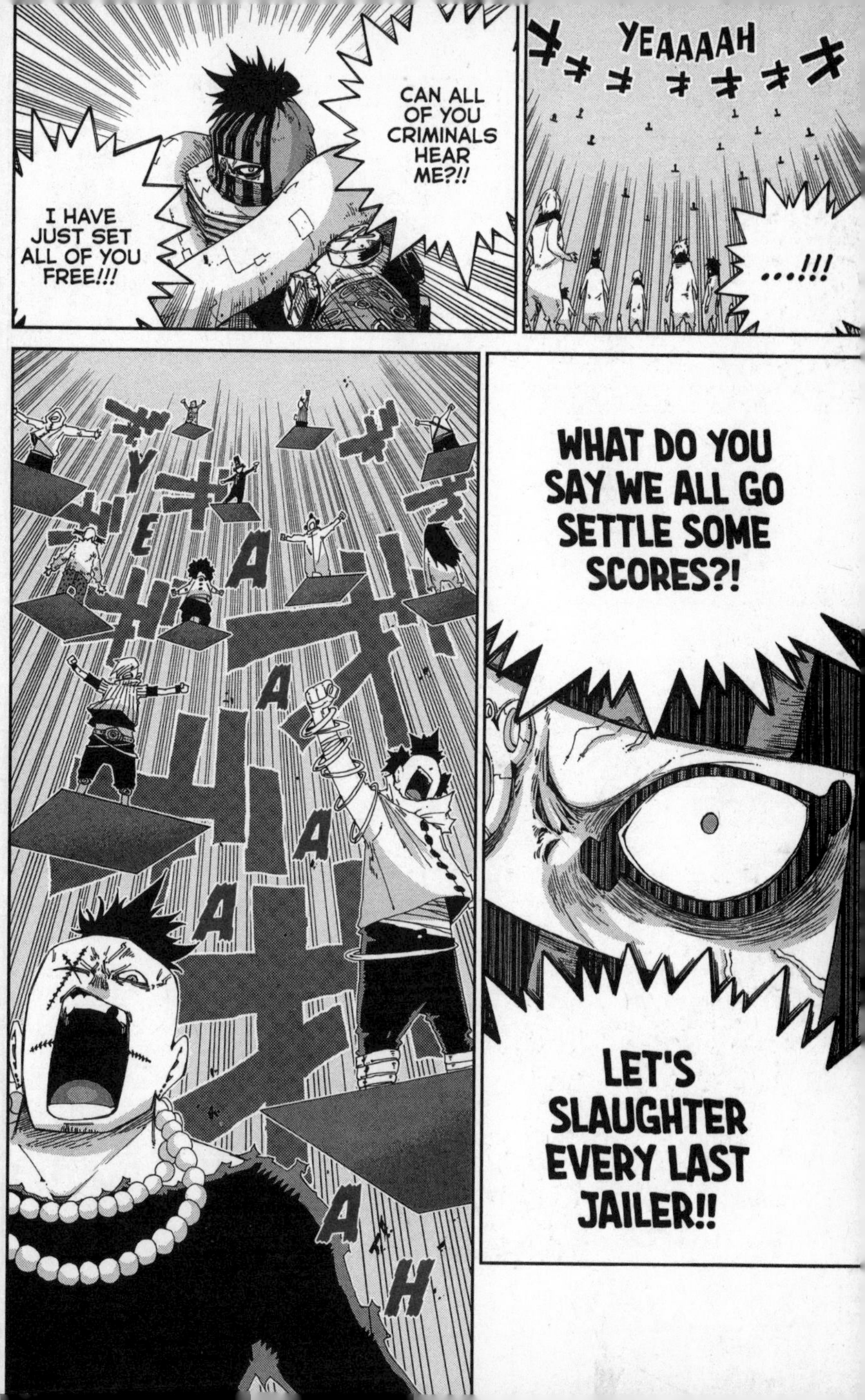

YEAAAAH
...!!!
CAN ALL OF YOU CRIMINALS HEAR ME?!!
I HAVE JUST SET ALL OF YOU FREE!!!
WHAT DO YOU SAY WE ALL GO SETTLE SOME SCORES?!
LET'S SLAUGHTER EVERY LAST JAILER!!
YEAAAAAH

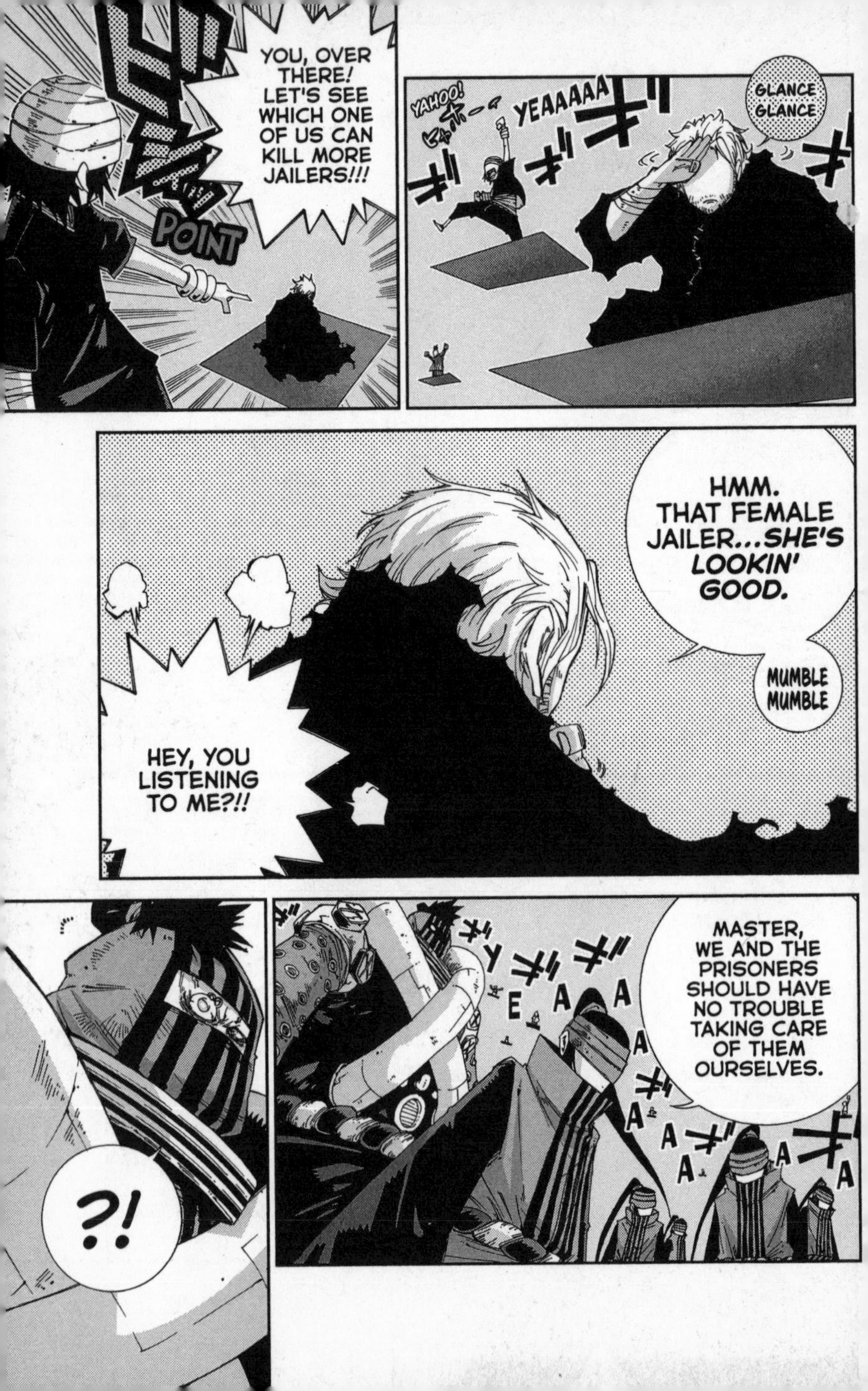
GLANCE GLANCE
YEAAAAA
YAHOO!
YOU, OVER THERE! LET'S SEE WHICH ONE OF US CAN KILL MORE JAILERS!!!
POINT
HMM. THAT FEMALE JAILER...SHE'S LOOKIN' GOOD.
MUMBLE MUMBLE
HEY, YOU LISTENING TO ME?!!
MASTER, WE AND THE PRISONERS SHOULD HAVE NO TROUBLE TAKING CARE OF THEM OURSELVES.
?!

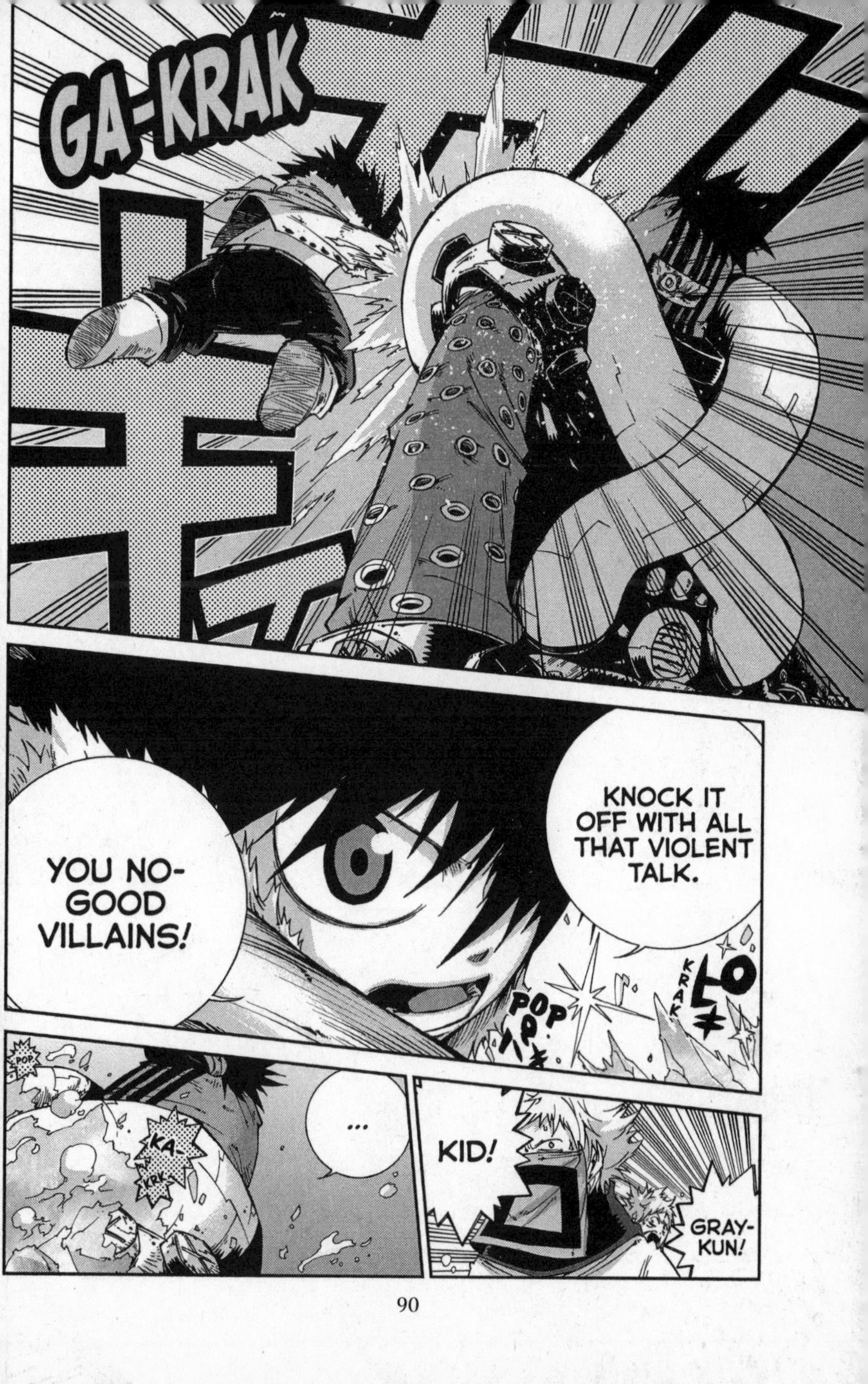
GA-KRAK
KNOCK IT OFF WITH ALL THAT VIOLENT TALK.
YOU NO-GOOD VILLAINS!
KRAK
POP
KID!
GRAY-KUN!
...
KA-KRK
POP

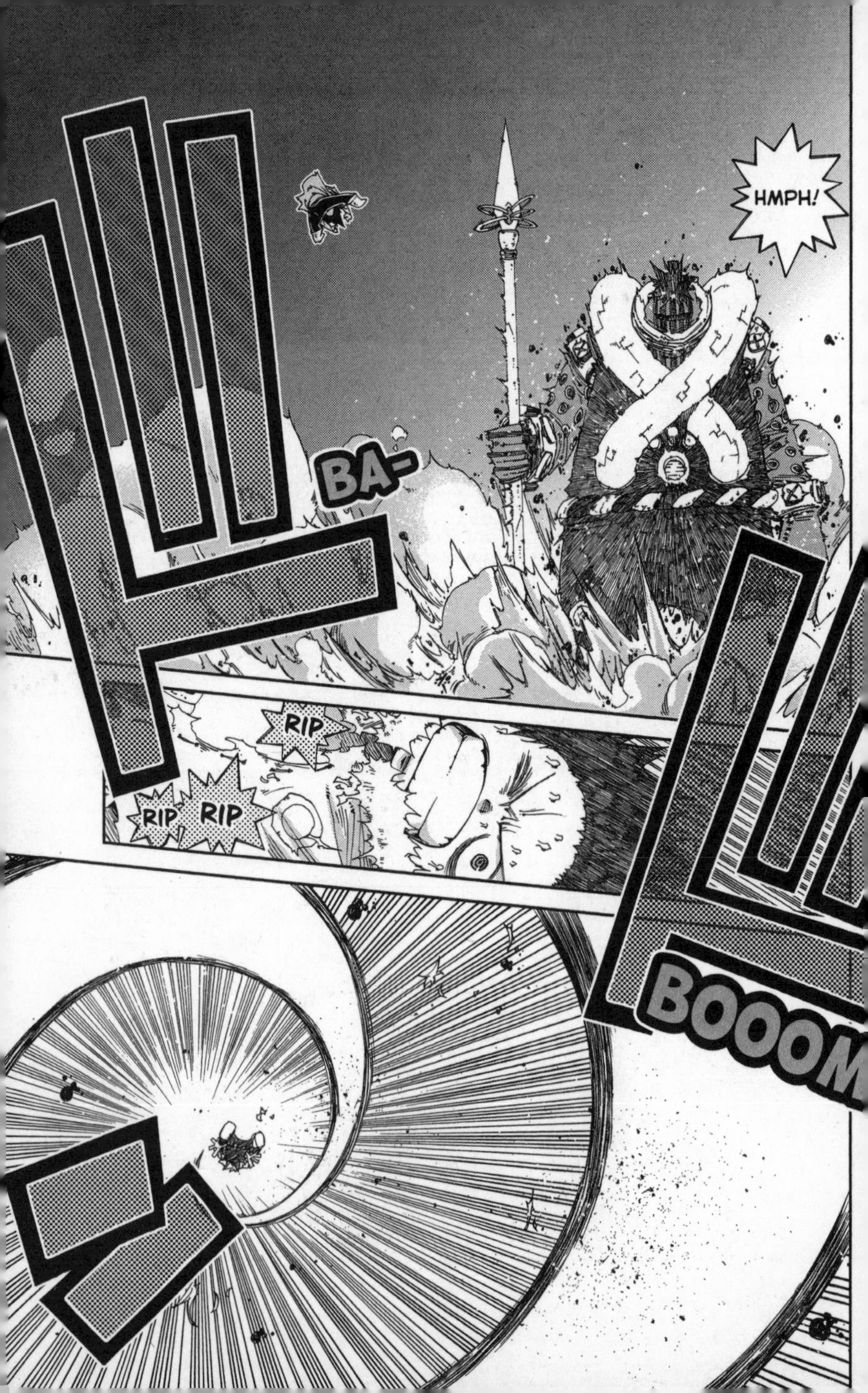
HMPH!
BA-
RIP
RIP
RIP
BOOOM

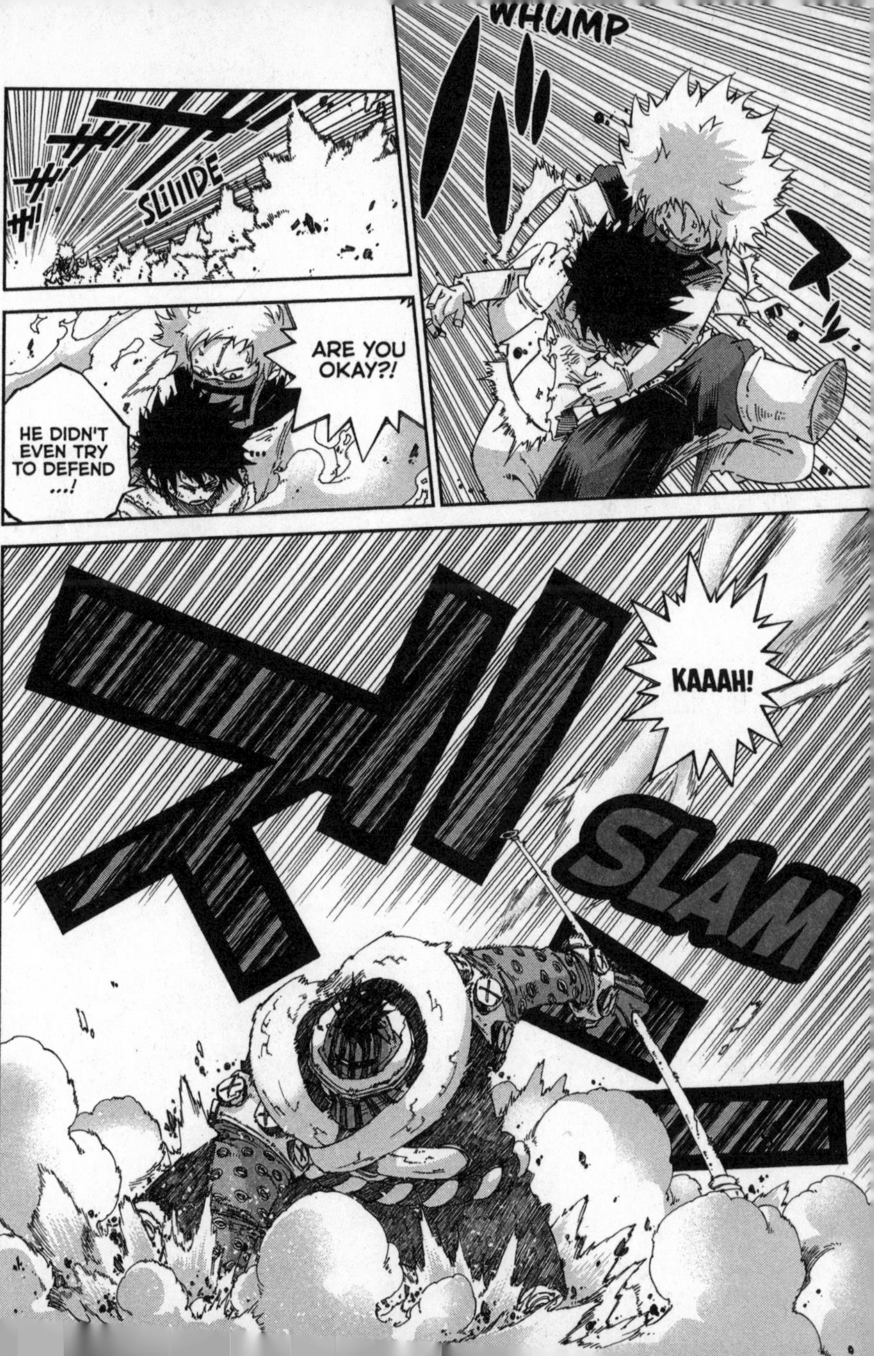

WHUMP
SLIIIDE
ARE YOU OKAY?!
HE DIDN'T EVEN TRY TO DEFEND ...!
KAAAH!
SLAM

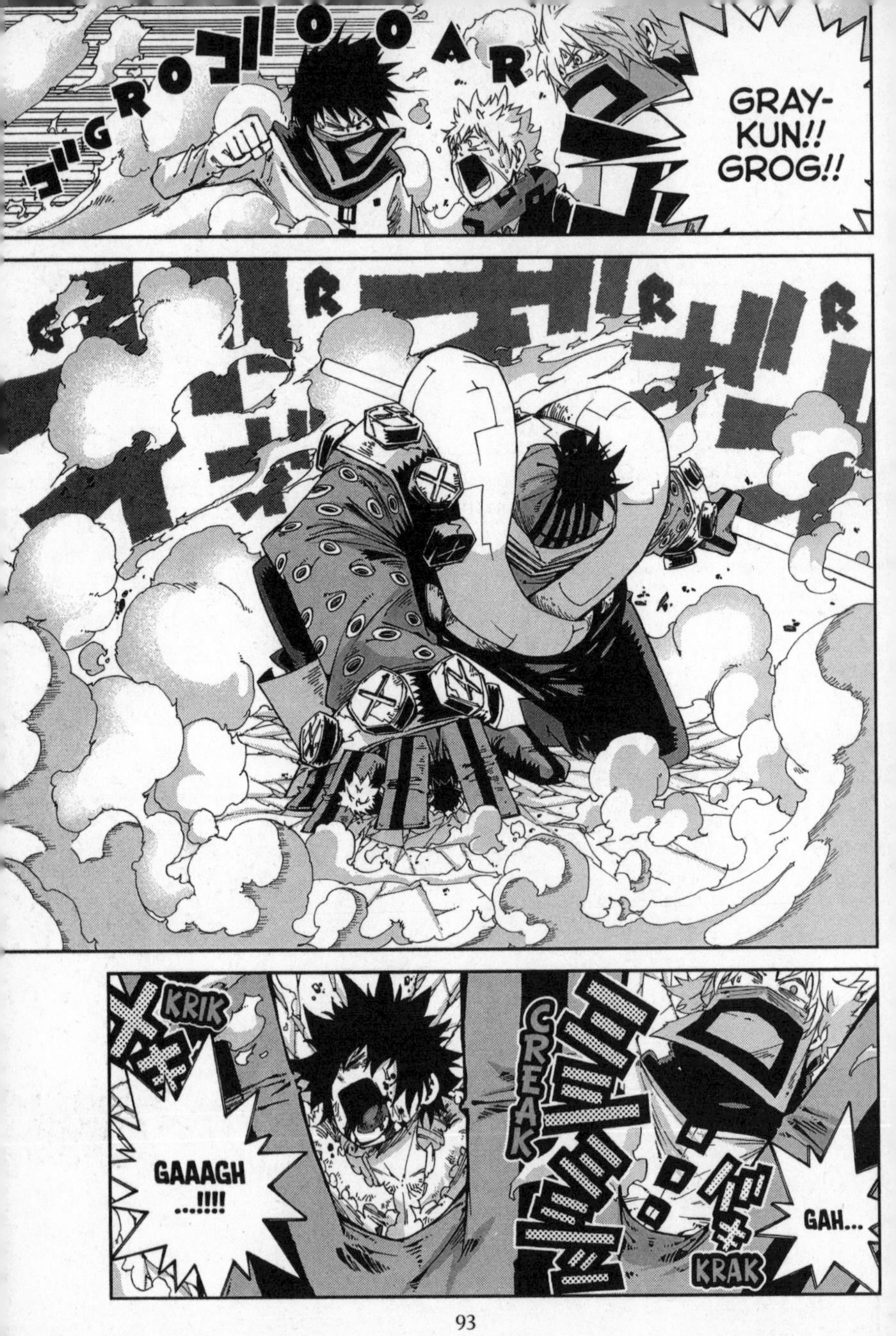
GRAY-KUN!! GROG!!
GROOOAR
GAH...
KRAK
CREAK
KRIK
GAAAGH ...!!!!

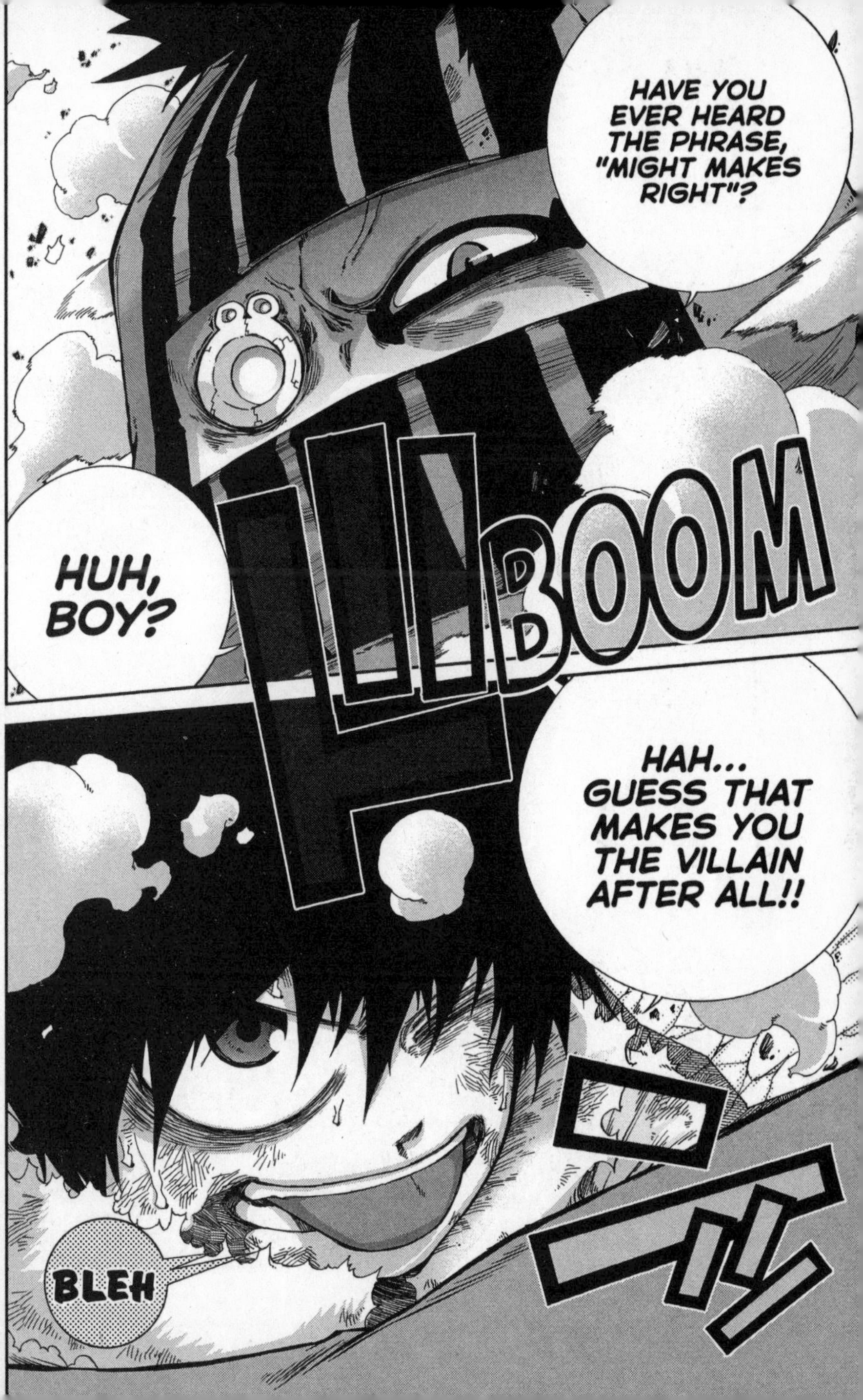
HAVE YOU EVER HEARD THE PHRASE, "MIGHT MAKES RIGHT"?
HUH, BOY?
BOOM
HAH... GUESS THAT MAKES YOU THE VILLAIN AFTER ALL!!
BLEH

Chapter 4: Fleeting Glimpses

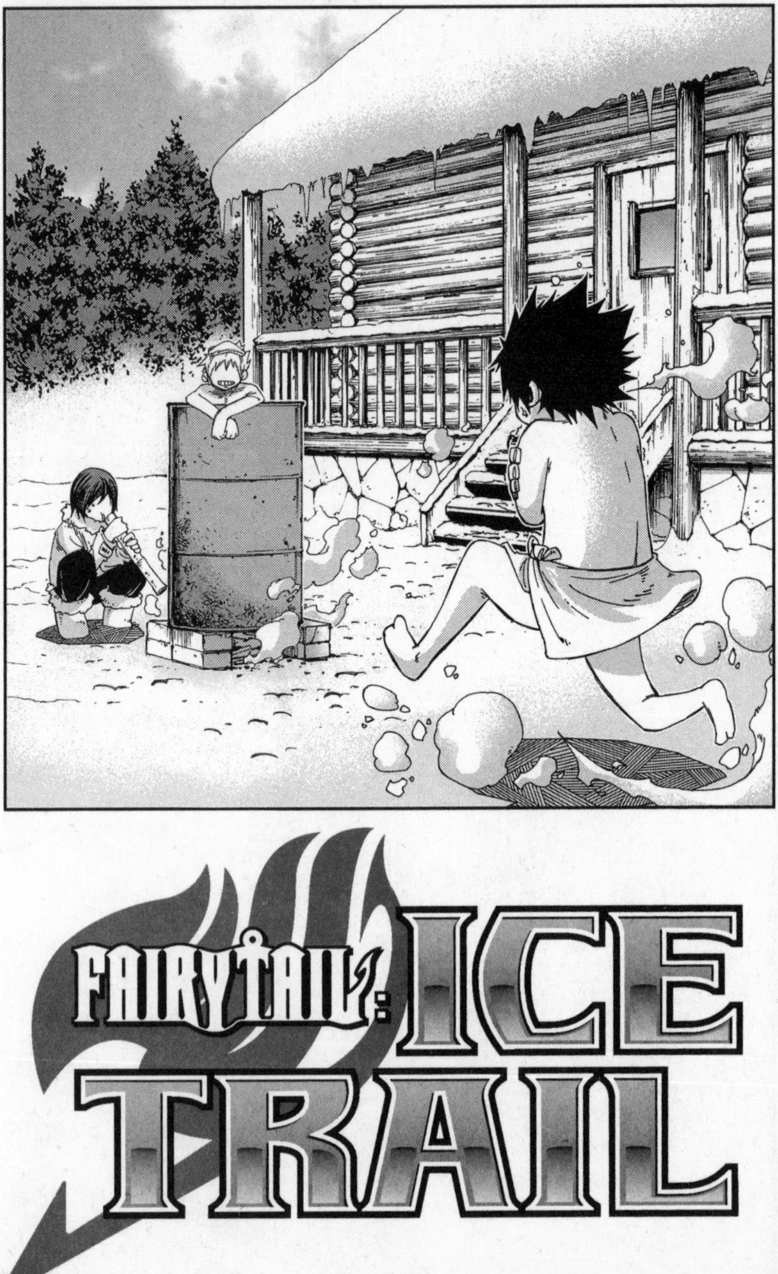

FAIRY TAIL: ICE TRAIL

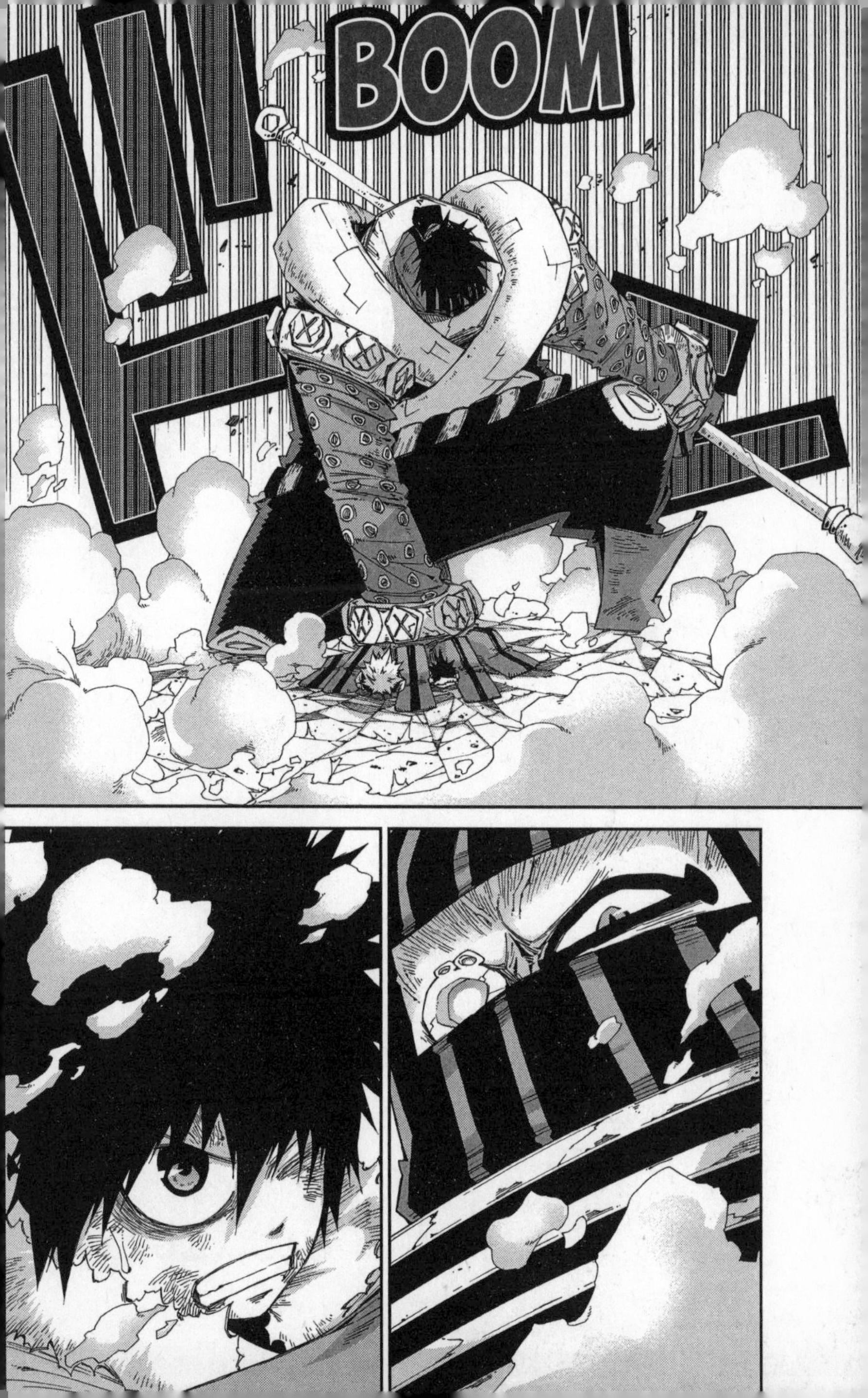
BOOM

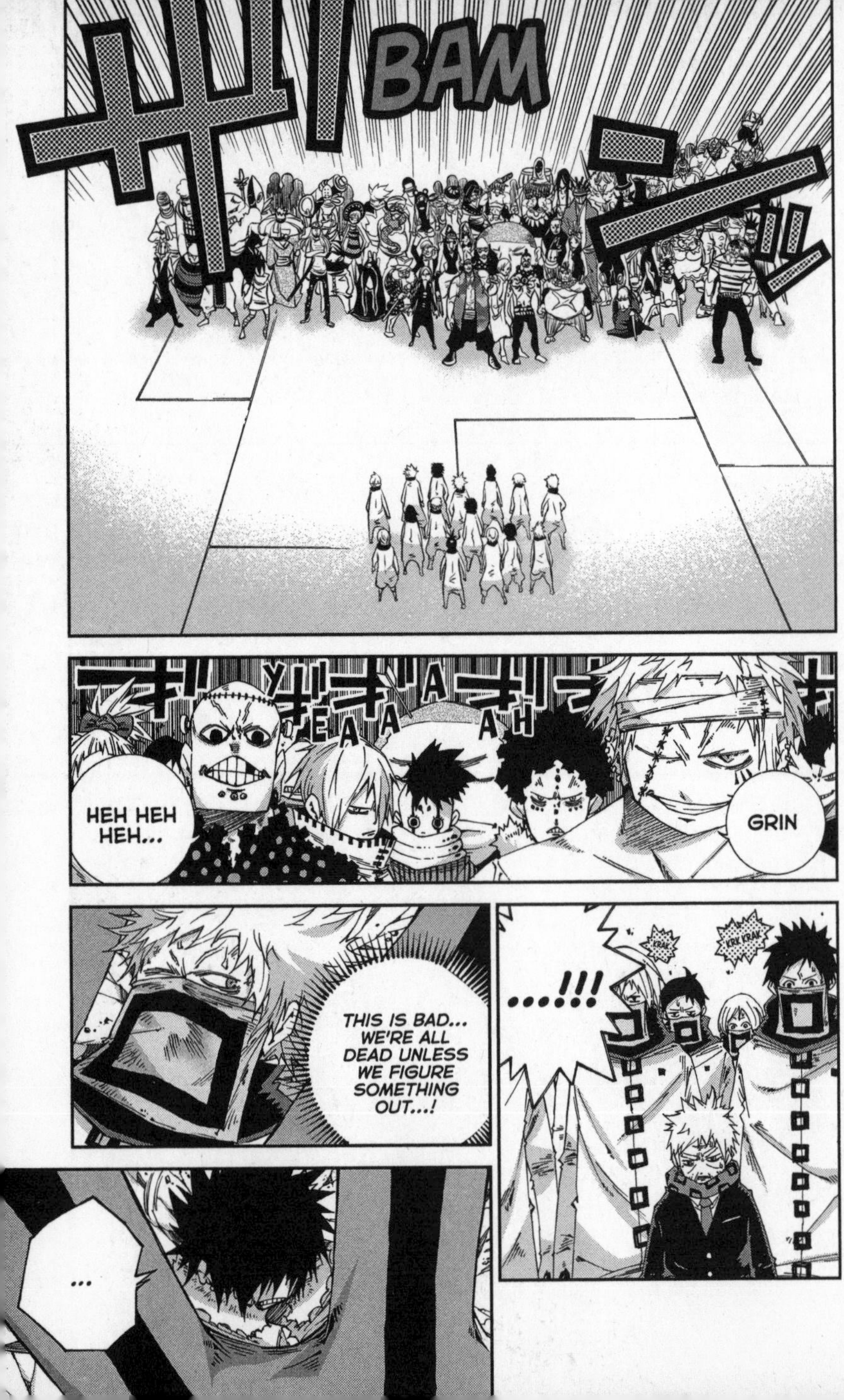
BAM
GRIN
YEAAAAH
HEH HEH HEH...
KRK KRAK
KRAK
...!!!
THIS IS BAD... WE'RE ALL DEAD UNLESS WE FIGURE SOMETHING OUT...!
...

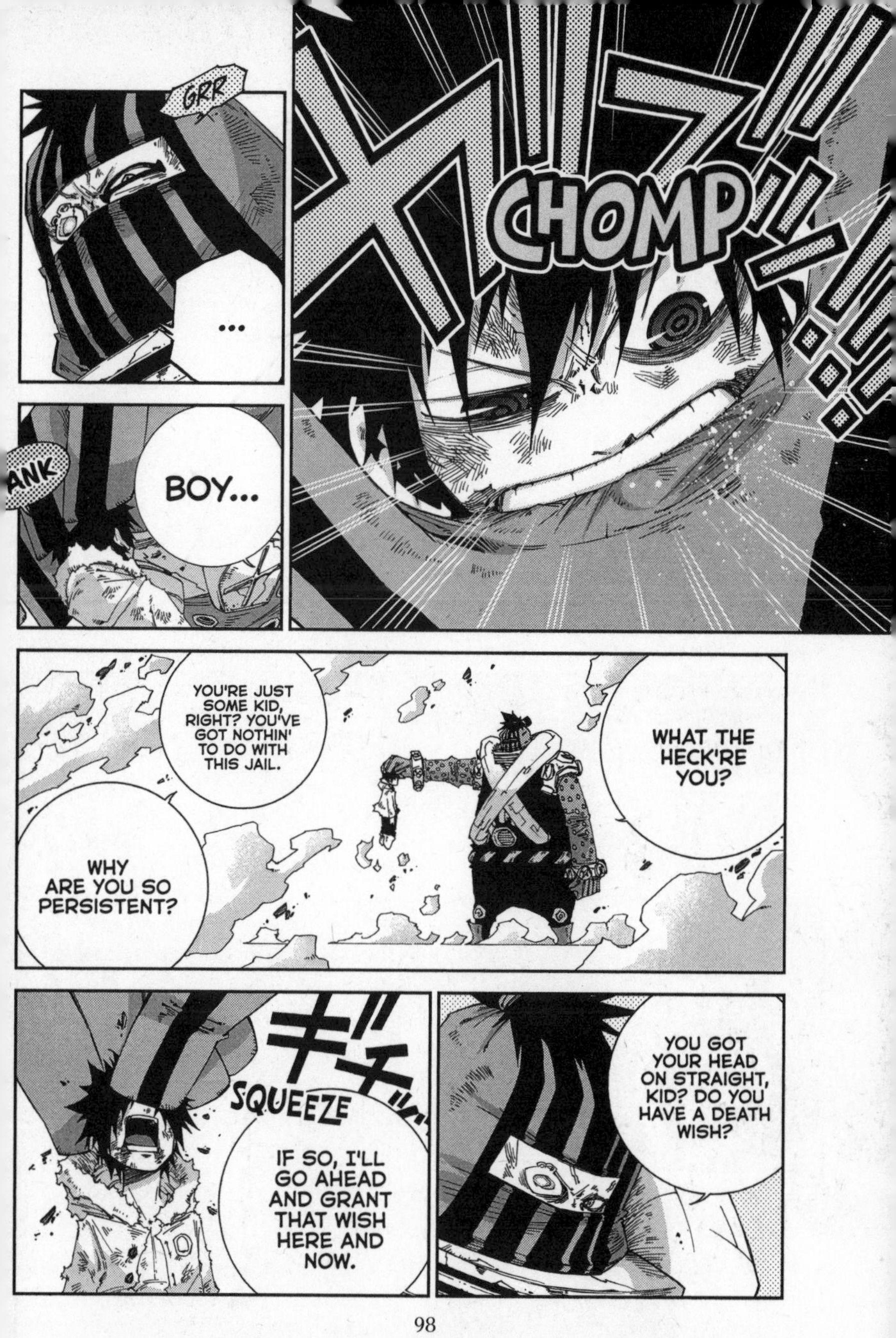
CHOMP!!
GRR
...
BOY...
WHAT THE HECK'RE YOU?
YOU'RE JUST SOME KID, RIGHT? YOU'VE GOT NOTHIN' TO DO WITH THIS JAIL.
WHY ARE YOU SO PERSISTENT?
YOU GOT YOUR HEAD ON STRAIGHT, KID? DO YOU HAVE A DEATH WISH?
SQUEEZE
IF SO, I'LL GO AHEAD AND GRANT THAT WISH HERE AND NOW.

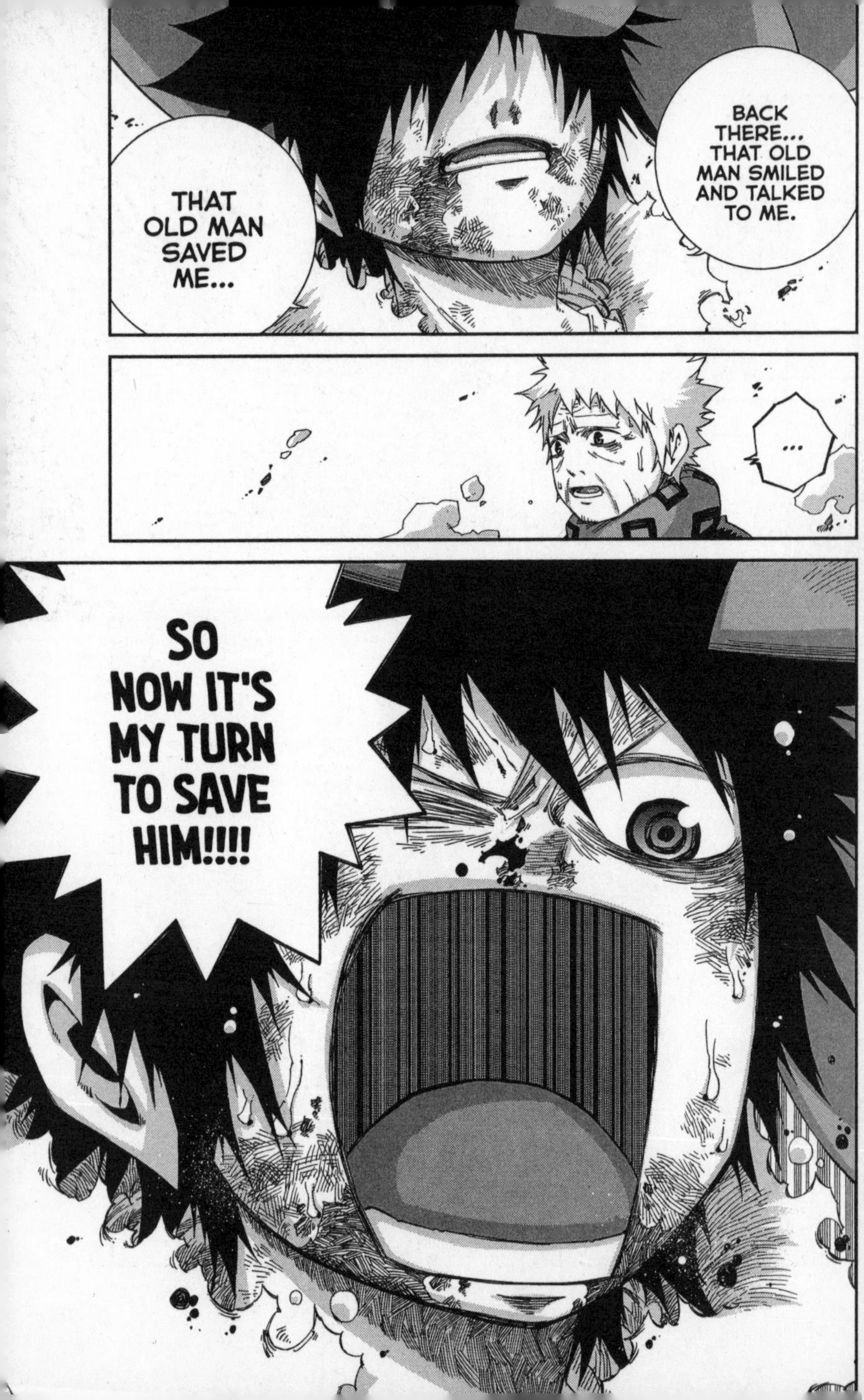
BACK THERE... THAT OLD MAN SMILED AND TALKED TO ME.
THAT OLD MAN SAVED ME...
...
SO NOW IT'S MY TURN TO SAVE HIM!!!!

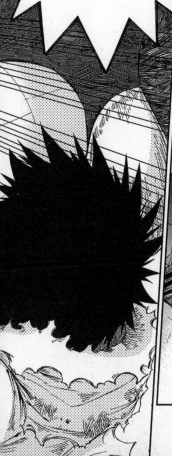

LANCE !!!!••••

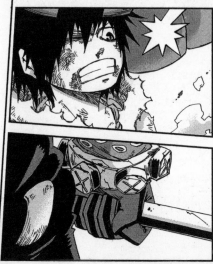

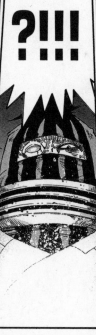

?!!!••••

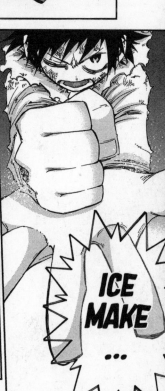

ICE MAKE ...

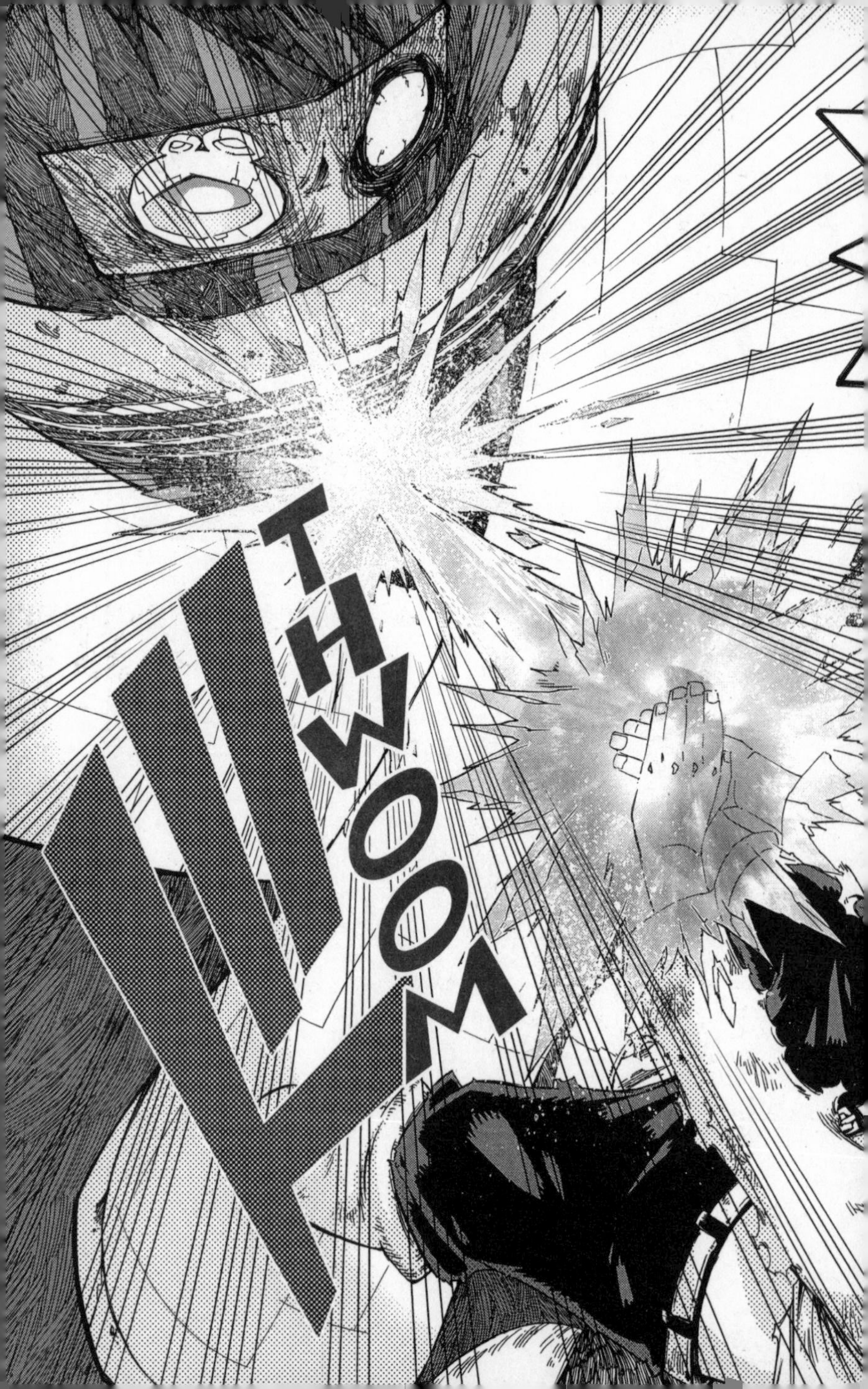
THWOOM

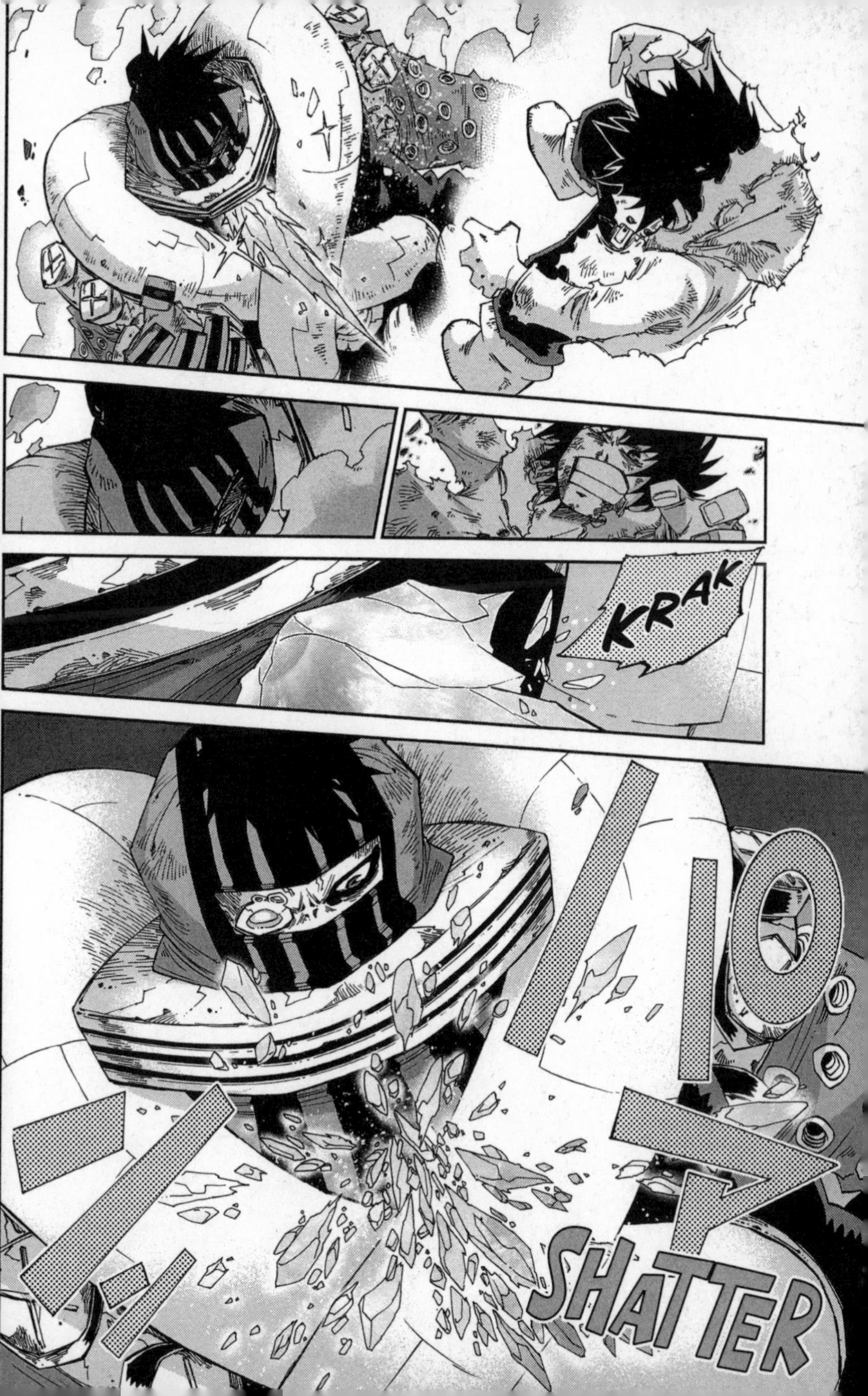
KRAK
SHATTER

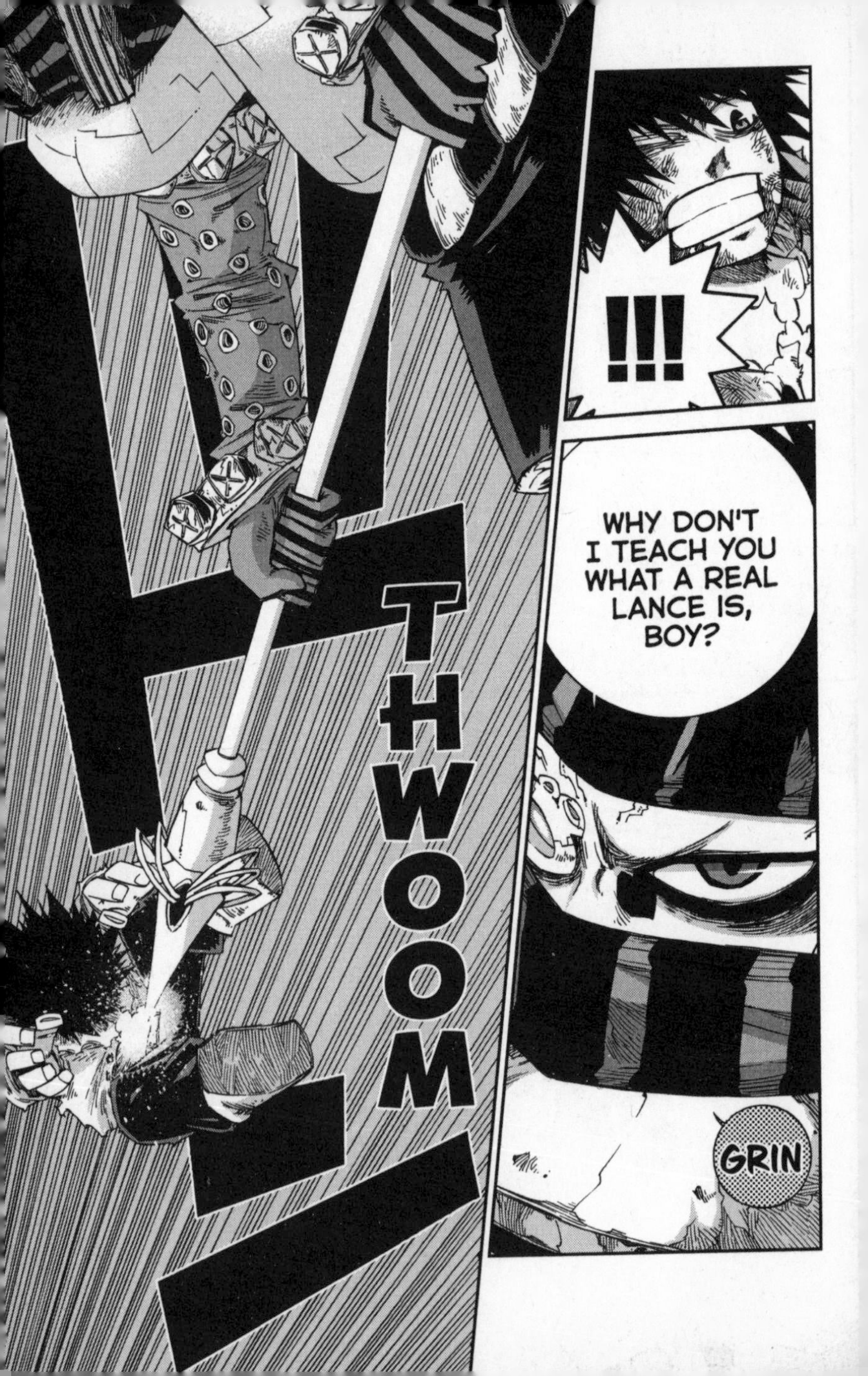
!!!
WHY DON'T I TEACH YOU WHAT A REAL LANCE IS, BOY?
GRIN
THWOOM

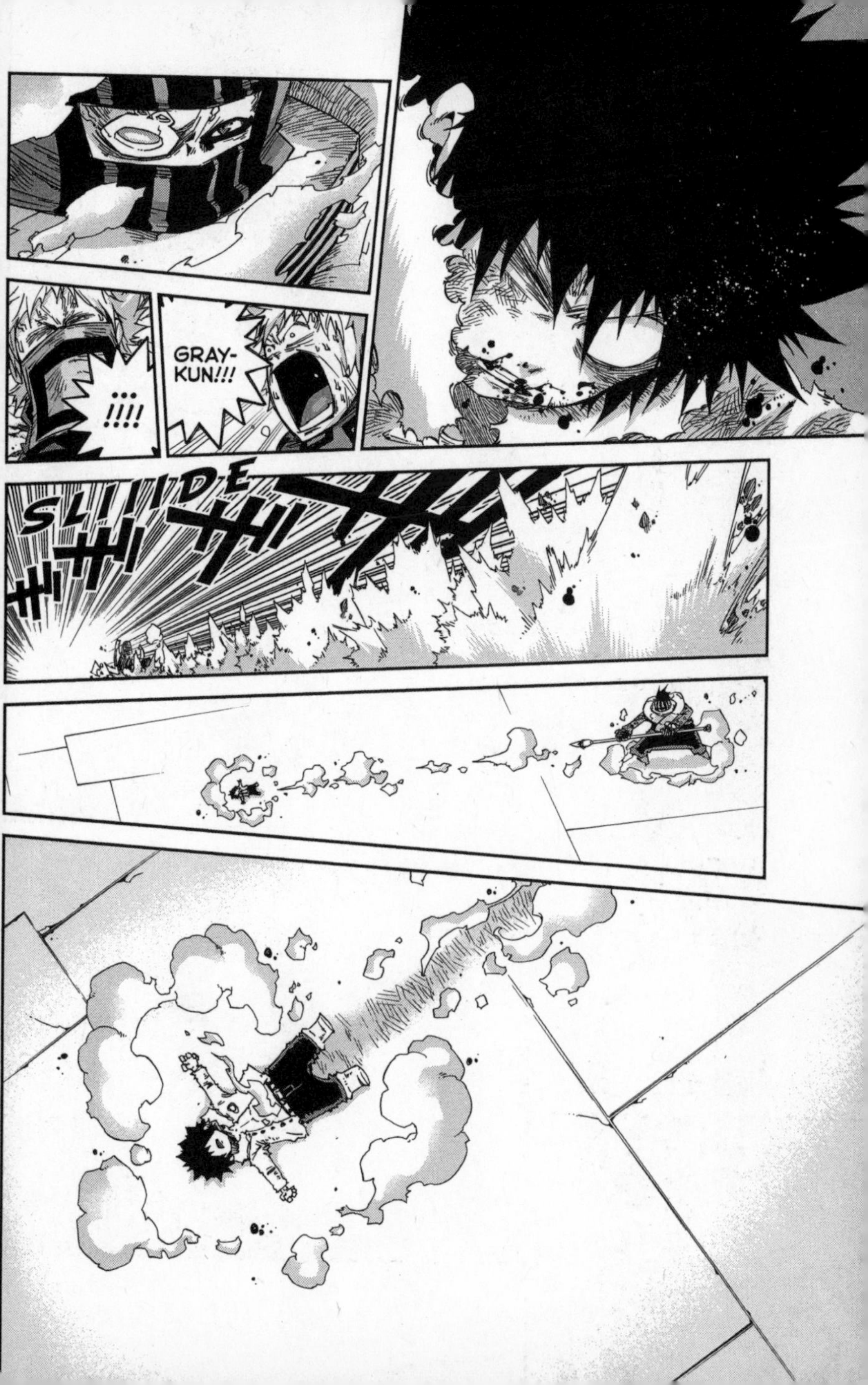
GRAY-KUN!!!
...!!!!
SLIIIDE

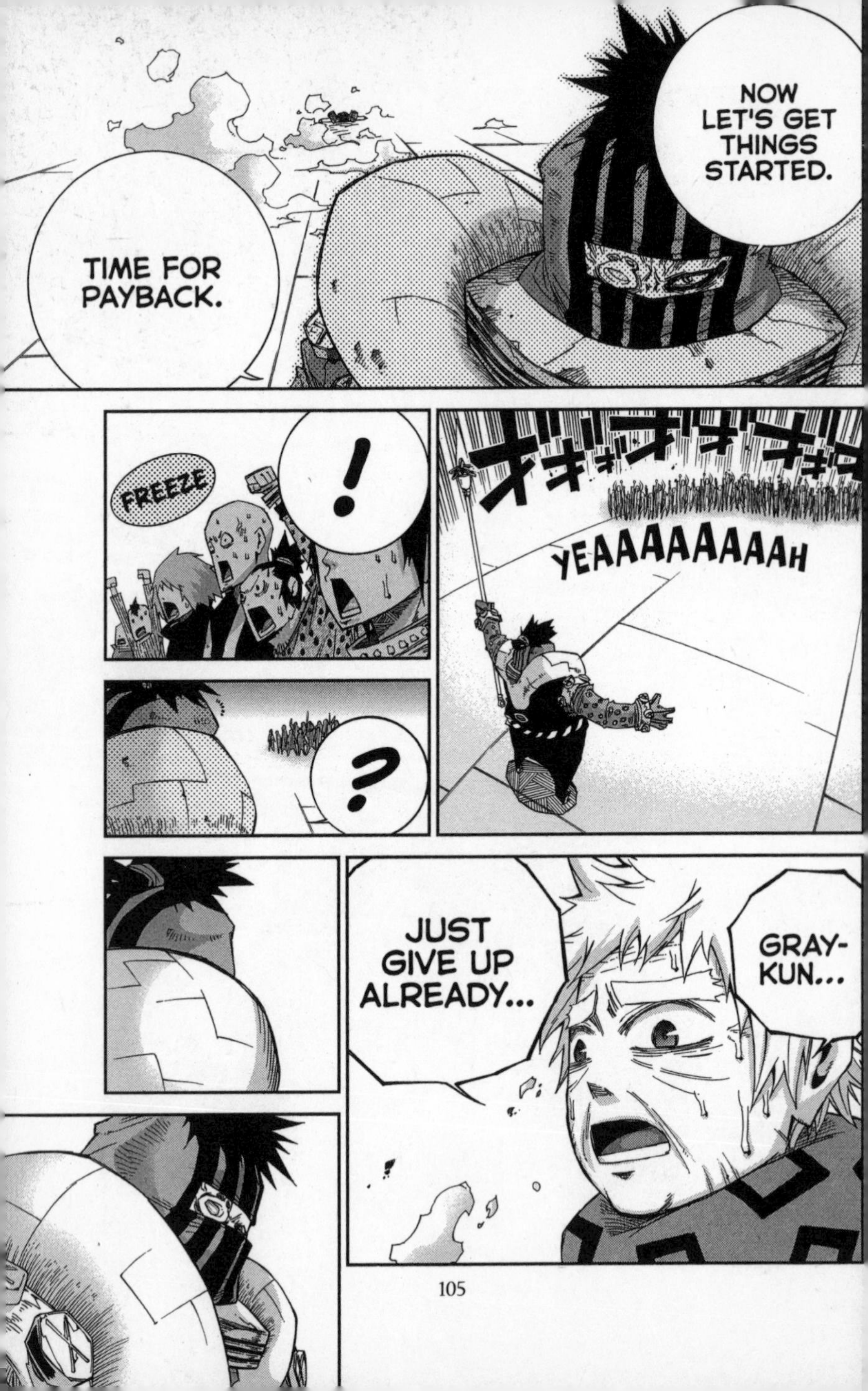
NOW LET'S GET THINGS STARTED.
TIME FOR PAYBACK.
YEAAAAAAAAAH
!
FREEZE
?
GRAY-KUN...
JUST GIVE UP ALREADY...

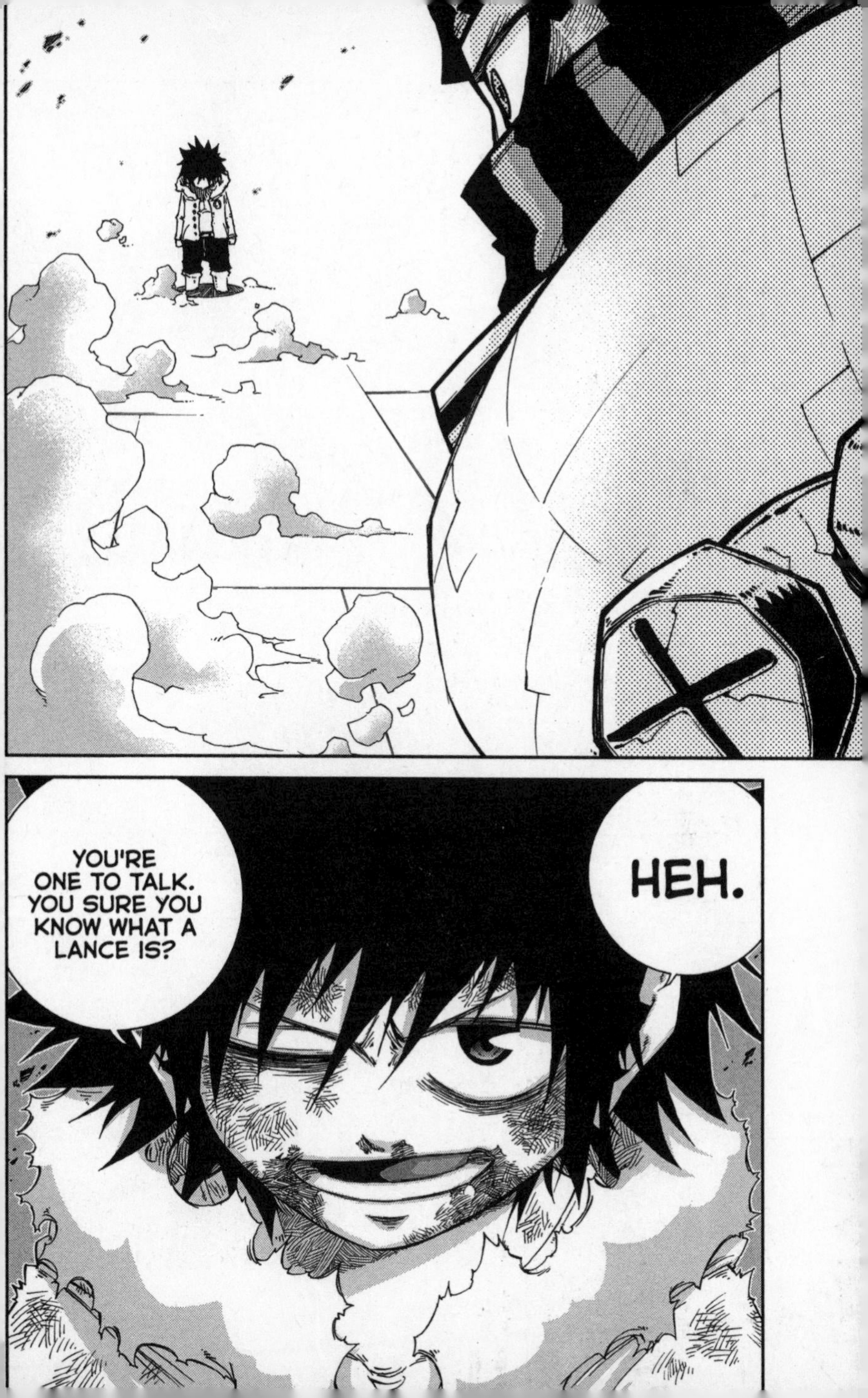
HEH.
YOU'RE ONE TO TALK. YOU SURE YOU KNOW WHAT A LANCE IS?

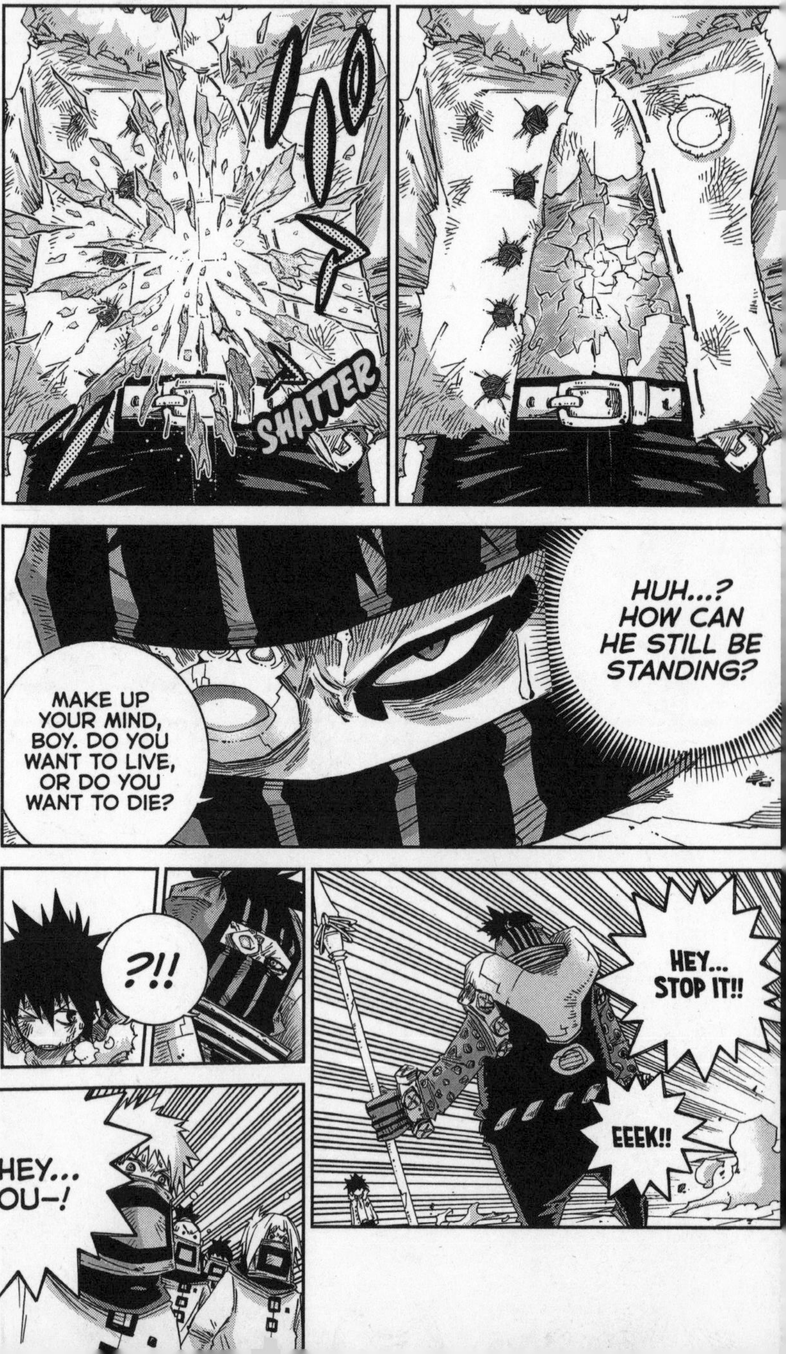
SHATTER
HUH...? HOW CAN HE STILL BE STANDING?
MAKE UP YOUR MIND, BOY. DO YOU WANT TO LIVE, OR DO YOU WANT TO DIE?
HEY... STOP IT!!
EEEK!!
?!!
H-HEY... YOU–!

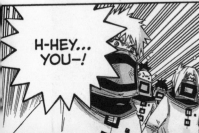

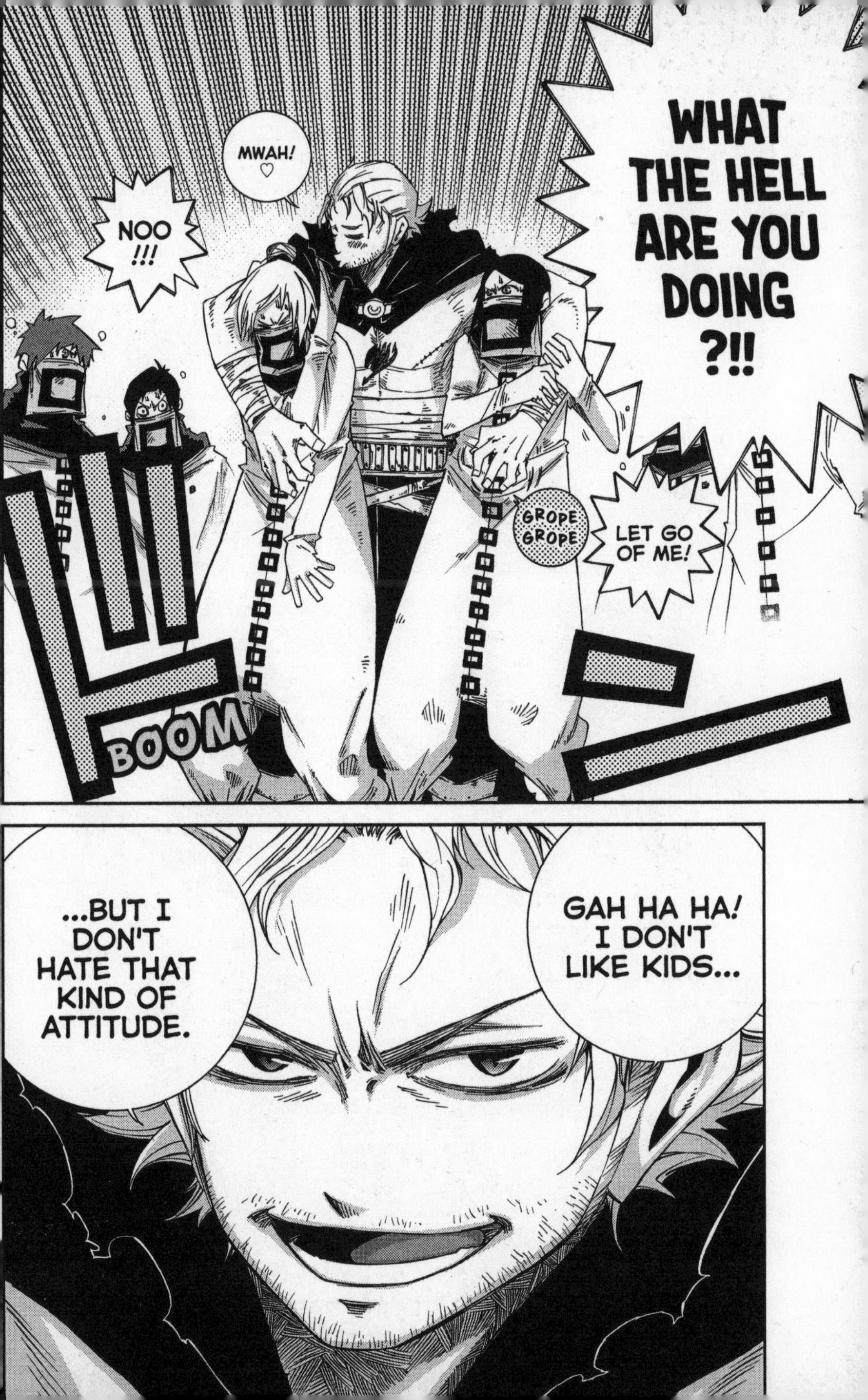
WHAT THE HELL ARE YOU DOING ?!!
MWAH! ♡
NOO !!!
LET GO OF ME!
GROPE GROPE
BOOM
GAH HA HA! I DON'T LIKE KIDS...
...BUT I DON'T HATE THAT KIND OF ATTITUDE.

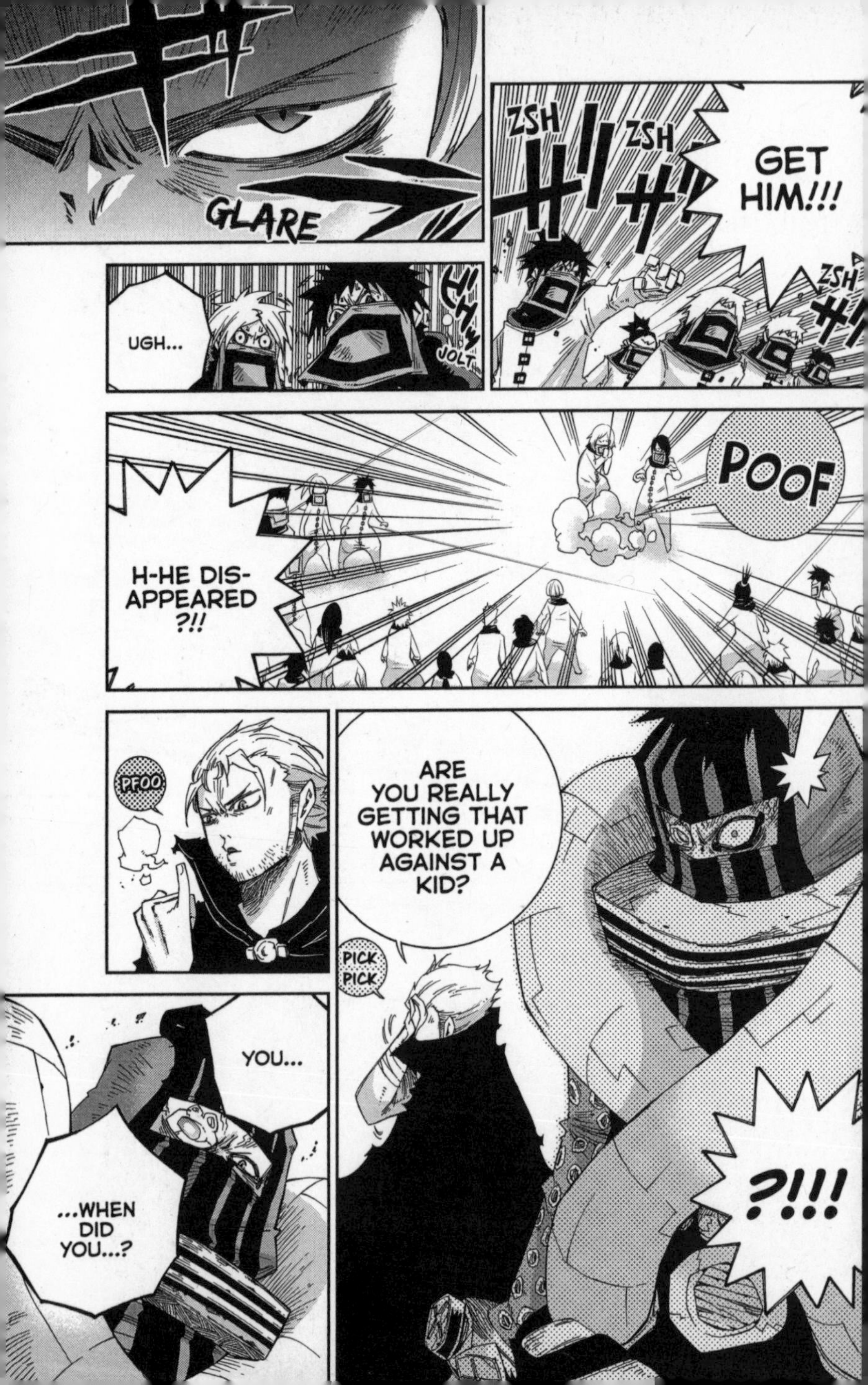
ZSH
ZSH
GET HIM!!!
ZSH
GLARE
JOLT
UGH...
POOF
H-HE DIS-APPEARED?!!
ARE YOU REALLY GETTING THAT WORKED UP AGAINST A KID?
PICK PICK
?!!!
PFOO
YOU...
...WHEN DID YOU...?

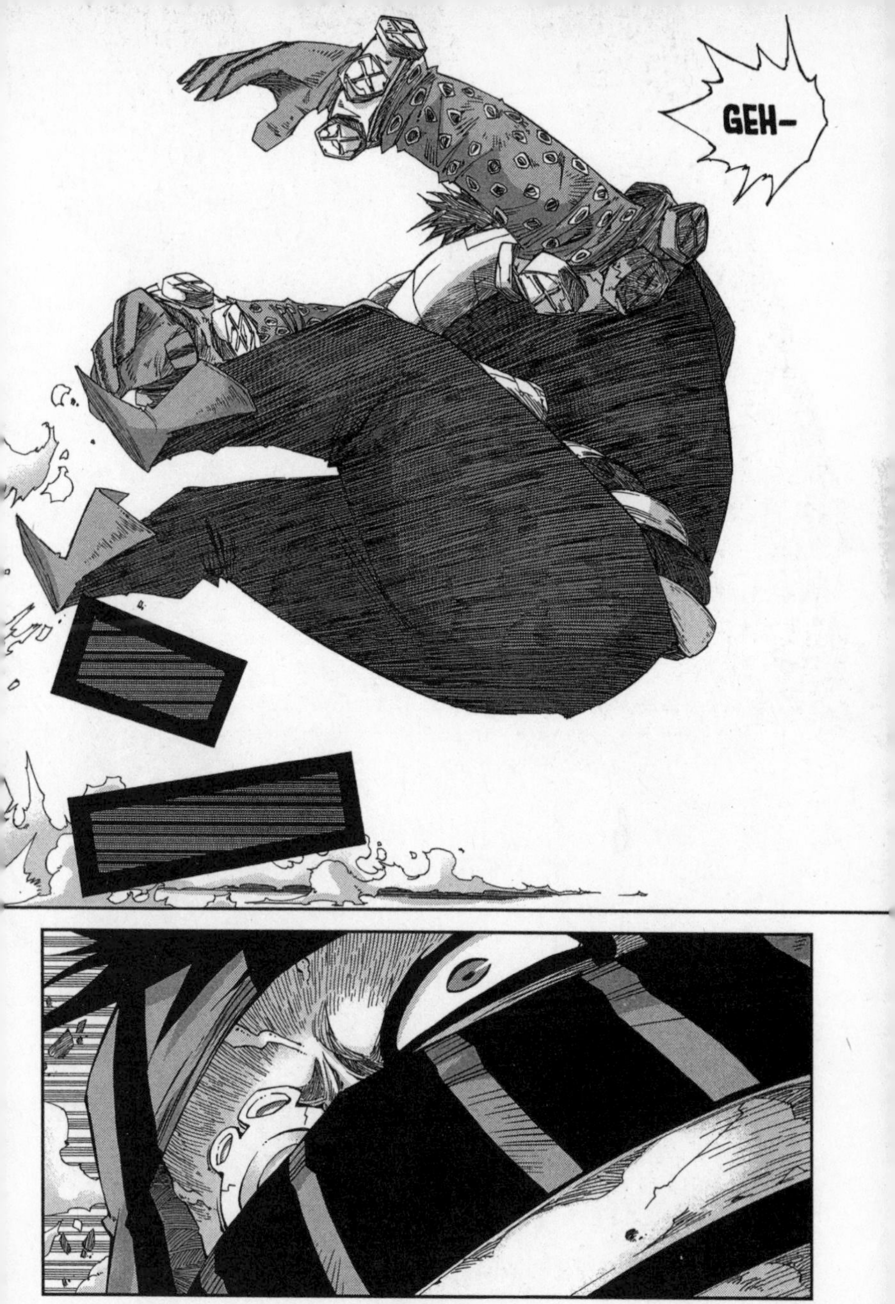
GEH-

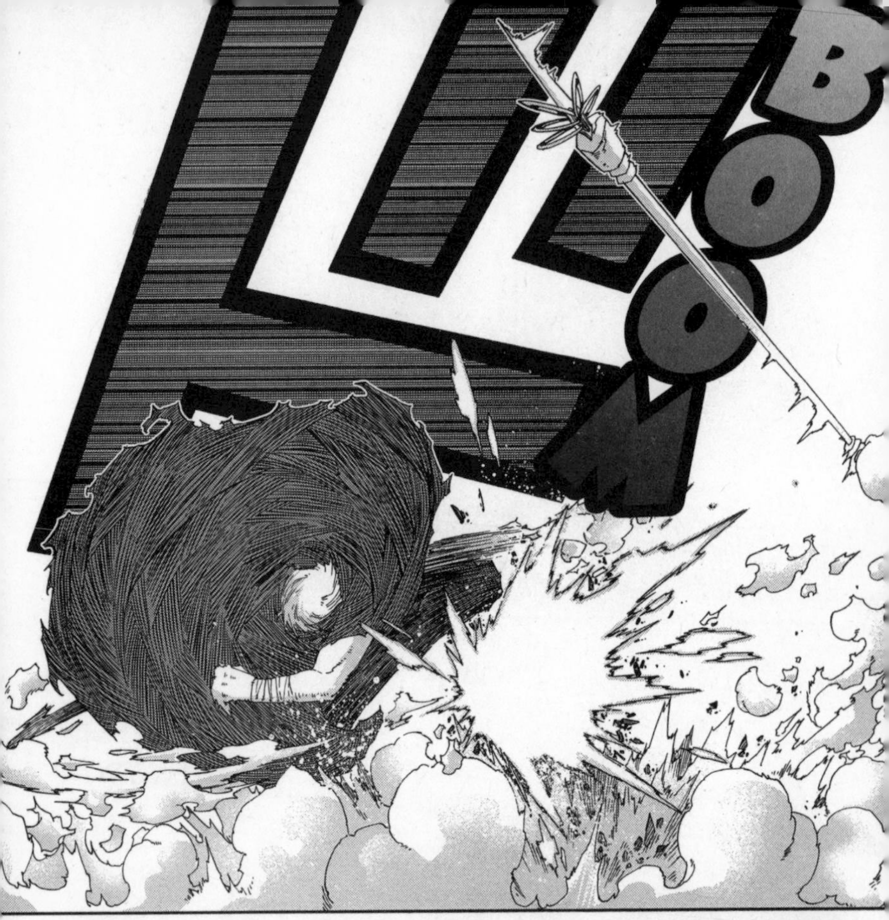
BOOM
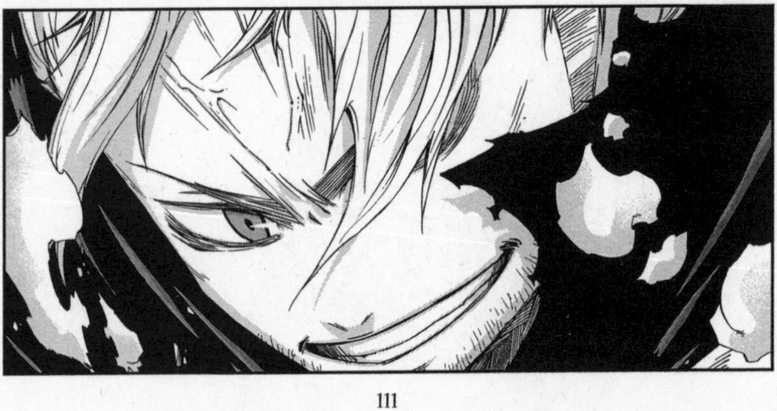

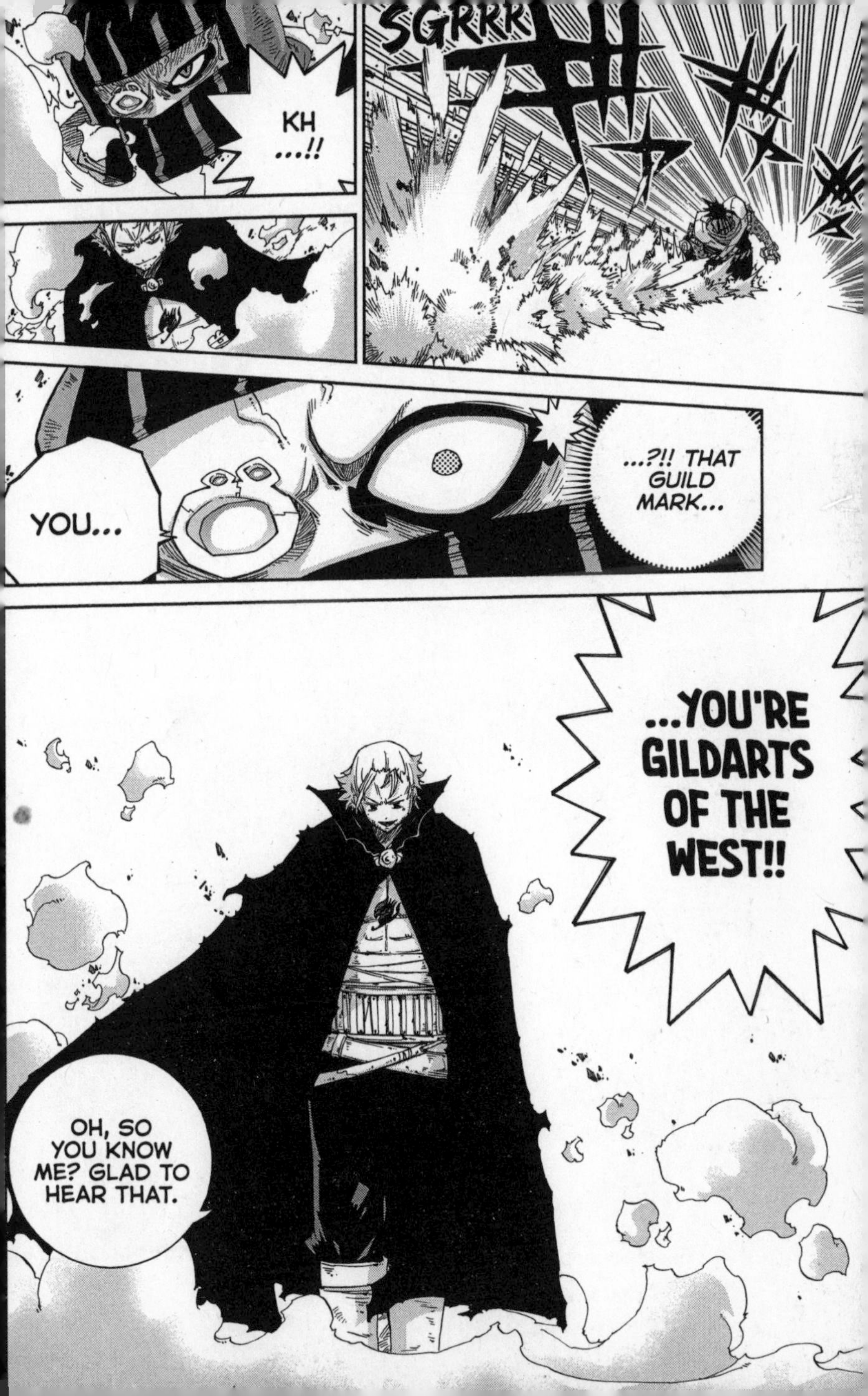
SGRRR
KH ...!!
...?!! THAT GUILD MARK...
YOU...
...YOU'RE GILDARTS OF THE WEST!!
OH, SO YOU KNOW ME? GLAD TO HEAR THAT.

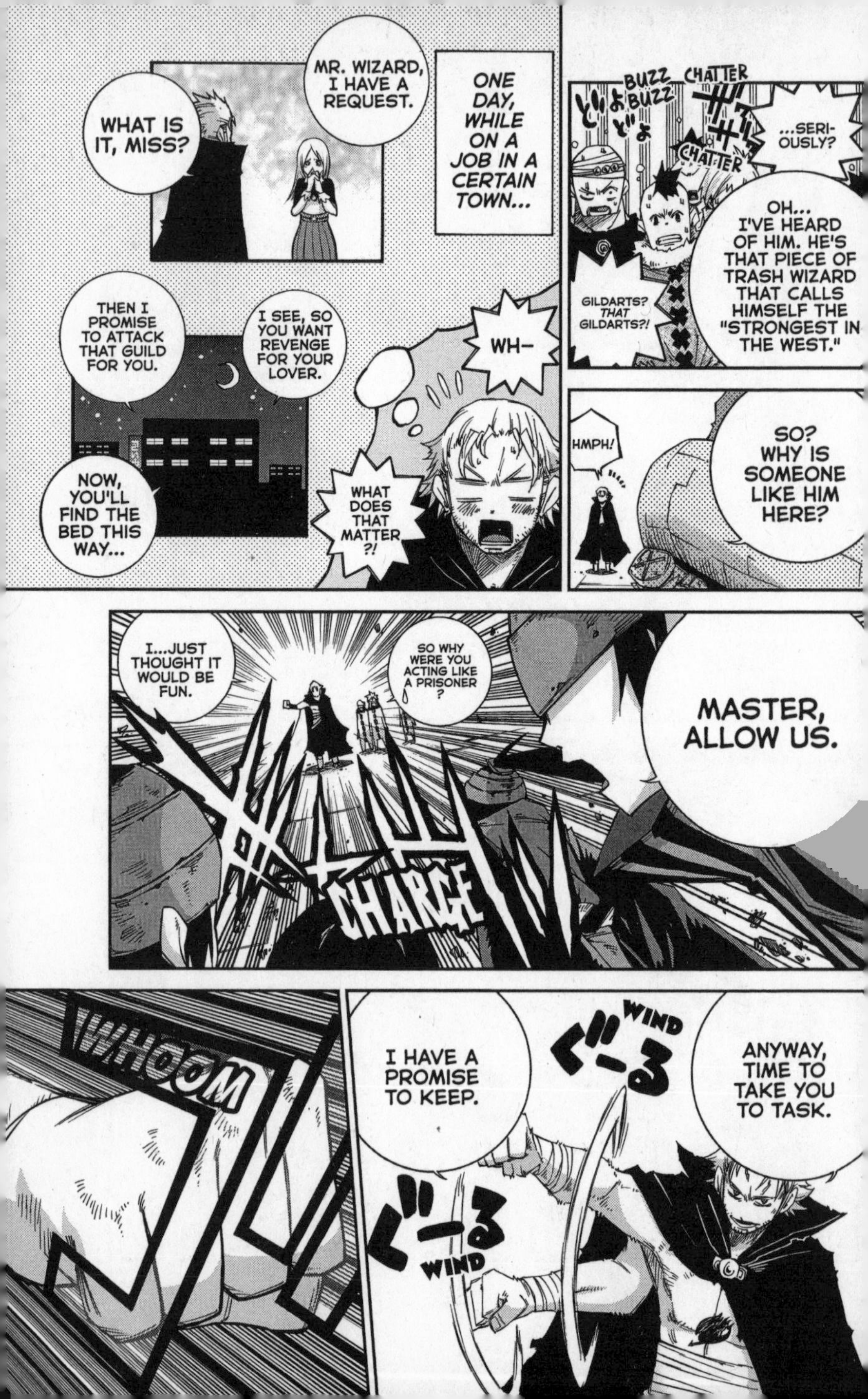
CHATTER
...SERIOUSLY?
BUZZ BUZZ
CHATTER
OH... I'VE HEARD OF HIM. HE'S THAT PIECE OF TRASH WIZARD THAT CALLS HIMSELF THE "STRONGEST IN THE WEST."
GILDARTS? THAT GILDARTS?!
SO? WHY IS SOMEONE LIKE HIM HERE?
HMPH!
ONE DAY, WHILE ON A JOB IN A CERTAIN TOWN...
MR. WIZARD, I HAVE A REQUEST.
WHAT IS IT, MISS?
WH-
I SEE, SO YOU WANT REVENGE FOR YOUR LOVER.
THEN I PROMISE TO ATTACK THAT GUILD FOR YOU.
NOW, YOU'LL FIND THE BED THIS WAY...
WHAT DOES THAT MATTER?!
MASTER, ALLOW US.
SO WHY WERE YOU ACTING LIKE A PRISONER?
I...JUST THOUGHT IT WOULD BE FUN.
CHARGE
ANYWAY, TIME TO TAKE YOU TO TASK.
WIND
I HAVE A PROMISE TO KEEP.
WIND
WHOOM

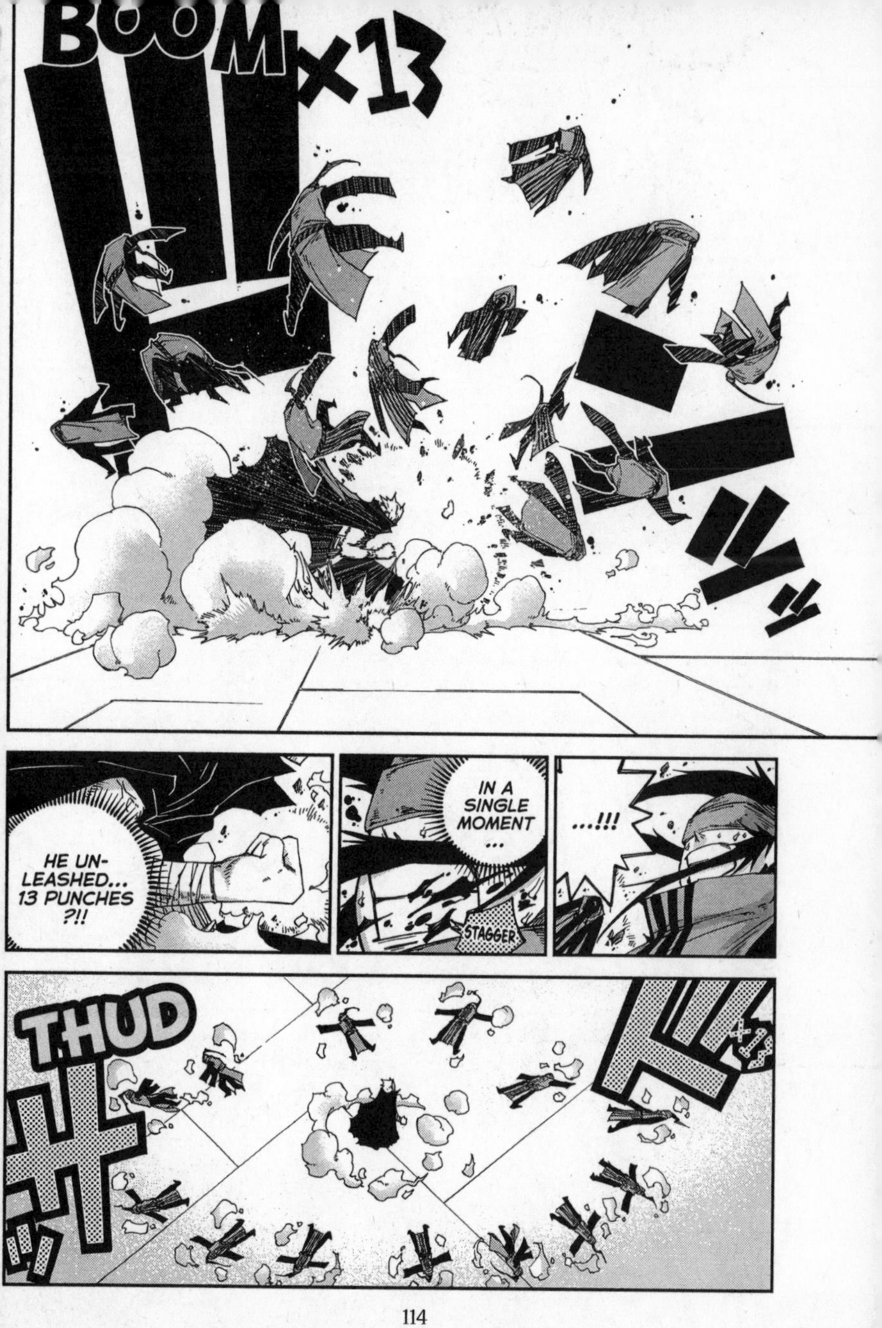
BOOM ×13
...!!!
IN A SINGLE MOMENT ...
STAGGER
HE UN-LEASHED... 13 PUNCHES ?!!
THUD

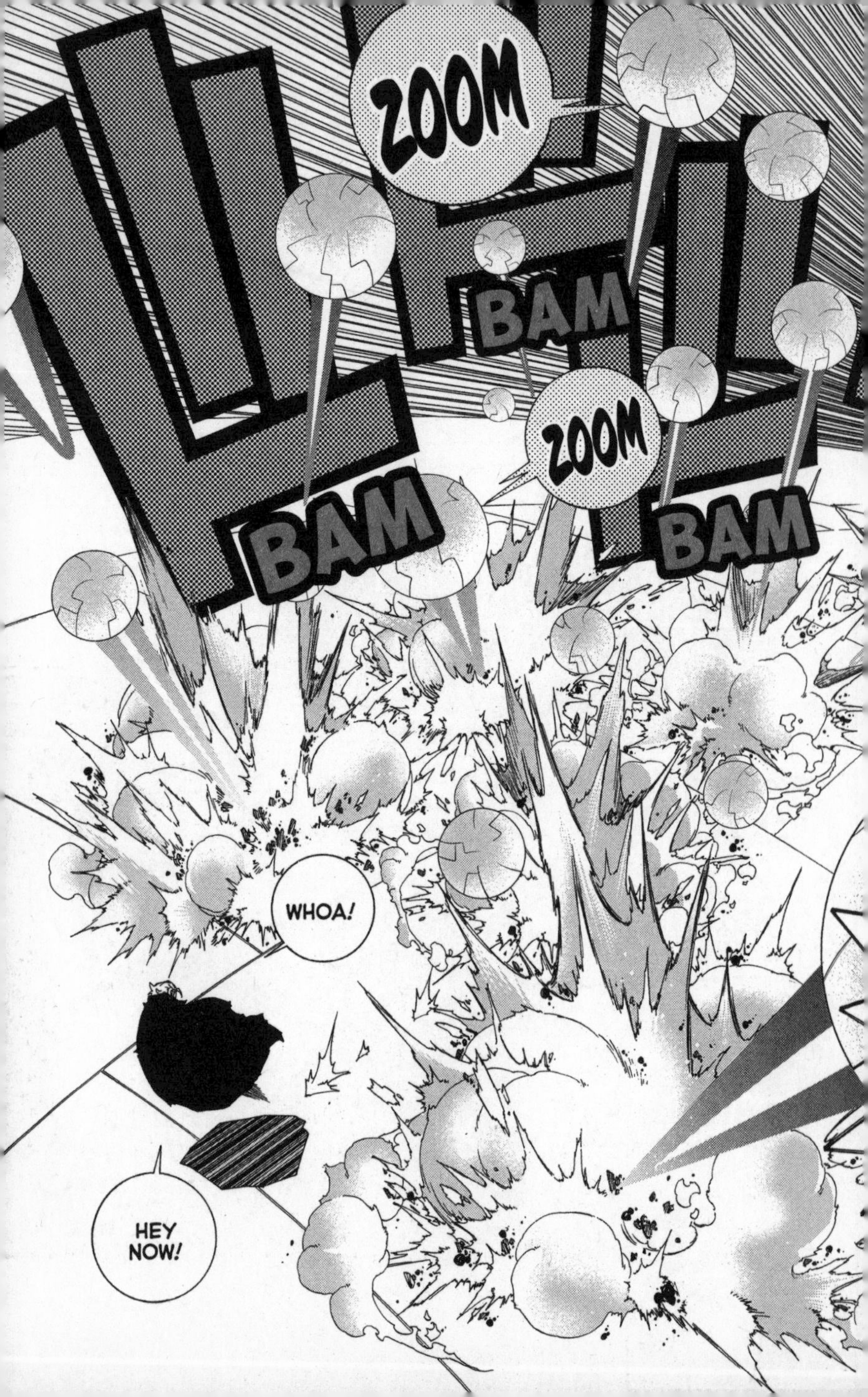
ZOOM
BAM
ZOOM
BAM
BAM
WHOA!
HEY NOW!

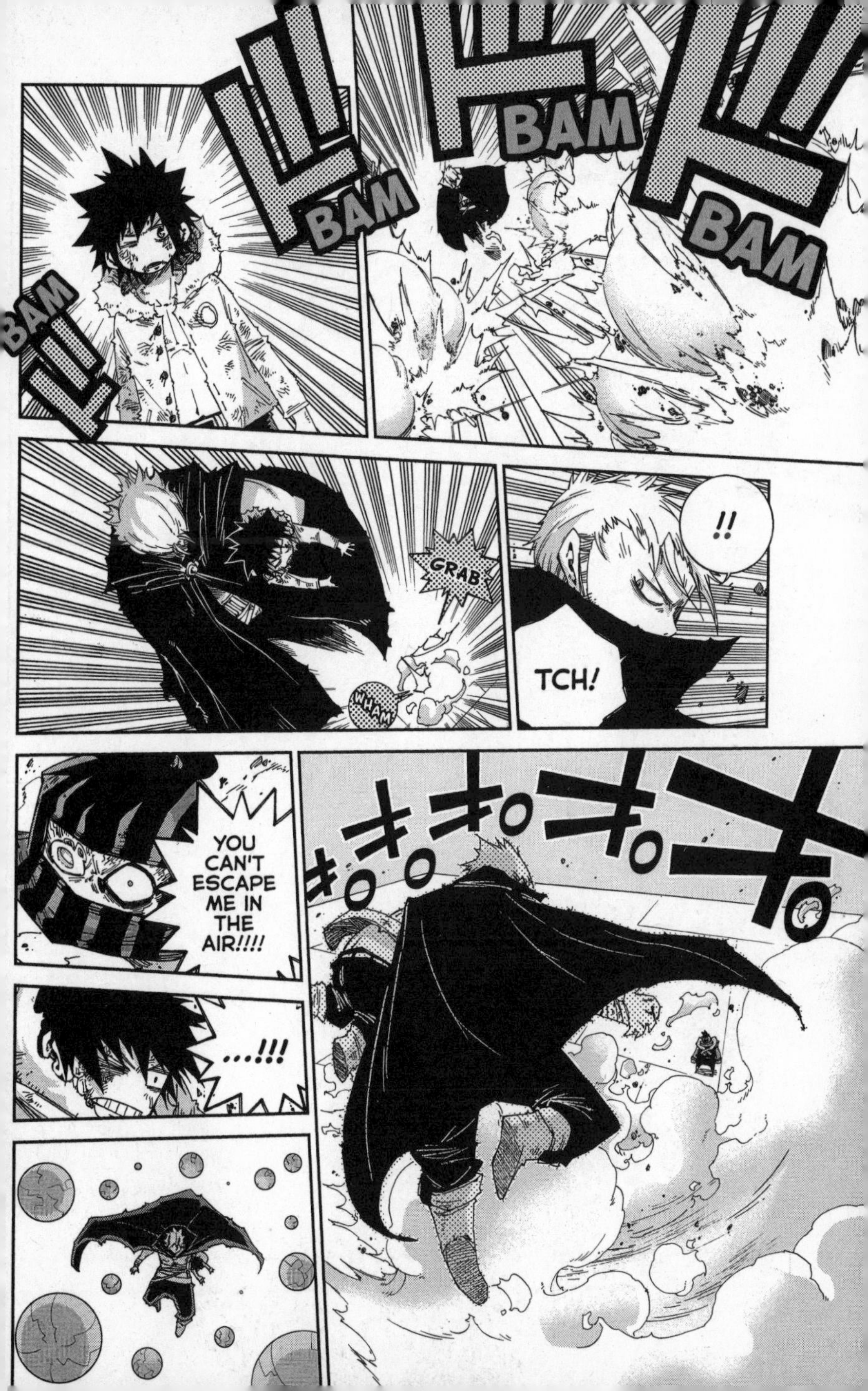

BAM
BAM
BAM
BAM
!!
TCH!
GRAB
WHAM!
YOU CAN'T ESCAPE ME IN THE AIR!!!!
...!!!

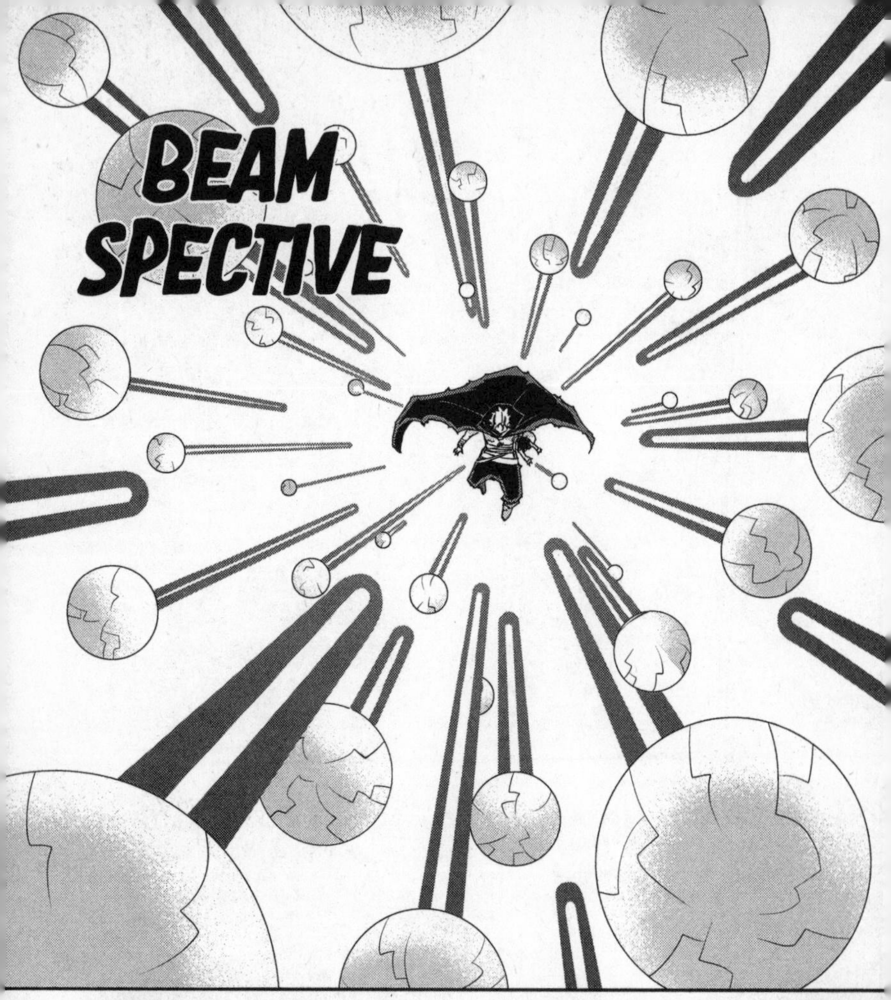
BEAM
SPECTIVE
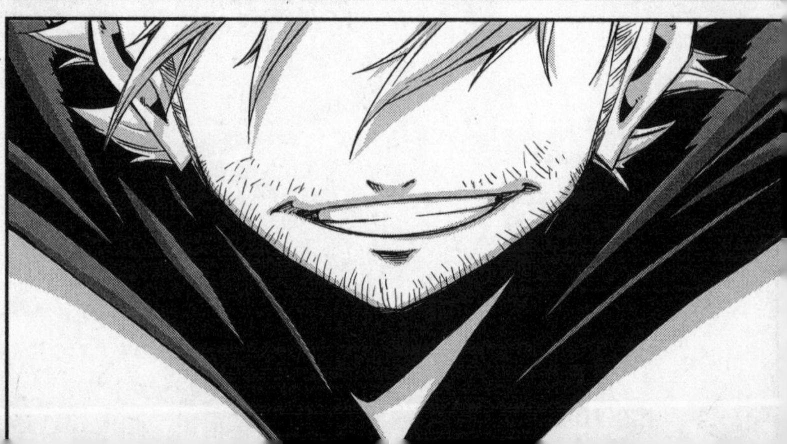

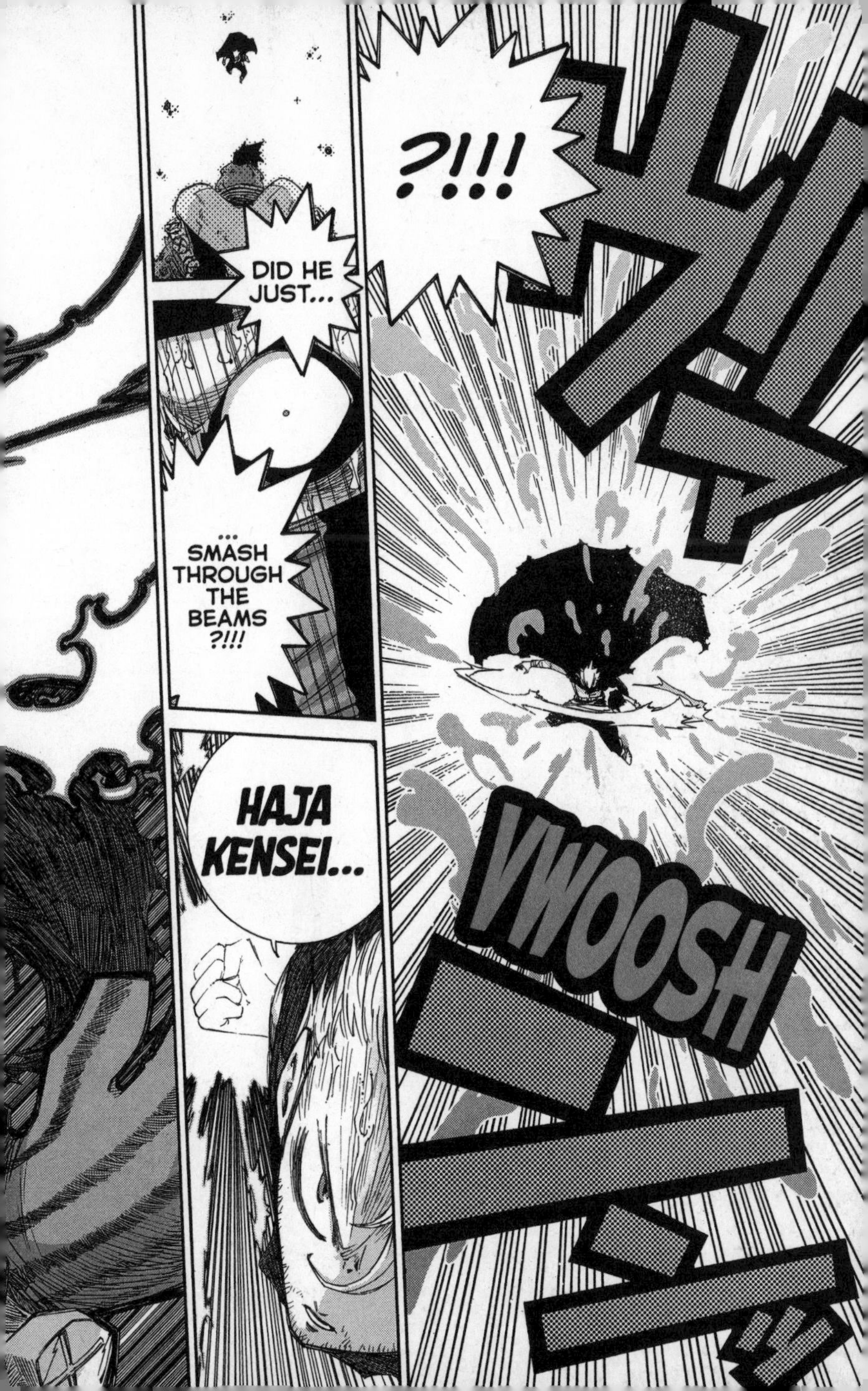
?!!!
VWOOSH
DID HE JUST...
...SMASH THROUGH THE BEAMS ?!!!
HAJA KENSEI...

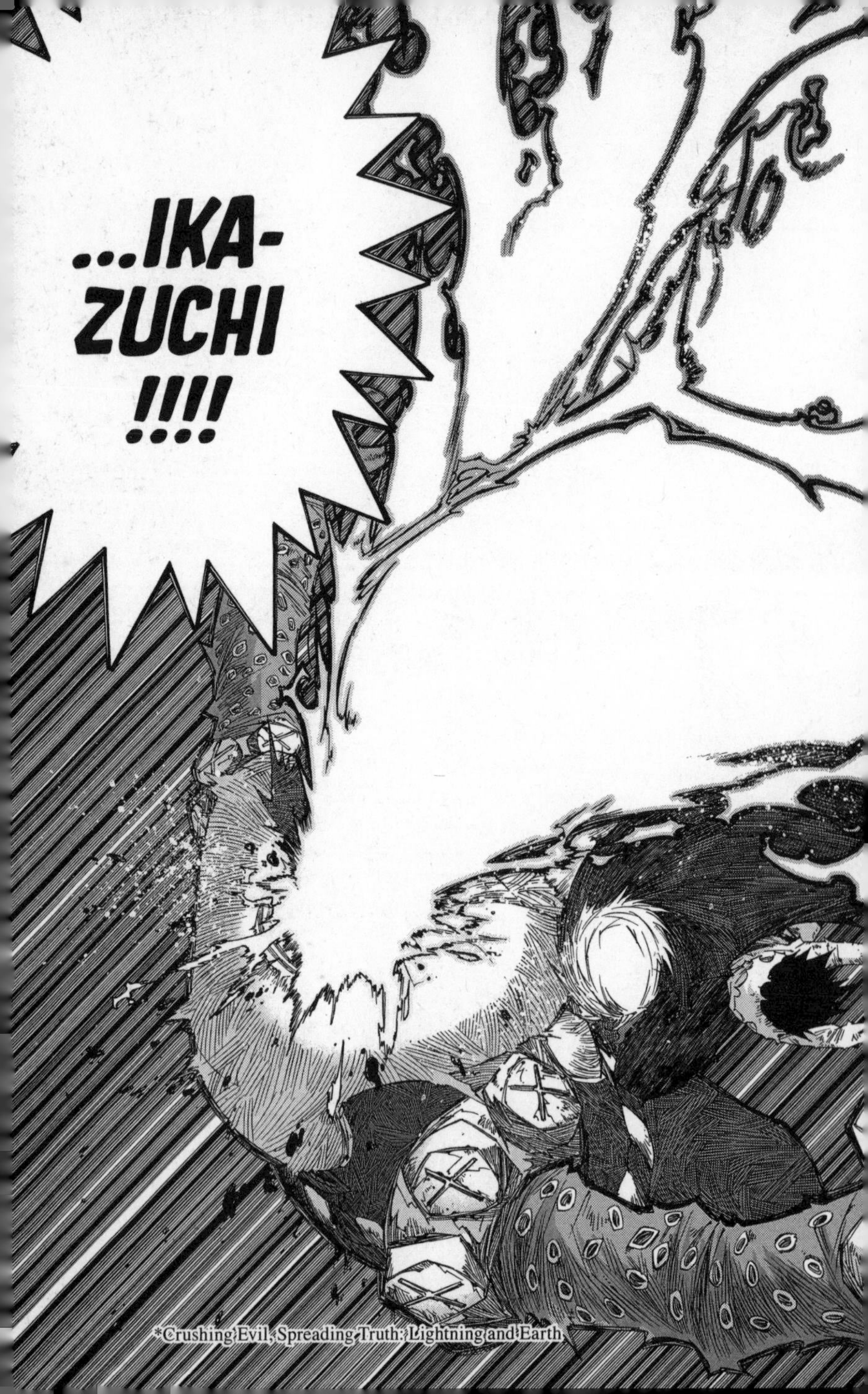
...IKA-
ZUCHI
!!!!
*Crushing Evil, Spreading Truth: Lightning and Earth

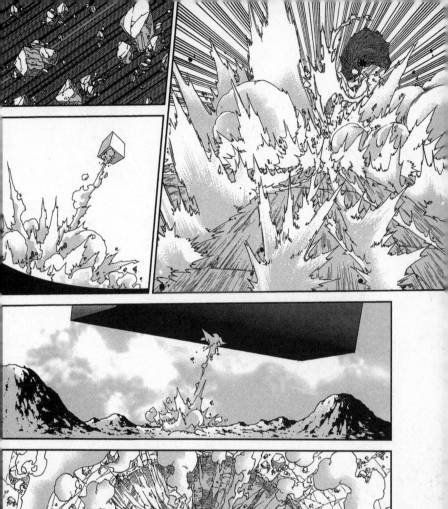
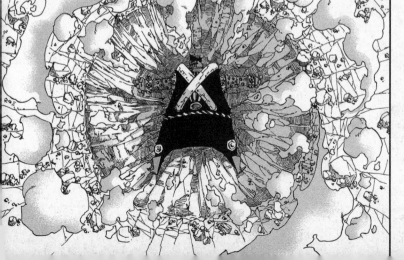

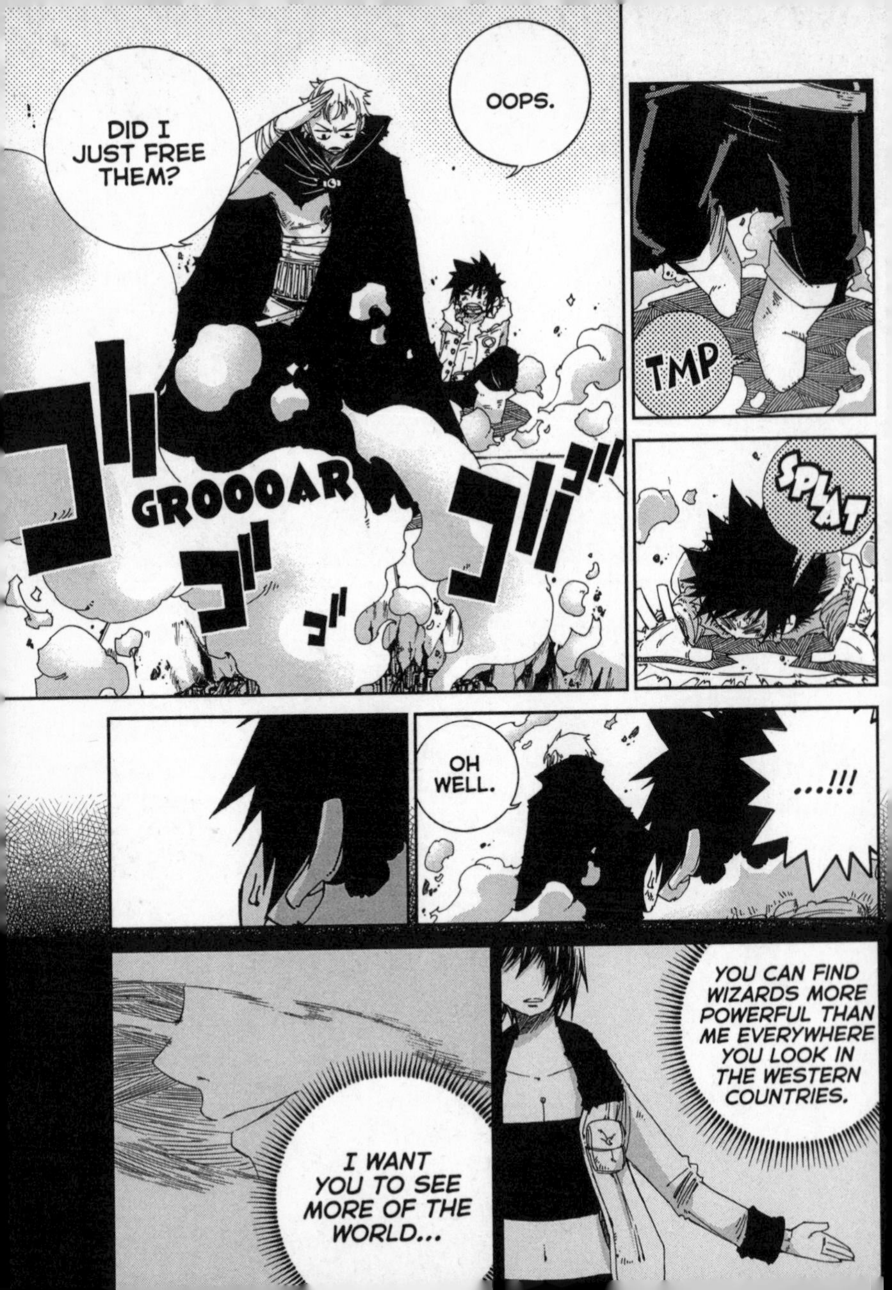
TMP
SPLAT
OOPS.
DID I JUST FREE THEM?
GROOOAR
...!!!
OH WELL.
YOU CAN FIND WIZARDS MORE POWERFUL THAN ME EVERYWHERE YOU LOOK IN THE WESTERN COUNTRIES.
I WANT YOU TO SEE MORE OF THE WORLD...

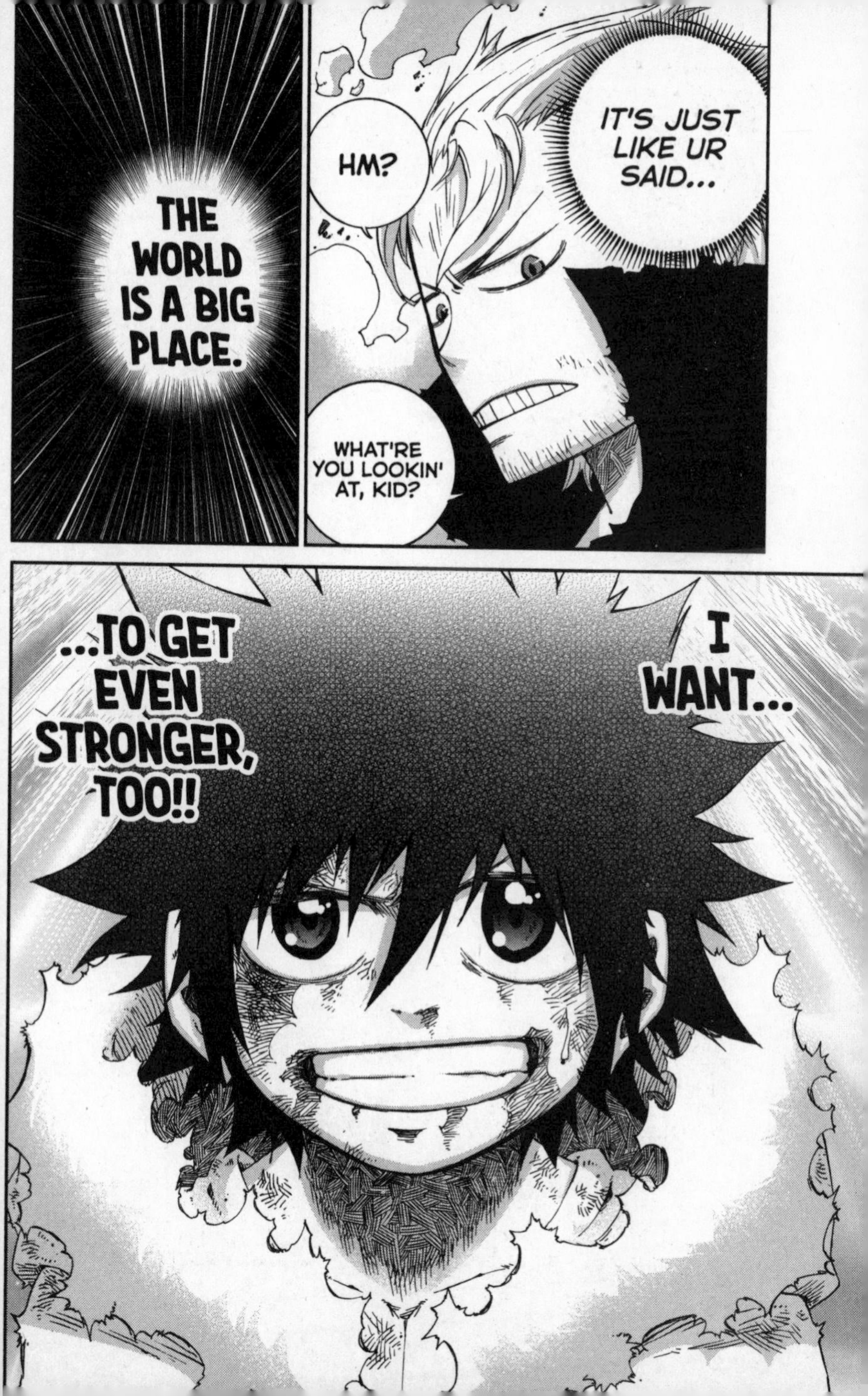
IT'S JUST LIKE UR SAID...
HM?
WHAT'RE YOU LOOKIN' AT, KID?
THE WORLD IS A BIG PLACE.
I WANT...
...TO GET EVEN STRONGER, TOO!!

Chapter 5: Meetings and Memories

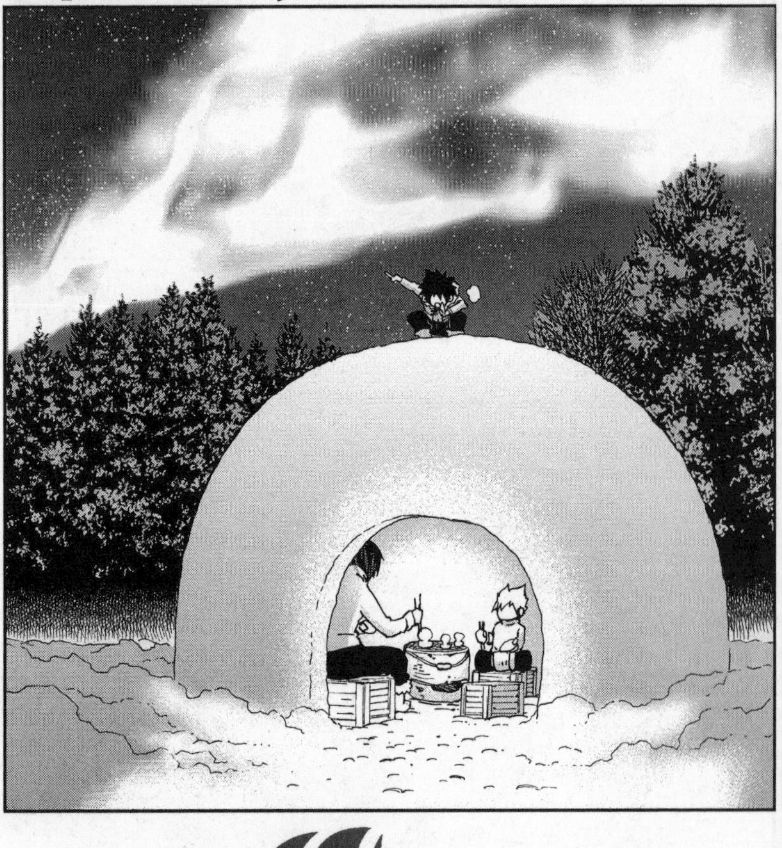

FAIRY TAIL: ICE TRAIL

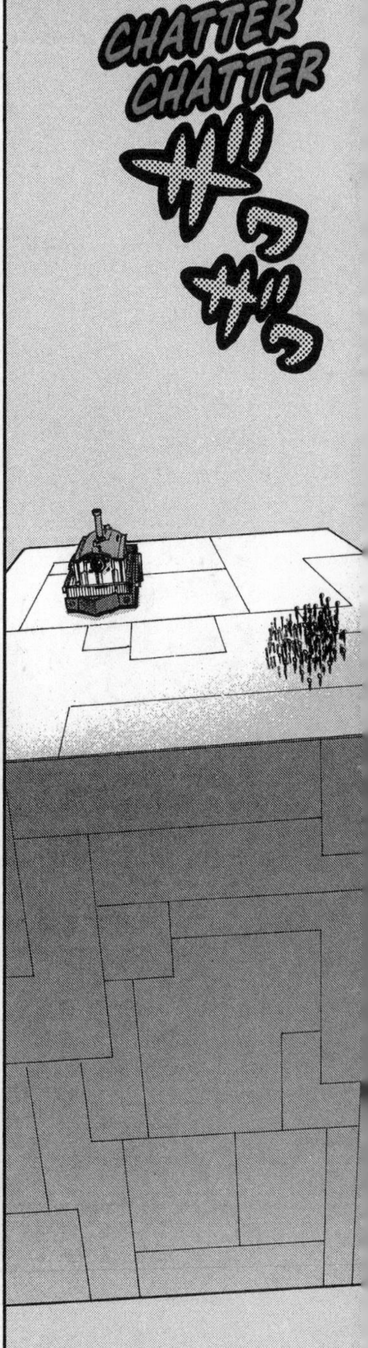
CHATTER CHATTER
ザワザワ

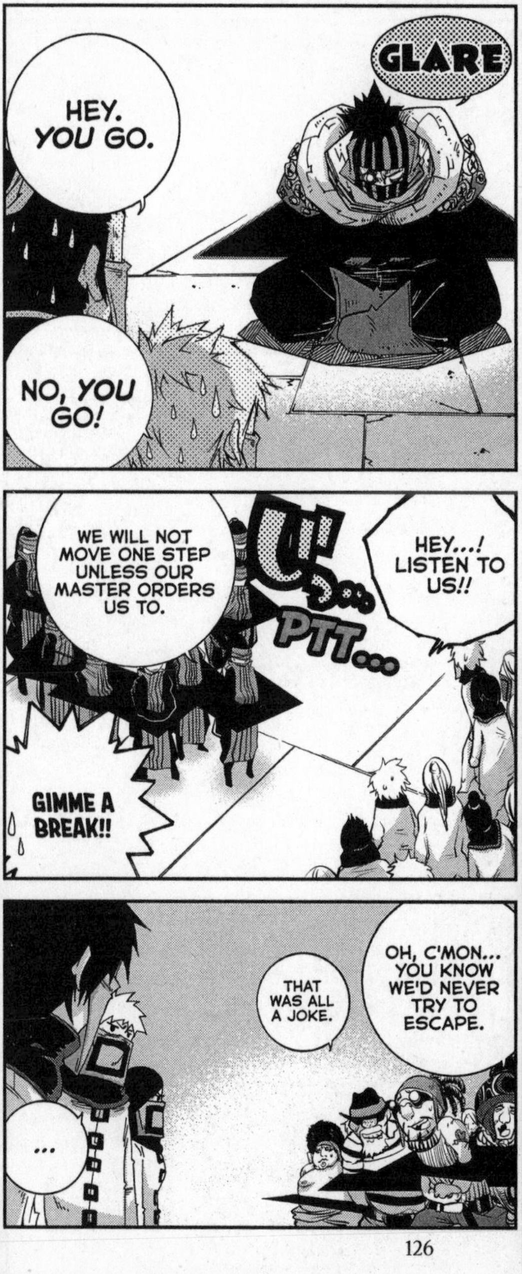
GLARE
HEY. *YOU* GO.
NO, *YOU* GO!
HEY...! LISTEN TO US!!
PTT...
WE WILL NOT MOVE ONE STEP UNLESS OUR MASTER ORDERS US TO.
GIMME A BREAK!!
OH, C'MON... YOU KNOW WE'D NEVER TRY TO ESCAPE.
THAT WAS ALL A JOKE.
...

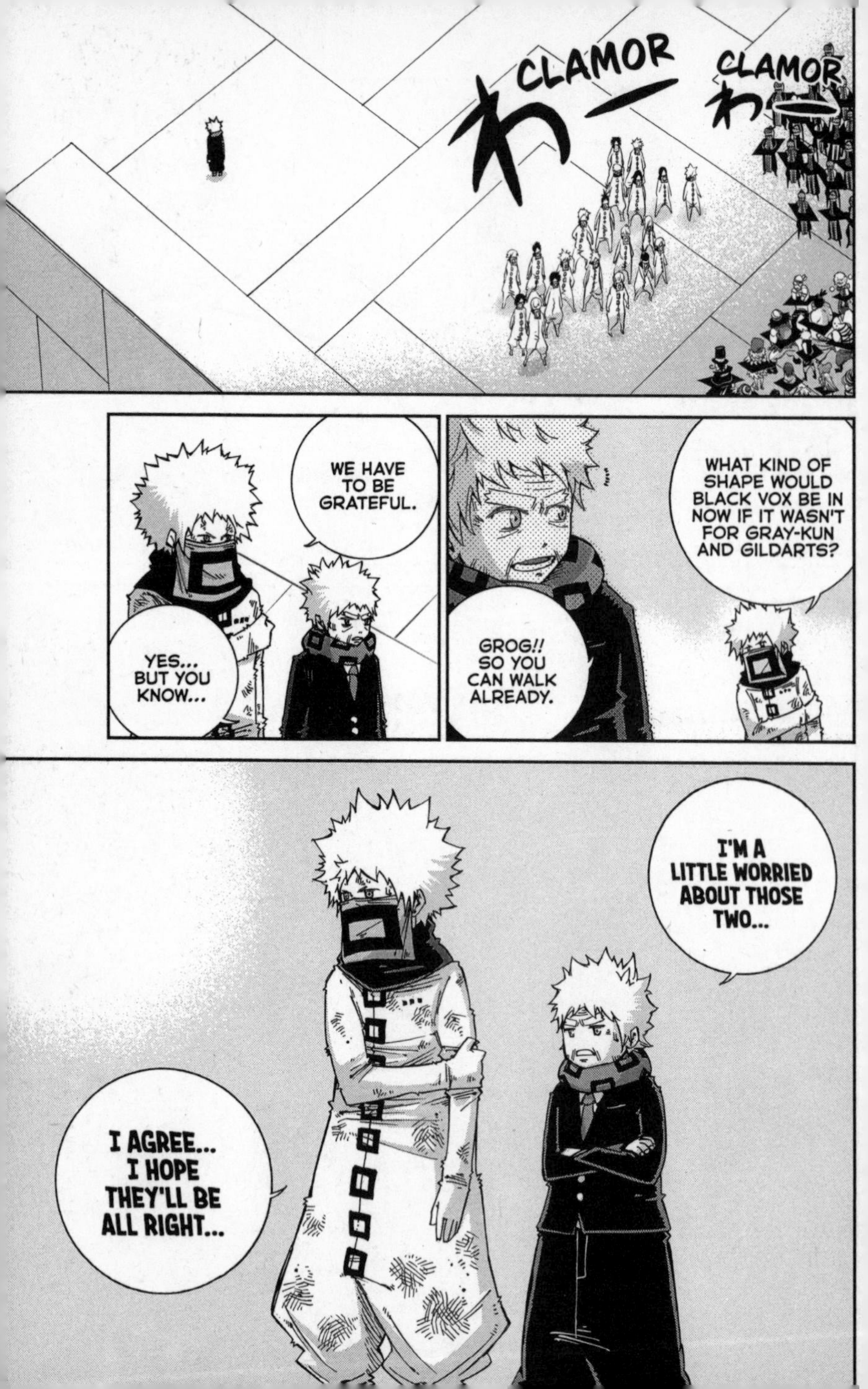

CLAMOR
わー
CLAMOR
わー
WHAT KIND OF SHAPE WOULD BLACK VOX BE IN NOW IF IT WASN'T FOR GRAY-KUN AND GILDARTS?
GROG!! SO YOU CAN WALK ALREADY.
WE HAVE TO BE GRATEFUL.
YES... BUT YOU KNOW...
I'M A LITTLE WORRIED ABOUT THOSE TWO...
I AGREE... I HOPE THEY'LL BE ALL RIGHT...

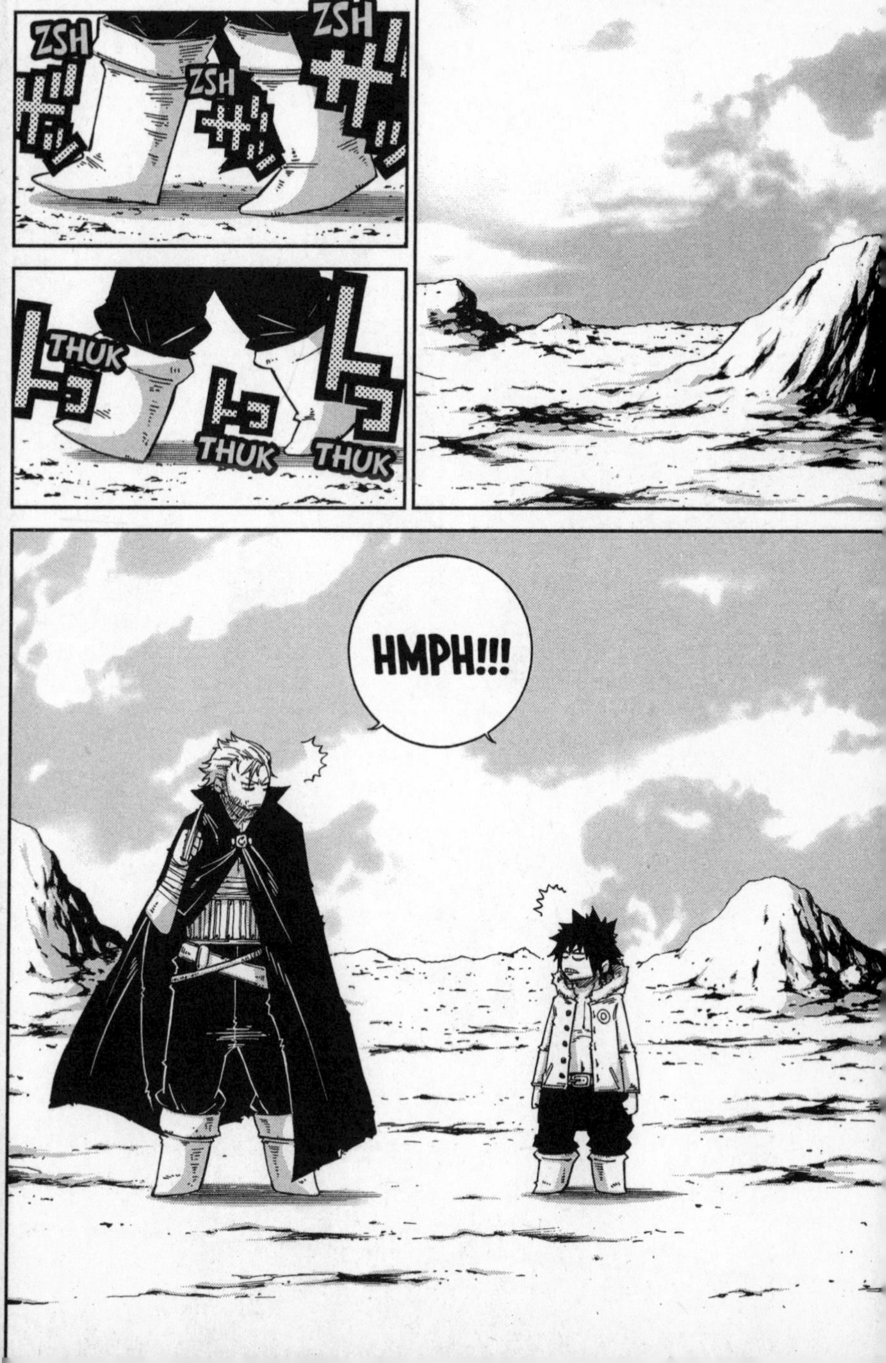
ZSH
ZSH
ZSH
THUK
THUK
THUK
HMPH!!!

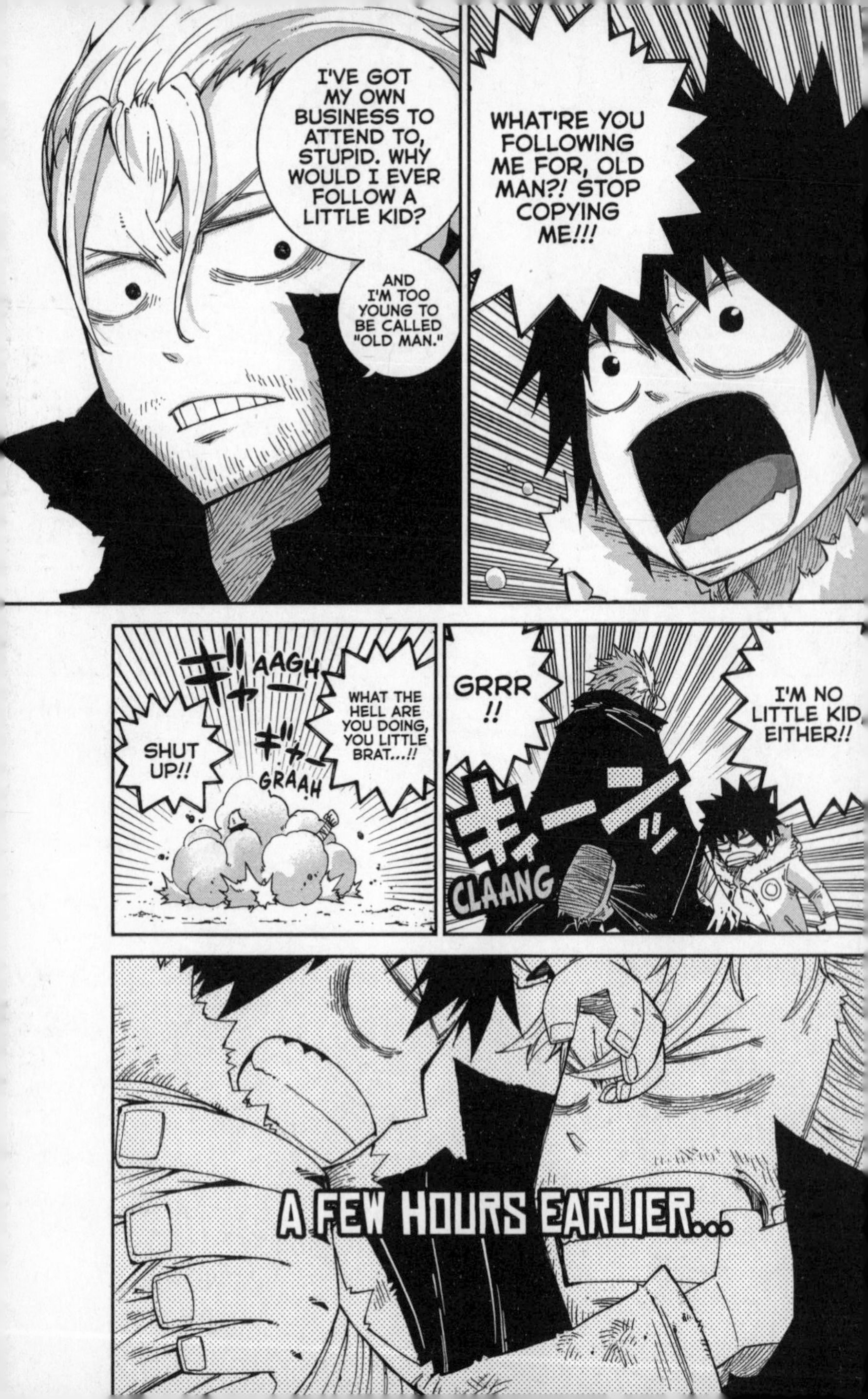
WHAT'RE YOU FOLLOWING ME FOR, OLD MAN?! STOP COPYING ME!!!
I'VE GOT MY OWN BUSINESS TO ATTEND TO, STUPID. WHY WOULD I EVER FOLLOW A LITTLE KID?
AND I'M TOO YOUNG TO BE CALLED "OLD MAN."
I'M NO LITTLE KID EITHER!!
GRRR !!
CLAANG
WHAT THE HELL ARE YOU DOING, YOU LITTLE BRAT...!!
AAGH
SHUT UP!!
GRAAH
A FEW HOURS EARLIER...

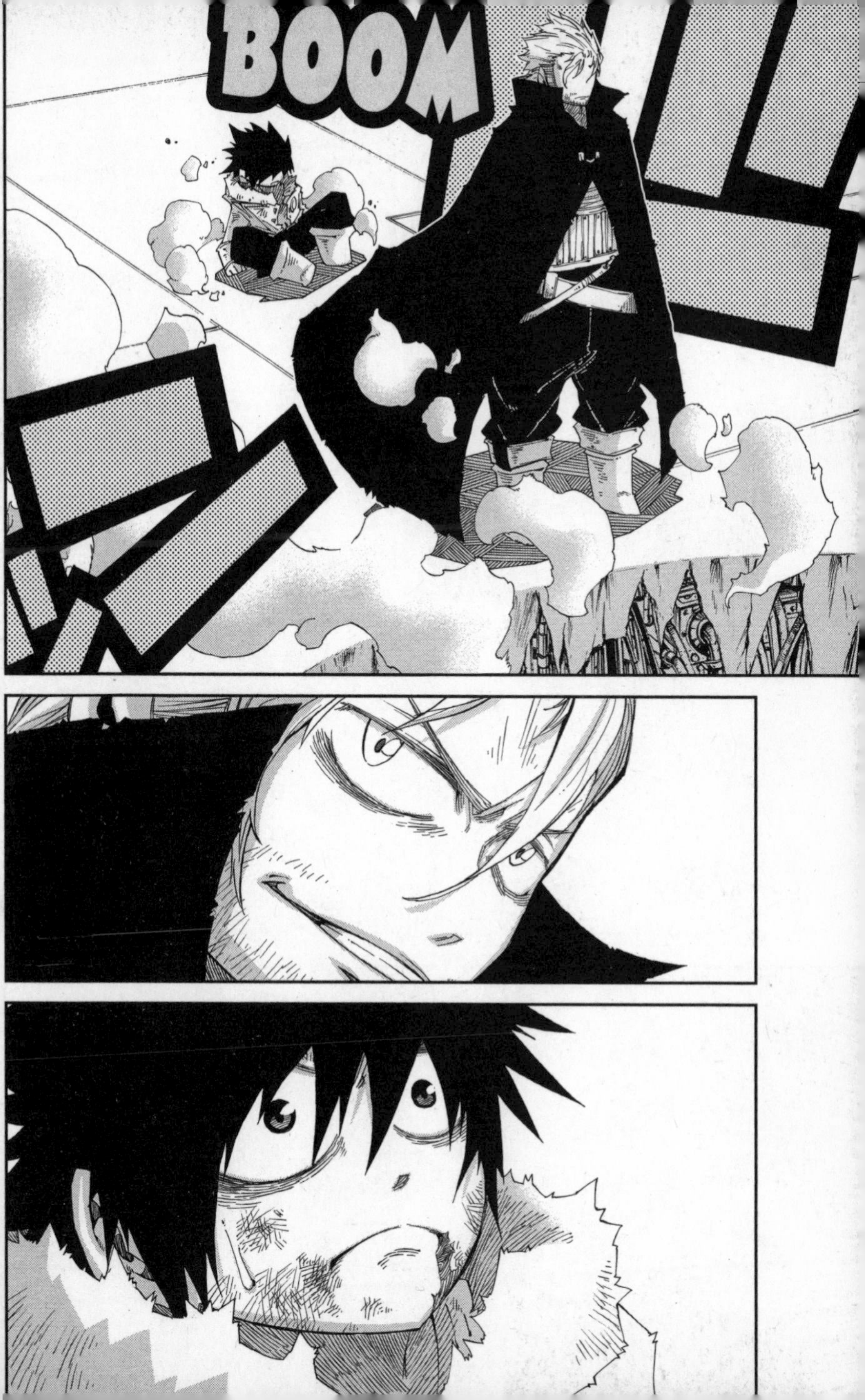
BOOM

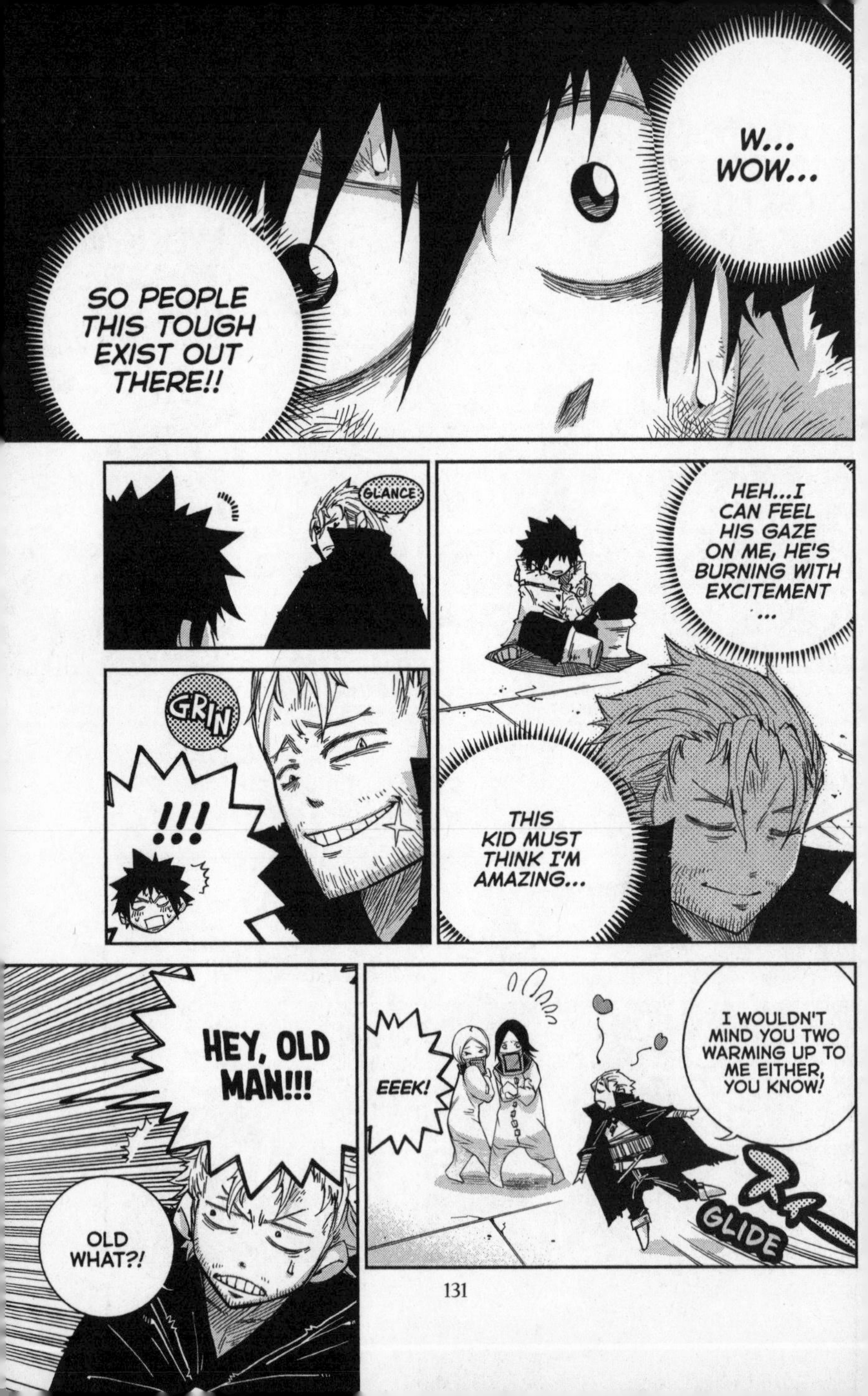
W... WOW...
SO PEOPLE THIS TOUGH EXIST OUT THERE!!
HEH...I CAN FEEL HIS GAZE ON ME, HE'S BURNING WITH EXCITEMENT ...
THIS KID MUST THINK I'M AMAZING...
GLANCE
GRIN
!!!
I WOULDN'T MIND YOU TWO WARMING UP TO ME EITHER, YOU KNOW!
EEEK!
GLIDE
HEY, OLD MAN!!!
OLD WHAT?!

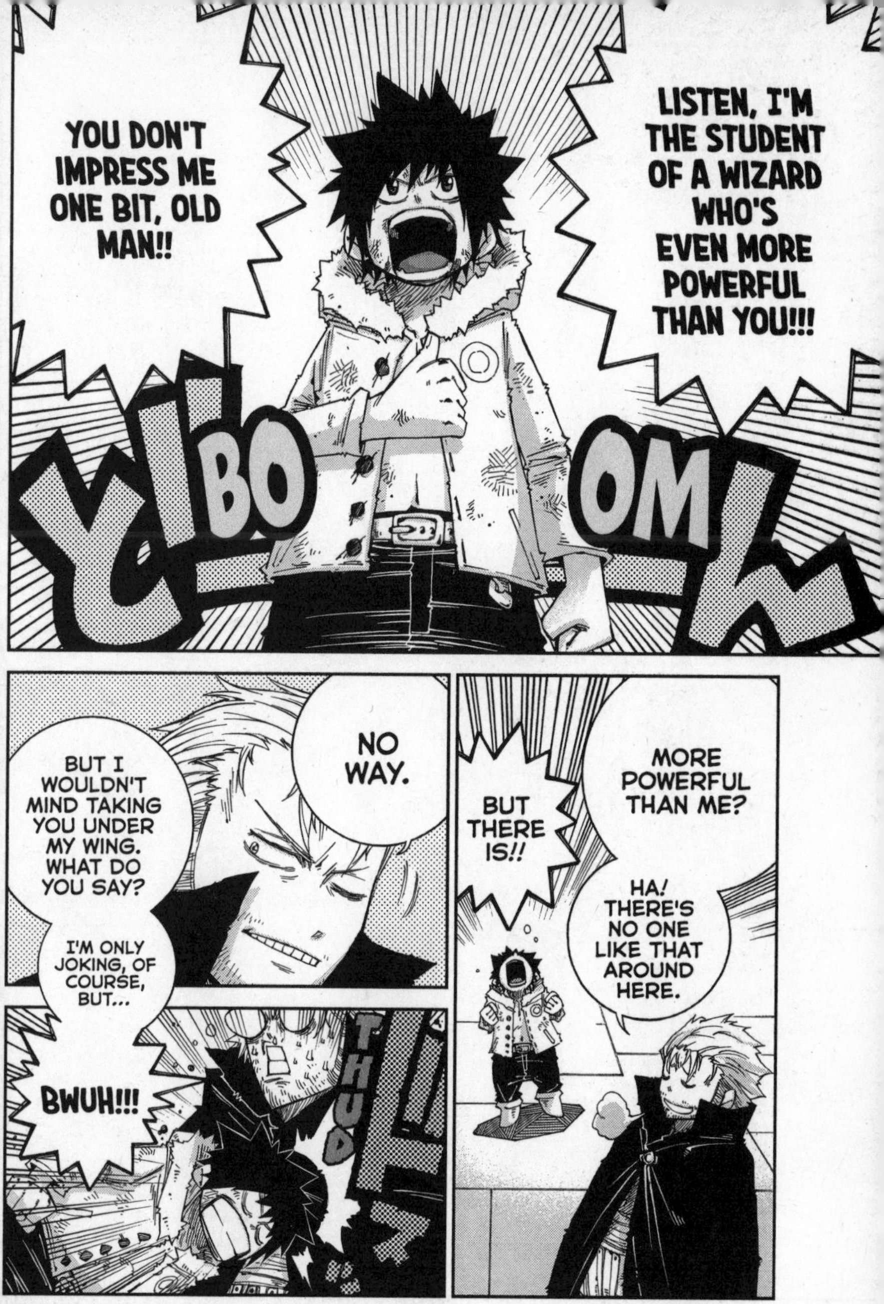

LISTEN, I'M THE STUDENT OF A WIZARD WHO'S EVEN MORE POWERFUL THAN YOU!!!
YOU DON'T IMPRESS ME ONE BIT, OLD MAN!!
BOOM
MORE POWERFUL THAN ME?
BUT THERE IS!!
HA! THERE'S NO ONE LIKE THAT AROUND HERE.
NO WAY.
BUT I WOULDN'T MIND TAKING YOU UNDER MY WING. WHAT DO YOU SAY?
I'M ONLY JOKING, OF COURSE, BUT...
THUD
BWUH!!!

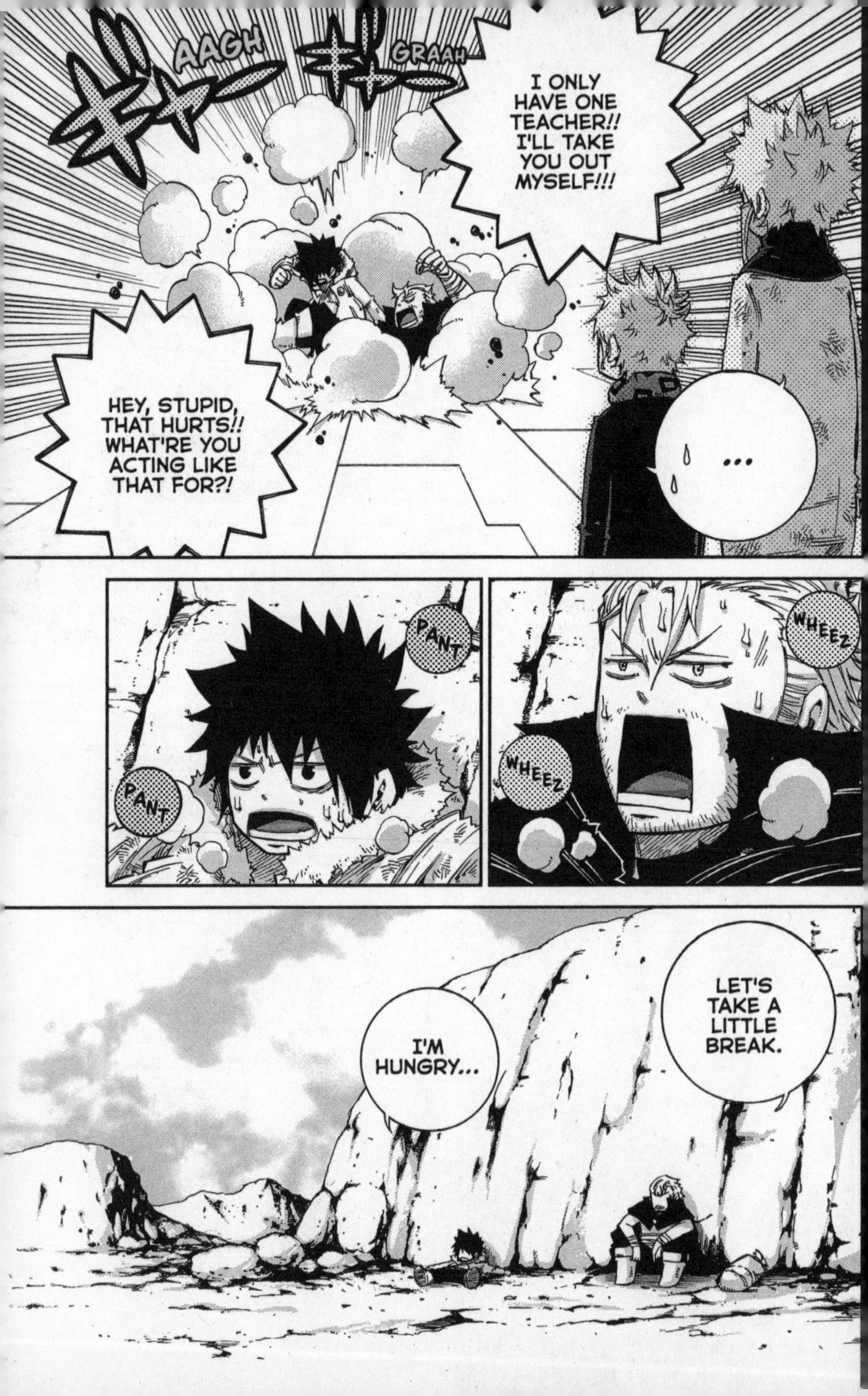
GRAAH
I ONLY HAVE ONE TEACHER!! I'LL TAKE YOU OUT MYSELF!!!
AAGH
...
HEY, STUPID, THAT HURTS!! WHAT'RE YOU ACTING LIKE THAT FOR?!
WHEEZ
WHEEZ
PANT
PANT
LET'S TAKE A LITTLE BREAK.
I'M HUNGRY...

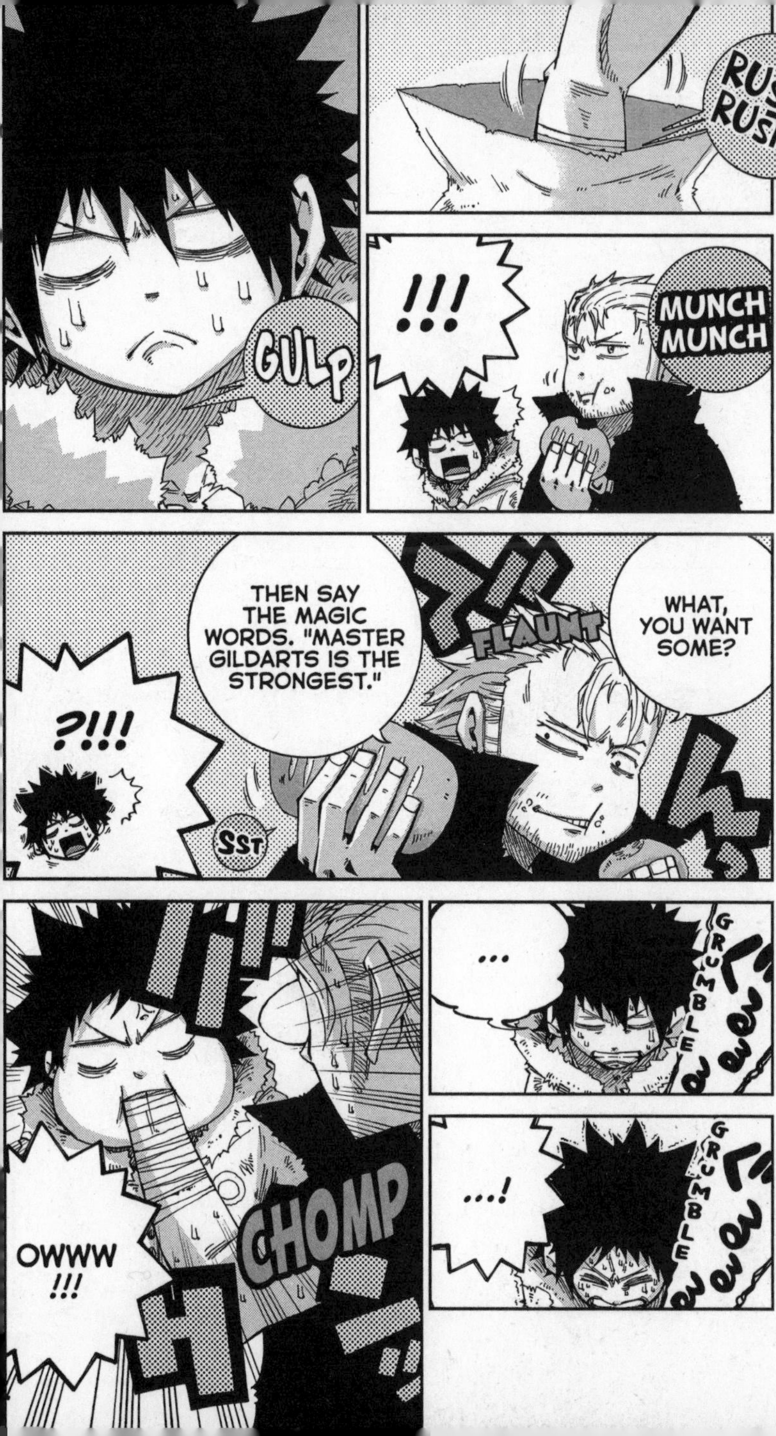
RUSTLE RUSTLE
!!!
MUNCH MUNCH
GULP
WHAT, YOU WANT SOME?
FLAUNT
THEN SAY THE MAGIC WORDS. "MASTER GILDARTS IS THE STRONGEST."
SST
?!!!
...
GRUMBLE
...!
GRUMBLE
CHOMP
OWWW !!!

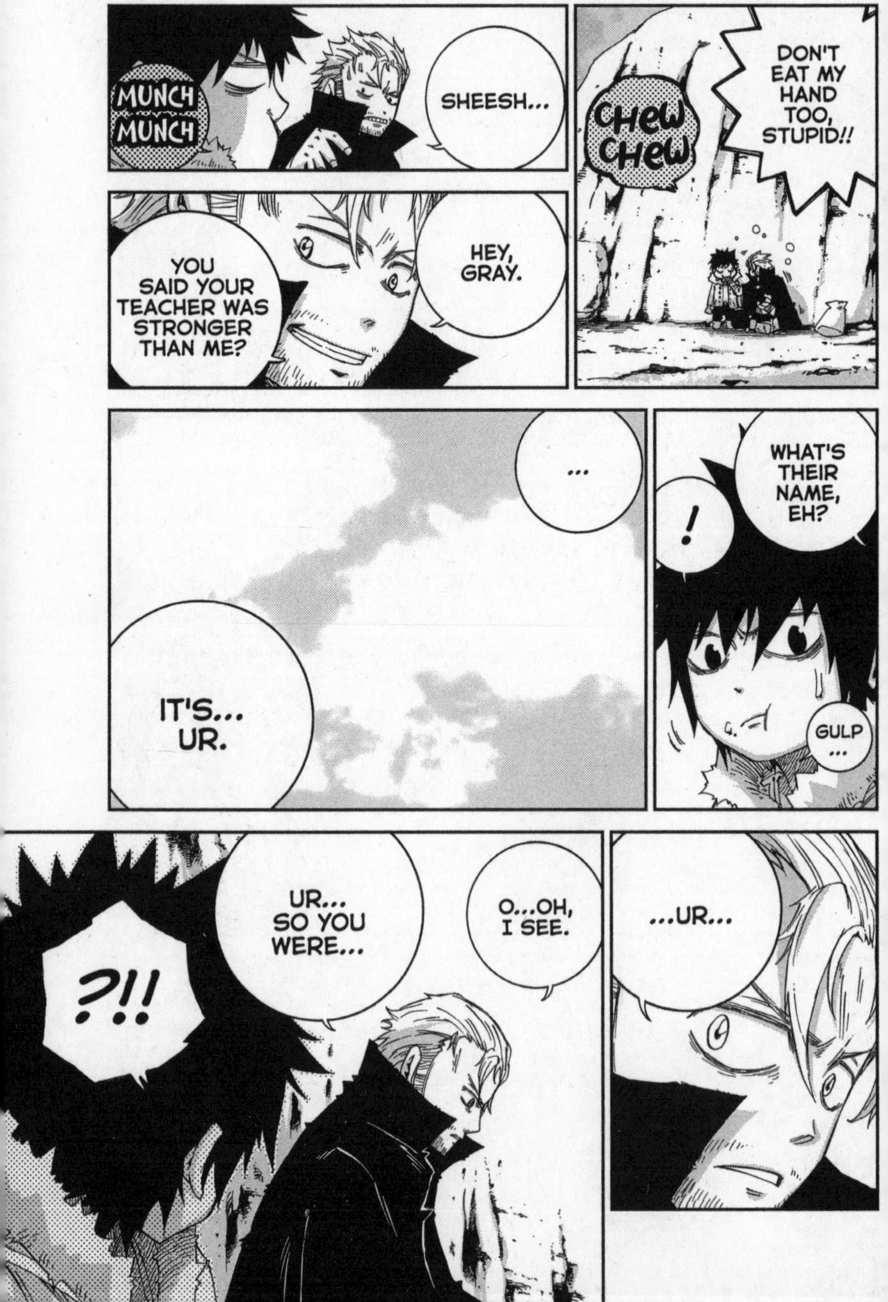
DON'T EAT MY HAND TOO, STUPID!!
CHEW CHEW
SHEESH...
MUNCH MUNCH
HEY, GRAY.
YOU SAID YOUR TEACHER WAS STRONGER THAN ME?
WHAT'S THEIR NAME, EH?
!
GULP...
...
IT'S... UR.
...UR...
O...OH, I SEE.
UR... SO YOU WERE...
?!!

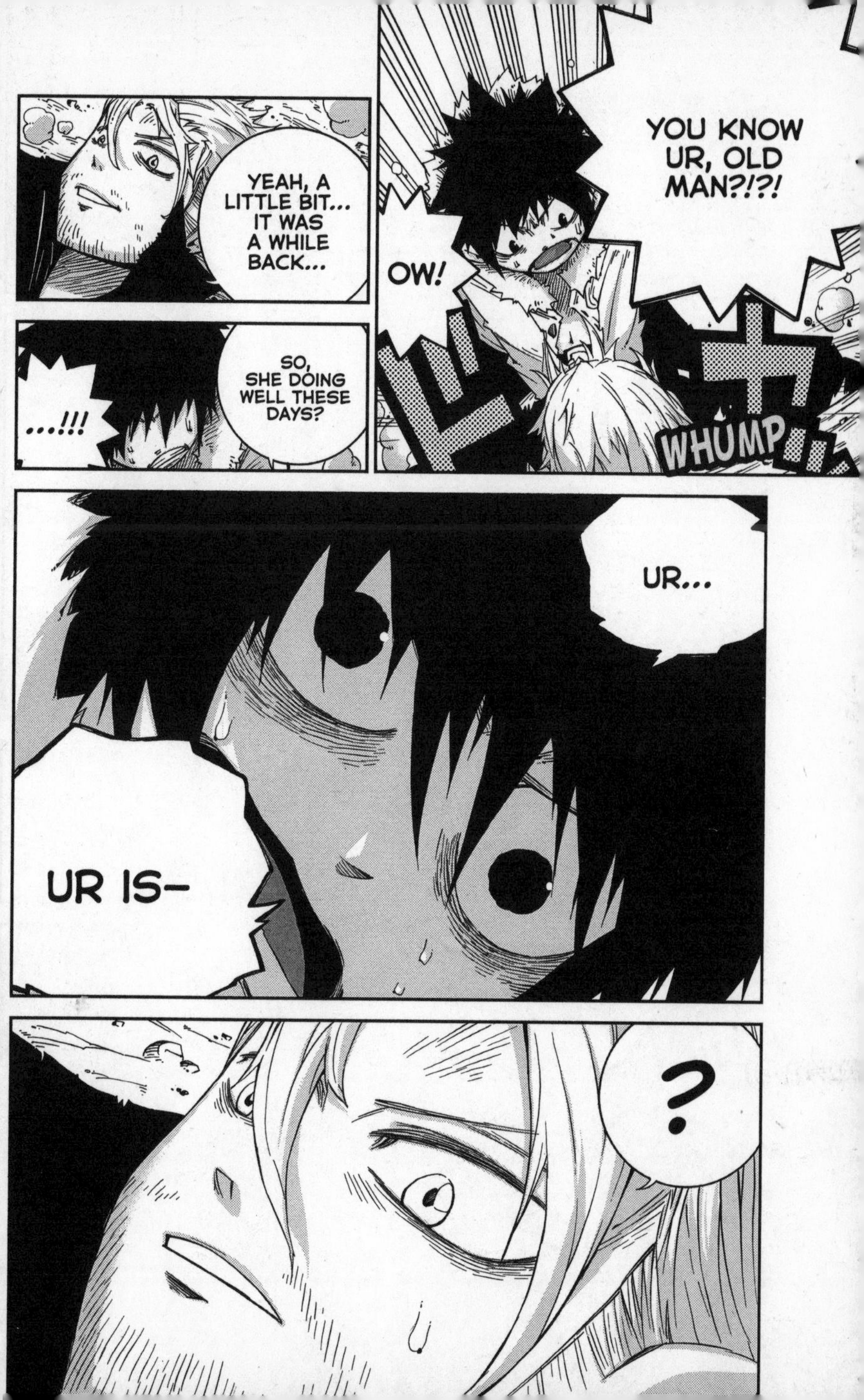
YOU KNOW UR, OLD MAN?!?!
OW!
WHUMP
YEAH, A LITTLE BIT... IT WAS A WHILE BACK...
SO, SHE DOING WELL THESE DAYS?
...!!!
UR...
UR IS-
?

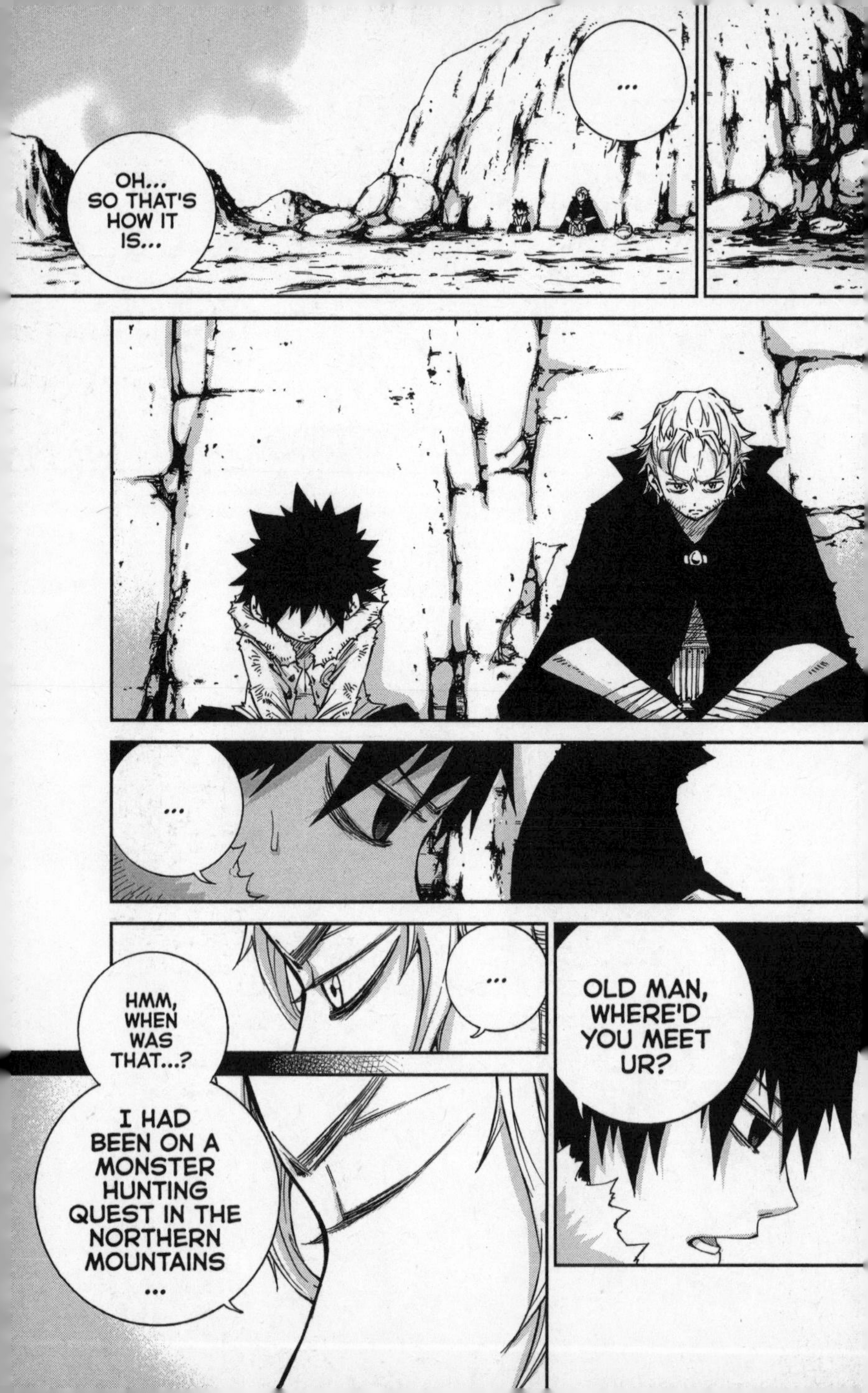
...
OH... SO THAT'S HOW IT IS...
...
OLD MAN, WHERE'D YOU MEET UR?
...
HMM, WHEN WAS THAT...?
I HAD BEEN ON A MONSTER HUNTING QUEST IN THE NORTHERN MOUNTAINS ...

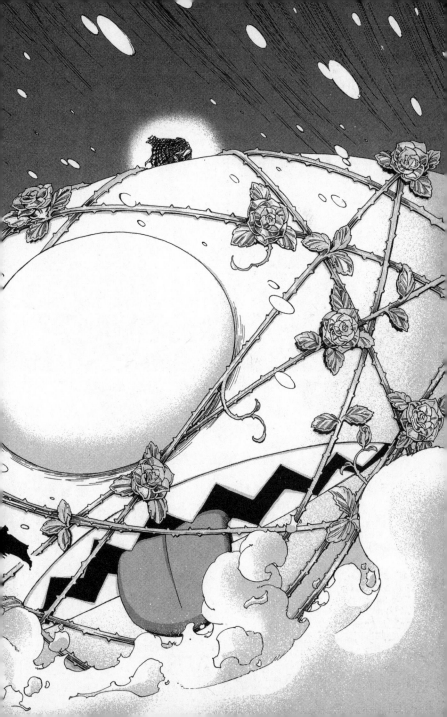

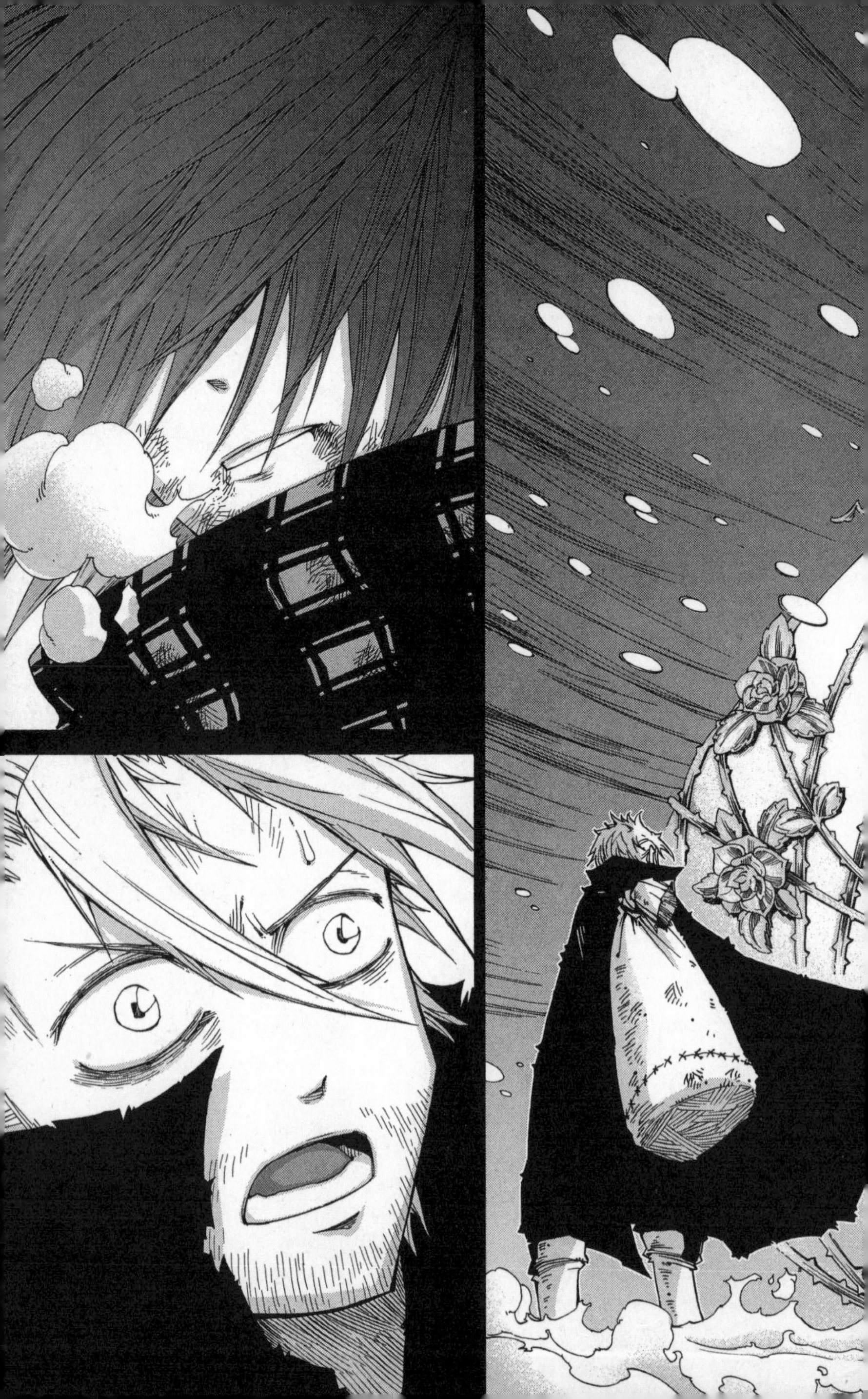

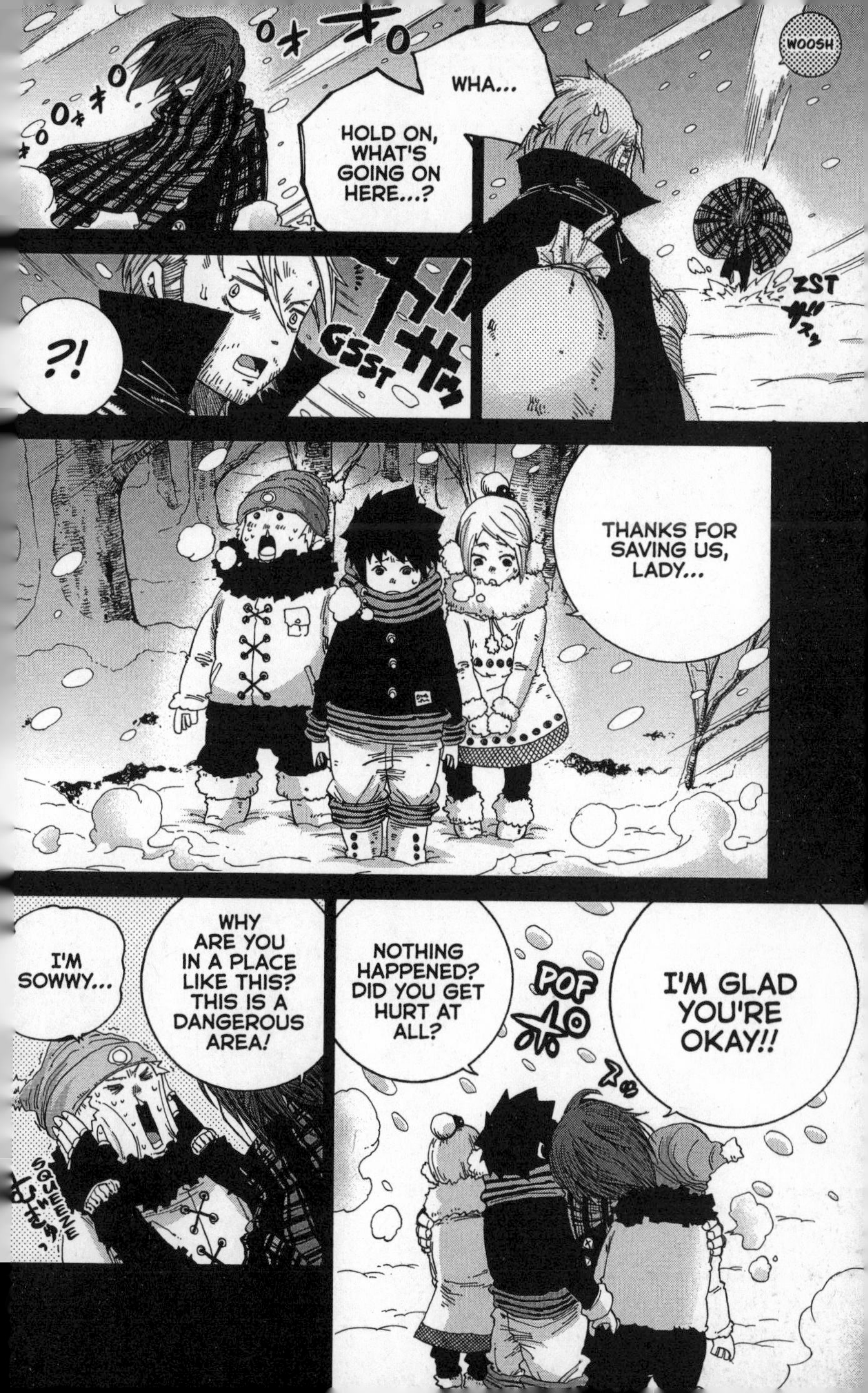
WOOSH
WHA...
HOLD ON, WHAT'S GOING ON HERE...?
ZST
?!
GSST
THANKS FOR SAVING US, LADY...
I'M GLAD YOU'RE OKAY!!
POF
NOTHING HAPPENED? DID YOU GET HURT AT ALL?
WHY ARE YOU IN A PLACE LIKE THIS? THIS IS A DANGEROUS AREA!
I'M SOWWY...
SQUEEZE

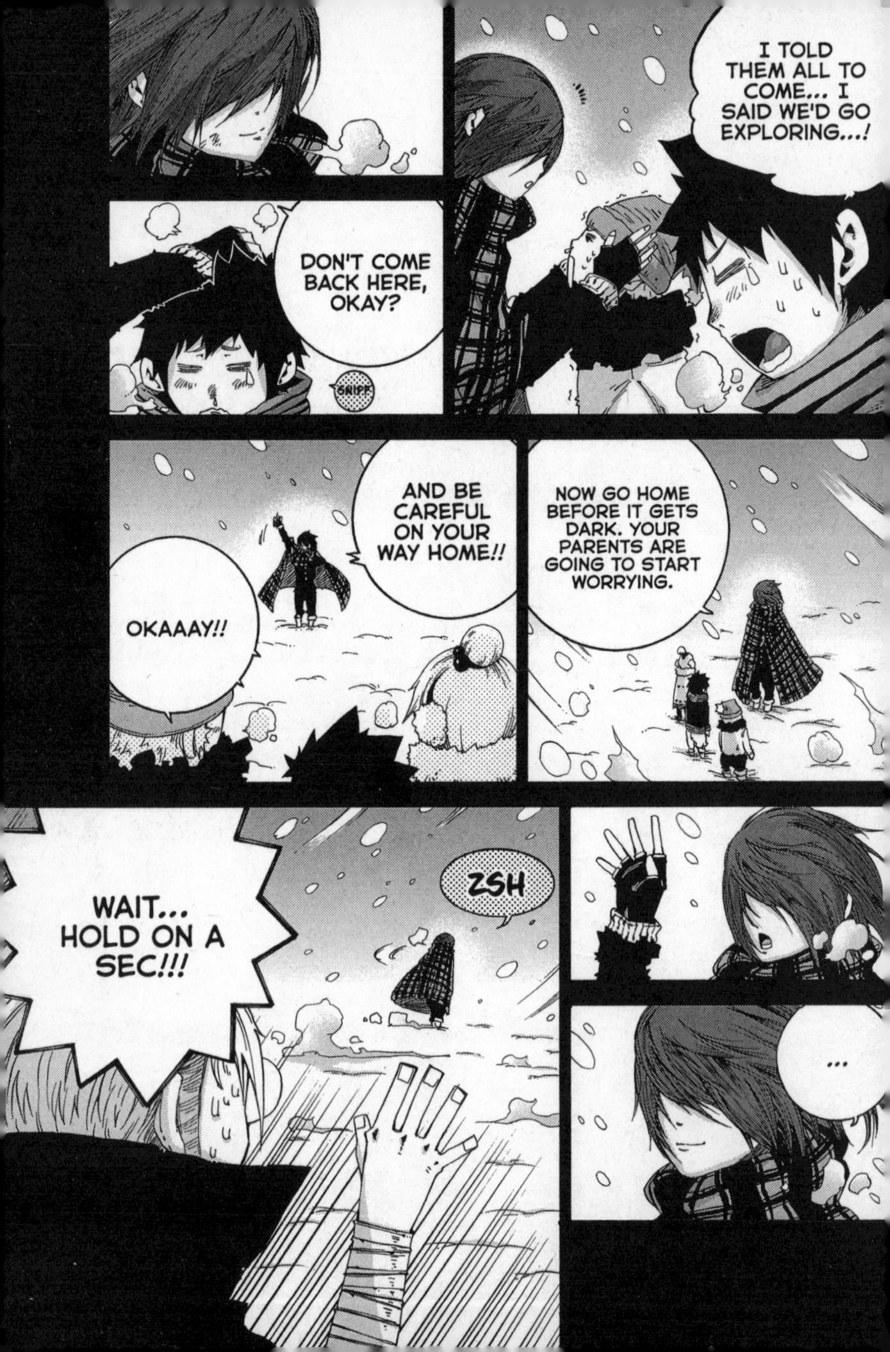
I TOLD THEM ALL TO COME... I SAID WE'D GO EXPLORING...!
DON'T COME BACK HERE, OKAY?
SNIFF
NOW GO HOME BEFORE IT GETS DARK. YOUR PARENTS ARE GOING TO START WORRYING.
AND BE CAREFUL ON YOUR WAY HOME!!
OKAAAY!!
...
ZSH
WAIT... HOLD ON A SEC!!!

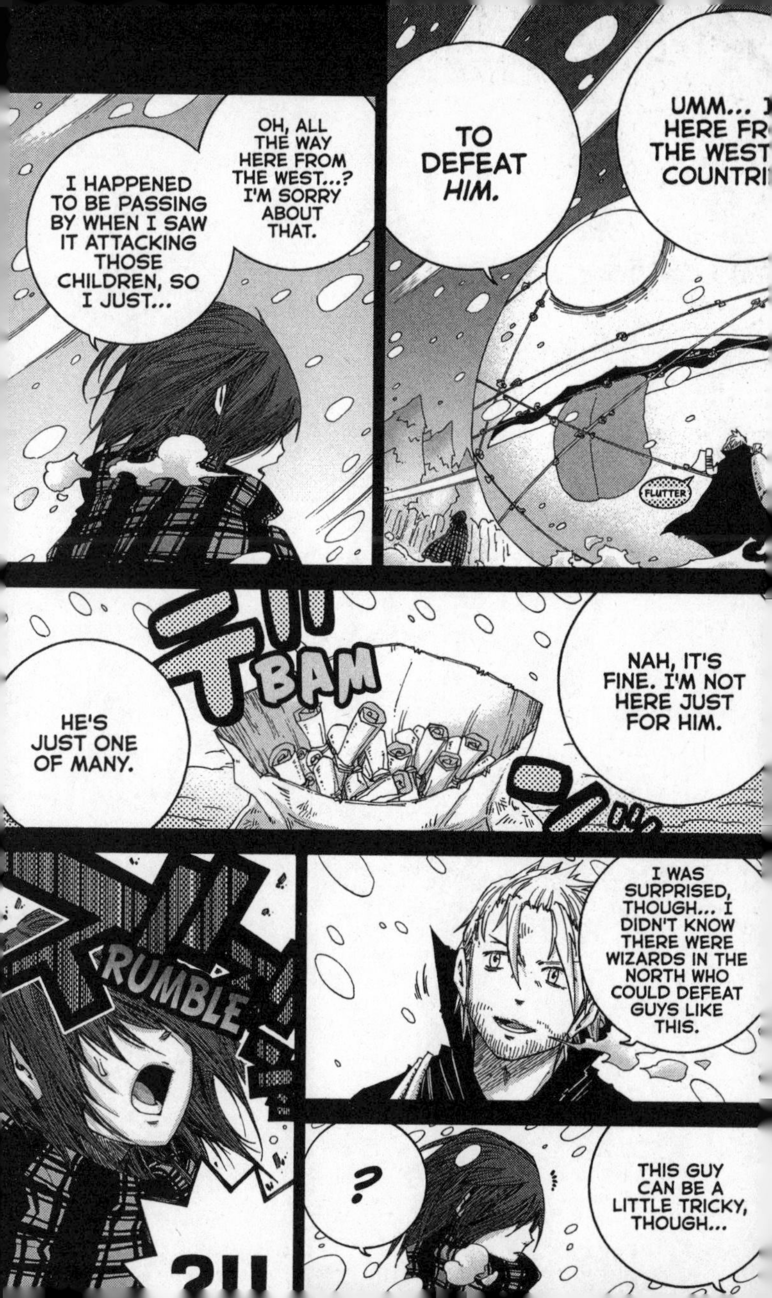
UMM... I HERE FR THE WEST COUNTRI
TO DEFEAT *HIM.*
FLUTTER
OH, ALL THE WAY HERE FROM THE WEST...? I'M SORRY ABOUT THAT.
I HAPPENED TO BE PASSING BY WHEN I SAW IT ATTACKING THOSE CHILDREN, SO I JUST...
NAH, IT'S FINE. I'M NOT HERE JUST FOR HIM.
BAM
HE'S JUST ONE OF MANY.
I WAS SURPRISED, THOUGH... I DIDN'T KNOW THERE WERE WIZARDS IN THE NORTH WHO COULD DEFEAT GUYS LIKE THIS.
THIS GUY CAN BE A LITTLE TRICKY, THOUGH...
?
RUMBLE
?!!

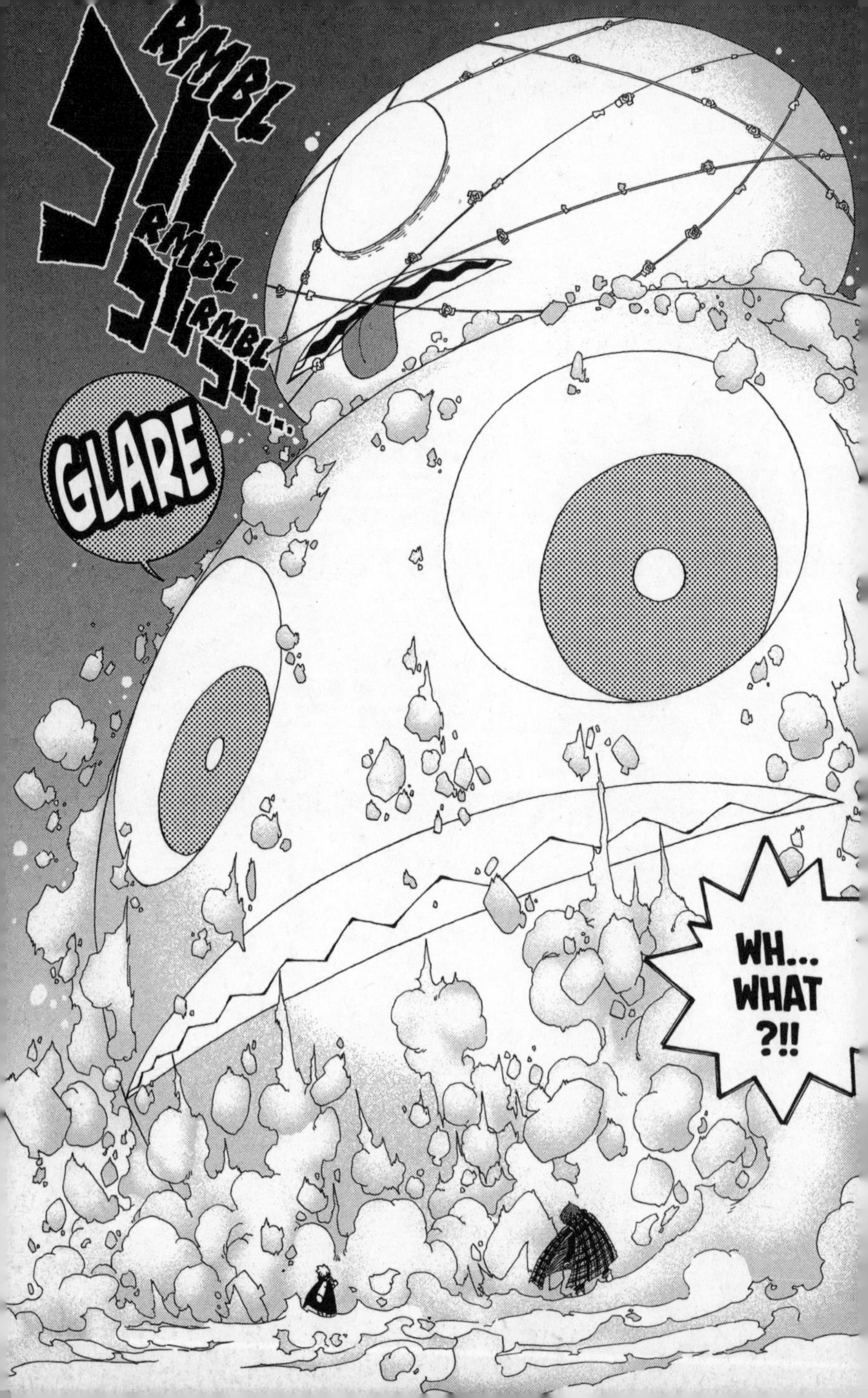
RMBL
RMBL
RMBL...
GLARE
WH... WHAT?!!

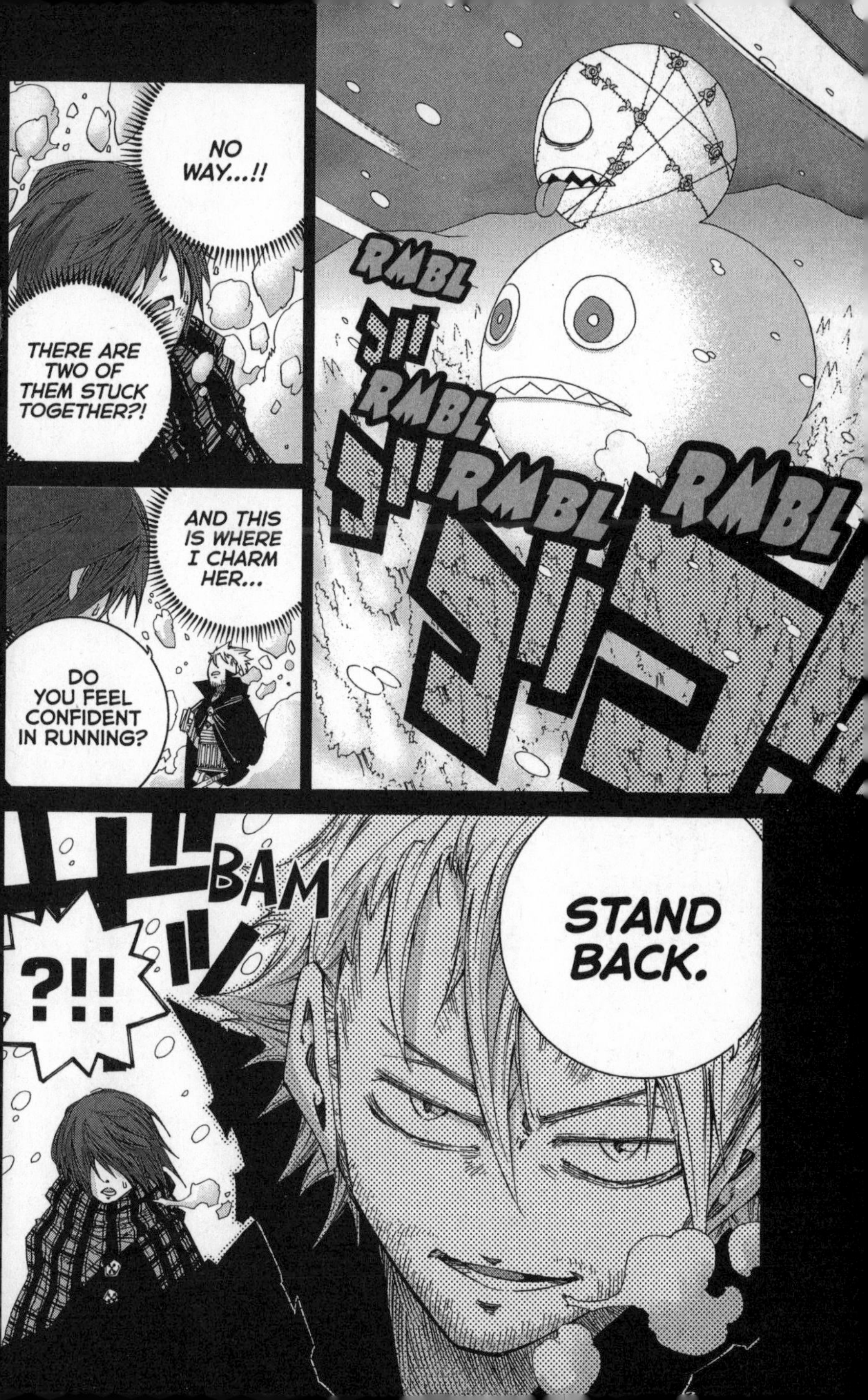
RMBL
RMBL
RMBL
RMBL
NO WAY...!!
THERE ARE TWO OF THEM STUCK TOGETHER?!
AND THIS IS WHERE I CHARM HER...
DO YOU FEEL CONFIDENT IN RUNNING?
STAND BACK.
BAM
?!!

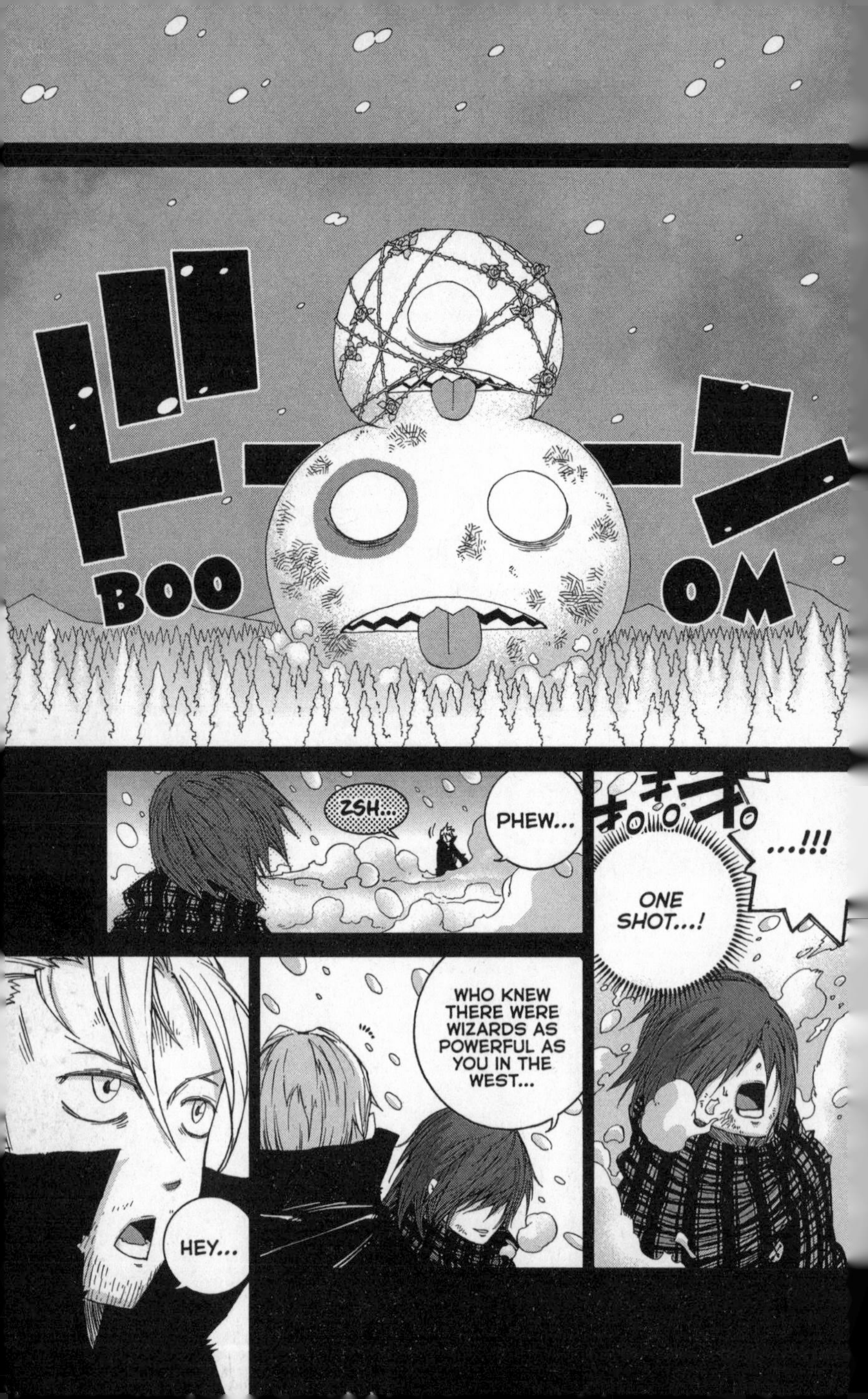
ドーーン
BOOOM
...!!!
ONE SHOT...!
ZSH...
PHEW...
WHO KNEW THERE WERE WIZARDS AS POWERFUL AS YOU IN THE WEST...
HEY...

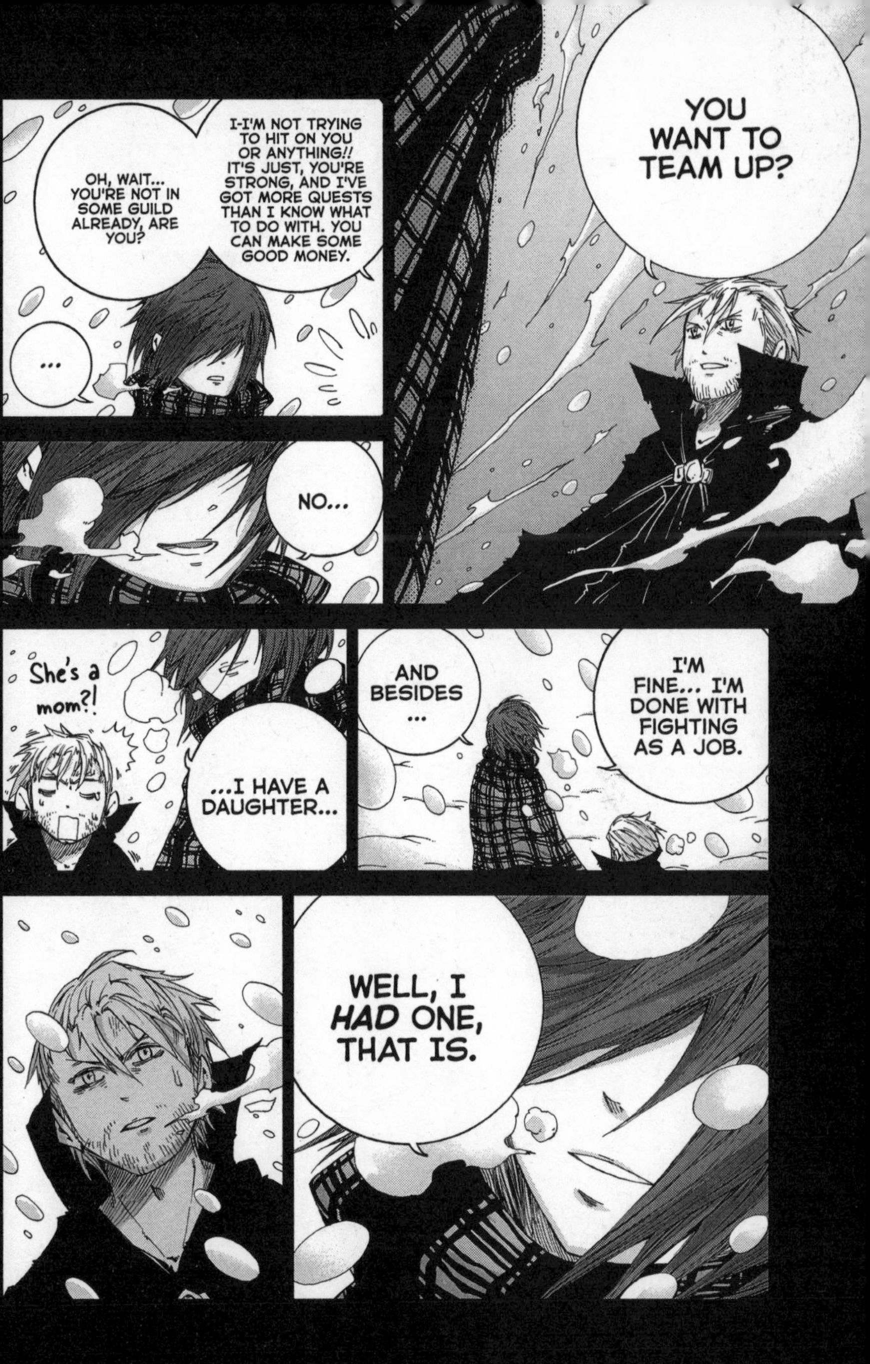
YOU WANT TO TEAM UP?
I-I'M NOT TRYING TO HIT ON YOU OR ANYTHING!! IT'S JUST, YOU'RE STRONG, AND I'VE GOT MORE QUESTS THAN I KNOW WHAT TO DO WITH. YOU CAN MAKE SOME GOOD MONEY.
OH, WAIT... YOU'RE NOT IN SOME GUILD ALREADY, ARE YOU?
...
NO...
I'M FINE... I'M DONE WITH FIGHTING AS A JOB.
AND BESIDES ...
...I HAVE A DAUGHTER...
She's a mom?!
WELL, I *HAD* ONE, THAT IS.

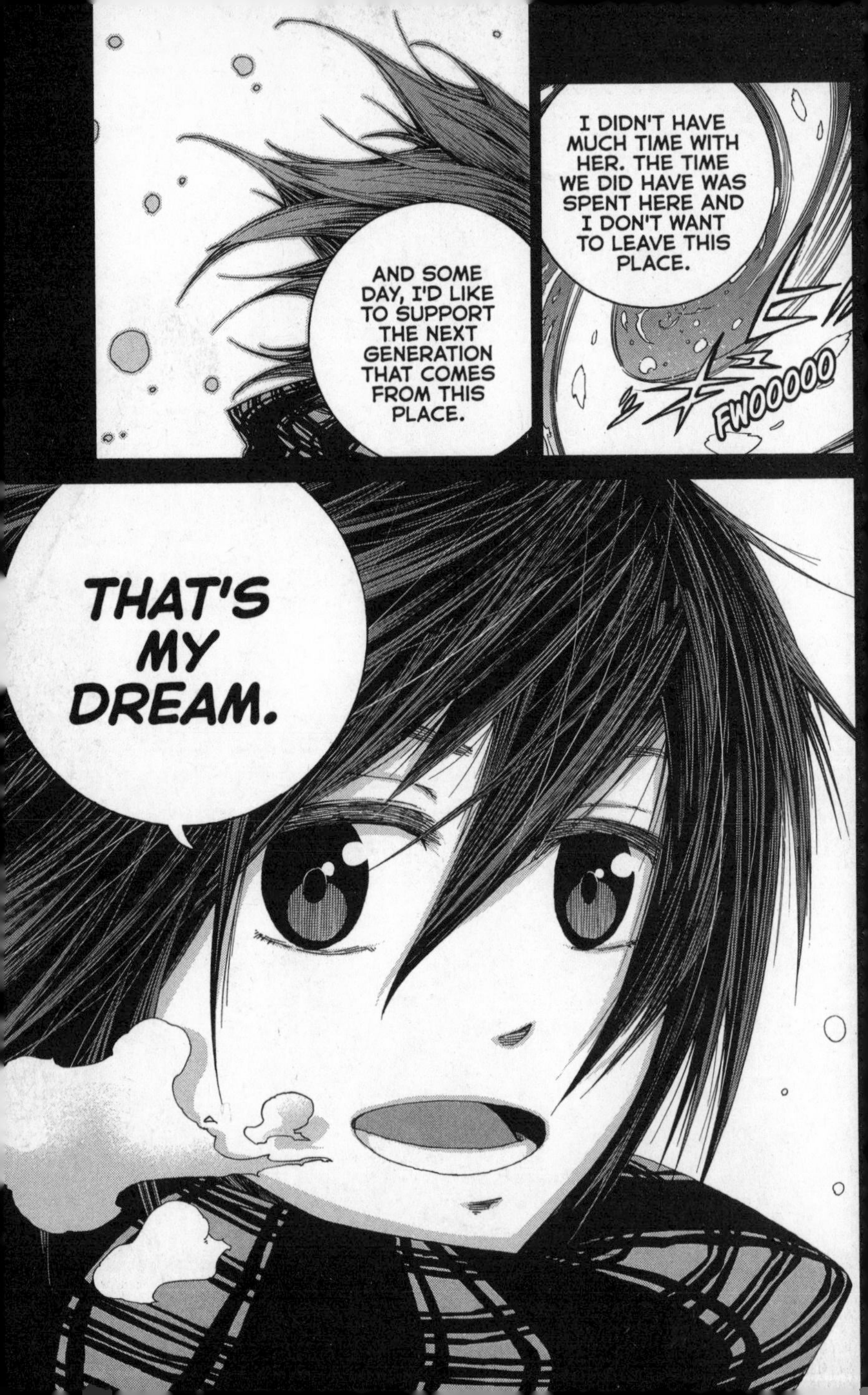
I DIDN'T HAVE MUCH TIME WITH HER. THE TIME WE DID HAVE WAS SPENT HERE AND I DON'T WANT TO LEAVE THIS PLACE.
FWOOOOO
AND SOME DAY, I'D LIKE TO SUPPORT THE NEXT GENERATION THAT COMES FROM THIS PLACE.
THAT'S MY DREAM.

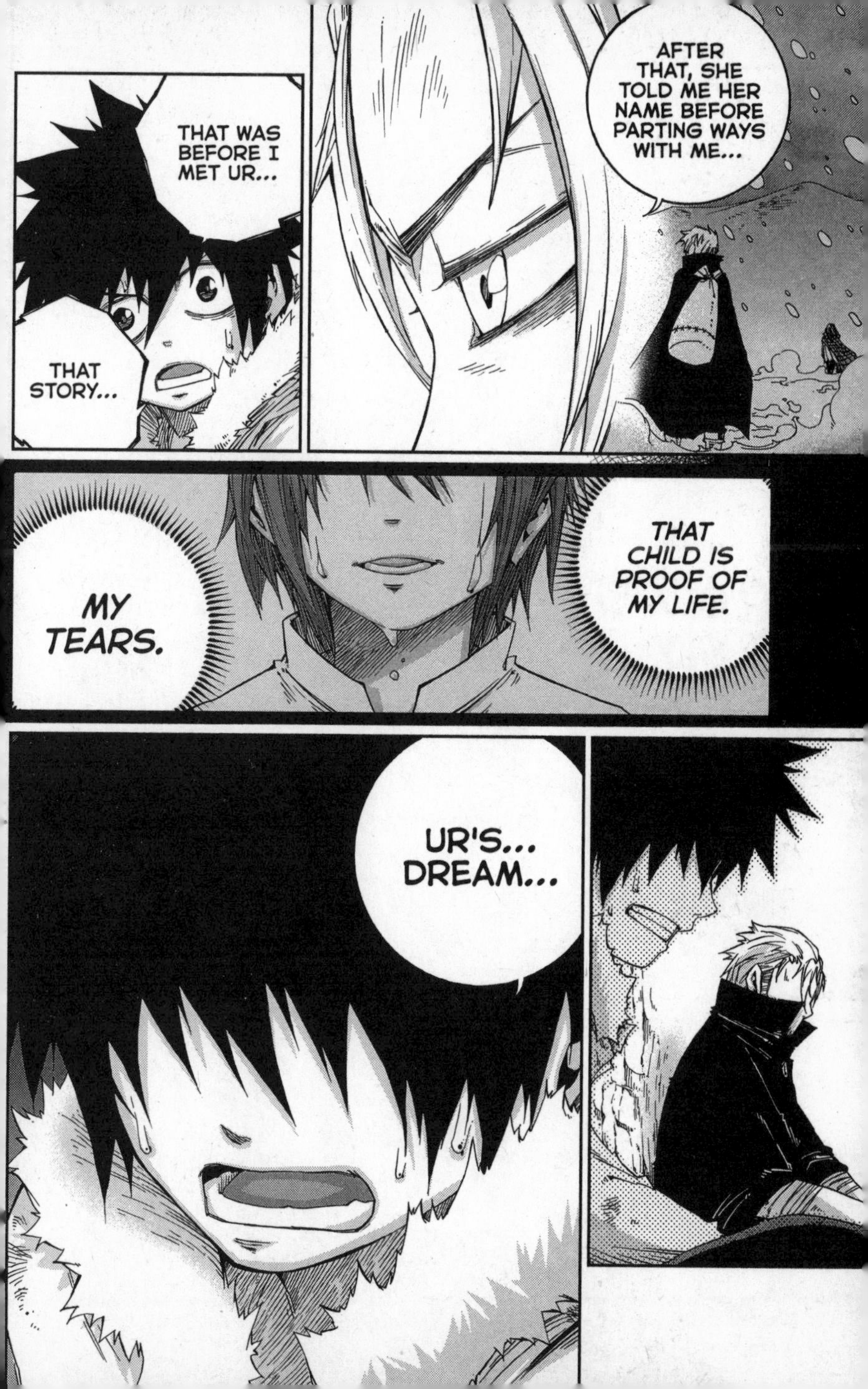
AFTER THAT, SHE TOLD ME HER NAME BEFORE PARTING WAYS WITH ME...
THAT WAS BEFORE I MET UR...
THAT STORY...
THAT CHILD IS PROOF OF MY LIFE.
MY TEARS.
UR'S... DREAM...

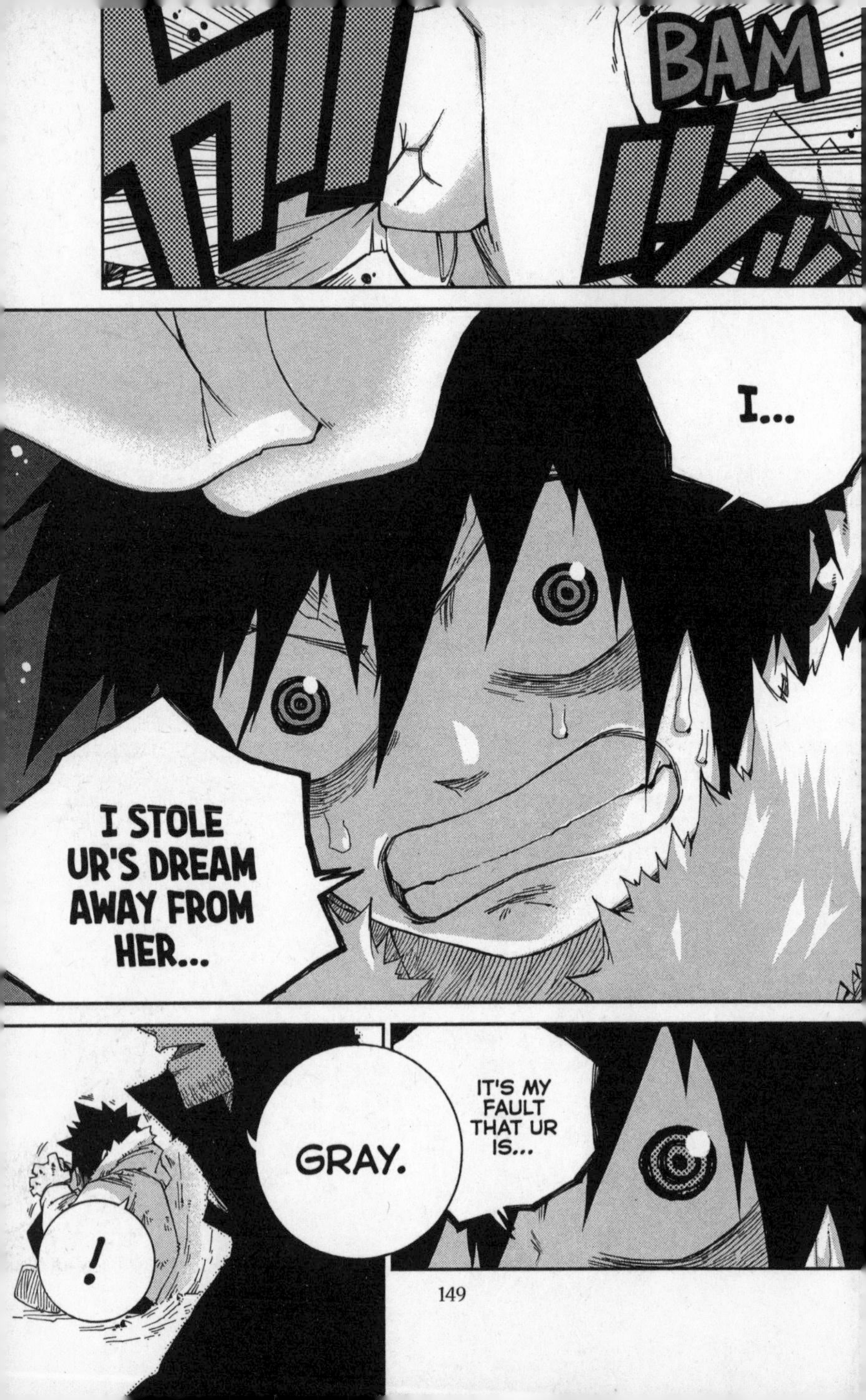
BAM
I...
I STOLE UR'S DREAM AWAY FROM HER...
IT'S MY FAULT THAT UR IS...
GRAY.
!

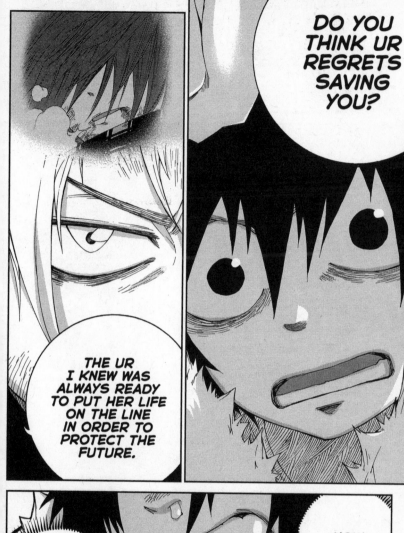

DO YOU THINK UR REGRETS SAVING YOU?

THE UR I KNEW WAS ALWAYS READY TO PUT HER LIFE ON THE LINE IN ORDER TO PROTECT THE FUTURE.

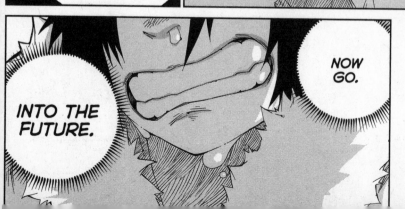

INTO THE FUTURE.

NOW GO.

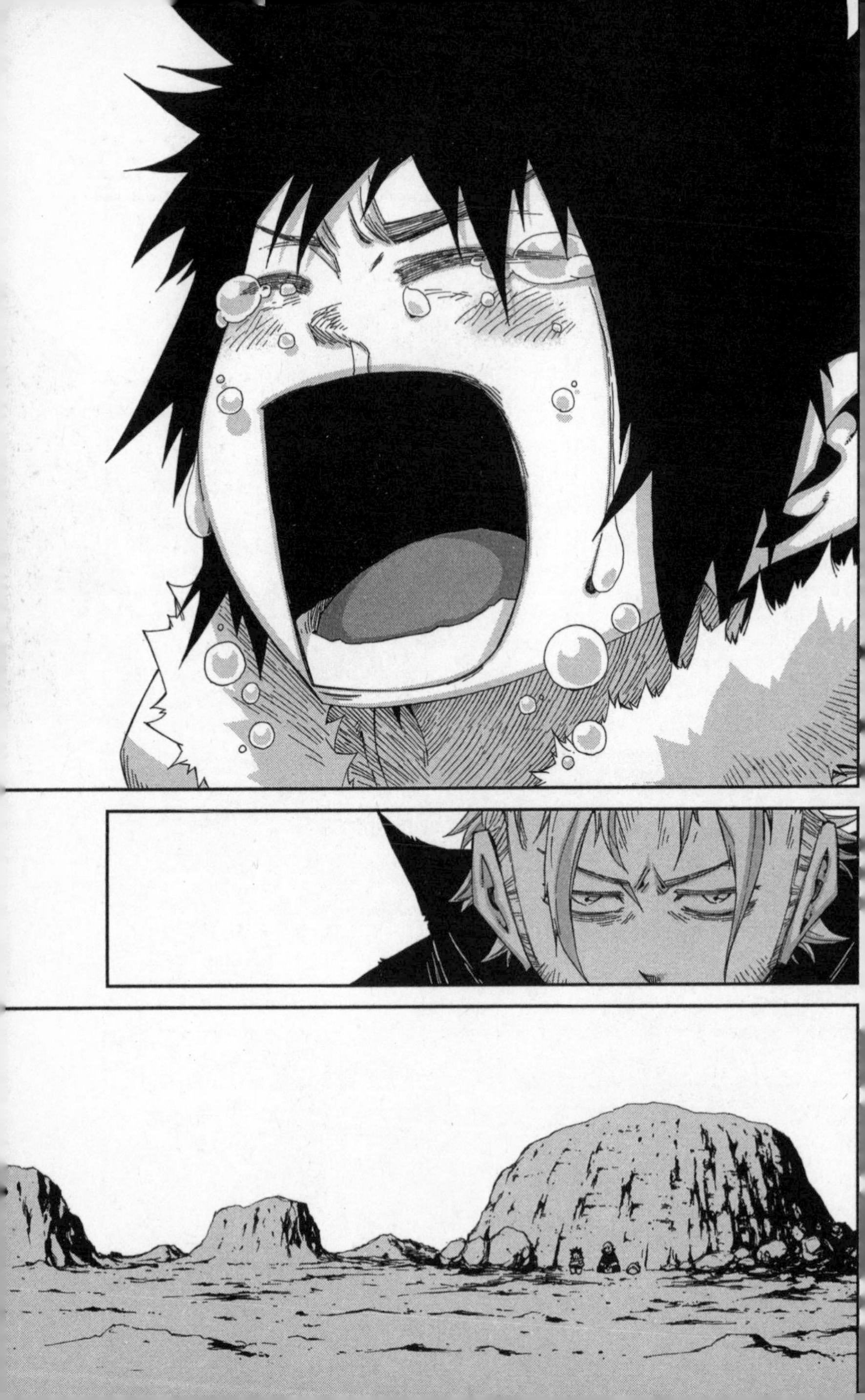

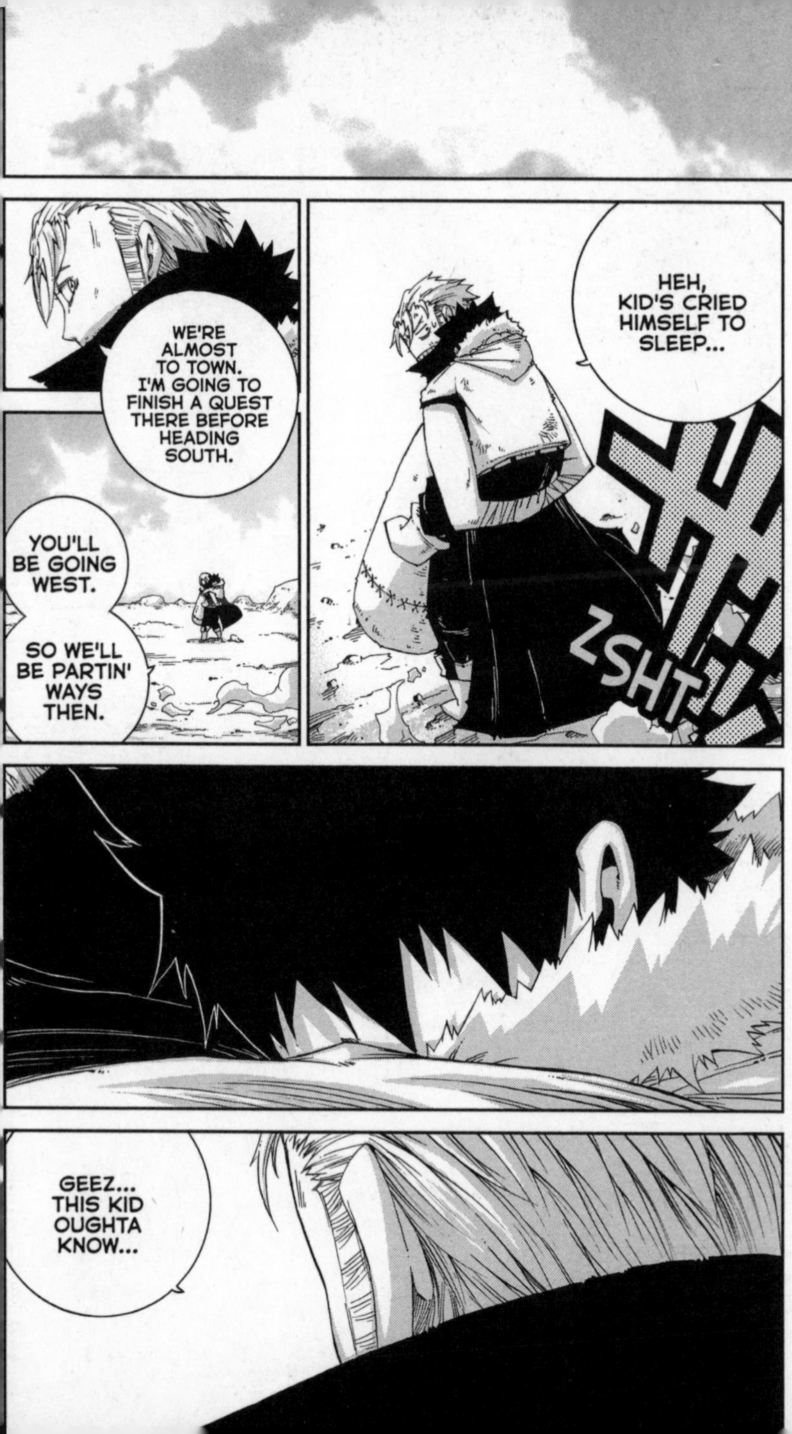
HEH, KID'S CRIED HIMSELF TO SLEEP...
ZSHT
WE'RE ALMOST TO TOWN. I'M GOING TO FINISH A QUEST THERE BEFORE HEADING SOUTH.
YOU'LL BE GOING WEST.
SO WE'LL BE PARTIN' WAYS THEN.
GEEZ... THIS KID OUGHTA KNOW...

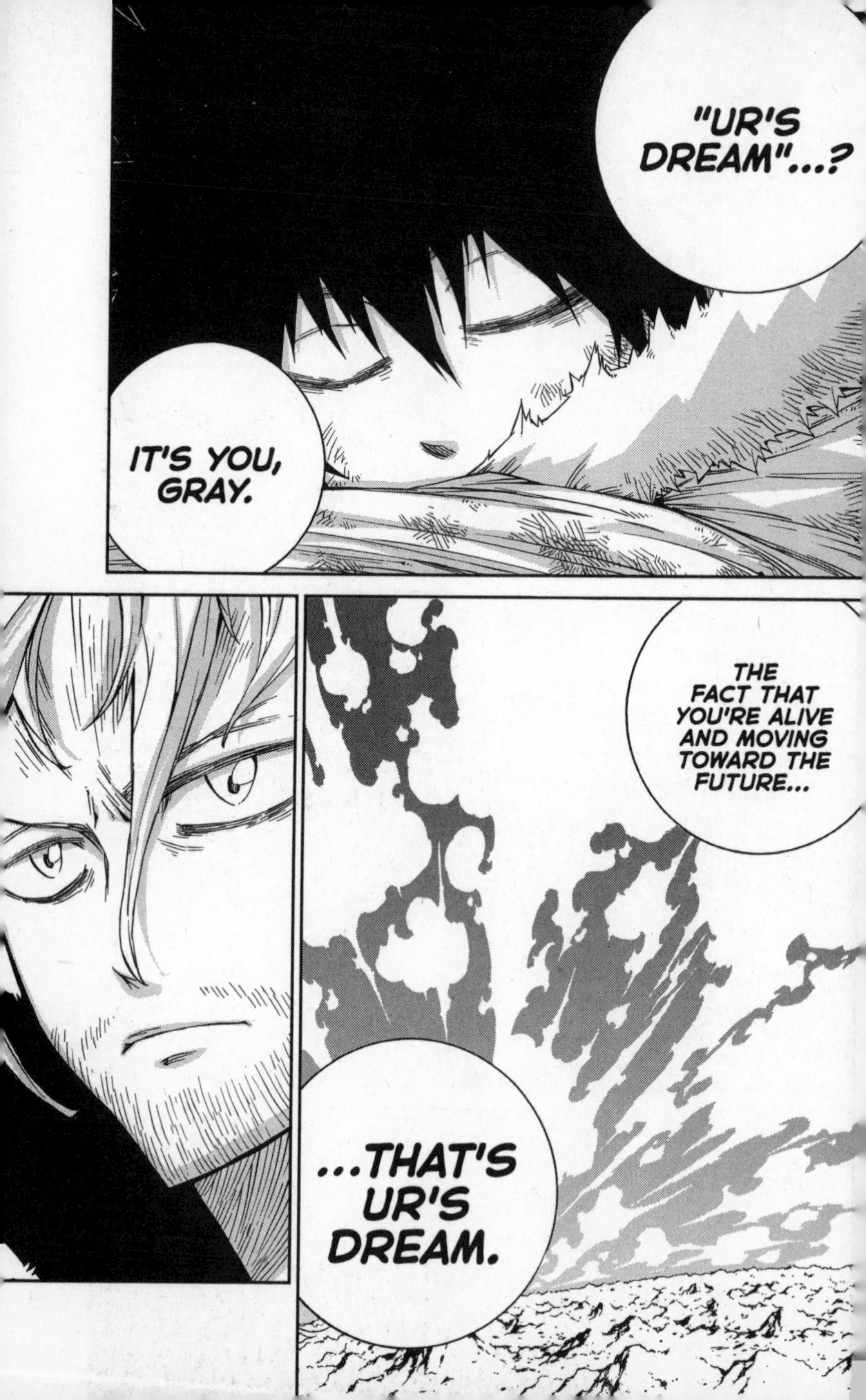
"UR'S DREAM"...?
IT'S YOU, GRAY.
THE FACT THAT YOU'RE ALIVE AND MOVING TOWARD THE FUTURE...
...THAT'S UR'S DREAM.

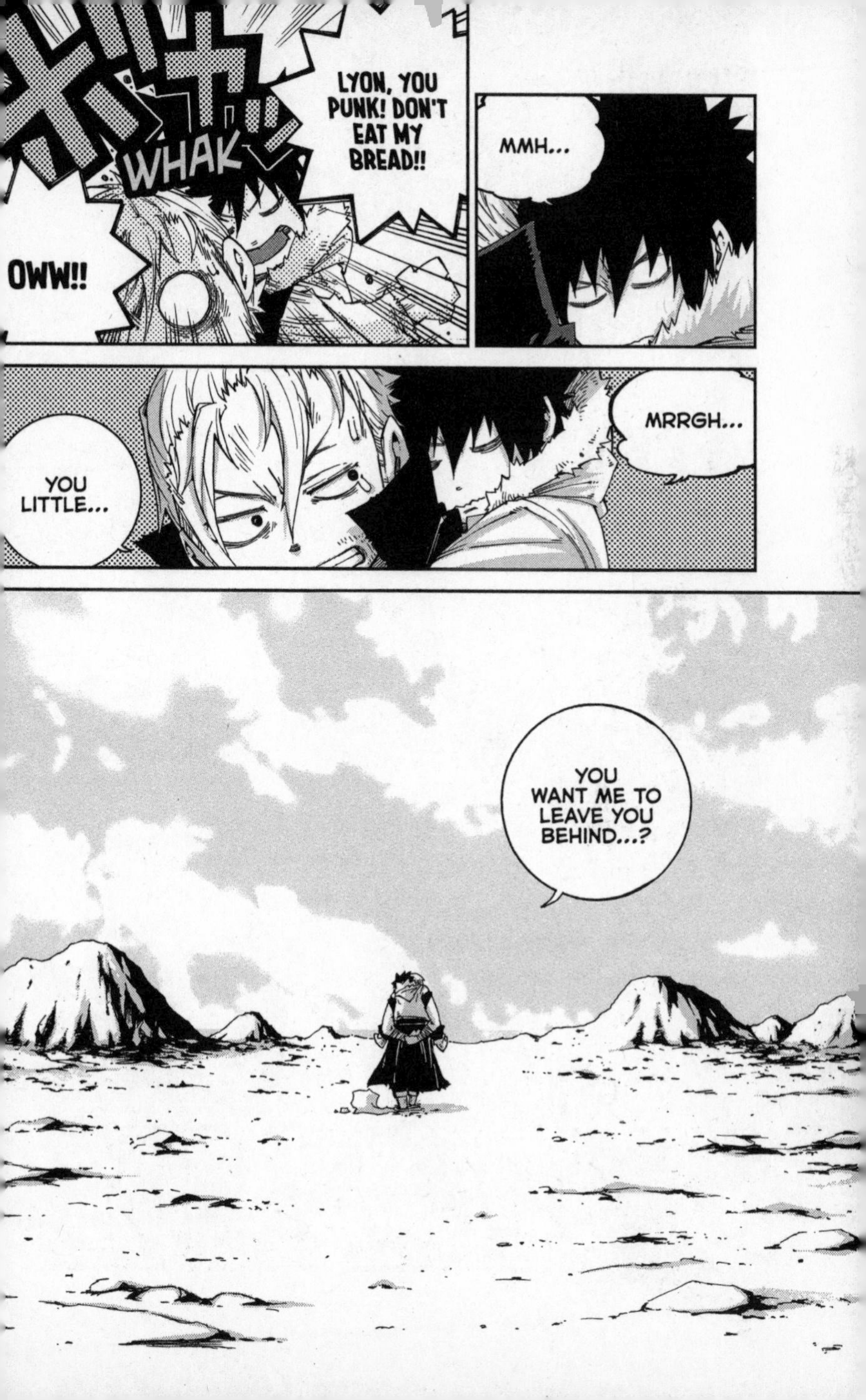
MMH...
LYON, YOU PUNK! DON'T EAT MY BREAD!!
WHAK
OWW!!
MRRGH...
YOU LITTLE...
YOU WANT ME TO LEAVE YOU BEHIND...?

Chapter 6: River

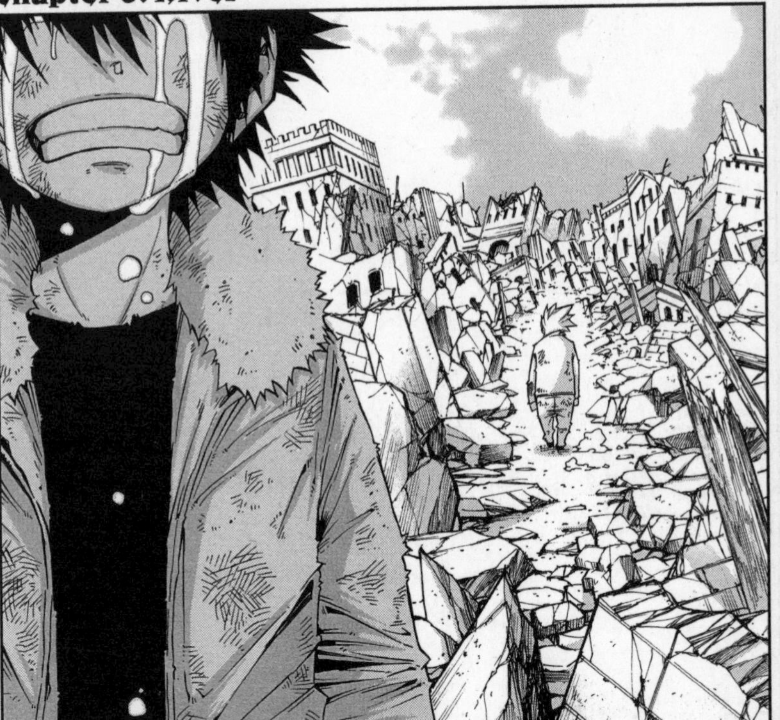

FAIRY TAIL: ICE TRAIL

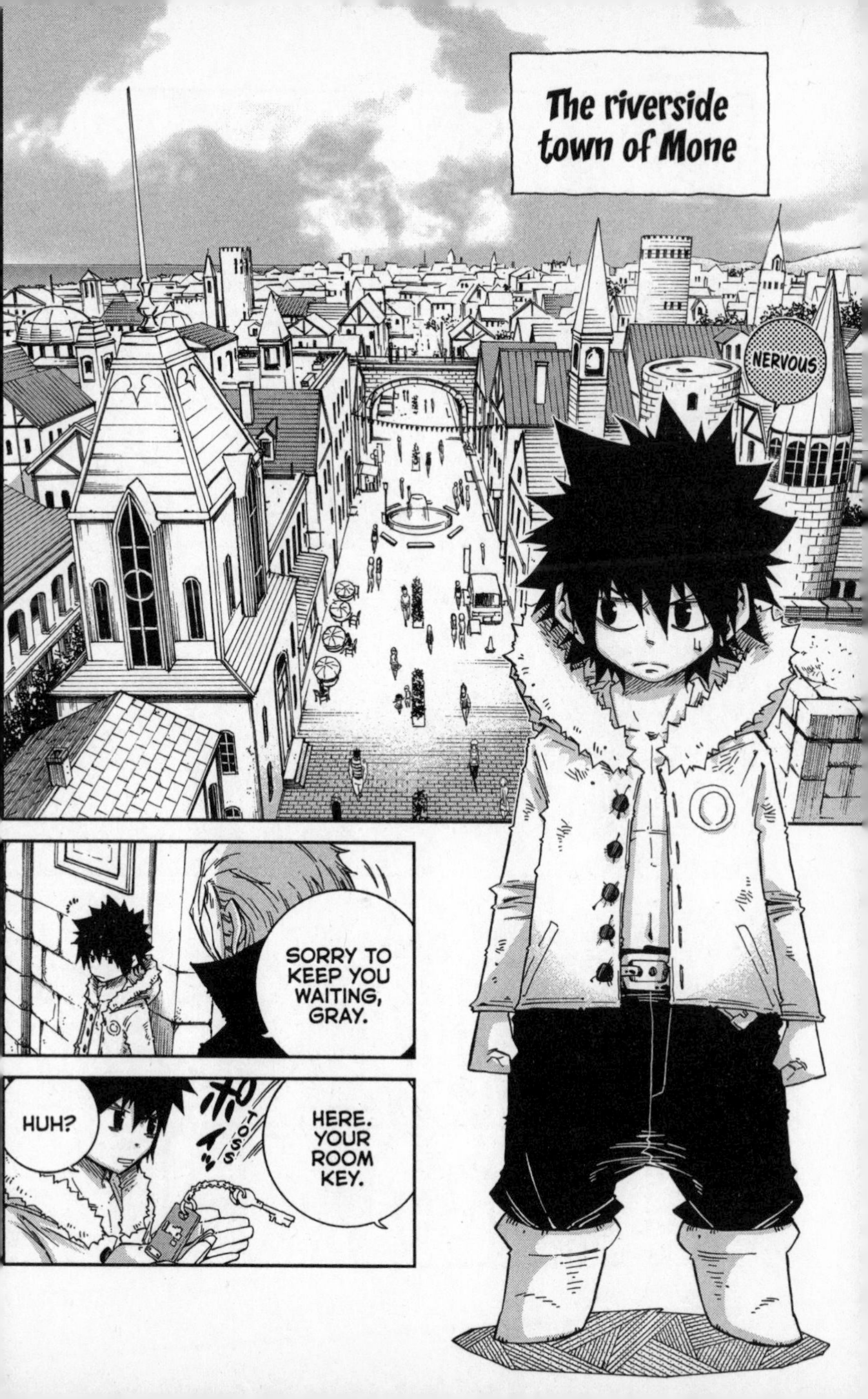
The riverside town of Mone
NERVOUS
SORRY TO KEEP YOU WAITING, GRAY.
HERE. YOUR ROOM KEY.
TOSS
HUH?

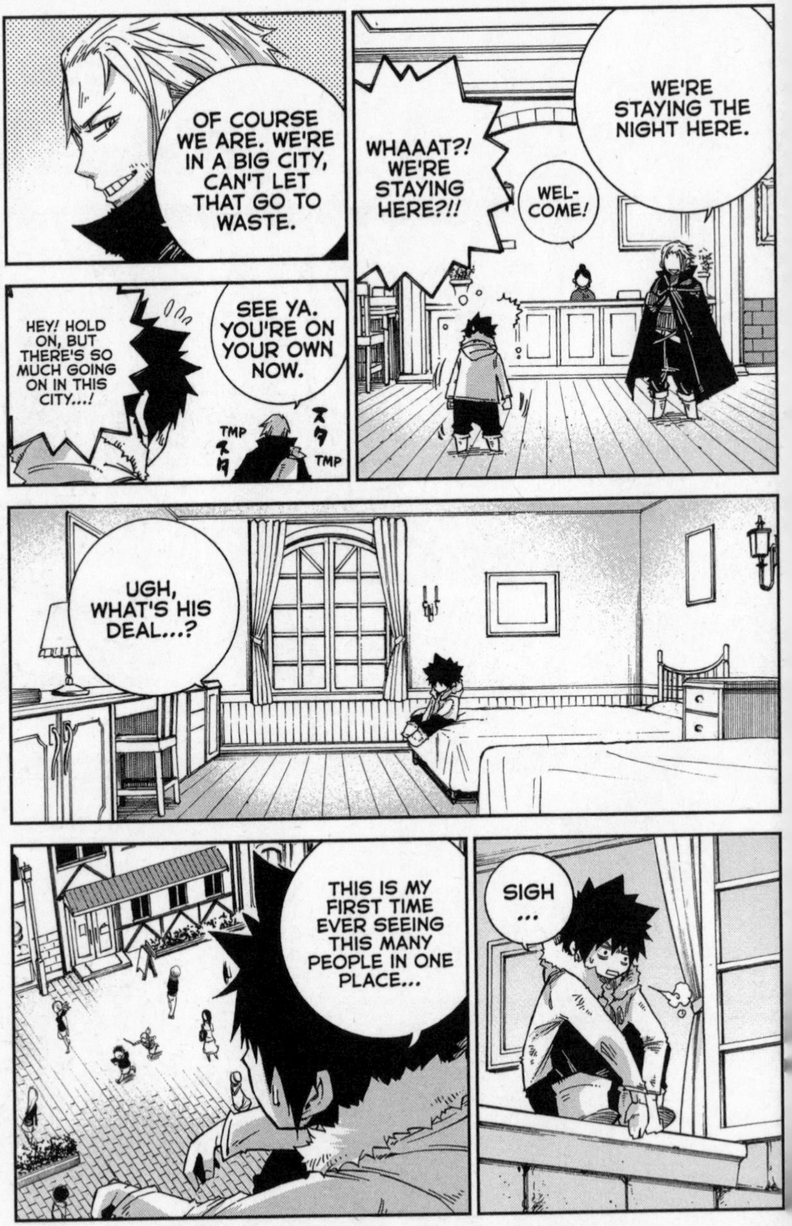
WE'RE STAYING THE NIGHT HERE.
WEL-COME!
WHAAAT?! WE'RE STAYING HERE?!!
OF COURSE WE ARE. WE'RE IN A BIG CITY, CAN'T LET THAT GO TO WASTE.
SEE YA. YOU'RE ON YOUR OWN NOW.
スタ TMP
スタ TMP
HEY! HOLD ON, BUT THERE'S SO MUCH GOING ON IN THIS CITY...!
UGH, WHAT'S HIS DEAL...?
SIGH...
THIS IS MY FIRST TIME EVER SEEING THIS MANY PEOPLE IN ONE PLACE...

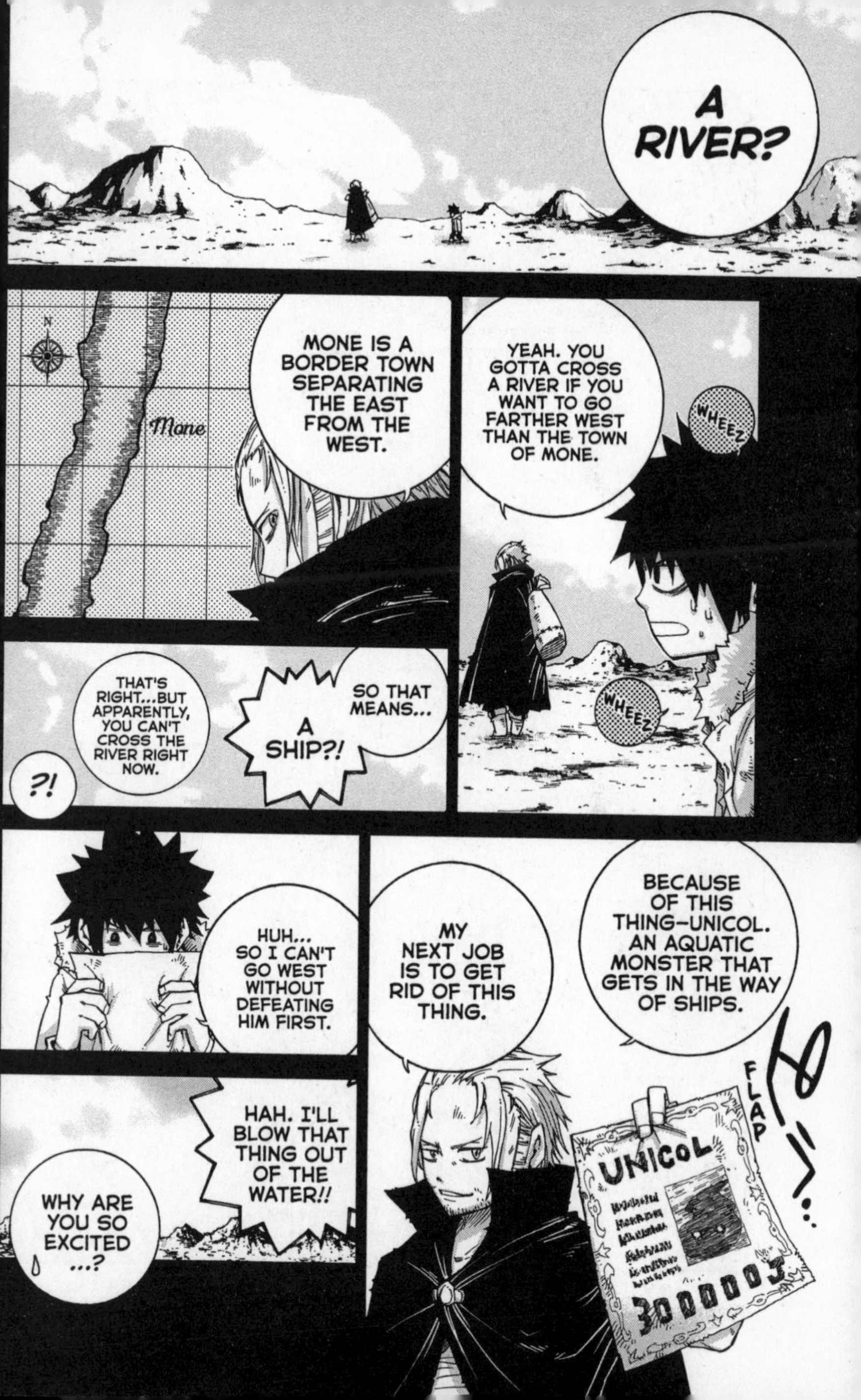
A RIVER?
WHEEZ
YEAH. YOU GOTTA CROSS A RIVER IF YOU WANT TO GO FARTHER WEST THAN THE TOWN OF MONE.
WHEEZ
MONE IS A BORDER TOWN SEPARATING THE EAST FROM THE WEST.
N
Mone
SO THAT MEANS...
A SHIP?!
THAT'S RIGHT...BUT APPARENTLY, YOU CAN'T CROSS THE RIVER RIGHT NOW.
?!
BECAUSE OF THIS THING—UNICOL. AN AQUATIC MONSTER THAT GETS IN THE WAY OF SHIPS.
MY NEXT JOB IS TO GET RID OF THIS THING.
FLAP
UNICOL
3000000J
HUH... SO I CAN'T GO WEST WITHOUT DEFEATING HIM FIRST.
HAH. I'LL BLOW THAT THING OUT OF THE WATER!!
WHY ARE YOU SO EXCITED ...?

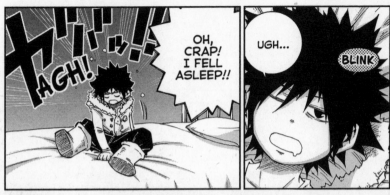

OH, CRAP! I FELL ASLEEP!!

AGH!

UGH...

BLINK

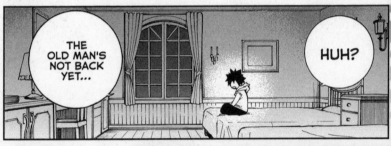

THE OLD MAN'S NOT BACK YET...

HUH?

GRRR

AGH... I'M HUNGRY, BUT I DON'T HAVE ANY MONEY. WHERE'D THAT OLD GUY GO...?

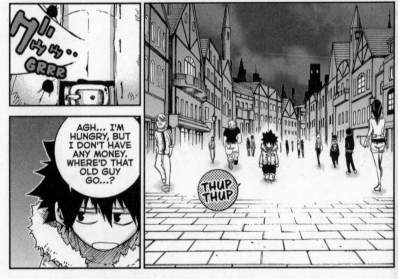

THUP THUP

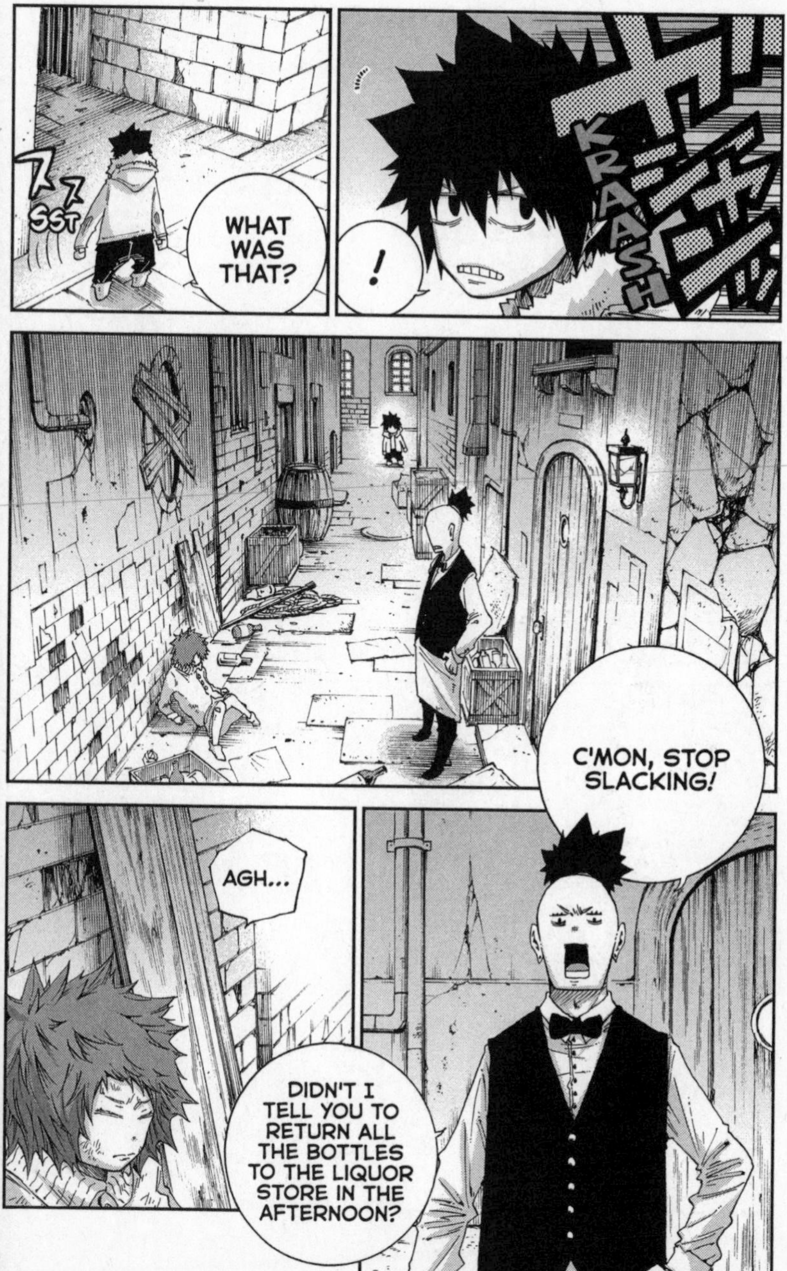
KRAASH
!
WHAT WAS THAT?
SST
C'MON, STOP SLACKING!
AGH...
DIDN'T I TELL YOU TO RETURN ALL THE BOTTLES TO THE LIQUOR STORE IN THE AFTERNOON?

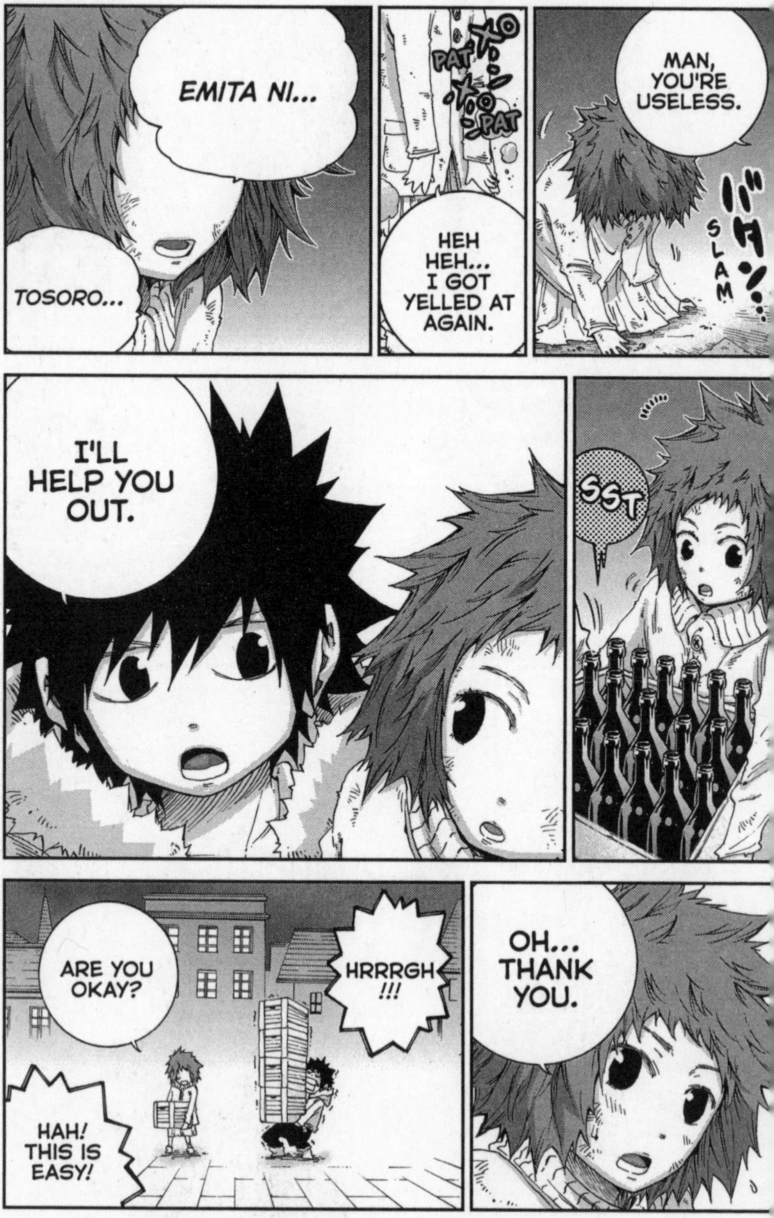
MAN, YOU'RE USELESS.
SLAM
PAT PAT
HEH HEH... I GOT YELLED AT AGAIN.
EMITA NI...
TOSORO...
SST
I'LL HELP YOU OUT.
OH... THANK YOU.
HRRRGH !!!
ARE YOU OKAY?
HAH! THIS IS EASY!

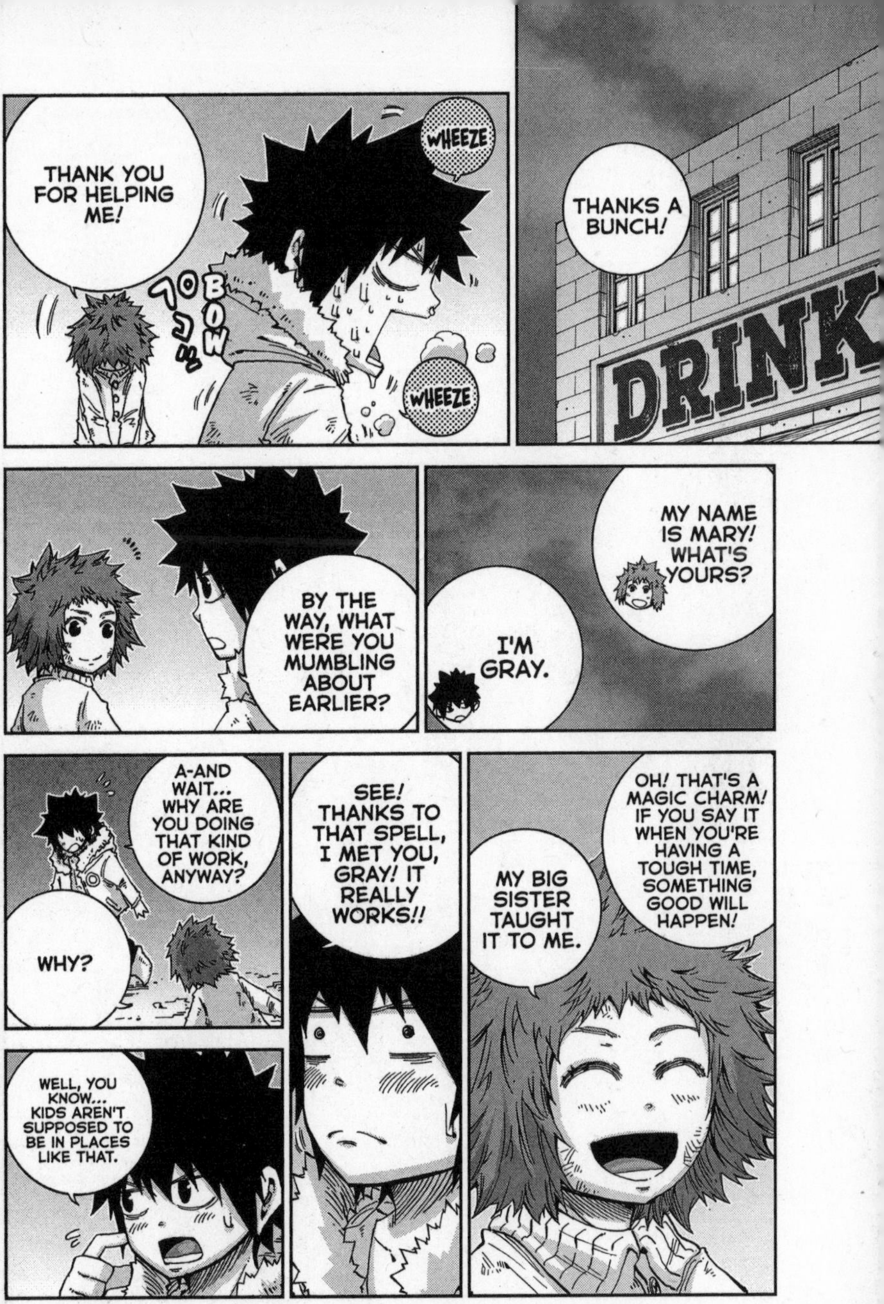
THANKS A BUNCH!
THANK YOU FOR HELPING ME!
WHEEZE
BOW
WHEEZE
MY NAME IS MARY! WHAT'S YOURS?
I'M GRAY.
BY THE WAY, WHAT WERE YOU MUMBLING ABOUT EARLIER?
OH! THAT'S A MAGIC CHARM! IF YOU SAY IT WHEN YOU'RE HAVING A TOUGH TIME, SOMETHING GOOD WILL HAPPEN!
MY BIG SISTER TAUGHT IT TO ME.
SEE! THANKS TO THAT SPELL, I MET YOU, GRAY! IT REALLY WORKS!!
A-AND WAIT... WHY ARE YOU DOING THAT KIND OF WORK, ANYWAY?
WHY?
WELL, YOU KNOW... KIDS AREN'T SUPPOSED TO BE IN PLACES LIKE THAT.

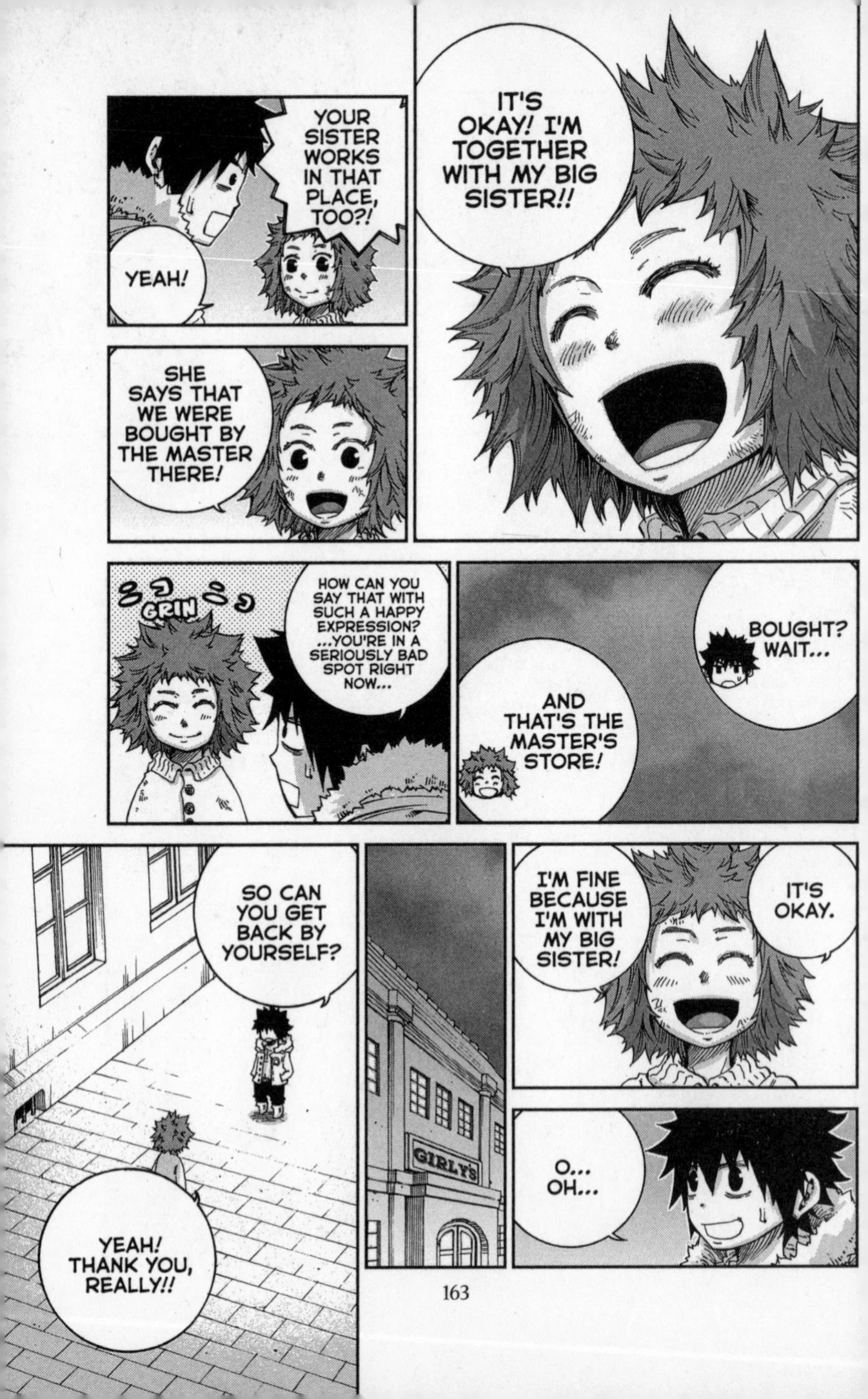
IT'S OKAY! I'M TOGETHER WITH MY BIG SISTER!!
YOUR SISTER WORKS IN THAT PLACE, TOO?!
YEAH!
SHE SAYS THAT WE WERE BOUGHT BY THE MASTER THERE!
BOUGHT? WAIT...
AND THAT'S THE MASTER'S STORE!
GRIN
HOW CAN YOU SAY THAT WITH SUCH A HAPPY EXPRESSION? ...YOU'RE IN A SERIOUSLY BAD SPOT RIGHT NOW...
IT'S OKAY.
I'M FINE BECAUSE I'M WITH MY BIG SISTER!
O... OH...
GIRLY'S
SO CAN YOU GET BACK BY YOURSELF?
YEAH! THANK YOU, REALLY!!

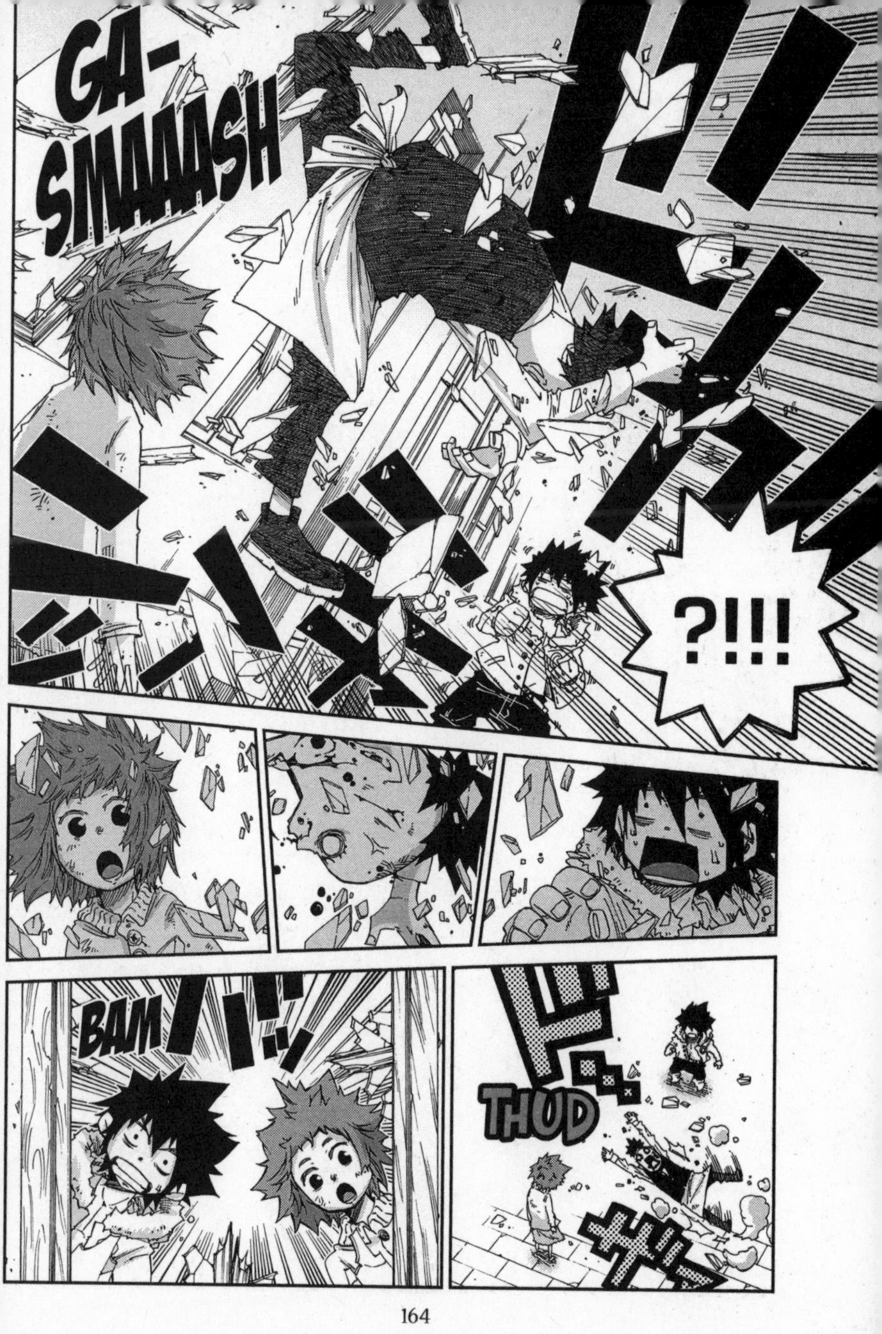
GA-SMAAASH
?!!!
THUD
BAM

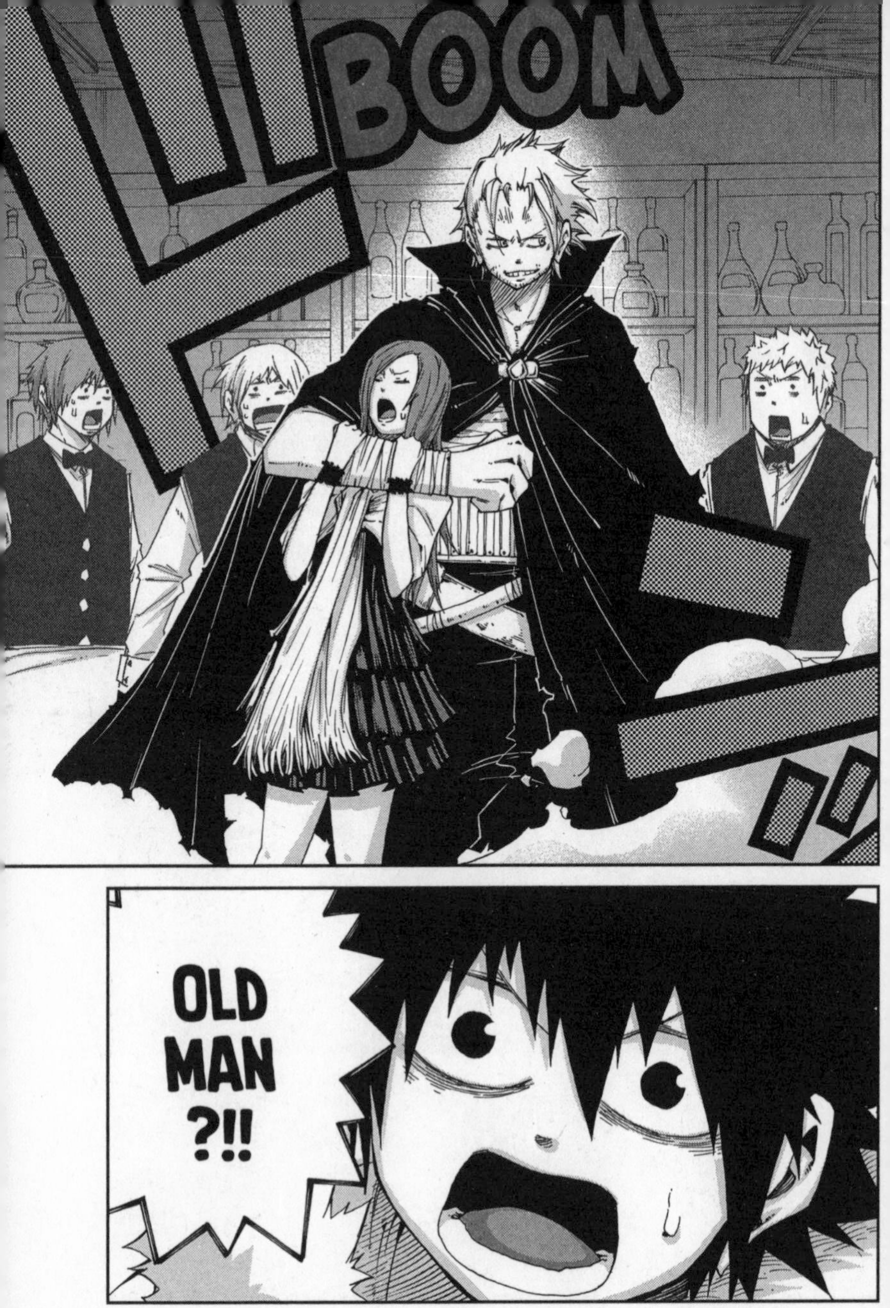
BOOM
OLD MAN ?!!

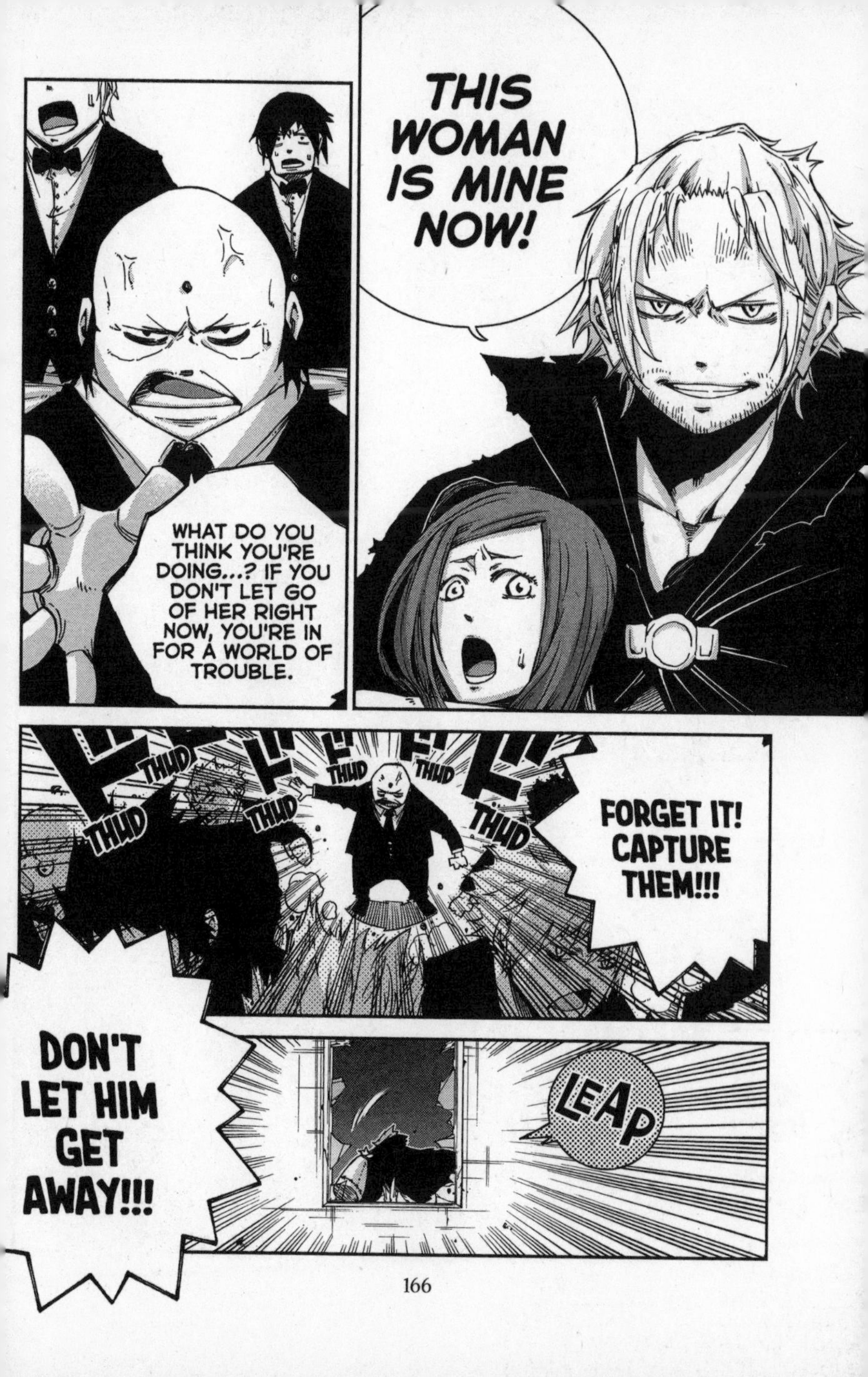
THIS WOMAN IS MINE NOW!
WHAT DO YOU THINK YOU'RE DOING...? IF YOU DON'T LET GO OF HER RIGHT NOW, YOU'RE IN FOR A WORLD OF TROUBLE.
THUD
THUD
THUD
THUD
THUD
THUD
FORGET IT! CAPTURE THEM!!!
LEAP
DON'T LET HIM GET AWAY!!!

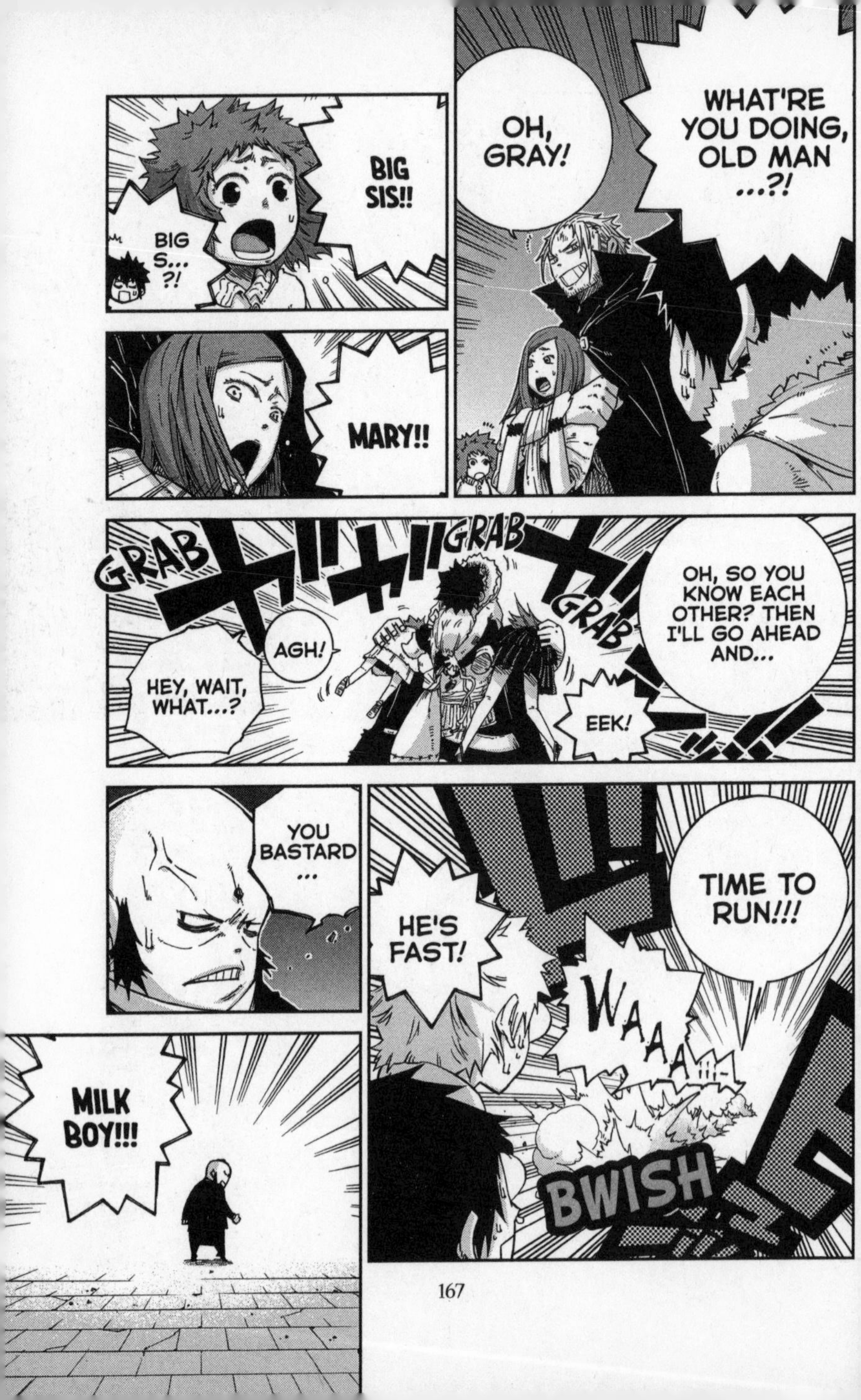
WHAT'RE YOU DOING, OLD MAN ...?!
OH, GRAY!
BIG SIS!!
BIG S... ?!
MARY!!
OH, SO YOU KNOW EACH OTHER? THEN I'LL GO AHEAD AND...
GRAB
EEK!
GRAB
AGH!
GRAB
HEY, WAIT, WHAT...?
TIME TO RUN!!!
HE'S FAST!
WAAAA!!!
BWISH
YOU BASTARD ...
MILK BOY!!!

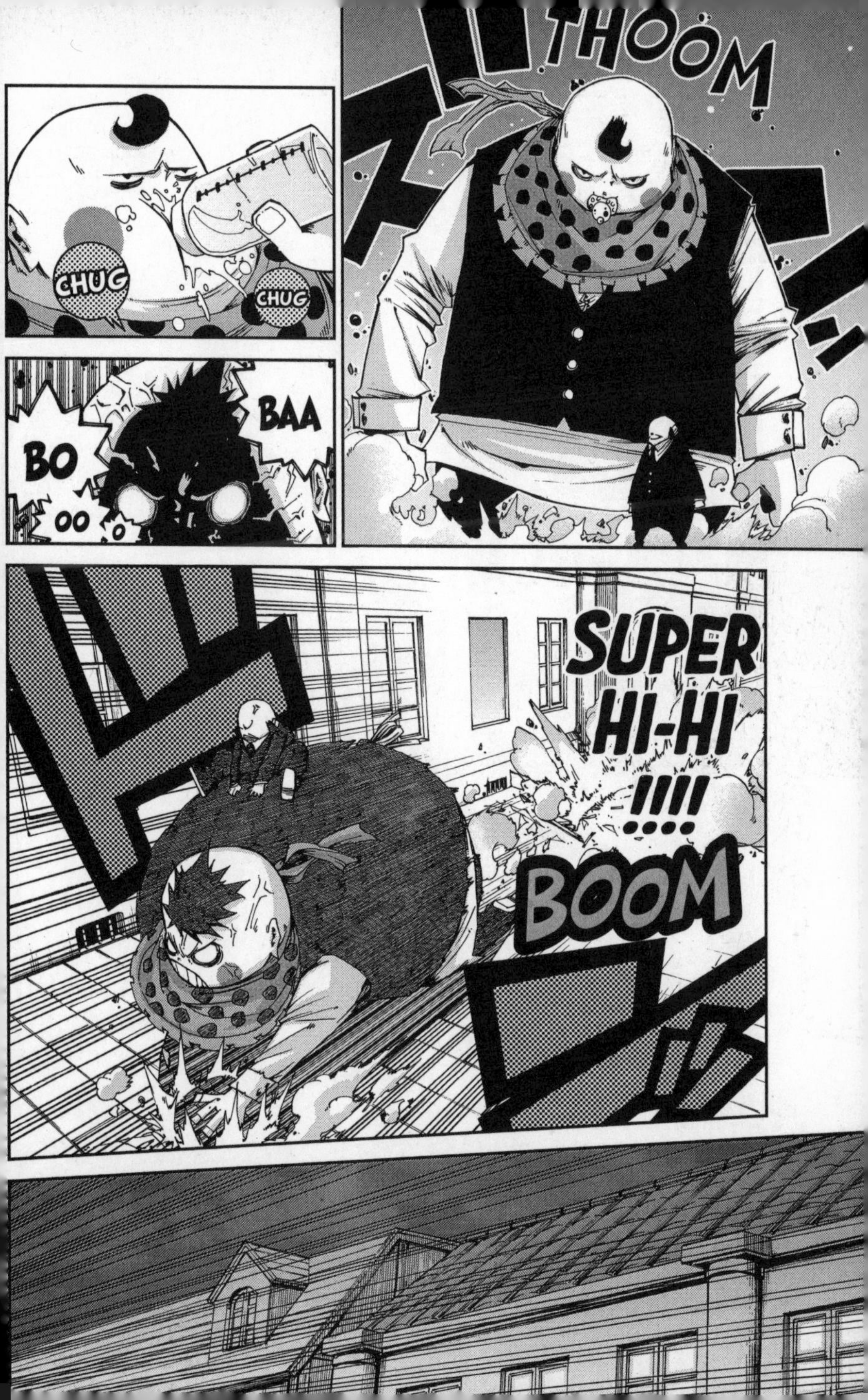
THOOM
CHUG
CHUG
BAA
BO
OO
O
SUPER HI-HI !!!!
BOOM

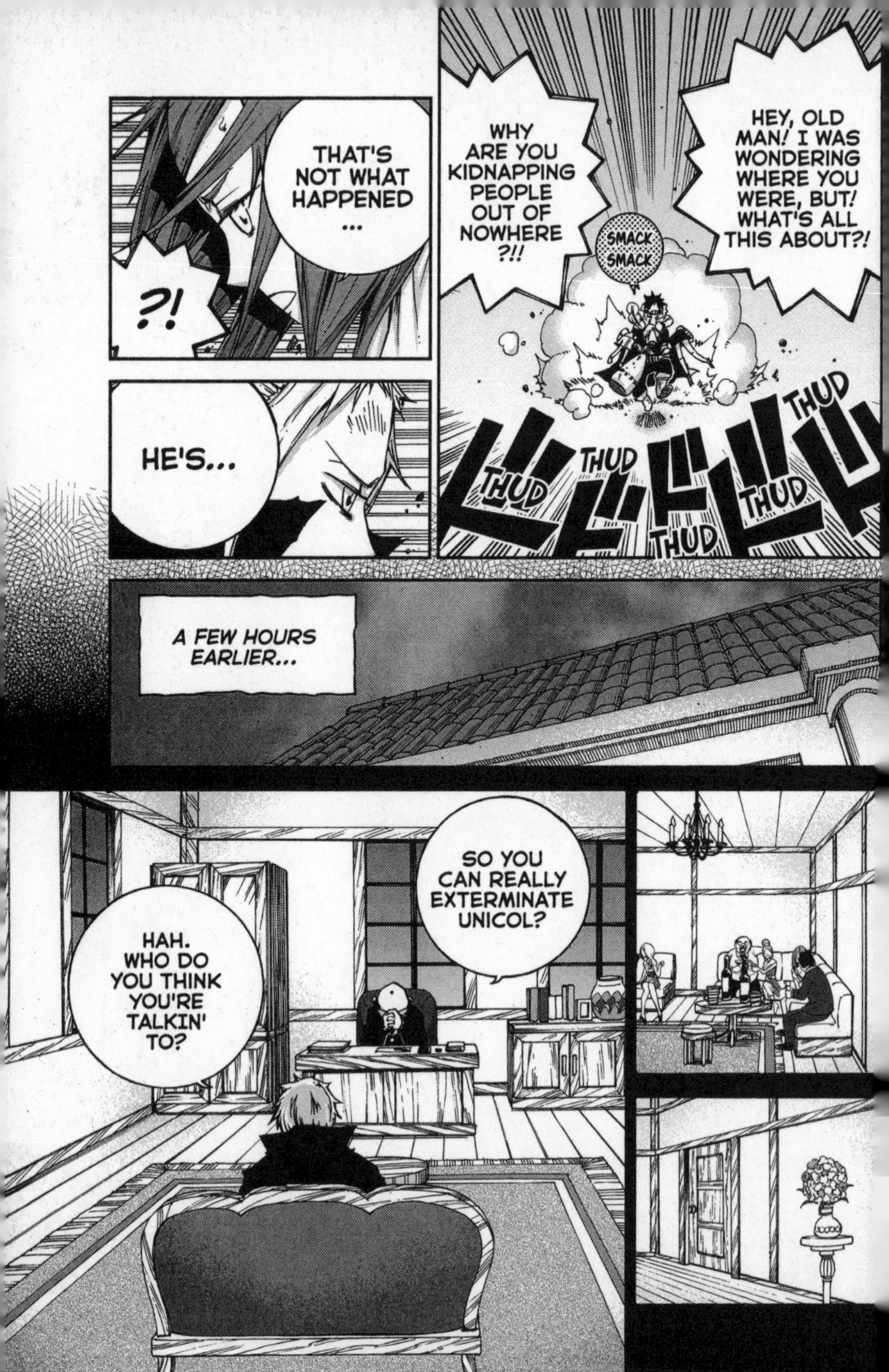
HEY, OLD MAN! I WAS WONDERING WHERE YOU WERE, BUT! WHAT'S ALL THIS ABOUT?!
WHY ARE YOU KIDNAPPING PEOPLE OUT OF NOWHERE ?!!
SMACK SMACK
THUD THUD THUD THUD THUD
THAT'S NOT WHAT HAPPENED ...
?!
HE'S...
A FEW HOURS EARLIER...
SO YOU CAN REALLY EXTERMINATE UNICOL?
HAH. WHO DO YOU THINK YOU'RE TALKIN' TO?

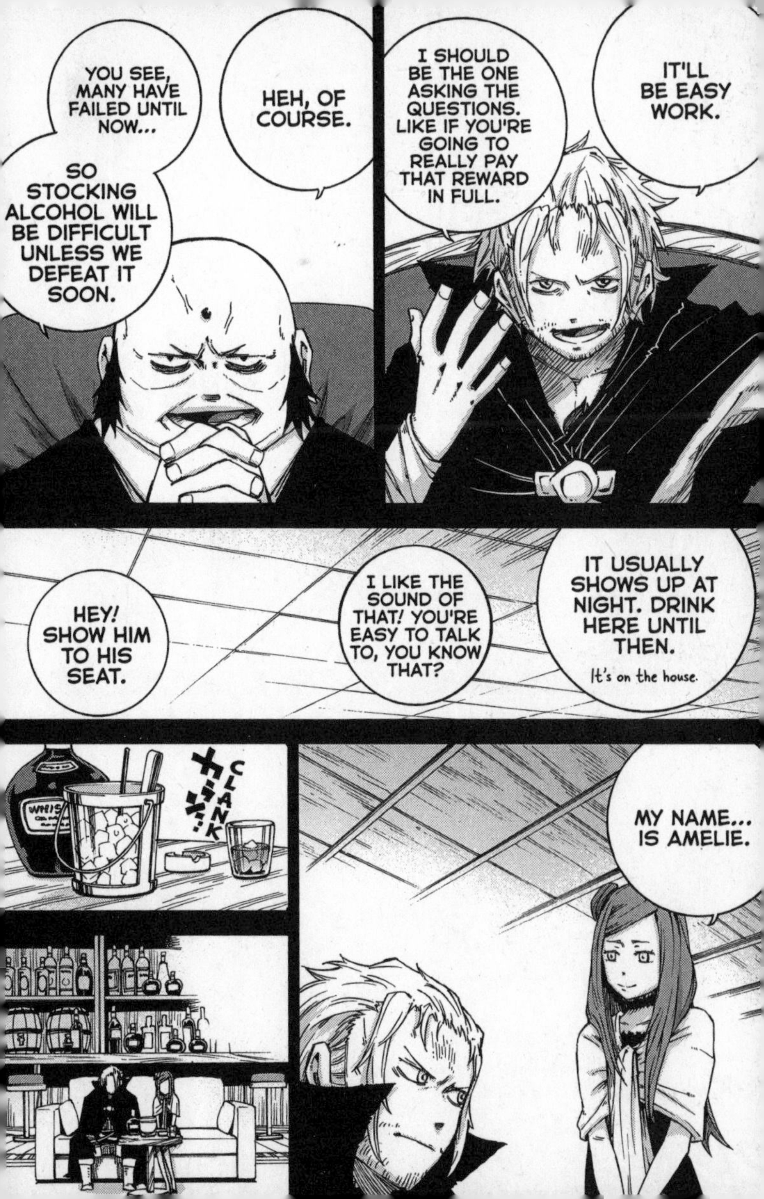
IT'LL BE EASY WORK.
I SHOULD BE THE ONE ASKING THE QUESTIONS. LIKE IF YOU'RE GOING TO REALLY PAY THAT REWARD IN FULL.
HEH, OF COURSE.
YOU SEE, MANY HAVE FAILED UNTIL NOW...
SO STOCKING ALCOHOL WILL BE DIFFICULT UNLESS WE DEFEAT IT SOON.
IT USUALLY SHOWS UP AT NIGHT. DRINK HERE UNTIL THEN.
It's on the house.
I LIKE THE SOUND OF THAT! YOU'RE EASY TO TALK TO, YOU KNOW THAT?
HEY! SHOW HIM TO HIS SEAT.
MY NAME... IS AMELIE.
CLANK

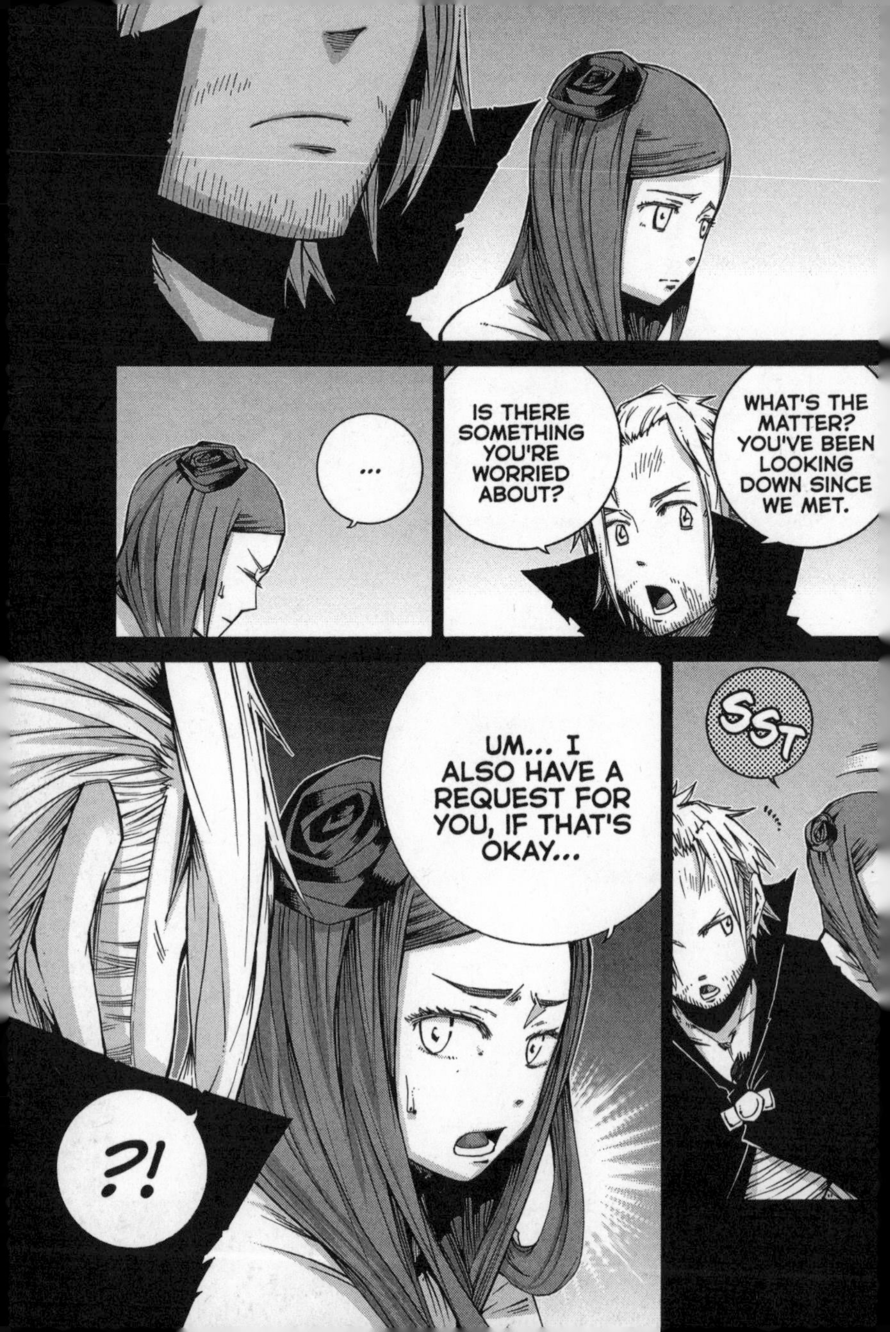
WHAT'S THE MATTER? YOU'VE BEEN LOOKING DOWN SINCE WE MET.
IS THERE SOMETHING YOU'RE WORRIED ABOUT?
...
SST
UM... I ALSO HAVE A REQUEST FOR YOU, IF THAT'S OKAY...
?!

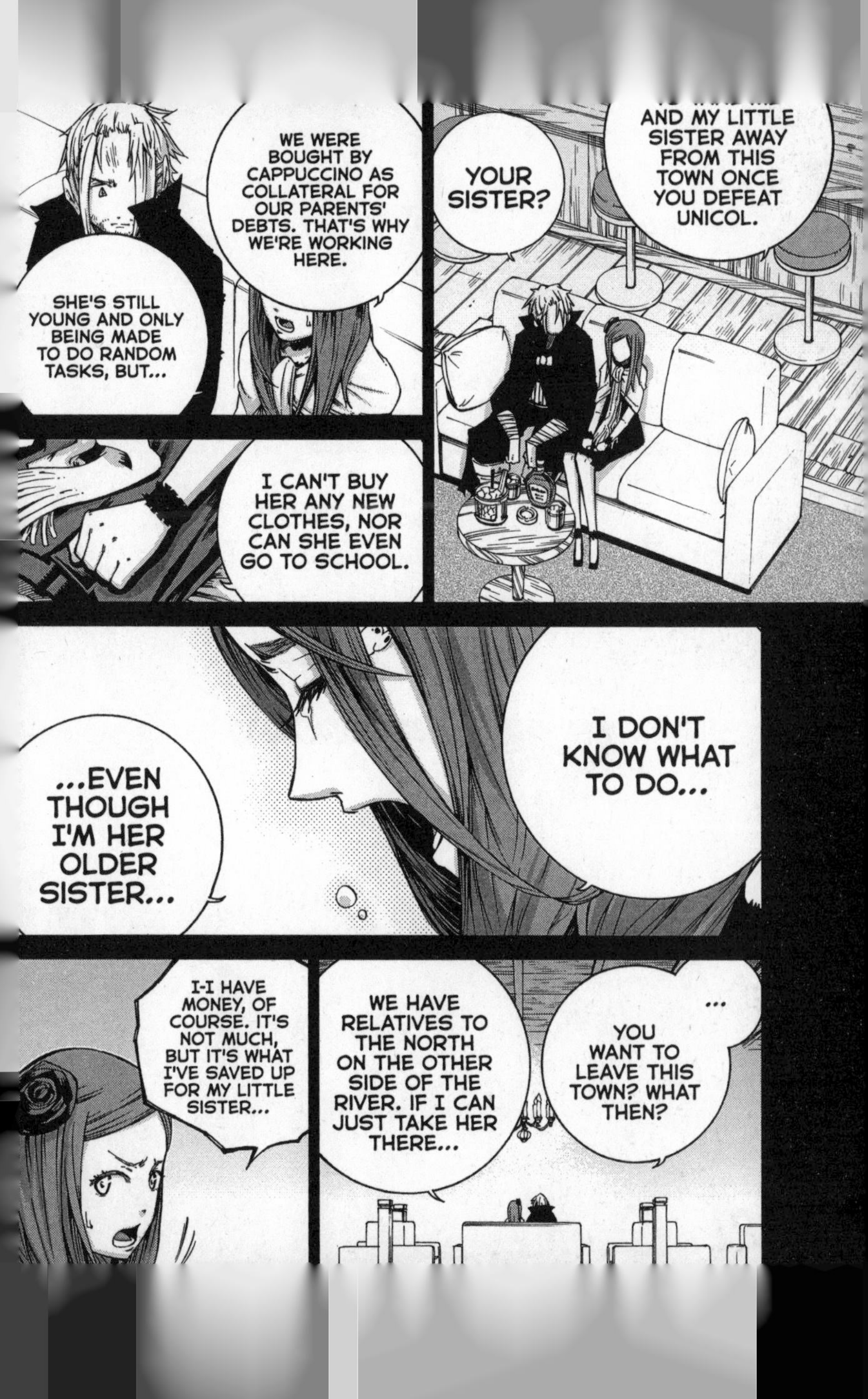
AND MY LITTLE SISTER AWAY FROM THIS TOWN ONCE YOU DEFEAT UNICOL.
YOUR SISTER?
WE WERE BOUGHT BY CAPPUCCINO AS COLLATERAL FOR OUR PARENTS' DEBTS. THAT'S WHY WE'RE WORKING HERE.
SHE'S STILL YOUNG AND ONLY BEING MADE TO DO RANDOM TASKS, BUT...
I CAN'T BUY HER ANY NEW CLOTHES, NOR CAN SHE EVEN GO TO SCHOOL.
I DON'T KNOW WHAT TO DO...
...EVEN THOUGH I'M HER OLDER SISTER...
...
YOU WANT TO LEAVE THIS TOWN? WHAT THEN?
WE HAVE RELATIVES TO THE NORTH ON THE OTHER SIDE OF THE RIVER. IF I CAN JUST TAKE HER THERE...
I-I HAVE MONEY, OF COURSE. IT'S NOT MUCH, BUT IT'S WHAT I'VE SAVED UP FOR MY LITTLE SISTER...

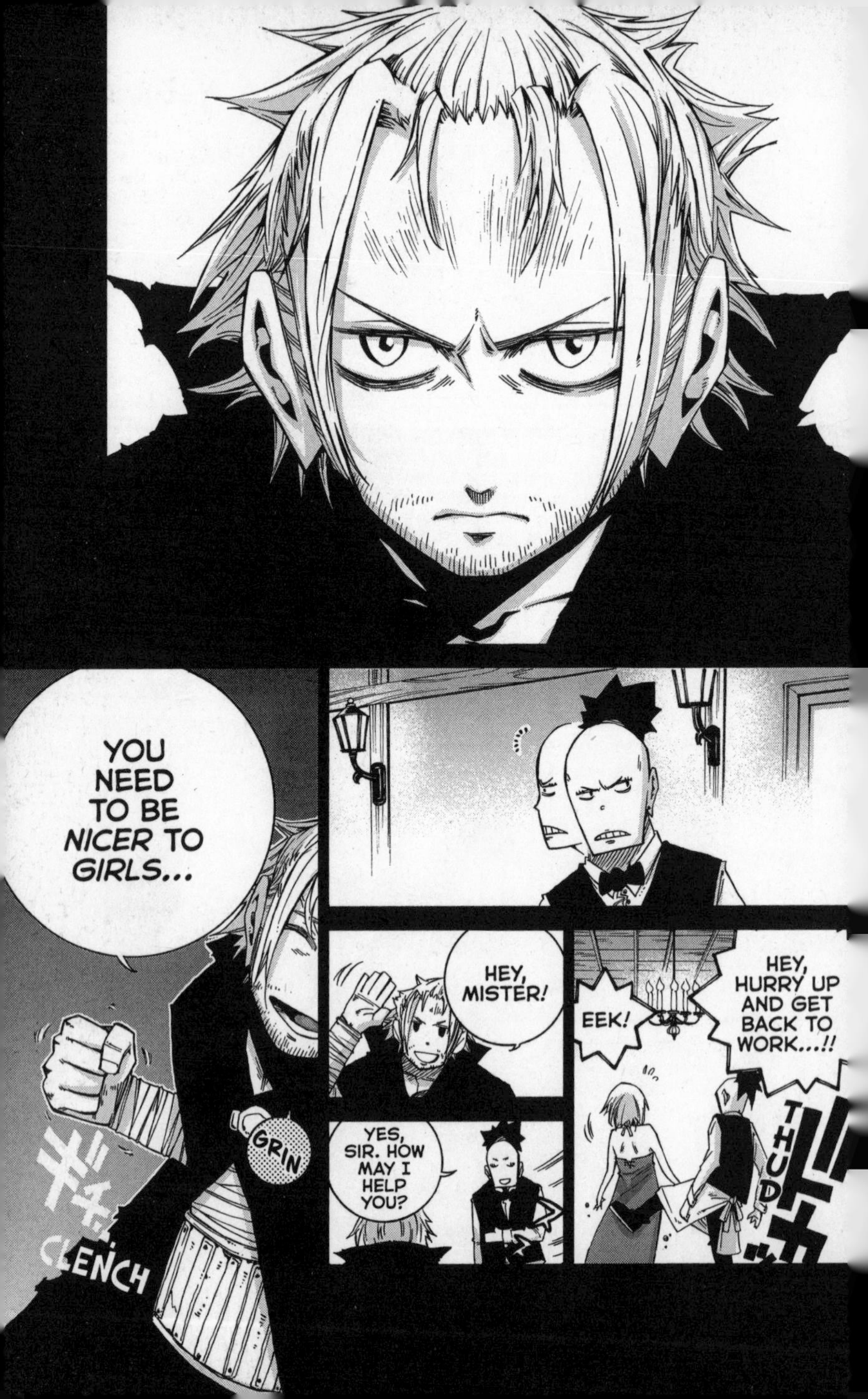
HEY, HURRY UP AND GET BACK TO WORK...!!
EEK!
THUD
HEY, MISTER!
YES, SIR. HOW MAY I HELP YOU?
YOU NEED TO BE *NICER* TO GIRLS...
GRIN
CLENCH

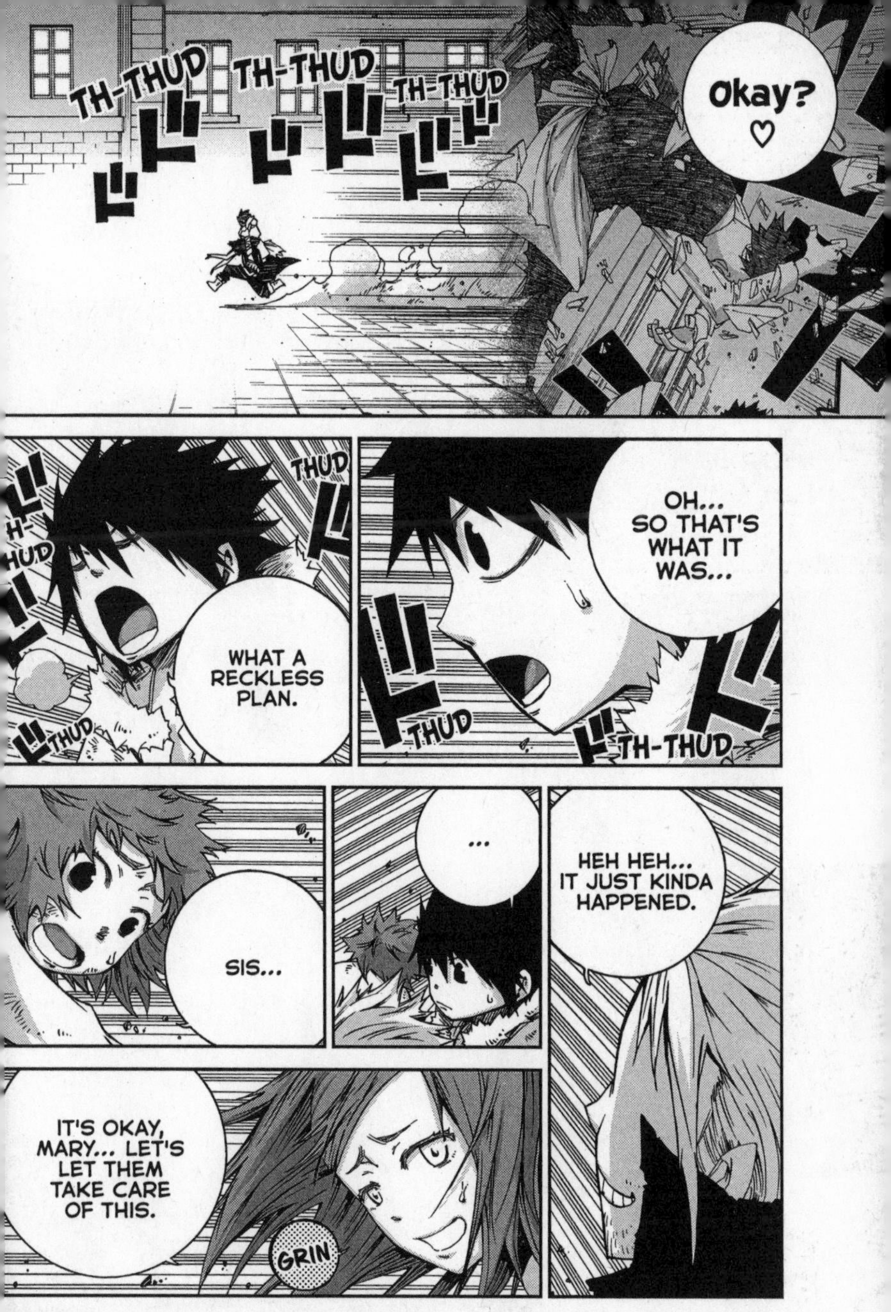
TH-THUD
TH-THUD
TH-THUD
Okay? ♡
OH... SO THAT'S WHAT IT WAS...
THUD
TH-THUD
THUD
WHAT A RECKLESS PLAN.
THUD
HEH HEH... IT JUST KINDA HAPPENED.
...
SIS...
IT'S OKAY, MARY... LET'S LET THEM TAKE CARE OF THIS.
GRIN

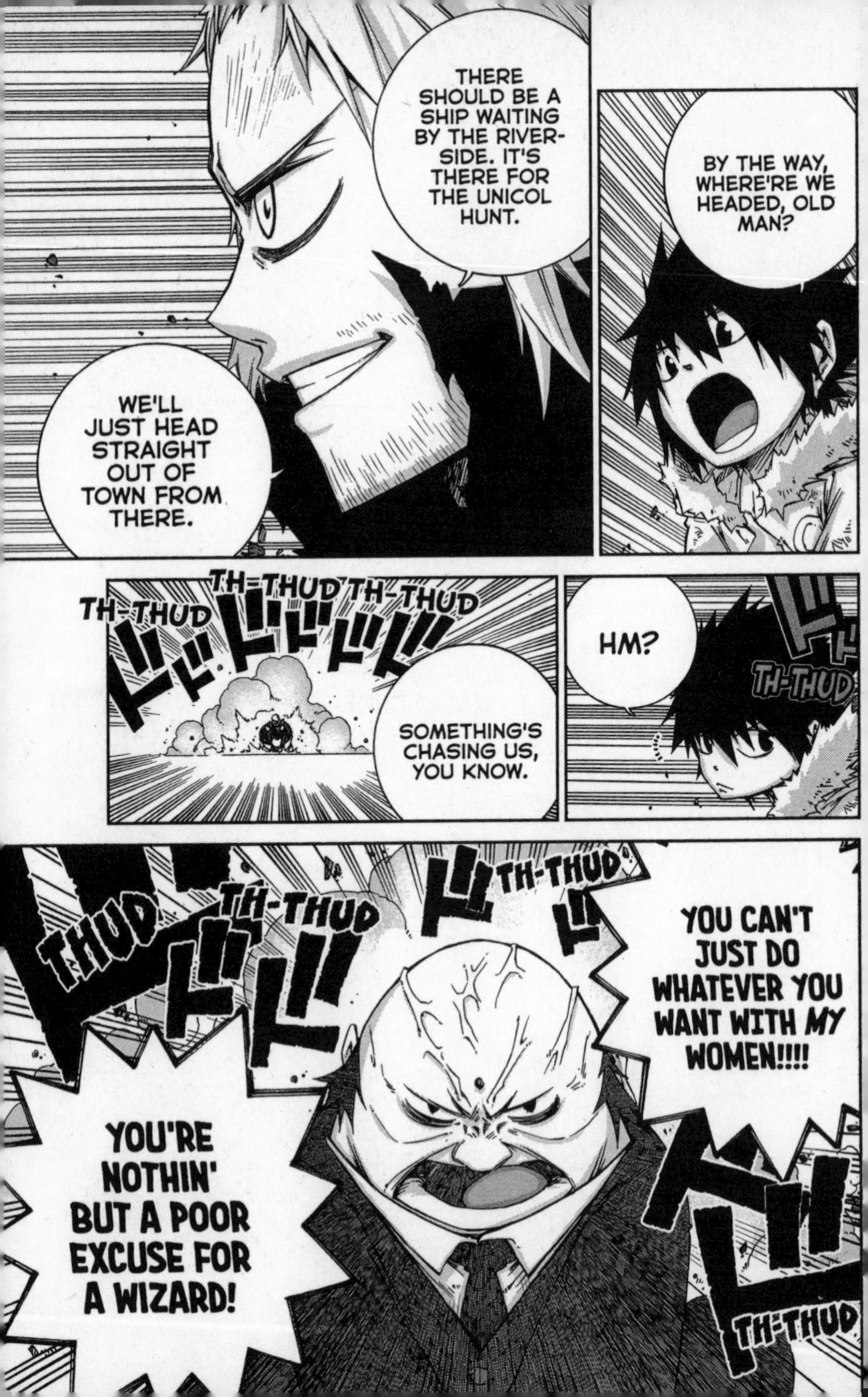
BY THE WAY, WHERE'RE WE HEADED, OLD MAN?
THERE SHOULD BE A SHIP WAITING BY THE RIVER-SIDE. IT'S THERE FOR THE UNICOL HUNT.
WE'LL JUST HEAD STRAIGHT OUT OF TOWN FROM THERE.
TH-THUD
HM?
TH-THUD TH-THUD
TH-THUD
SOMETHING'S CHASING US, YOU KNOW.
TH-THUD
YOU CAN'T JUST DO WHATEVER YOU WANT WITH MY WOMEN!!!!
TH-THUD
THUD
TH-THUD
YOU'RE NOTHIN' BUT A POOR EXCUSE FOR A WIZARD!

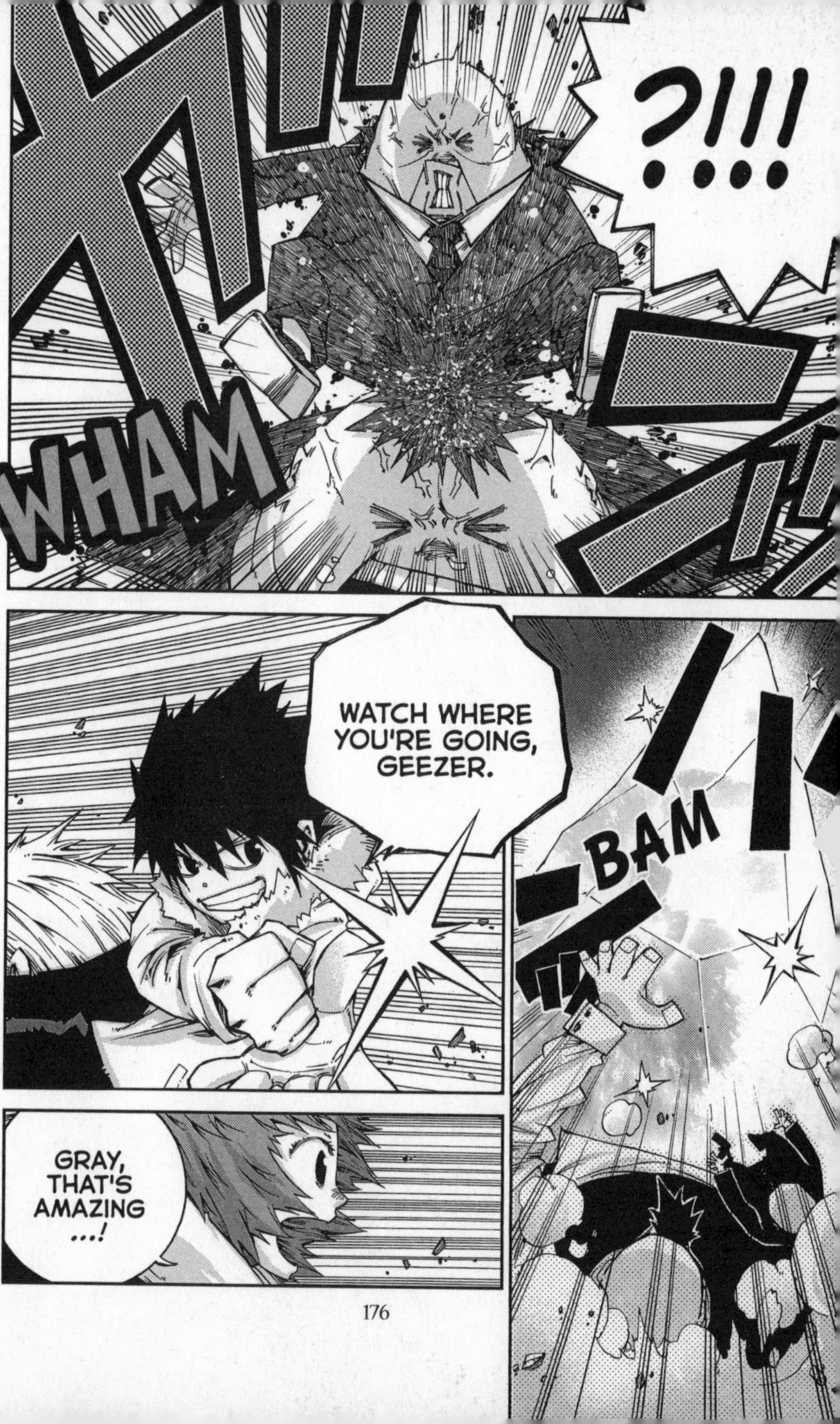
?!!!
WHAM
BAM
WATCH WHERE YOU'RE GOING, GEEZER.
GRAY, THAT'S AMAZING ...!

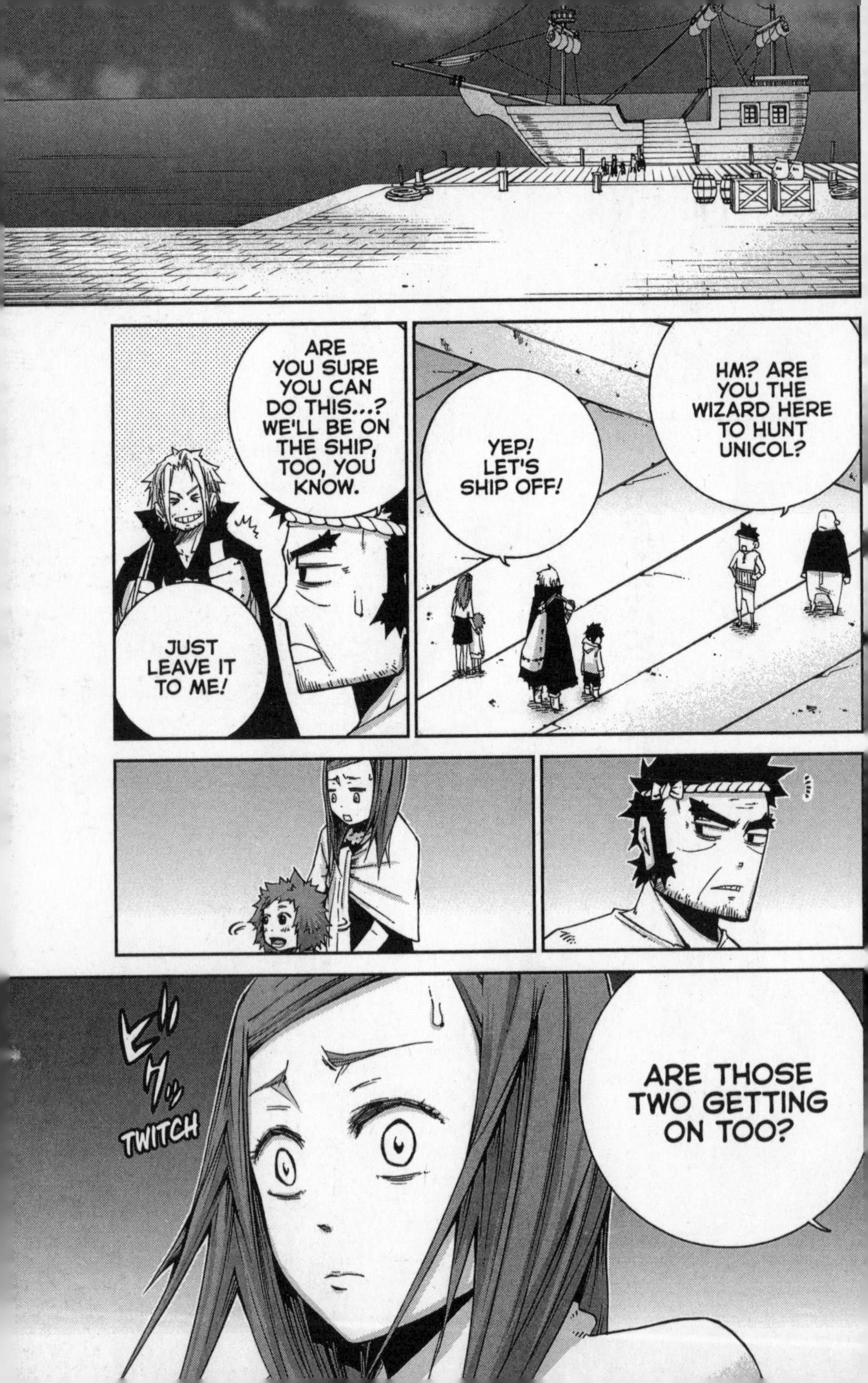
HM? ARE YOU THE WIZARD HERE TO HUNT UNICOL?
YEP! LET'S SHIP OFF!
ARE YOU SURE YOU CAN DO THIS...? WE'LL BE ON THE SHIP, TOO, YOU KNOW.
JUST LEAVE IT TO ME!
ARE THOSE TWO GETTING ON TOO?
ビクッ
TWITCH

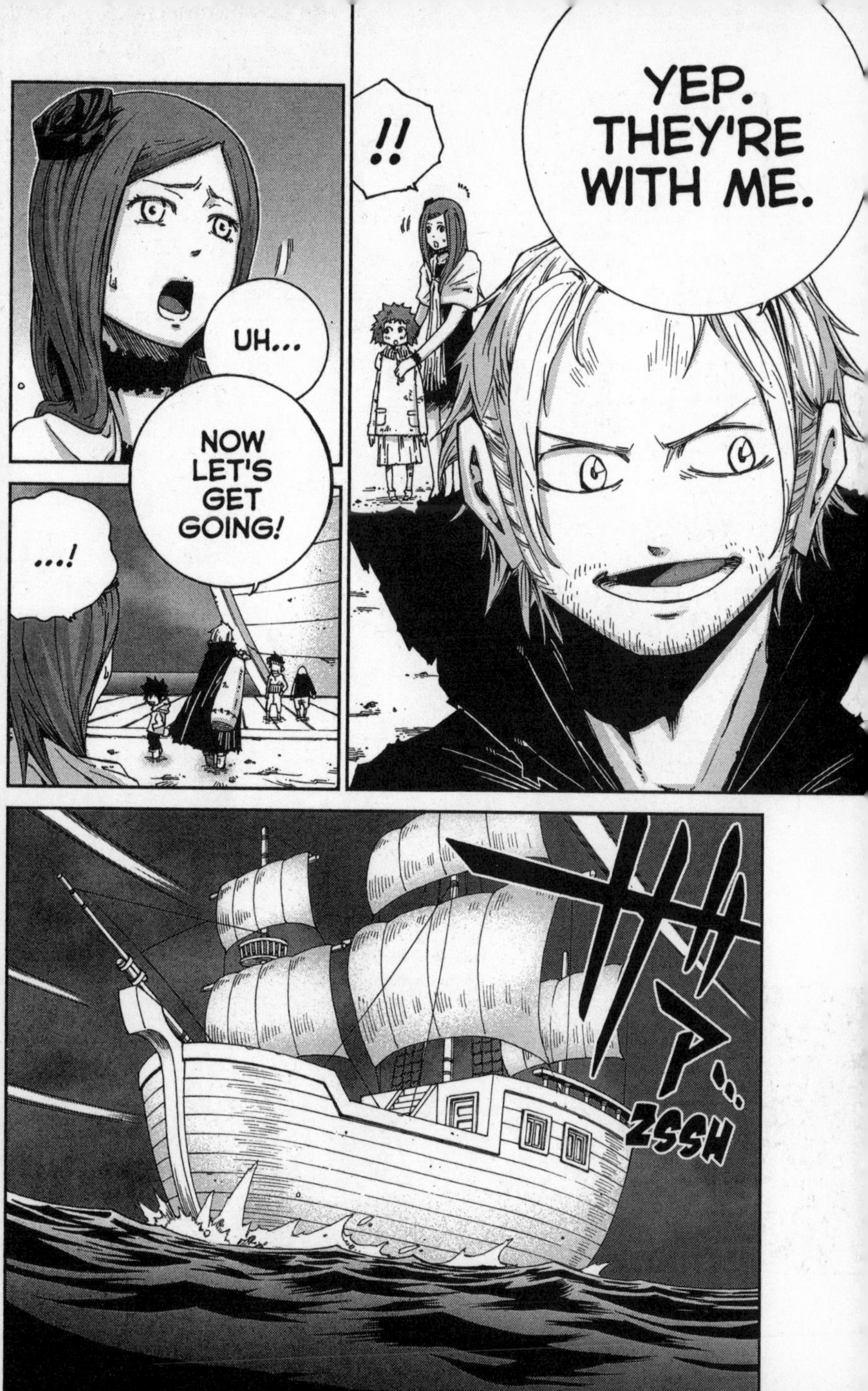
YEP. THEY'RE WITH ME.
!!
UH...
NOW LET'S GET GOING!
...!
ZSSH

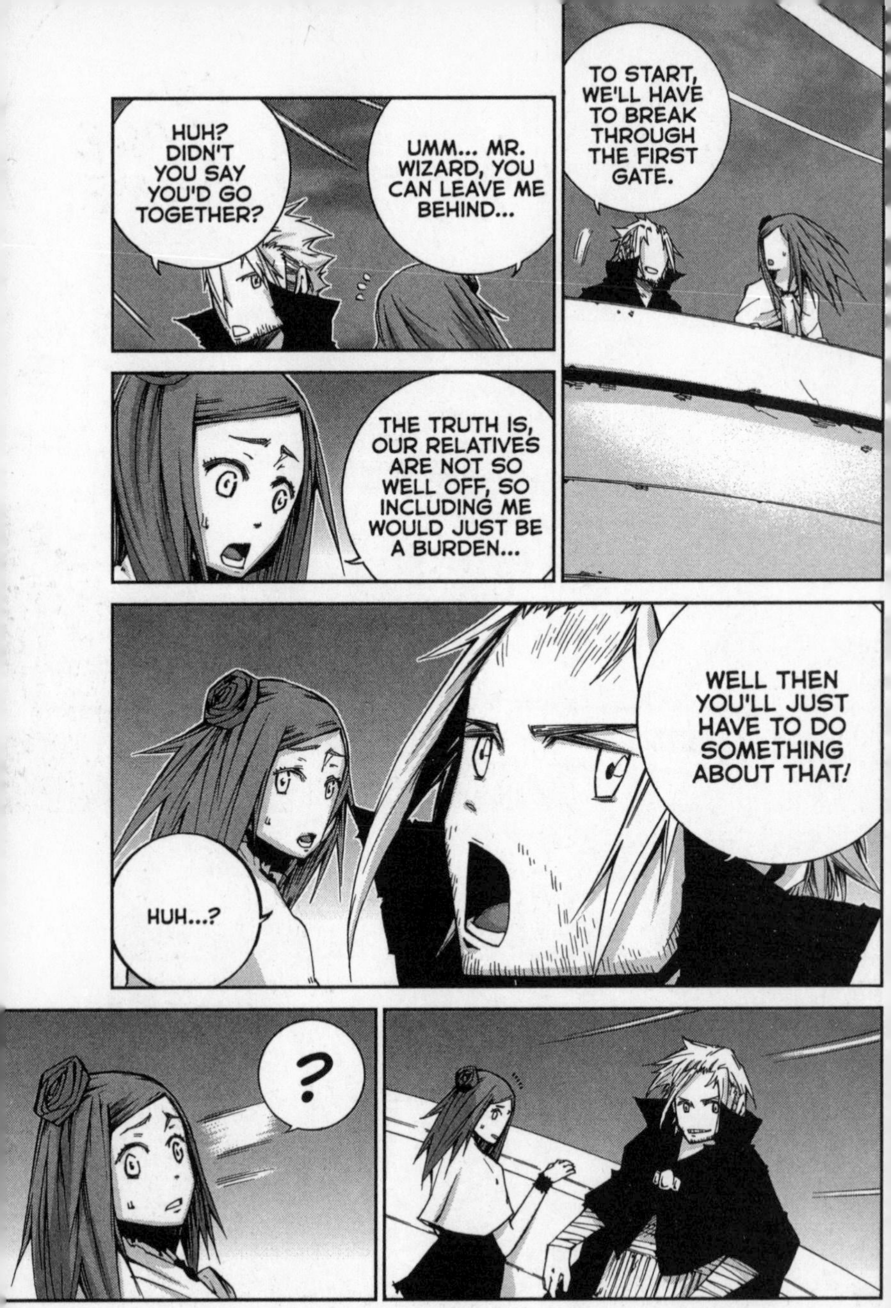

TO START, WE'LL HAVE TO BREAK THROUGH THE FIRST GATE.
UMM... MR. WIZARD, YOU CAN LEAVE ME BEHIND...
HUH? DIDN'T YOU SAY YOU'D GO TOGETHER?
THE TRUTH IS, OUR RELATIVES ARE NOT SO WELL OFF, SO INCLUDING ME WOULD JUST BE A BURDEN...
WELL THEN YOU'LL JUST HAVE TO DO SOMETHING ABOUT THAT!
HUH...?
?

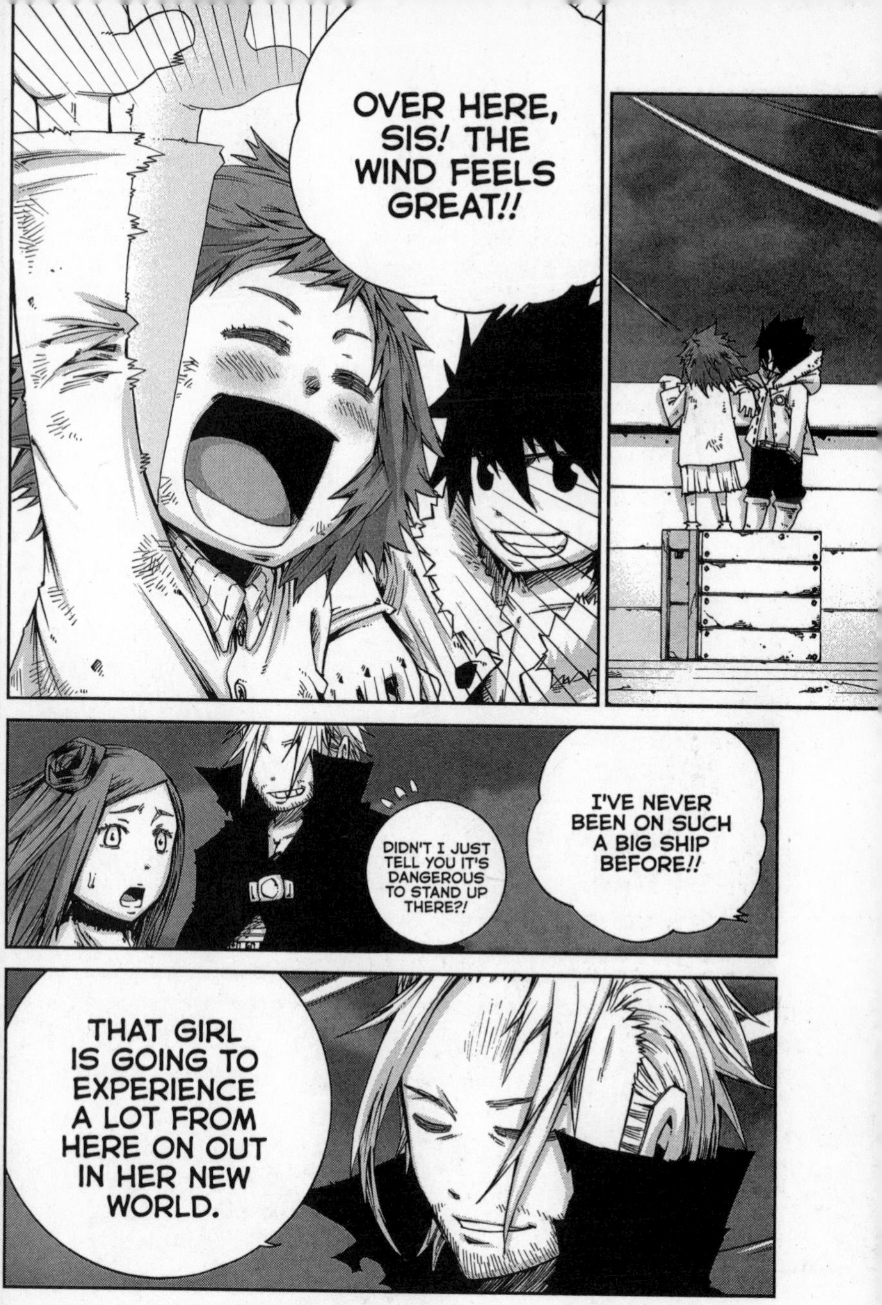
OVER HERE, SIS! THE WIND FEELS GREAT!!
I'VE NEVER BEEN ON SUCH A BIG SHIP BEFORE!!
DIDN'T I JUST TELL YOU IT'S DANGEROUS TO STAND UP THERE?!
THAT GIRL IS GOING TO EXPERIENCE A LOT FROM HERE ON OUT IN HER NEW WORLD.

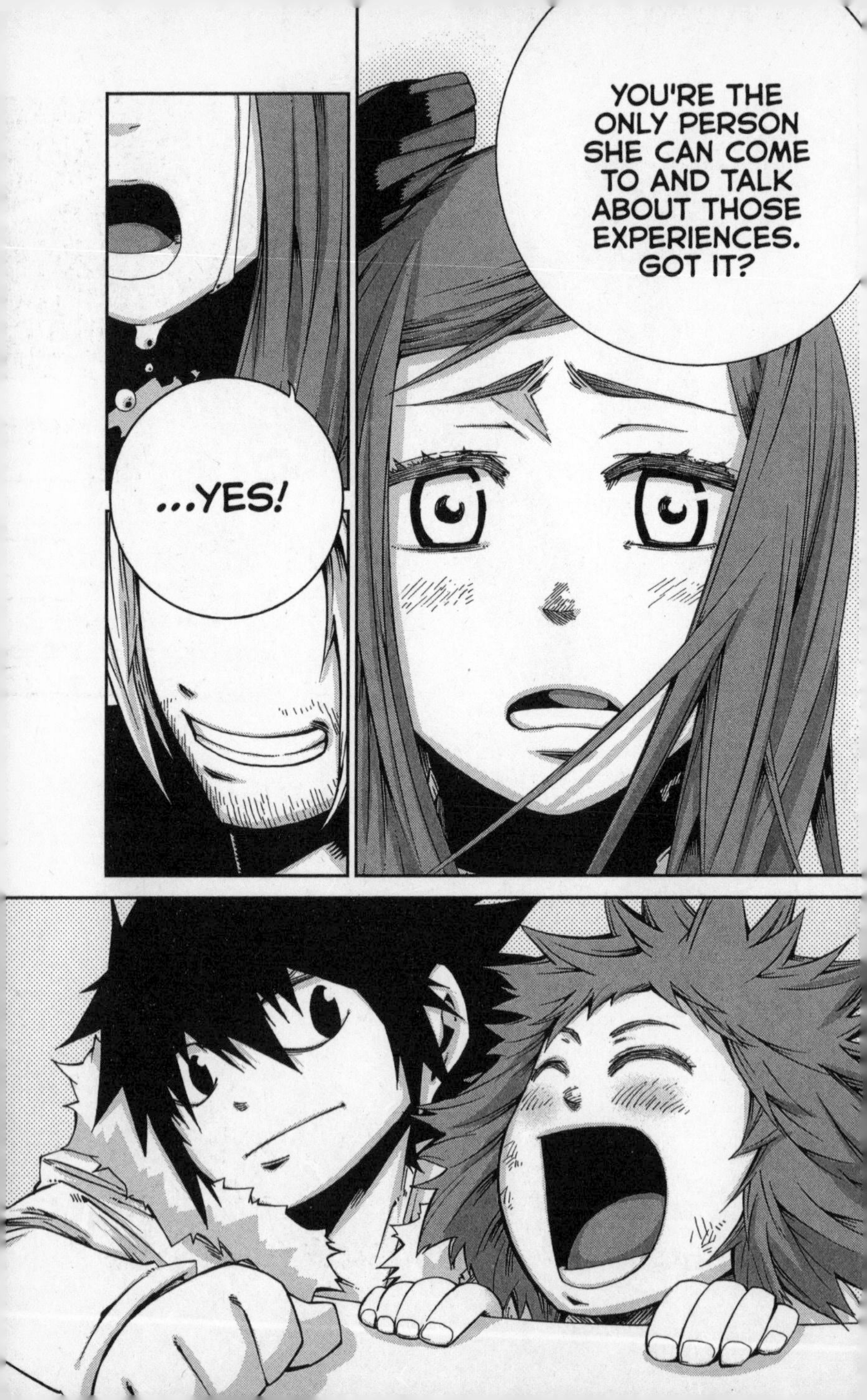
YOU'RE THE ONLY PERSON SHE CAN COME TO AND TALK ABOUT THOSE EXPERIENCES. GOT IT?
...YES!

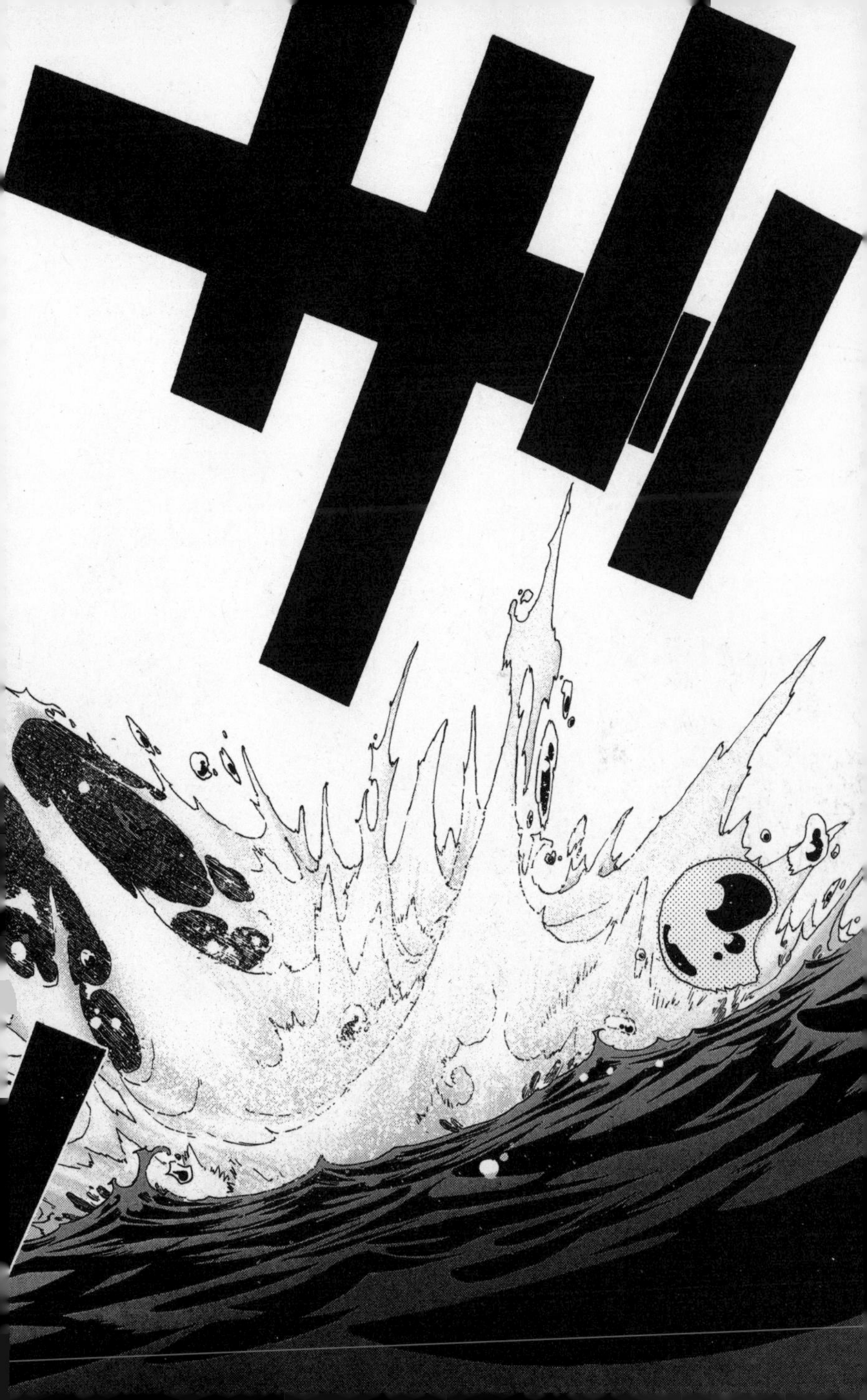
ザ

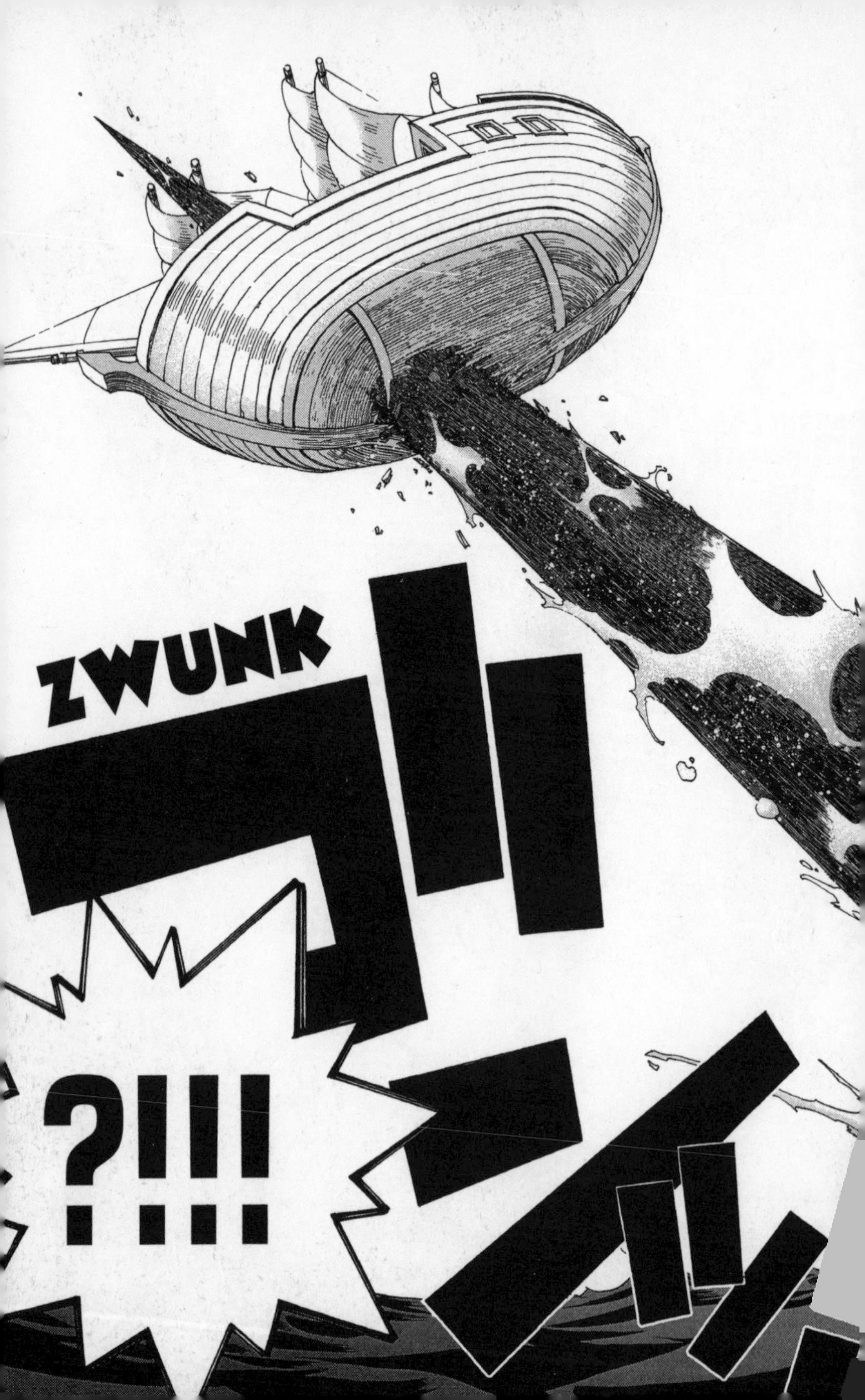
ZWUNK
?!!!

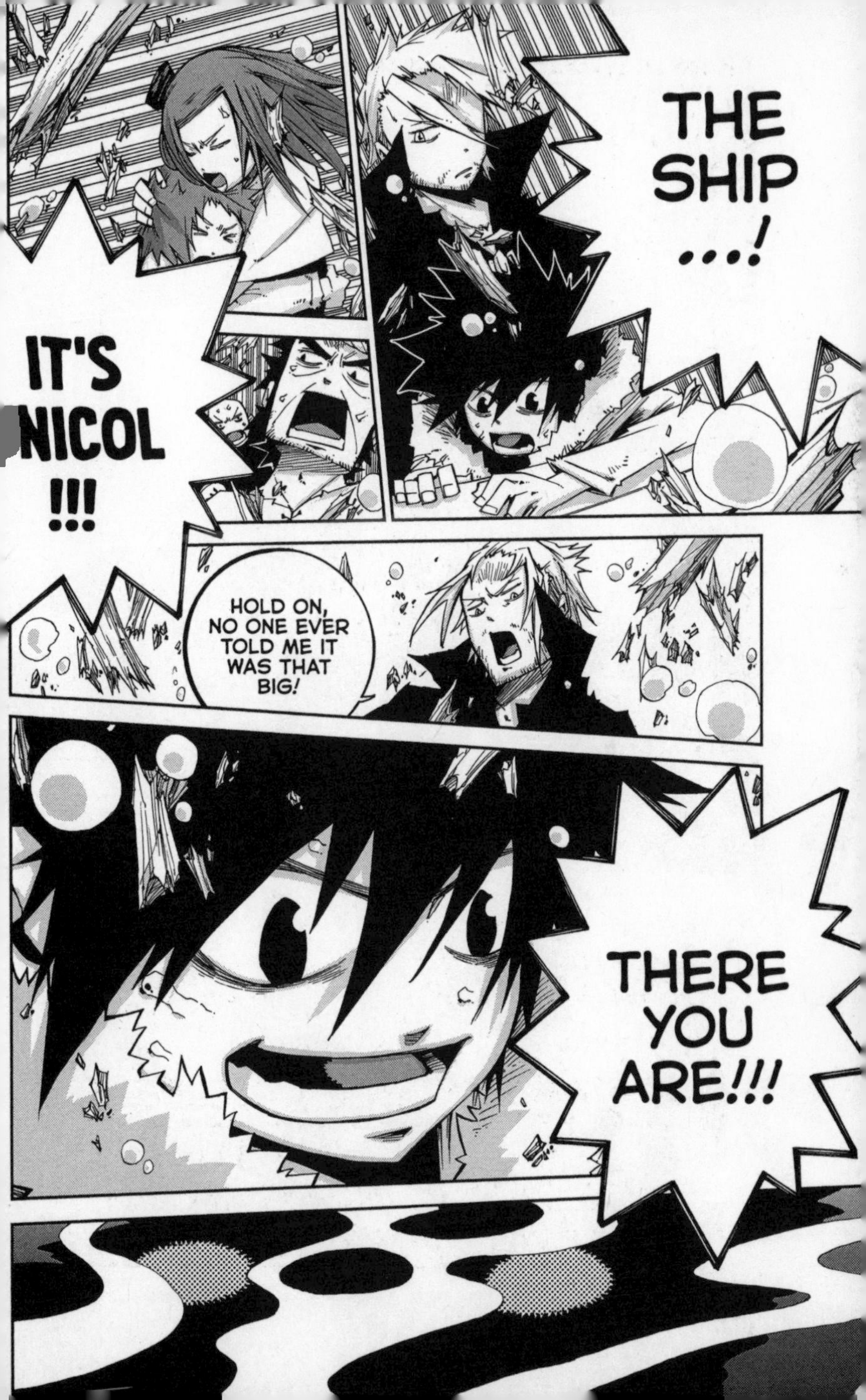
THE SHIP ...!
IT'S NICOL!!!
HOLD ON, NO ONE EVER TOLD ME IT WAS THAT BIG!
THERE YOU ARE!!!

Chapter 7: And Its Name is...

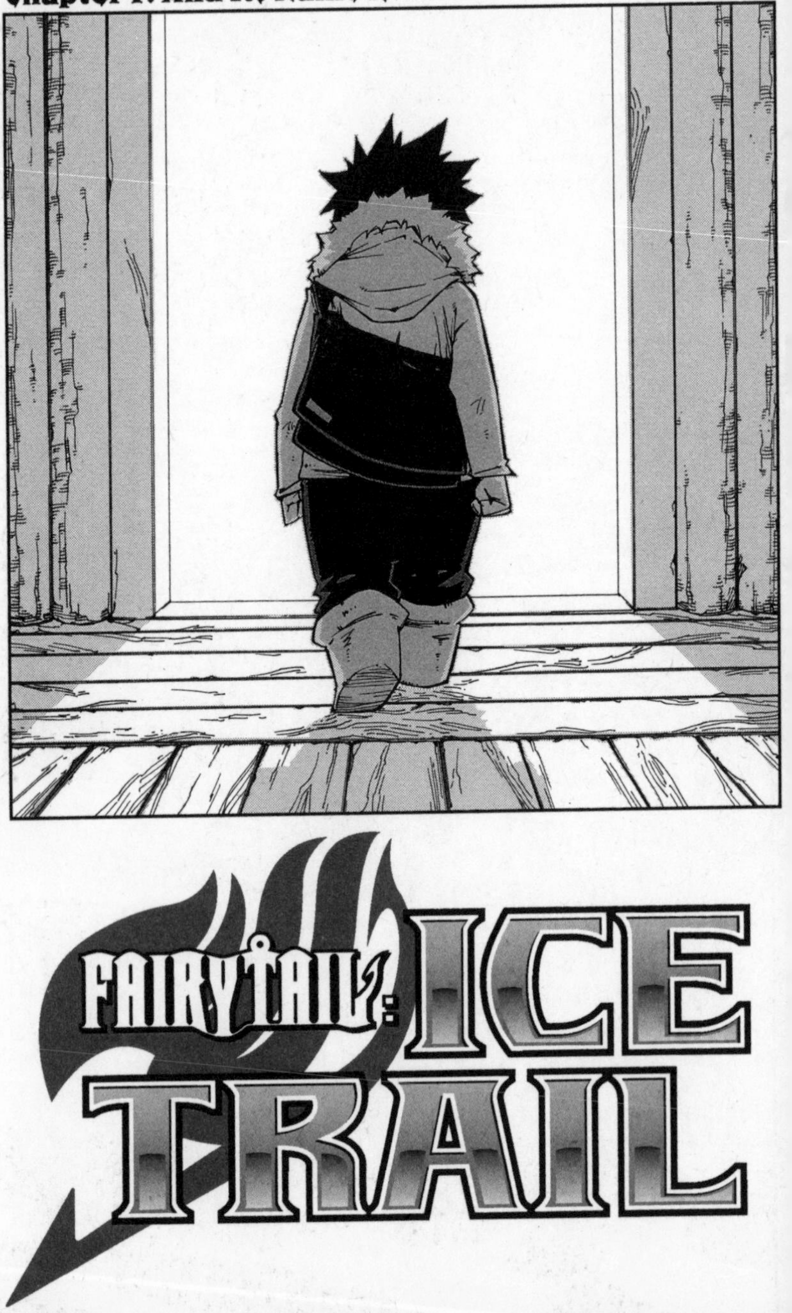

FAIRY TAIL: ICE TRAIL

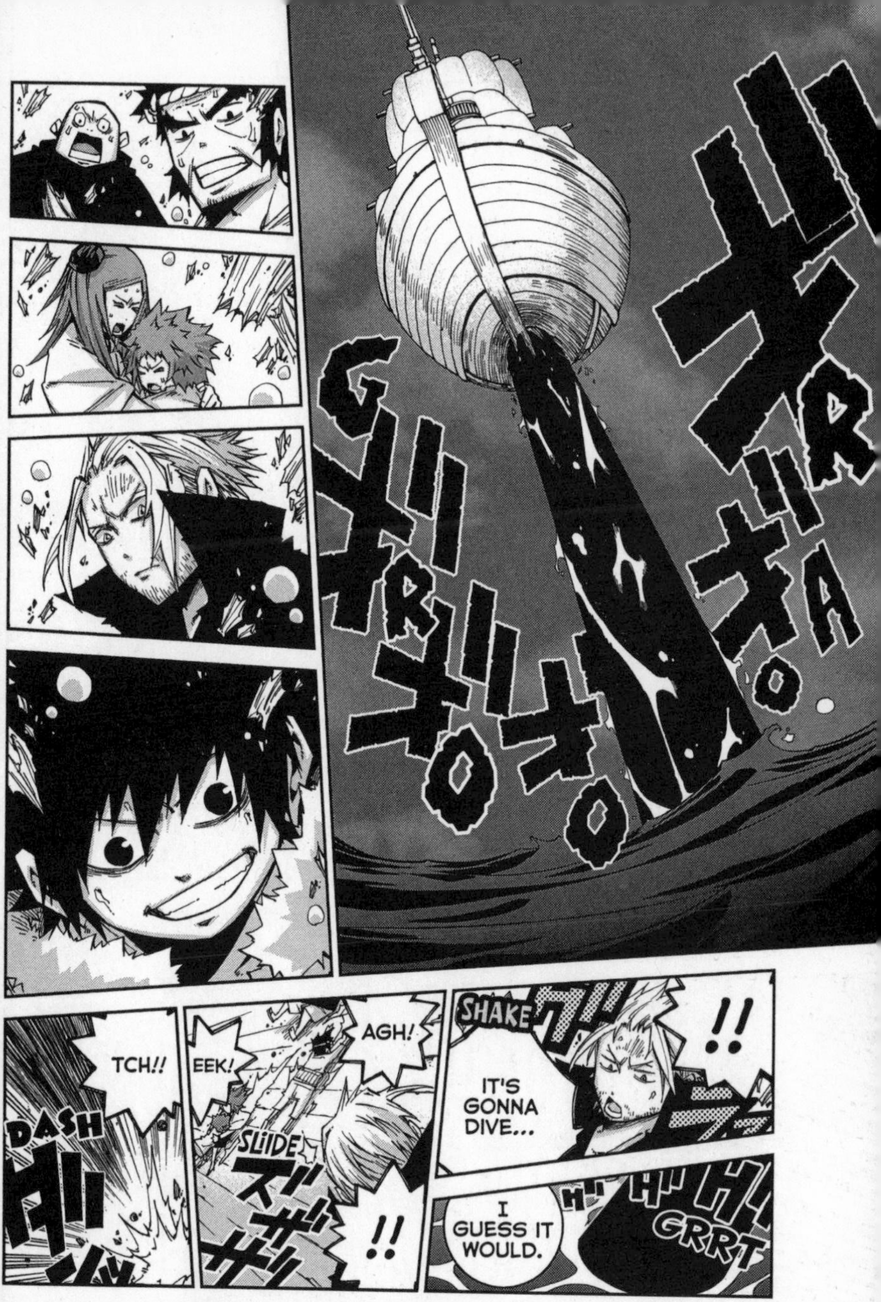
SHAKE
!!
IT'S GONNA DIVE...
I GUESS IT WOULD.
GRRT
AGH!
EEK!
SLIIDE
!!
TCH!!
DASH

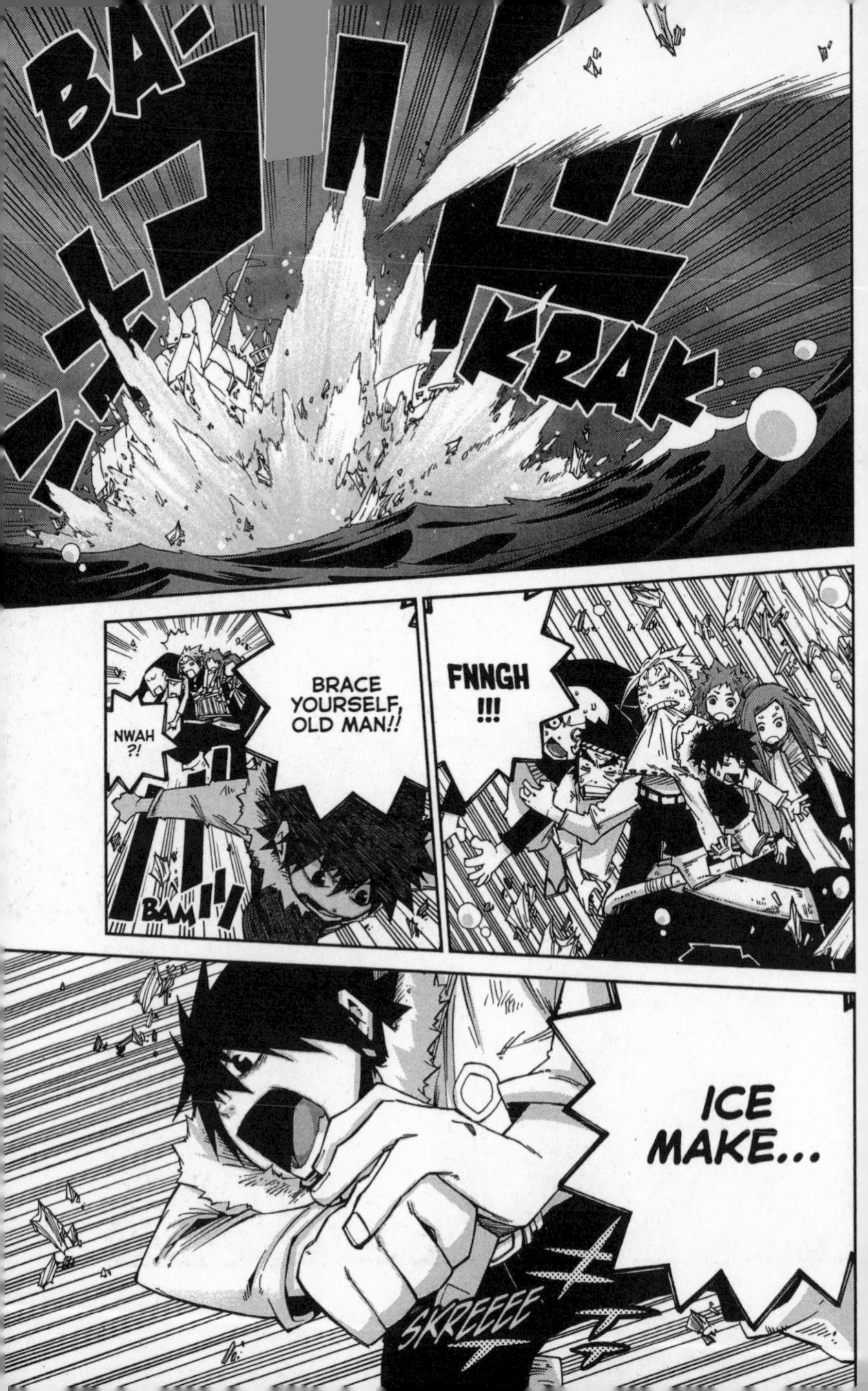
BA-
KRAK
FNNGH !!!
BRACE YOURSELF, OLD MAN!!
NWAH ?!
BAM !!
ICE MAKE...
SKREEEE

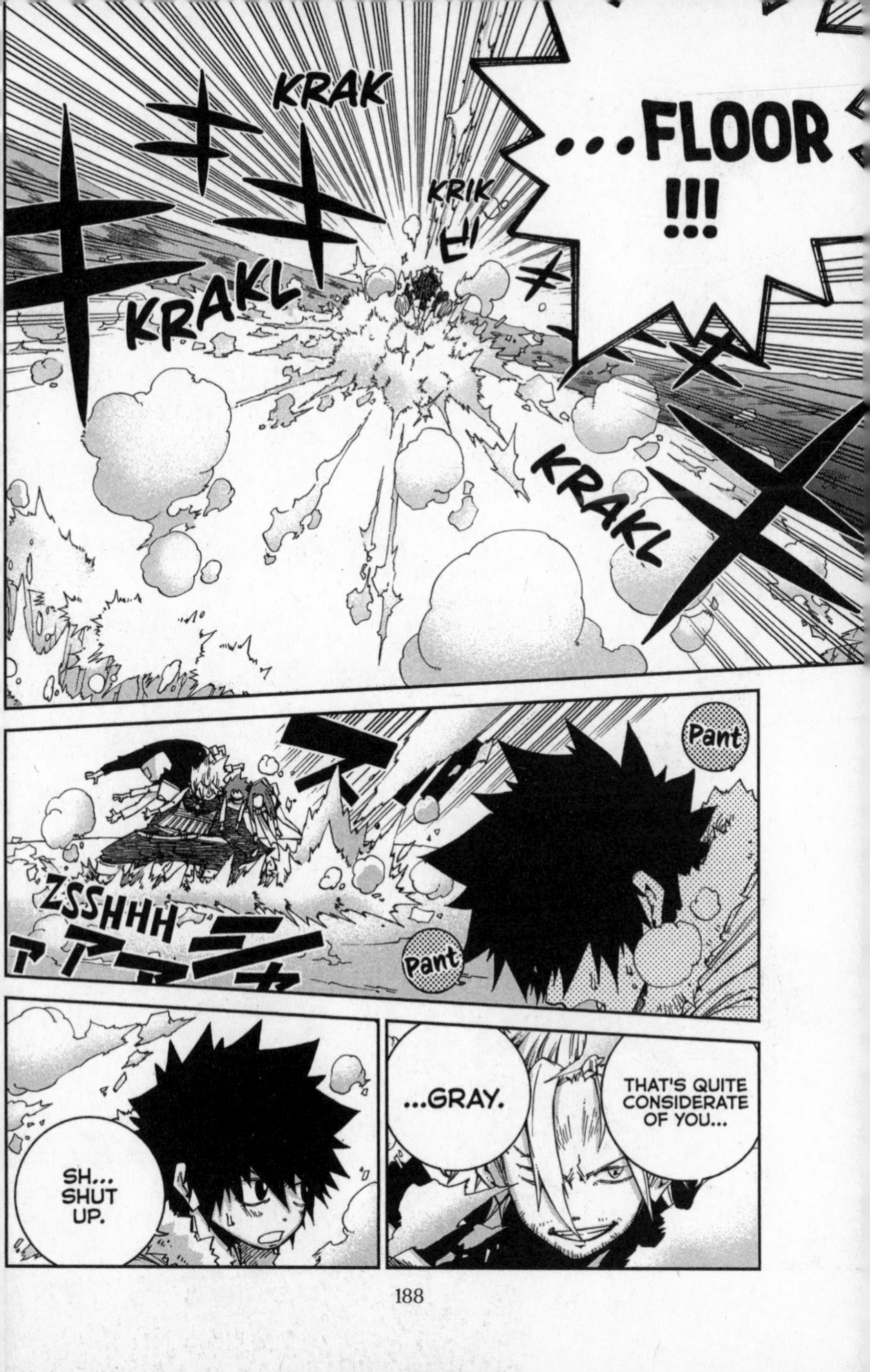
...FLOOR !!!
KRAK
KRIK
KRAKL
KRAKL
Pant
Pant
ZSSHHH
...GRAY.
THAT'S QUITE CONSIDERATE OF YOU...
SH... SHUT UP.

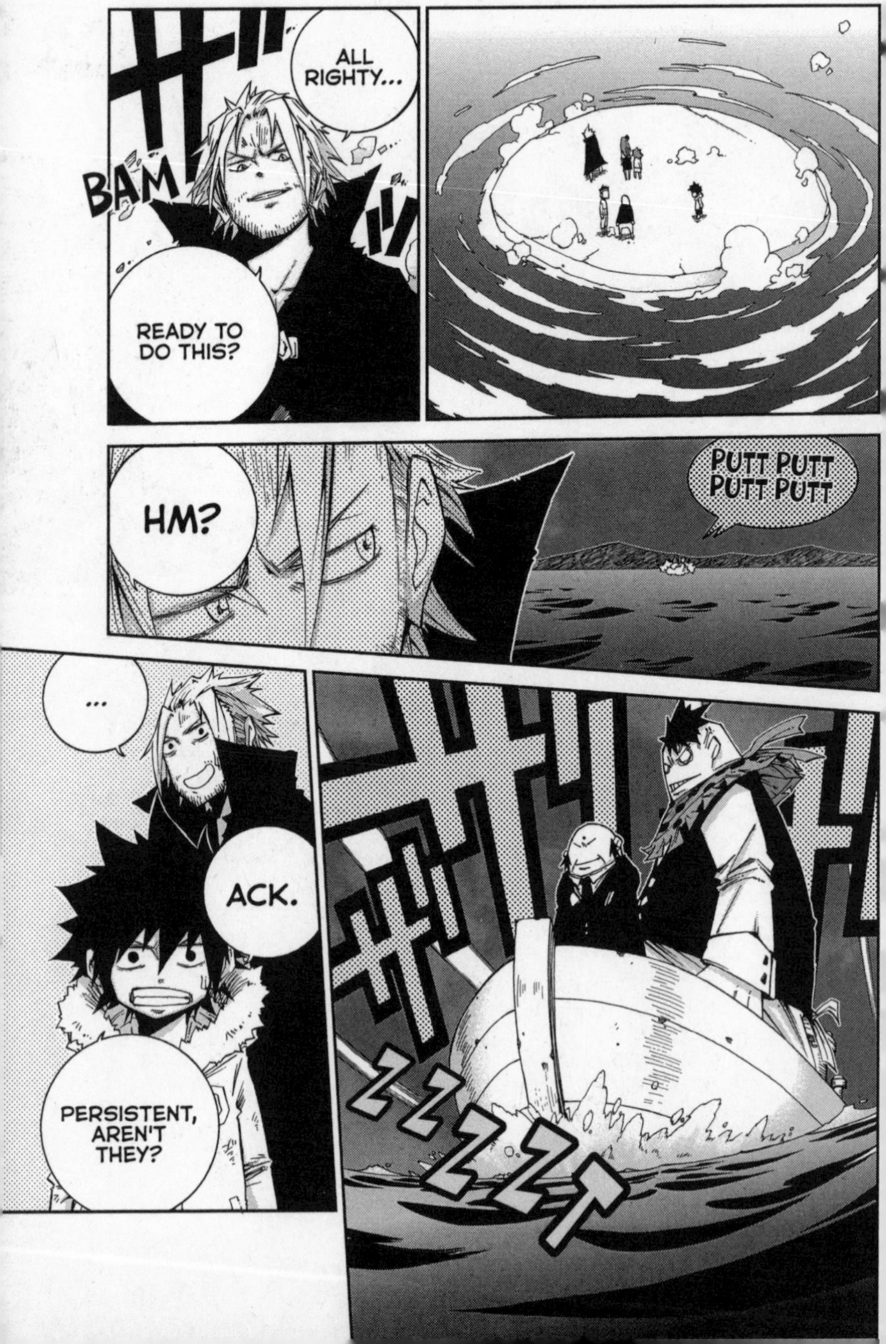
ALL RIGHTY...
BAM
READY TO DO THIS?
PUTT PUTT PUTT PUTT
HM?
ZZZZT
...
ACK.
PERSISTENT, AREN'T THEY?

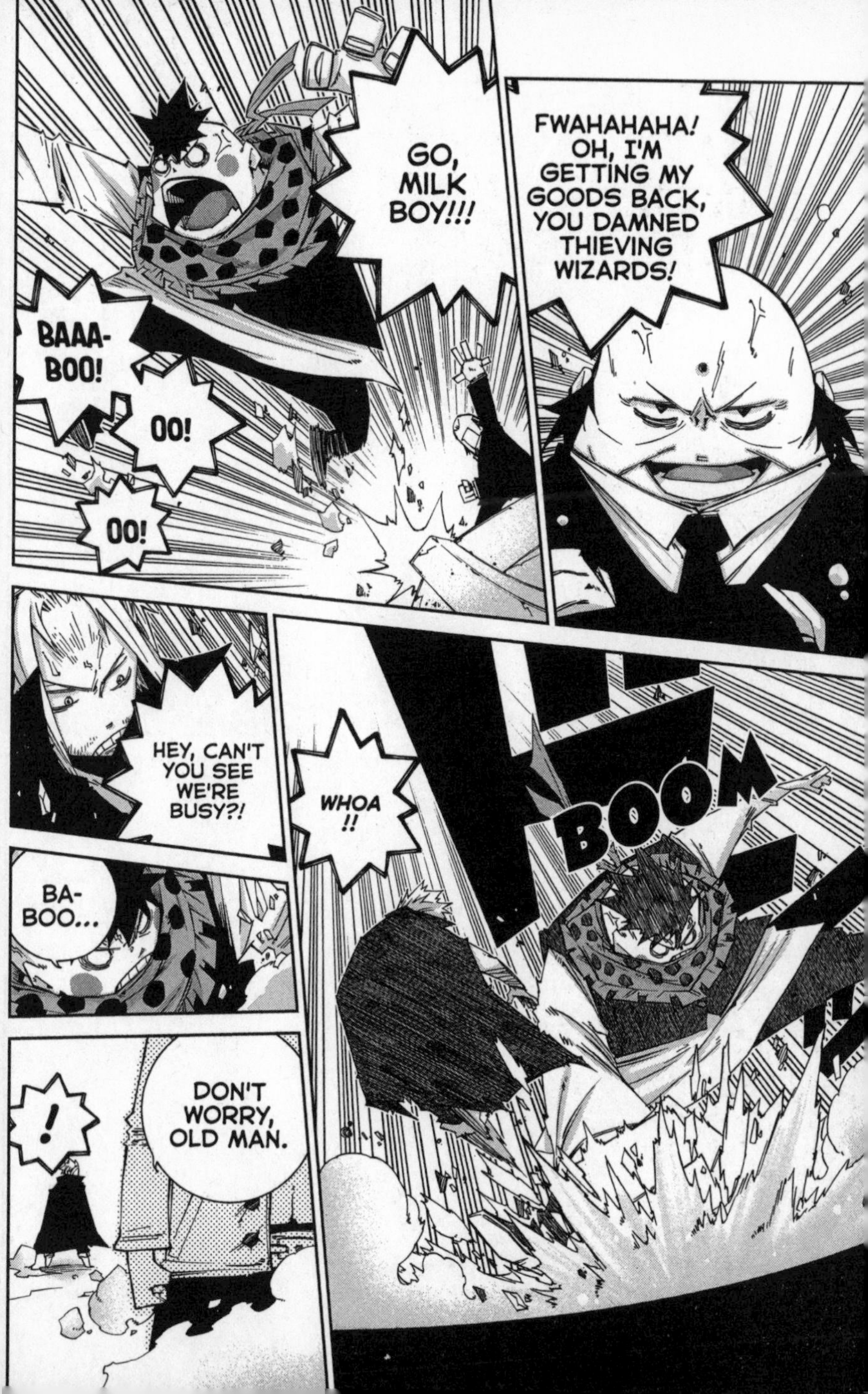
FWAHAHAHA! OH, I'M GETTING MY GOODS BACK, YOU DAMNED THIEVING WIZARDS!
GO, MILK BOY!!!
BAAA-BOO!
OO!
OO!
WHOA !!
BOOM
HEY, CAN'T YOU SEE WE'RE BUSY?!
BA-BOO...
!
DON'T WORRY, OLD MAN.

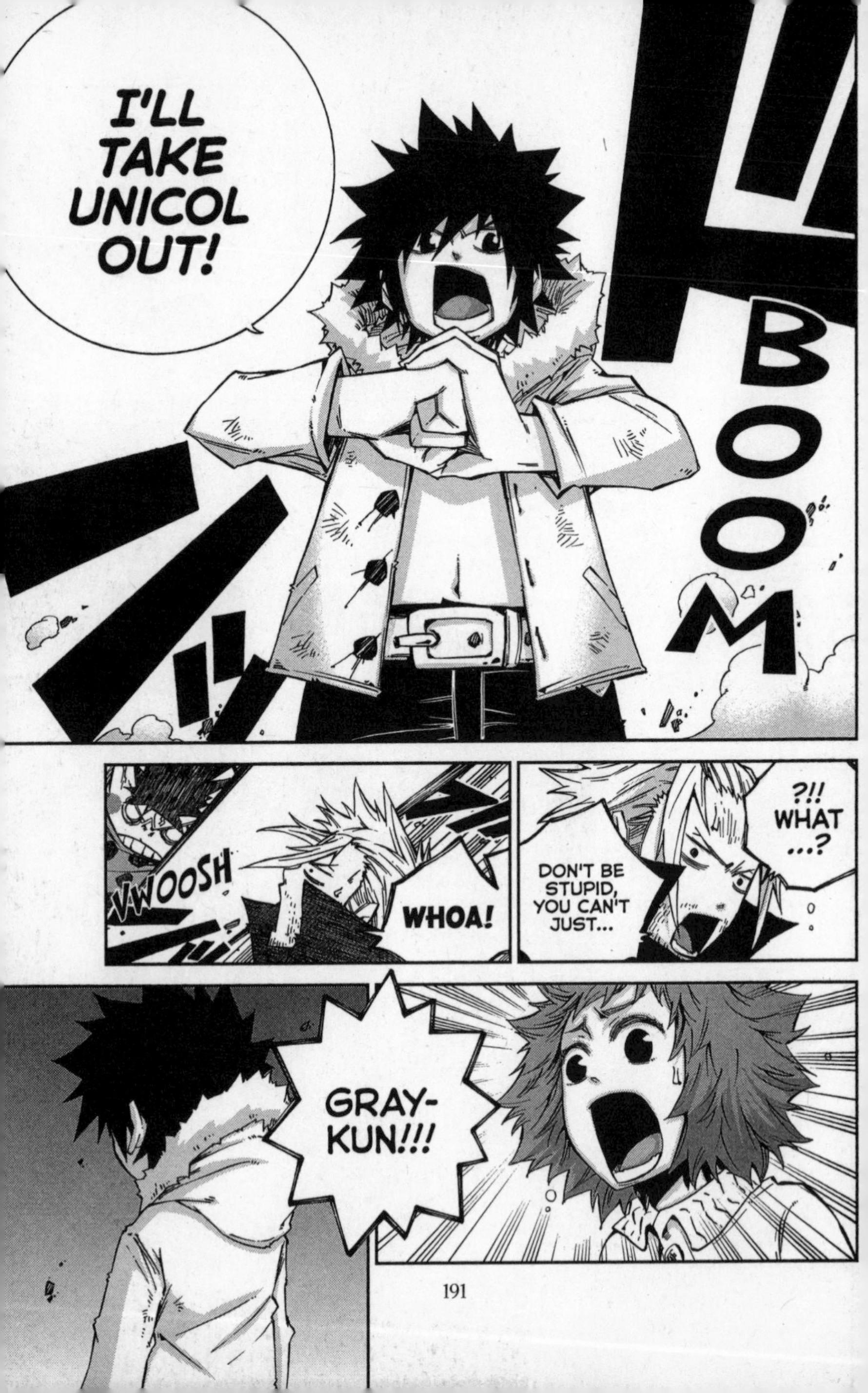
I'LL TAKE UNICOL OUT!
BOOM
?!! WHAT ...?
DON'T BE STUPID, YOU CAN'T JUST...
VWOOSH
WHOA!
GRAY-KUN!!!

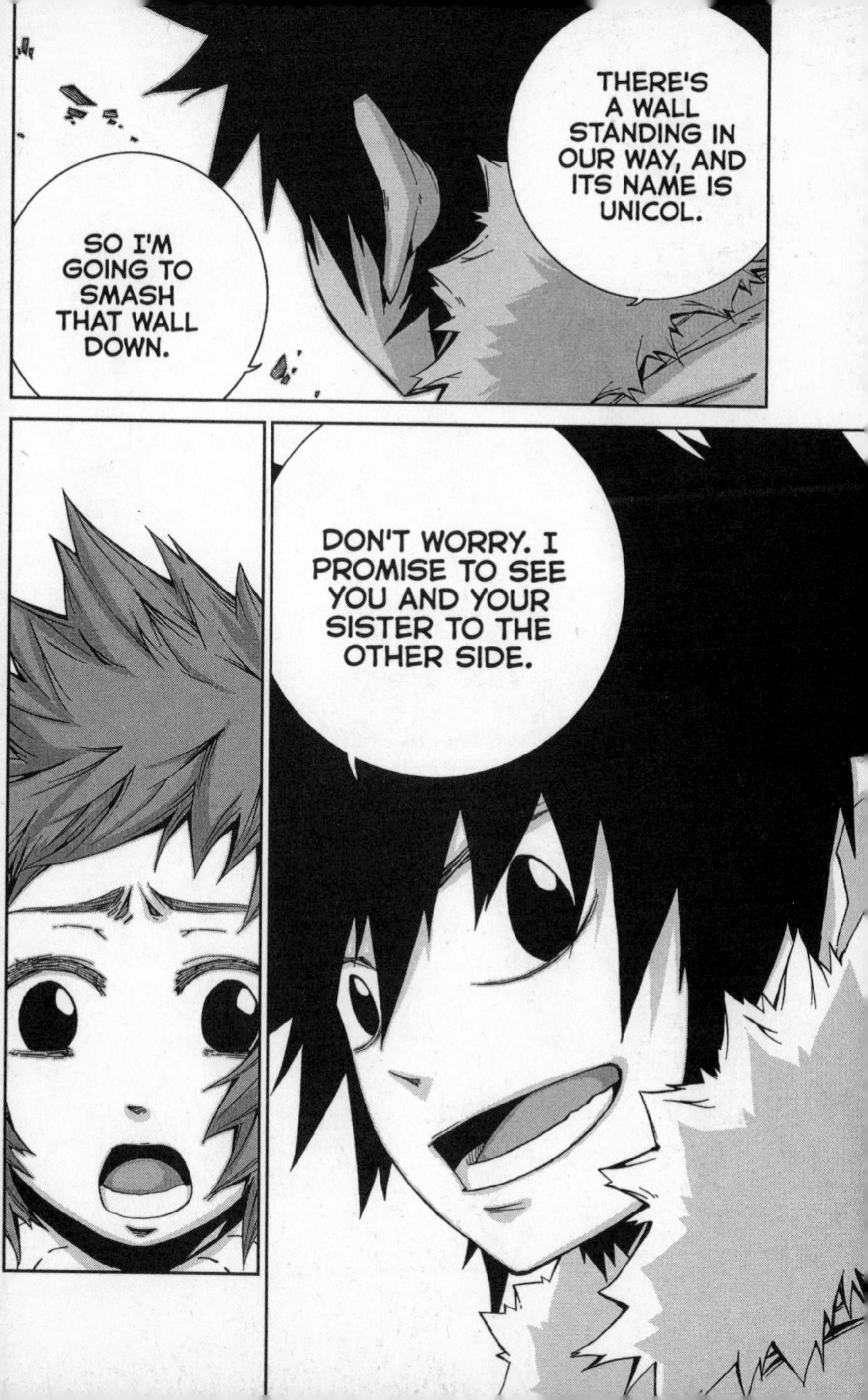
THERE'S A WALL STANDING IN OUR WAY, AND ITS NAME IS UNICOL.
SO I'M GOING TO SMASH THAT WALL DOWN.
DON'T WORRY. I PROMISE TO SEE YOU AND YOUR SISTER TO THE OTHER SIDE.

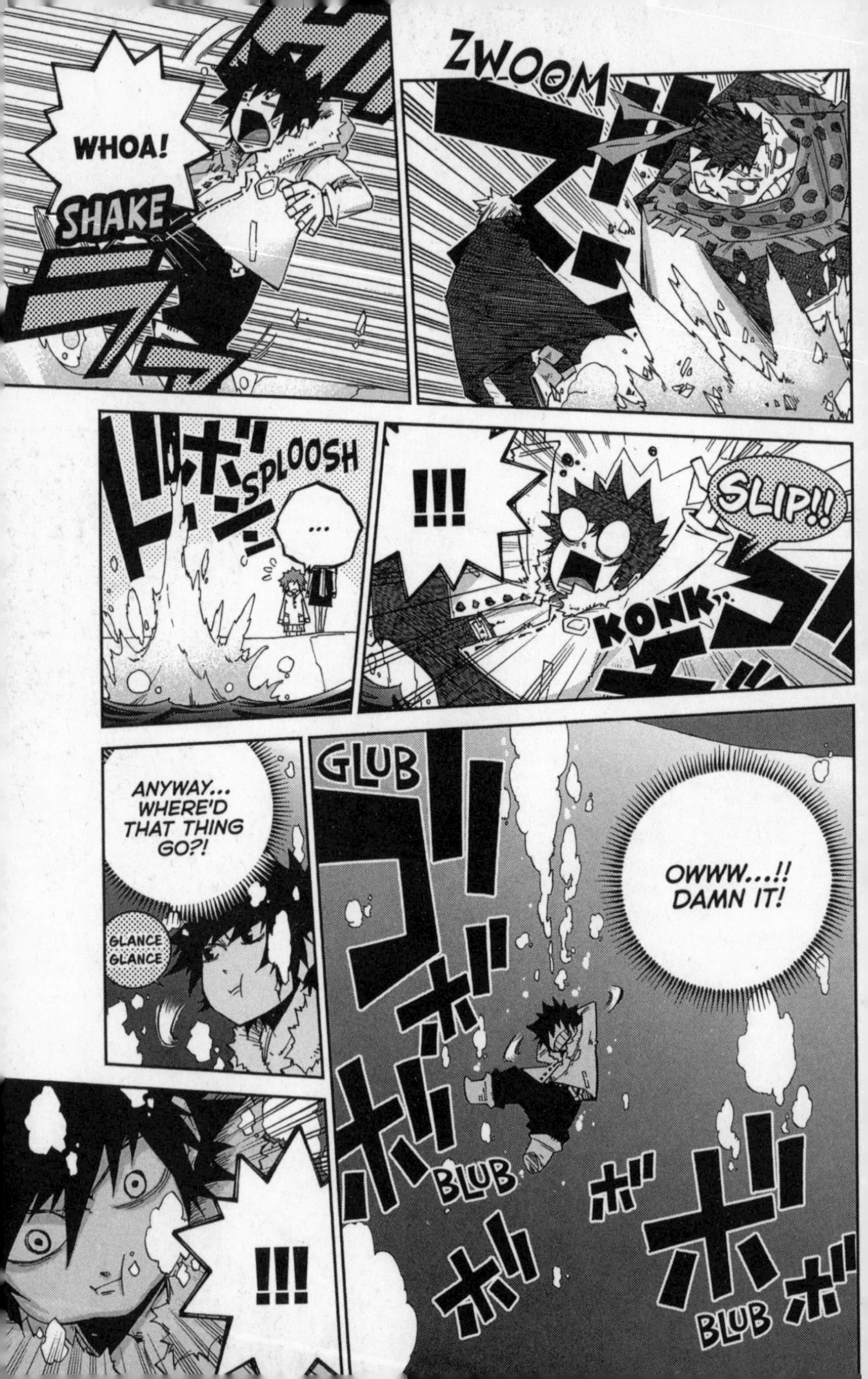
ZWOOM
WHOA!
SHAKE
SLIP!!
!!!
KONK
SPLOOSH
...
GLUB
OWWW...!! DAMN IT!
BLUB
BLUB
ANYWAY... WHERE'D THAT THING GO?!
GLANCE GLANCE
!!!

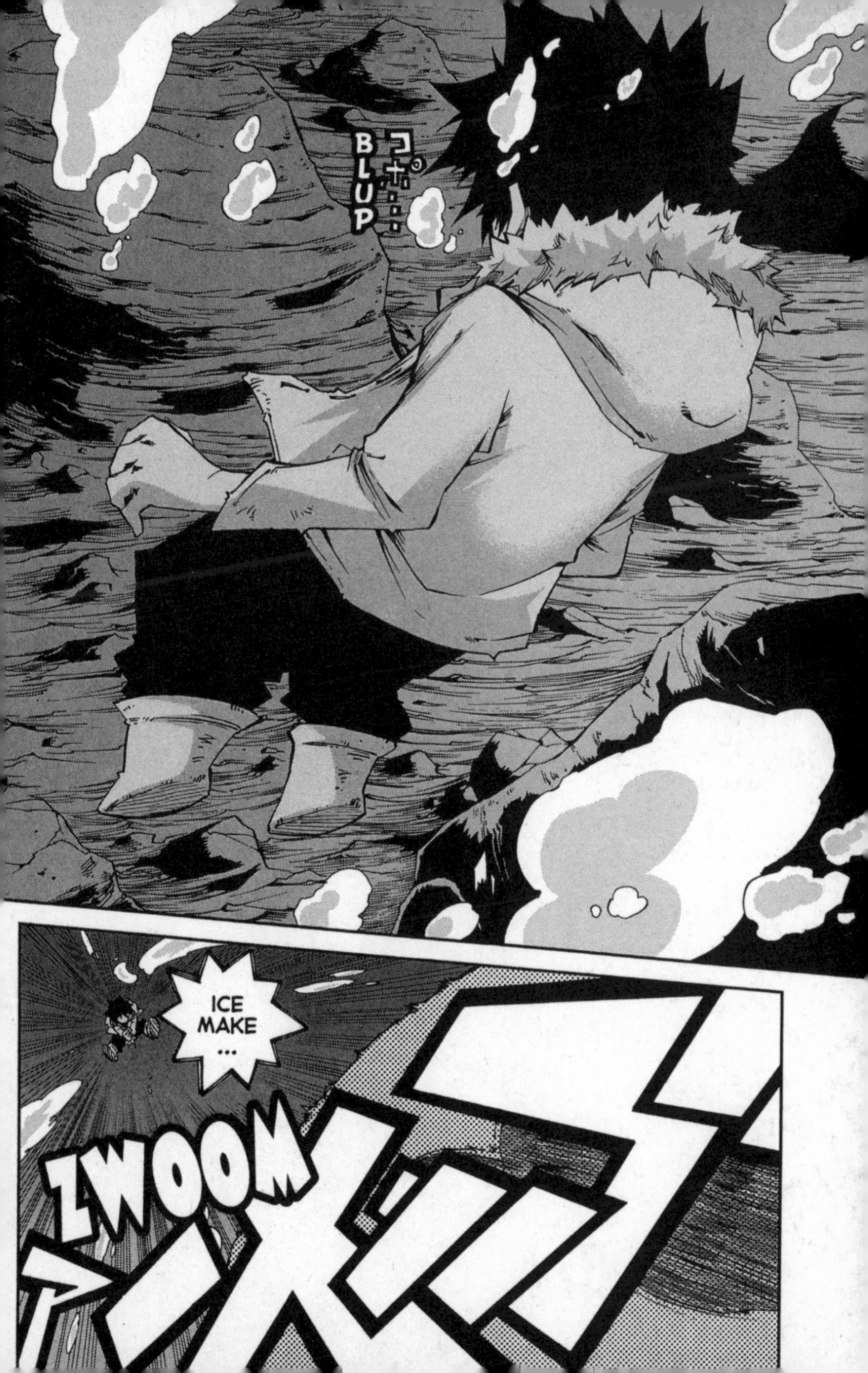
BLUP
ICE MAKE
...
ZWOOM

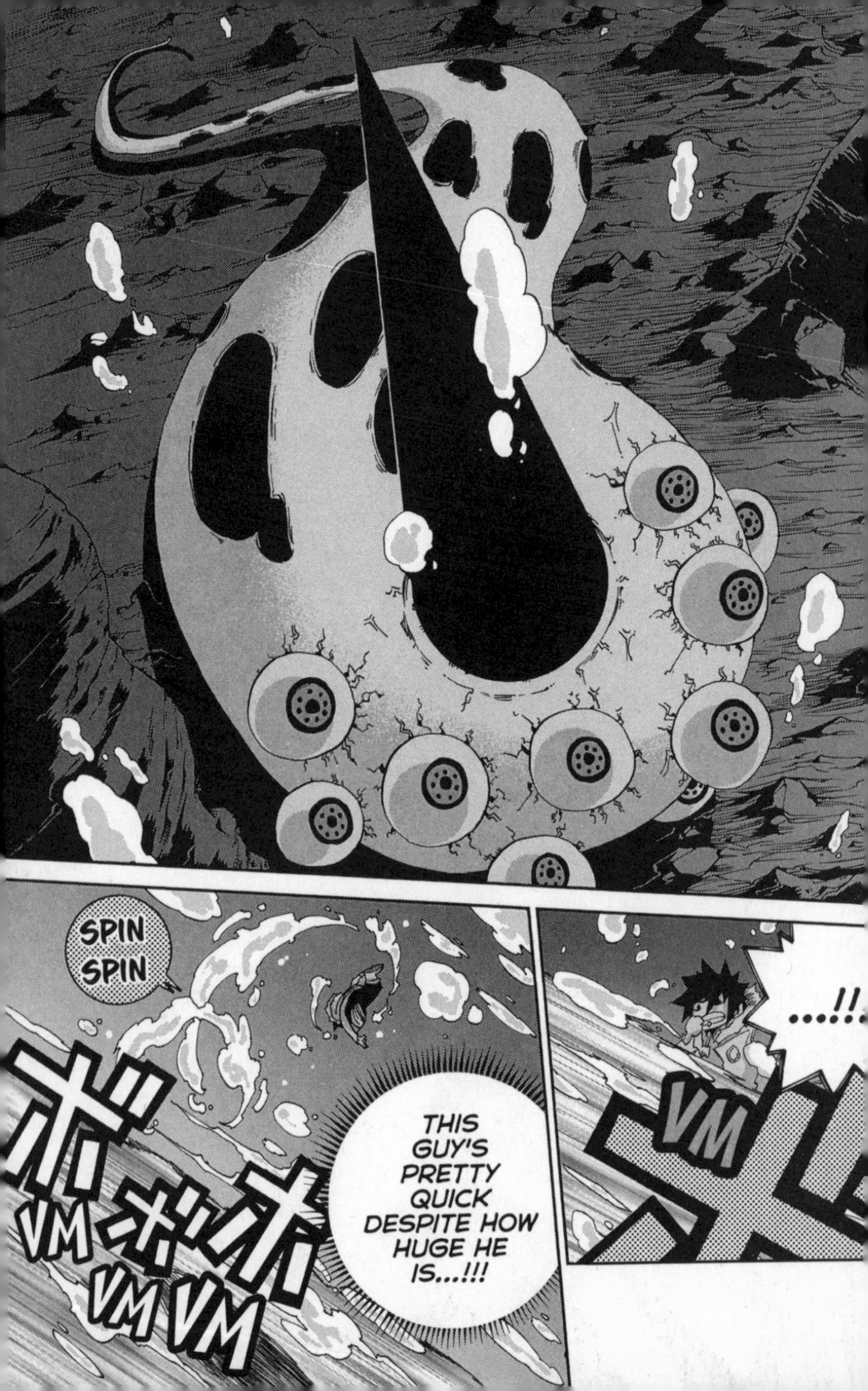
...!!
VM
SPIN SPIN
VM VM VM VM
THIS GUY'S PRETTY QUICK DESPITE HOW HUGE HE IS...!!!

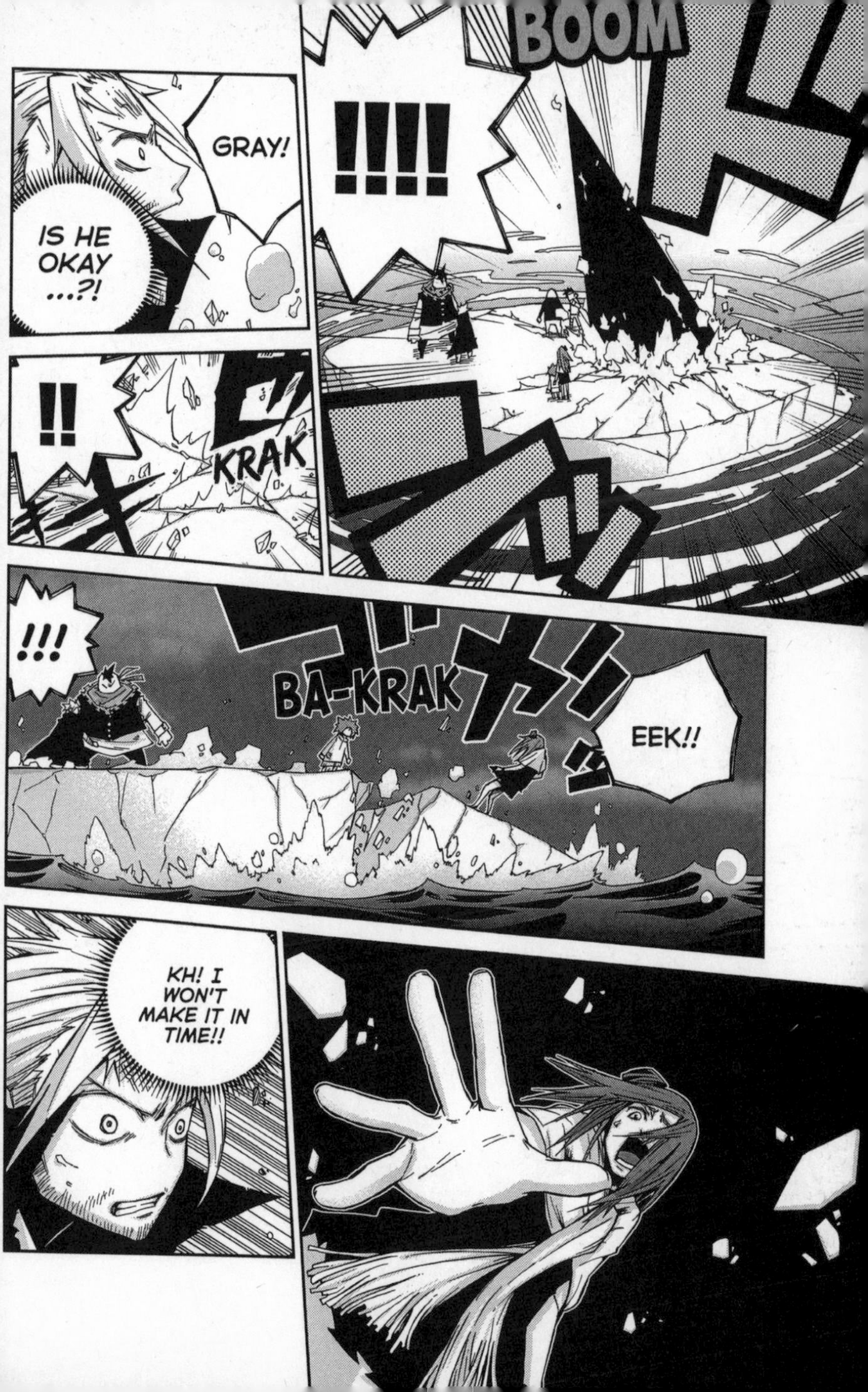
BOOM
!!!!
GRAY!
IS HE OKAY ...?!
!!
KRAK
EEK!!
BA-KRAK
!!!
KH! I WON'T MAKE IT IN TIME!!

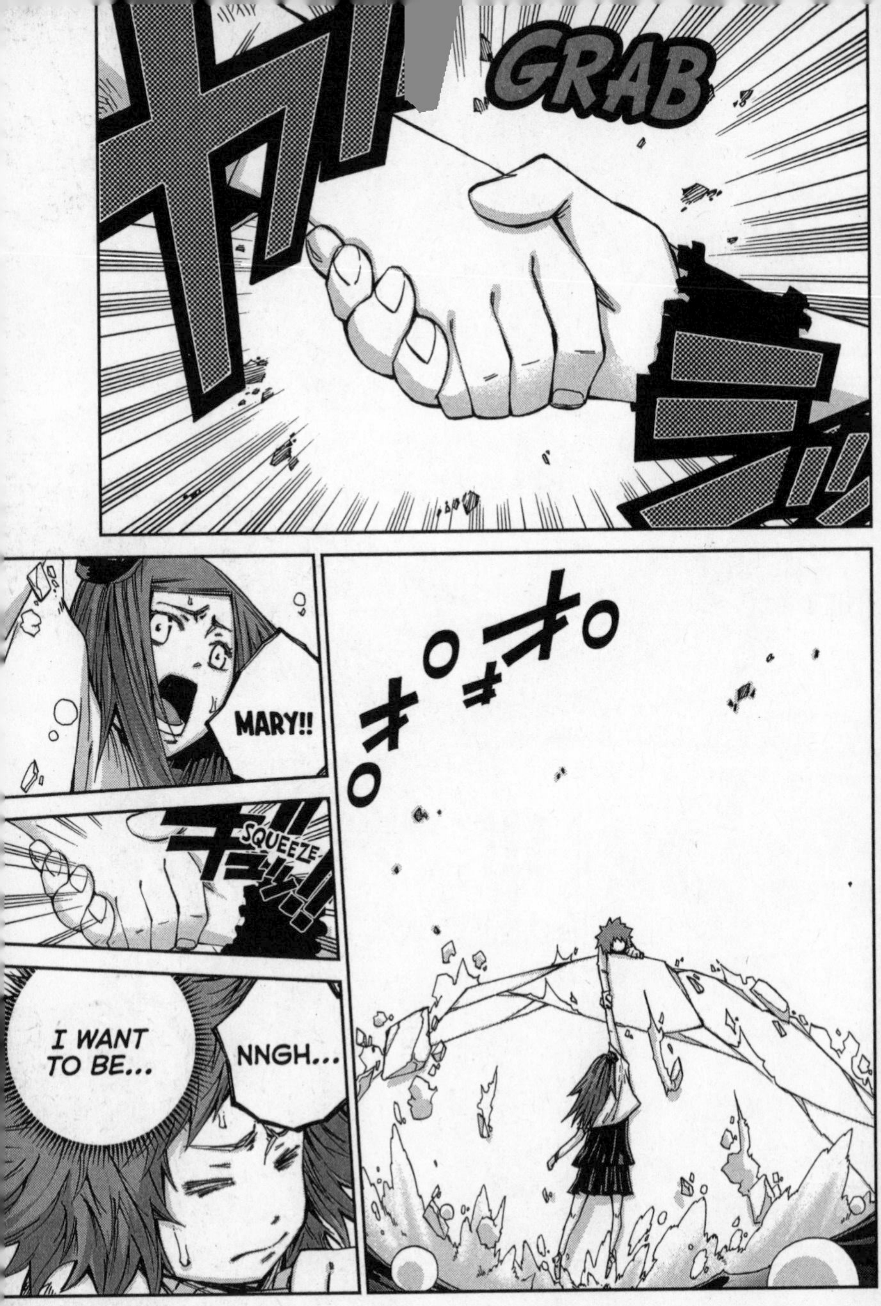
GRAB
MARY!!
SQUEEZE
NNGH...
I WANT TO BE...

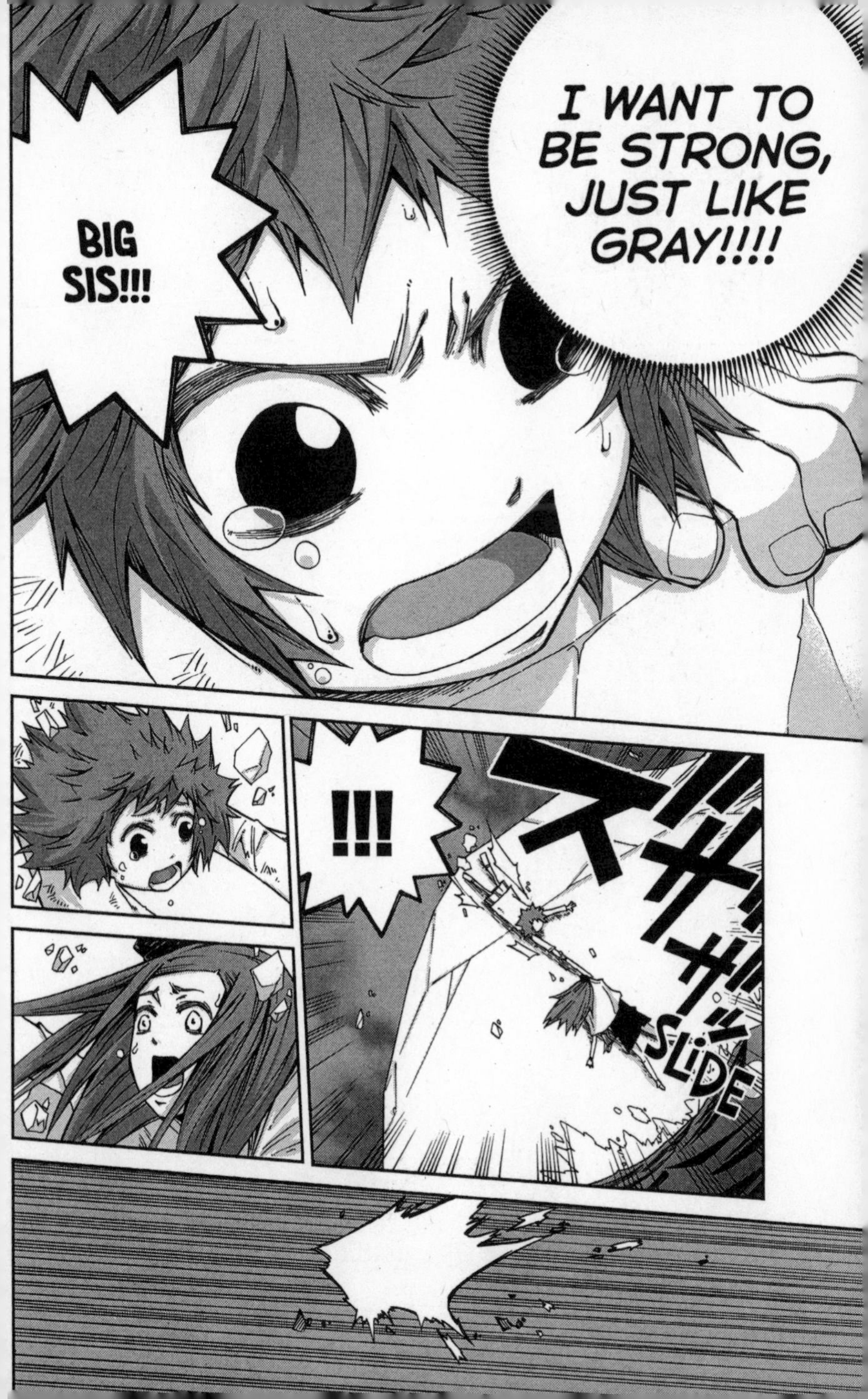
I WANT TO BE STRONG, JUST LIKE GRAY!!!!
BIG SIS!!!
!!!
SLIDE

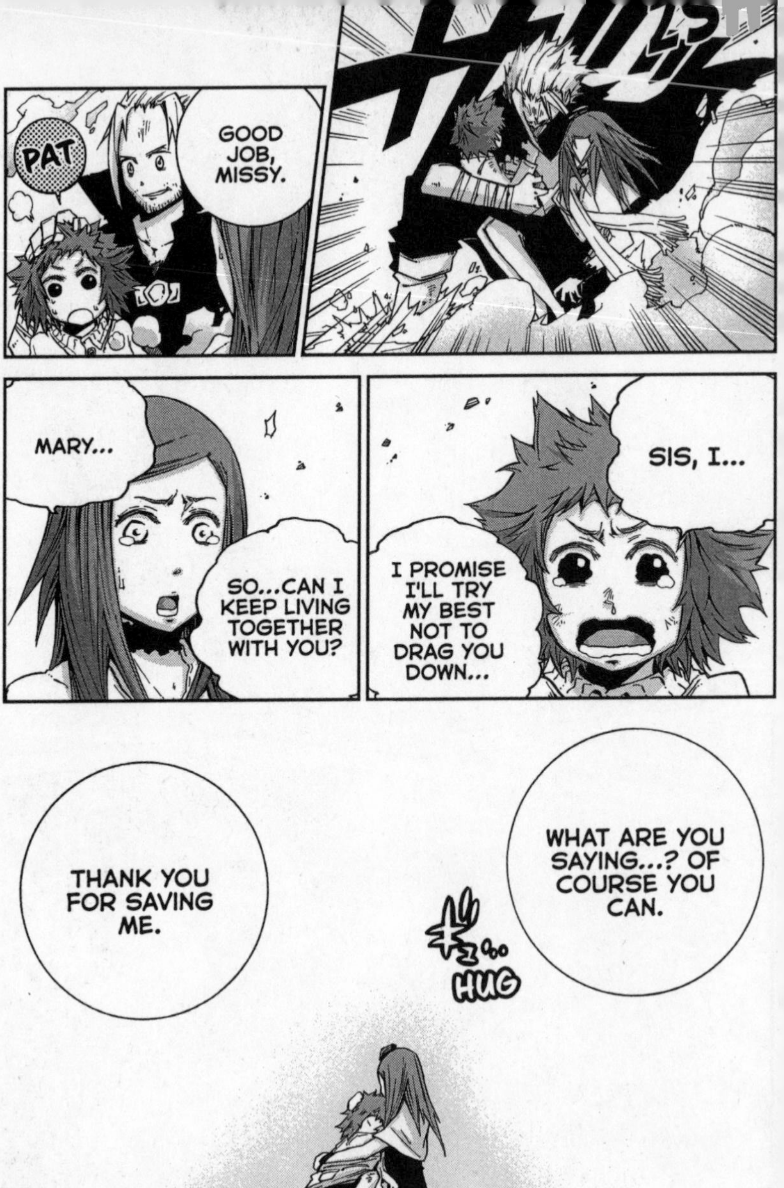
GOOD JOB, MISSY.
PAT
SIS, I...
I PROMISE I'LL TRY MY BEST NOT TO DRAG YOU DOWN...
MARY...
SO...CAN I KEEP LIVING TOGETHER WITH YOU?
WHAT ARE YOU SAYING...? OF COURSE YOU CAN.
HUG
THANK YOU FOR SAVING ME.

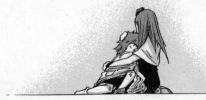

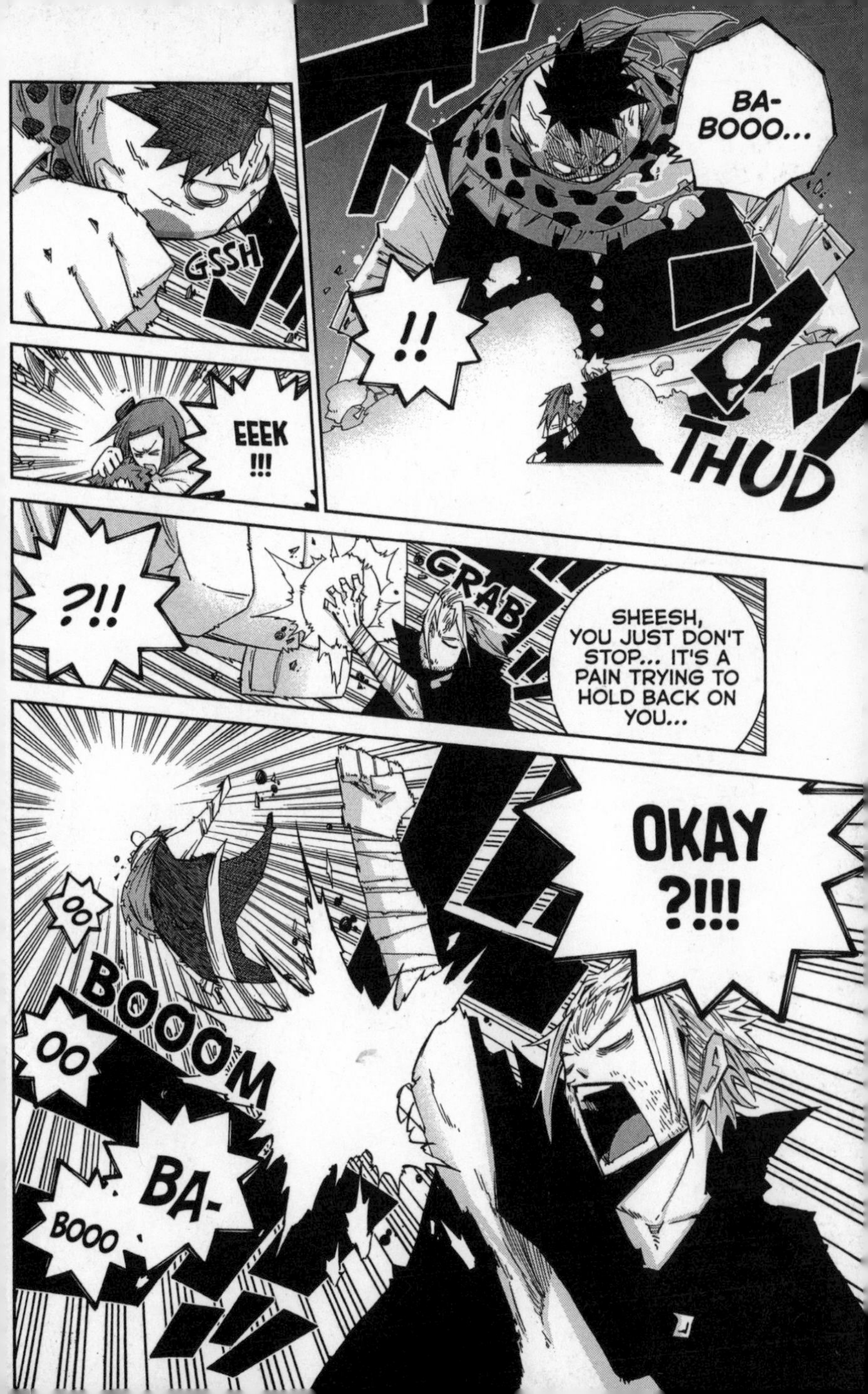
BA-BOOO...
!!
THUD
GSSH
EEEK!!!
SHEESH, YOU JUST DON'T STOP... IT'S A PAIN TRYING TO HOLD BACK ON YOU...
GRAB
?!!
OKAY?!!!
BOOOOOOM
BA-BOOO

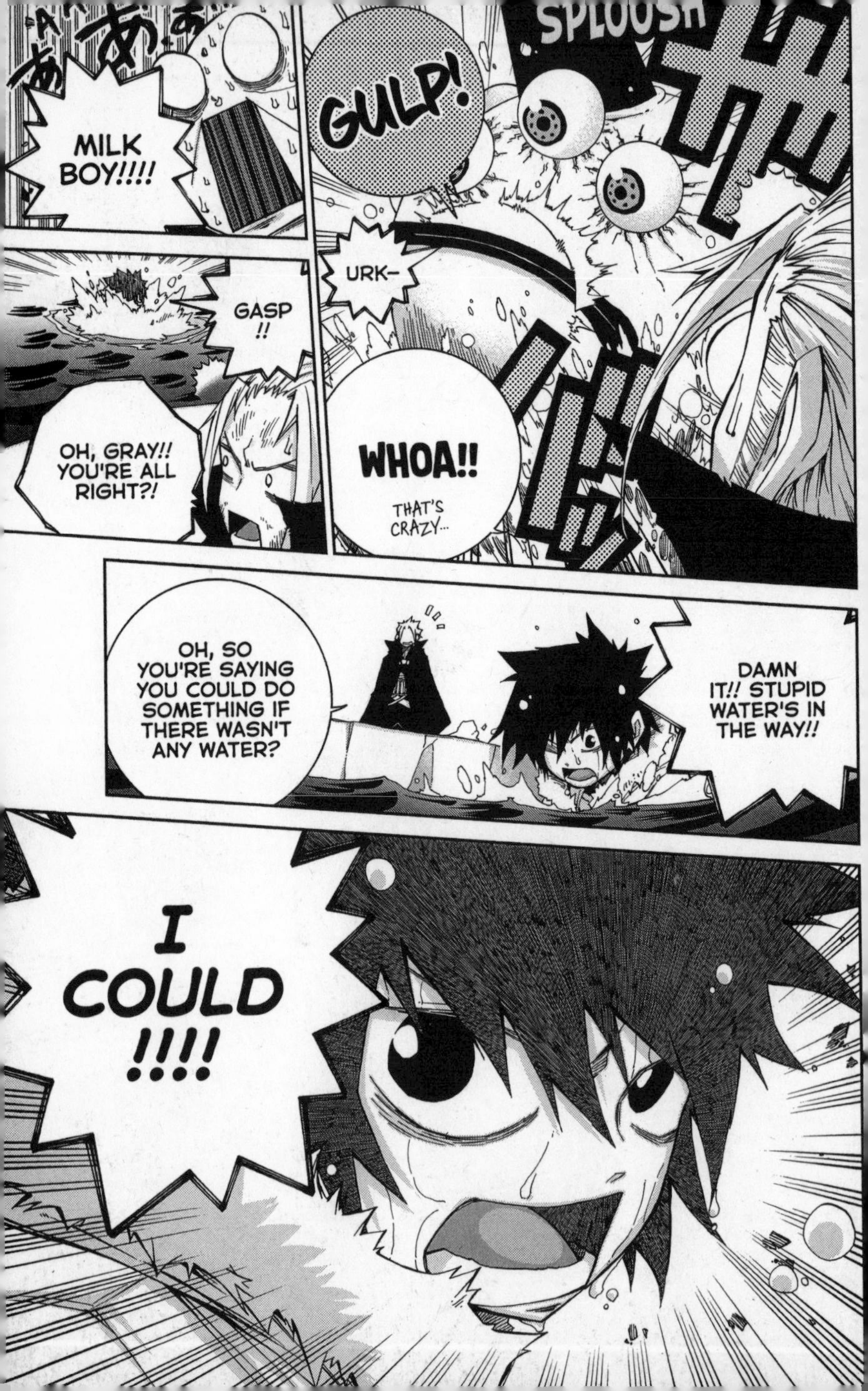
SPLOOSH
GULP!
URK–
WHOA!!
THAT'S CRAZY...
A
あ あ あ
MILK BOY!!!!
GASP !!
OH, GRAY!! YOU'RE ALL RIGHT?!
DAMN IT!! STUPID WATER'S IN THE WAY!!
OH, SO YOU'RE SAYING YOU COULD DO SOMETHING IF THERE WASN'T ANY WATER?
I COULD !!!!

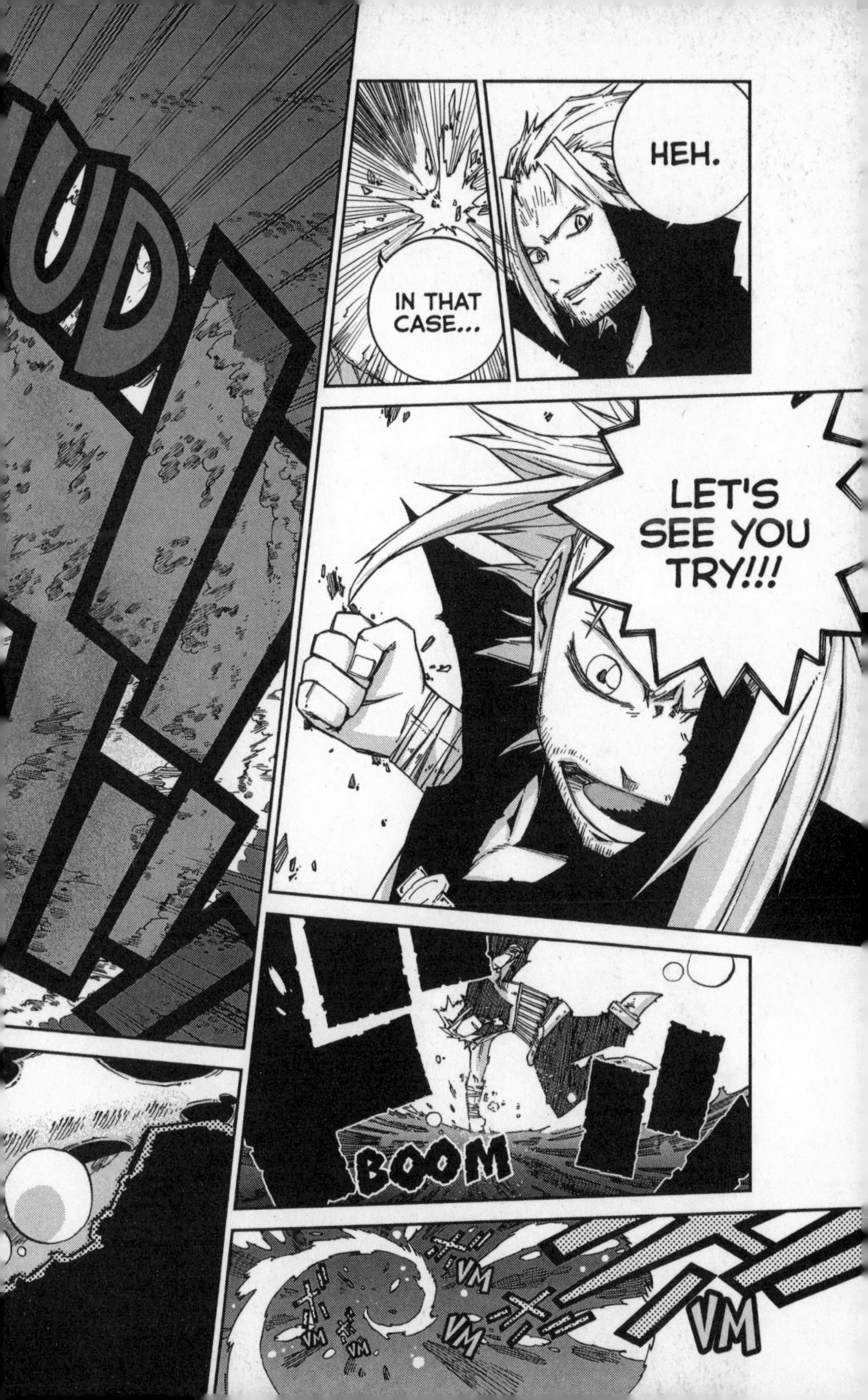
HEH.
IN THAT CASE...
LET'S SEE YOU TRY!!!
BOOM
UD
VM
VM
VM
VM
VM

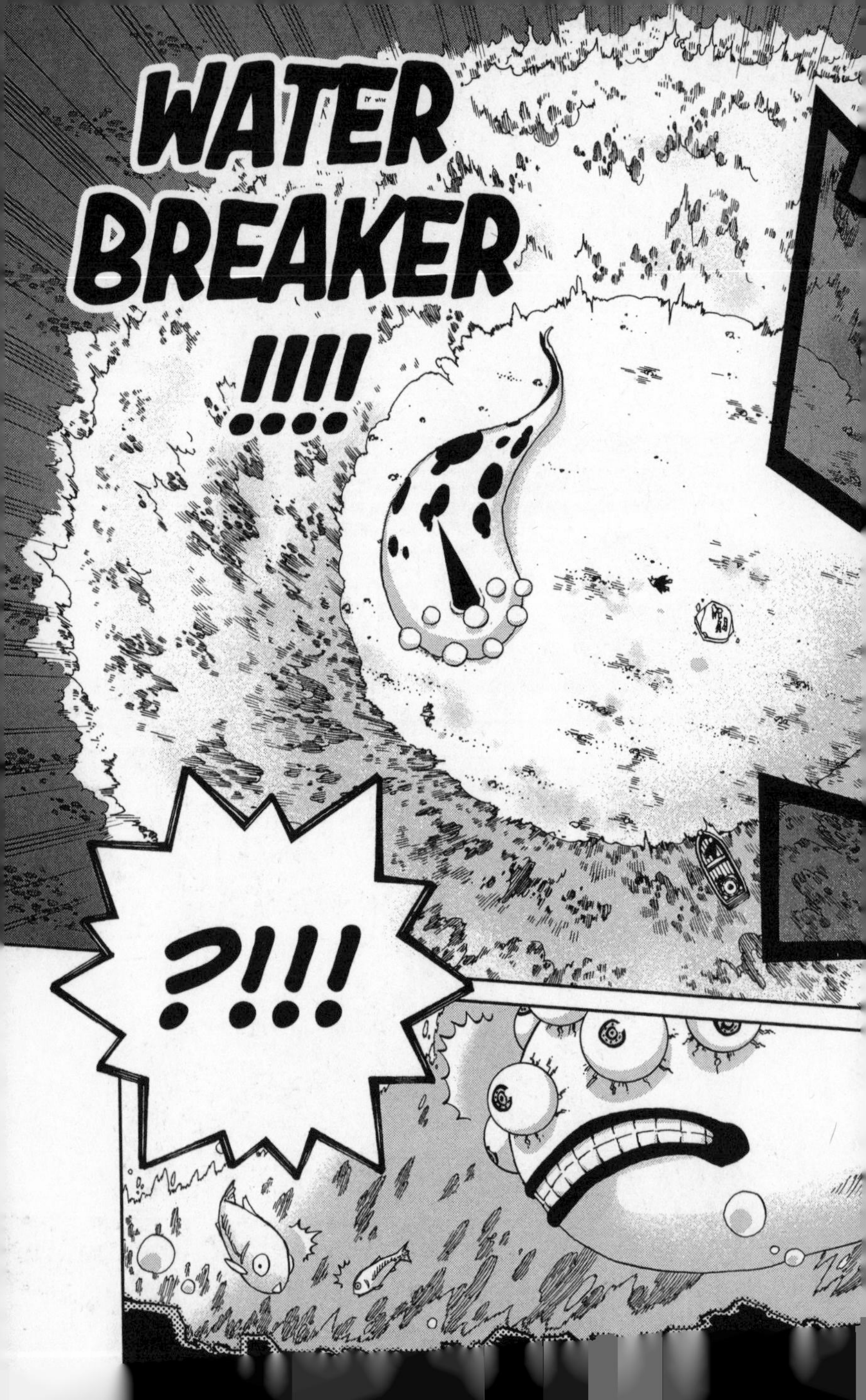
WATER BREAKER !!!!
?!!!

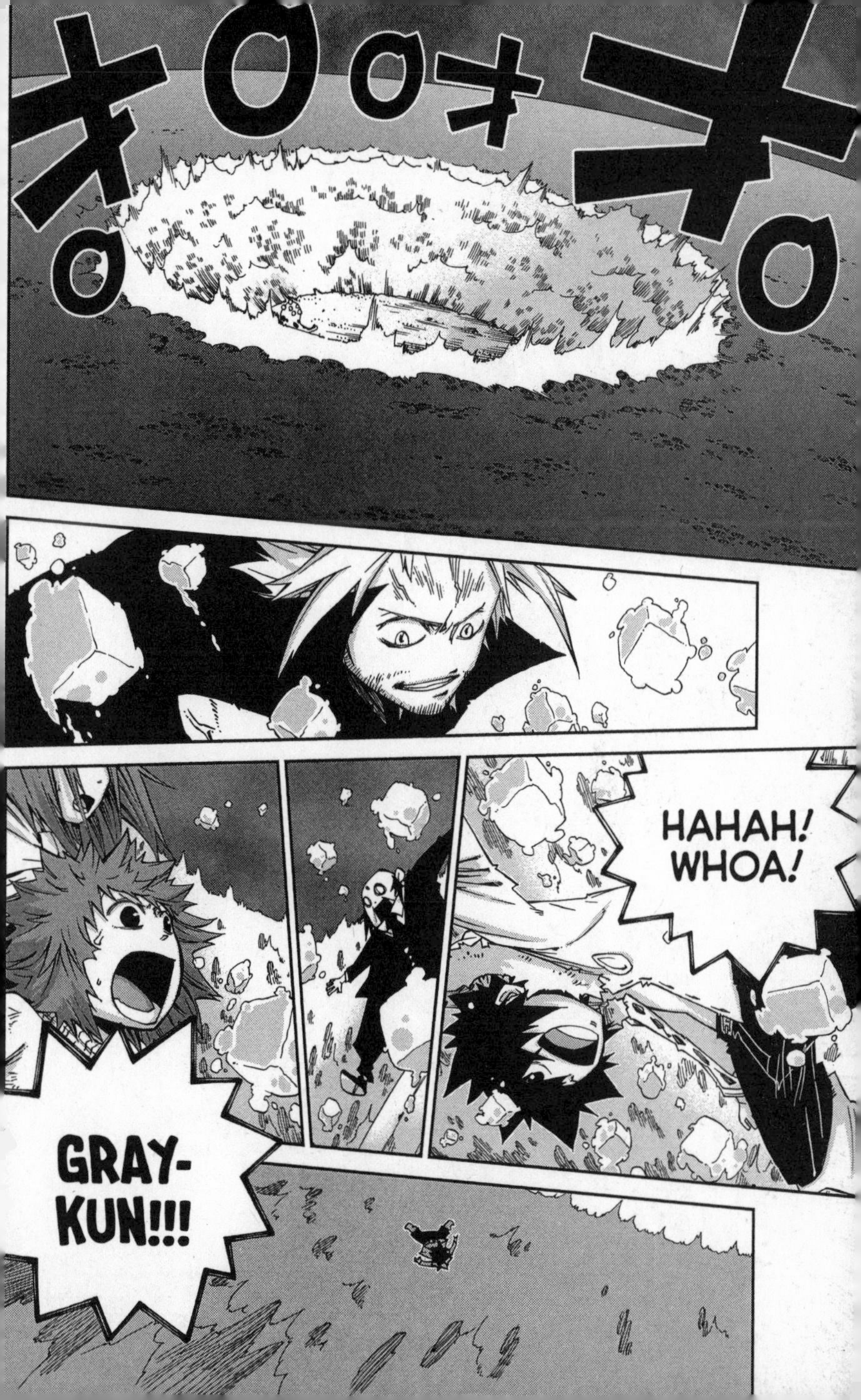
HAHAH! WHOA!
GRAY-KUN!!!

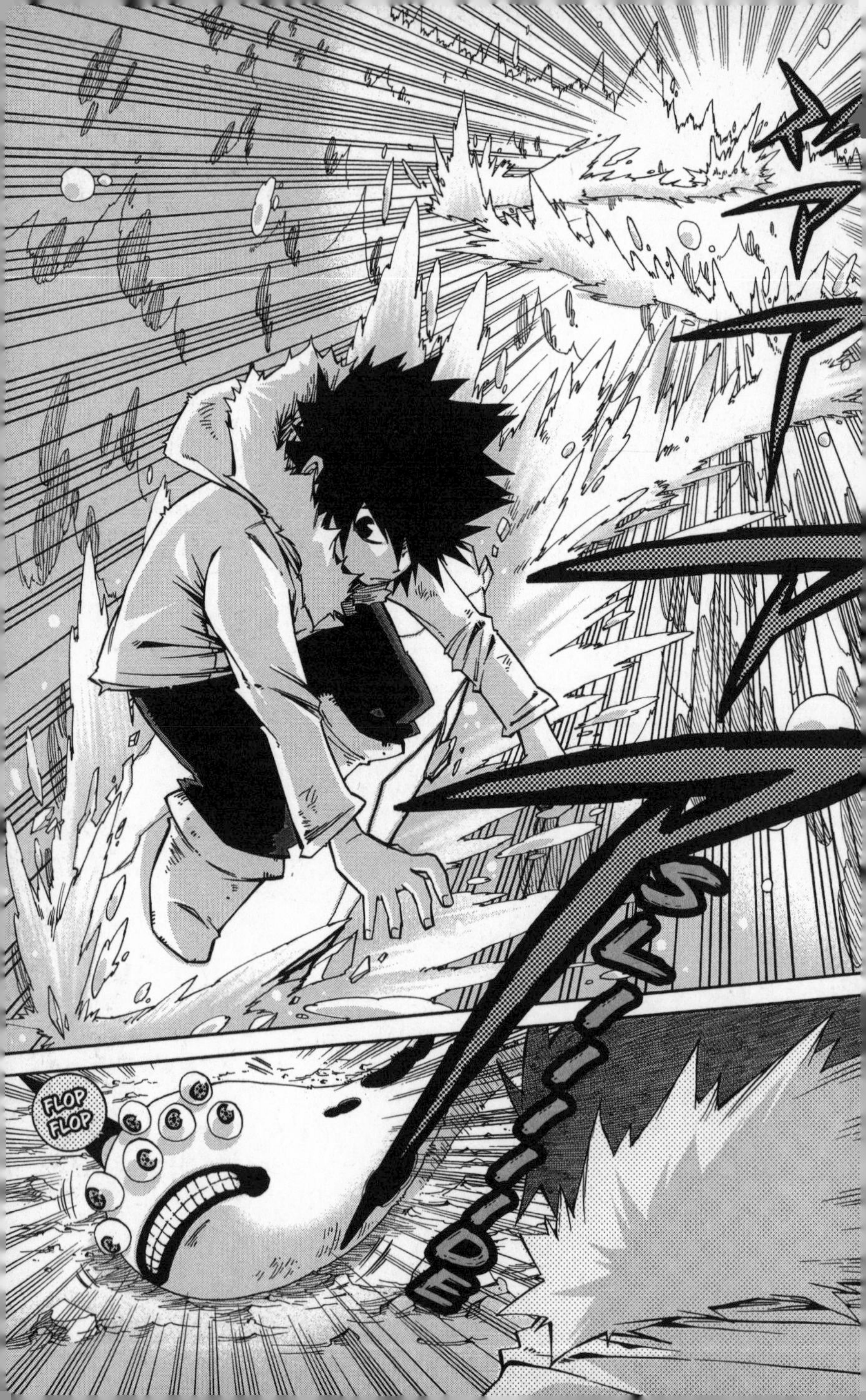
SLIIIIIDE
FLOP FLOP

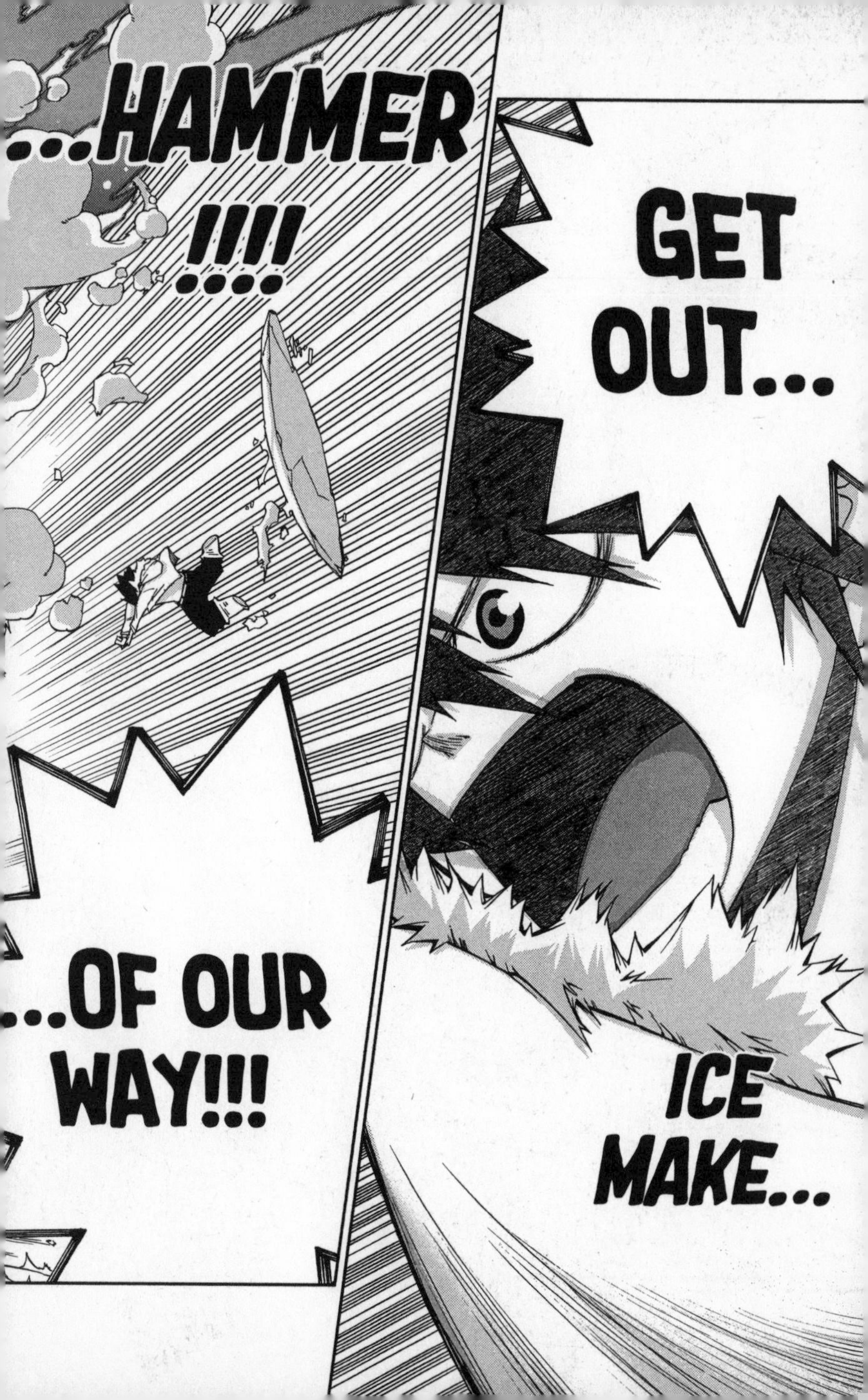
GET OUT...
ICE MAKE...
...HAMMER !!!!
...OF OUR WAY!!!

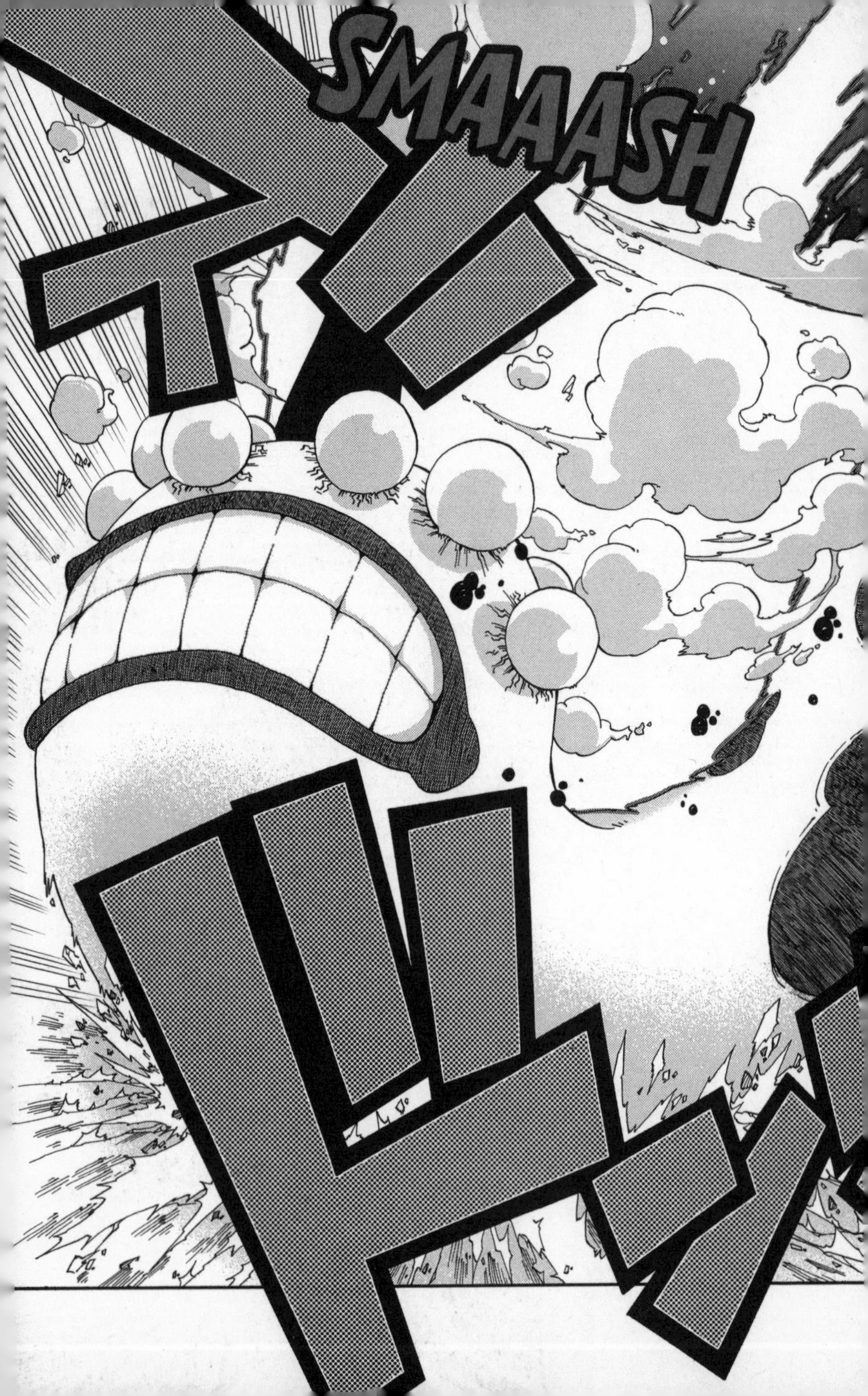
SMAAASH

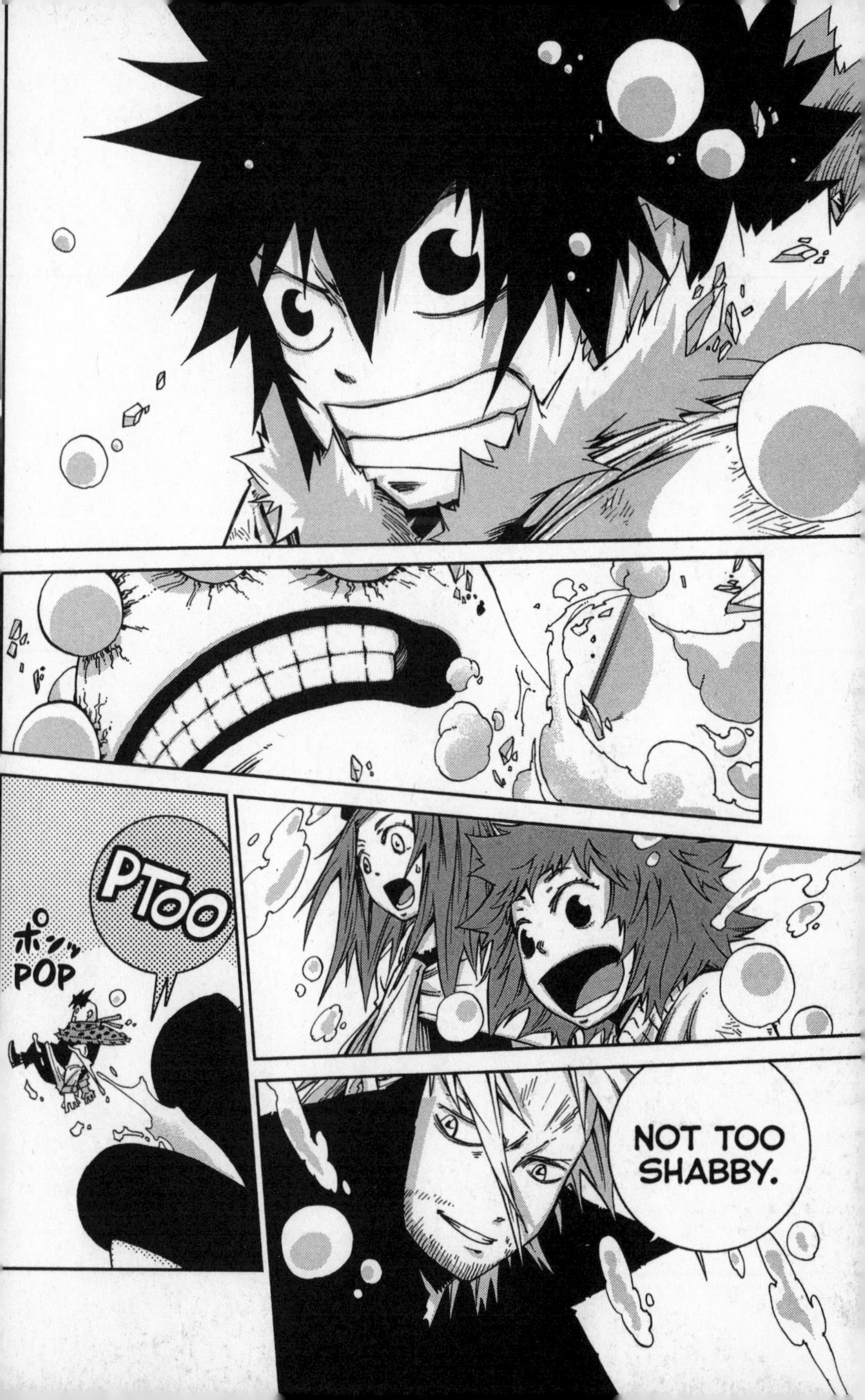
PTOO
ポンッ
POP
NOT TOO SHABBY.

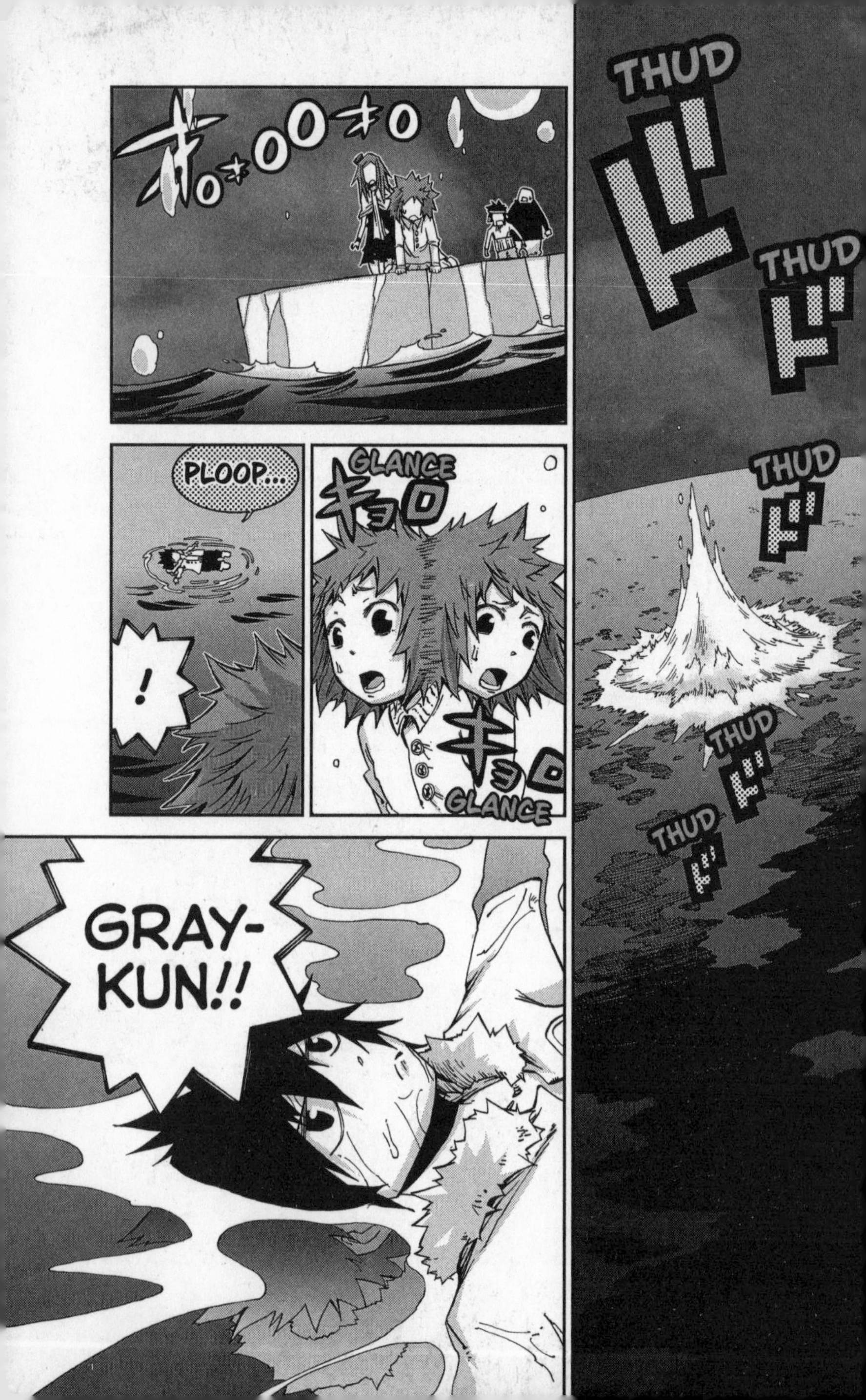
THUD
THUD
THUD
THUD
THUD
GLANCE
GLANCE
PLOOP...
!
GRAY-KUN!!

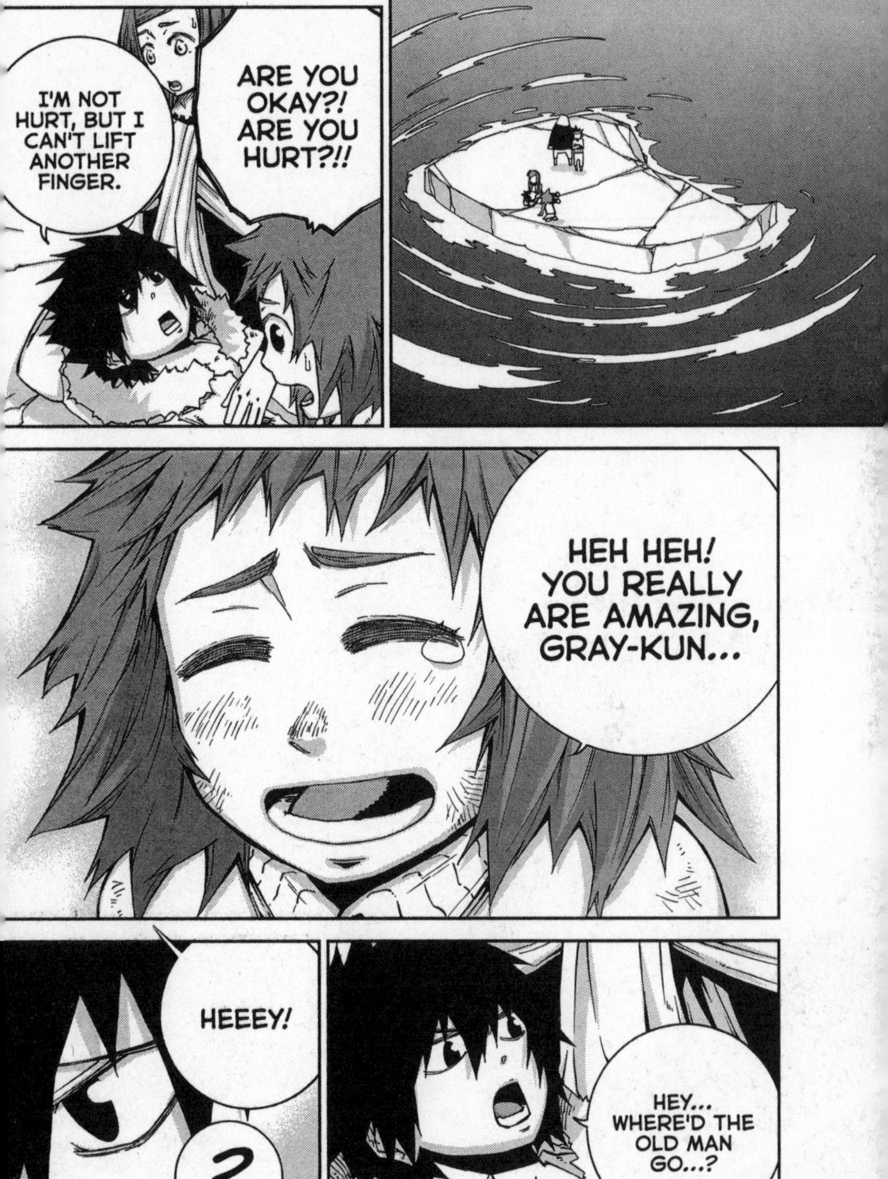
ARE YOU OKAY?! ARE YOU HURT?!!
I'M NOT HURT, BUT I CAN'T LIFT ANOTHER FINGER.
HEH HEH! YOU REALLY ARE AMAZING, GRAY-KUN...
HEY... WHERE'D THE OLD MAN GO...?
HEEEY!
?

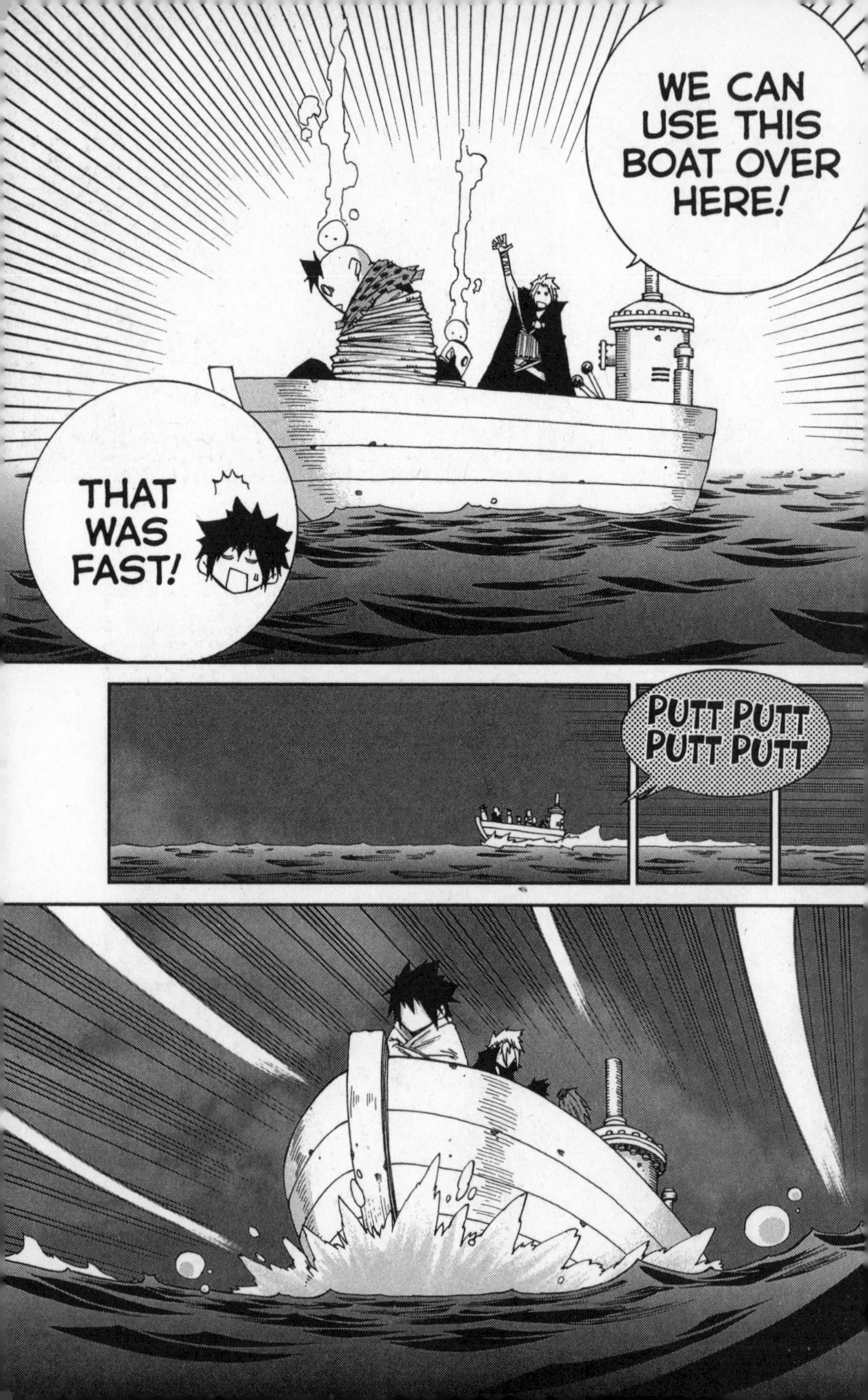
WE CAN USE THIS BOAT OVER HERE!
THAT WAS FAST!
PUTT PUTT PUTT PUTT

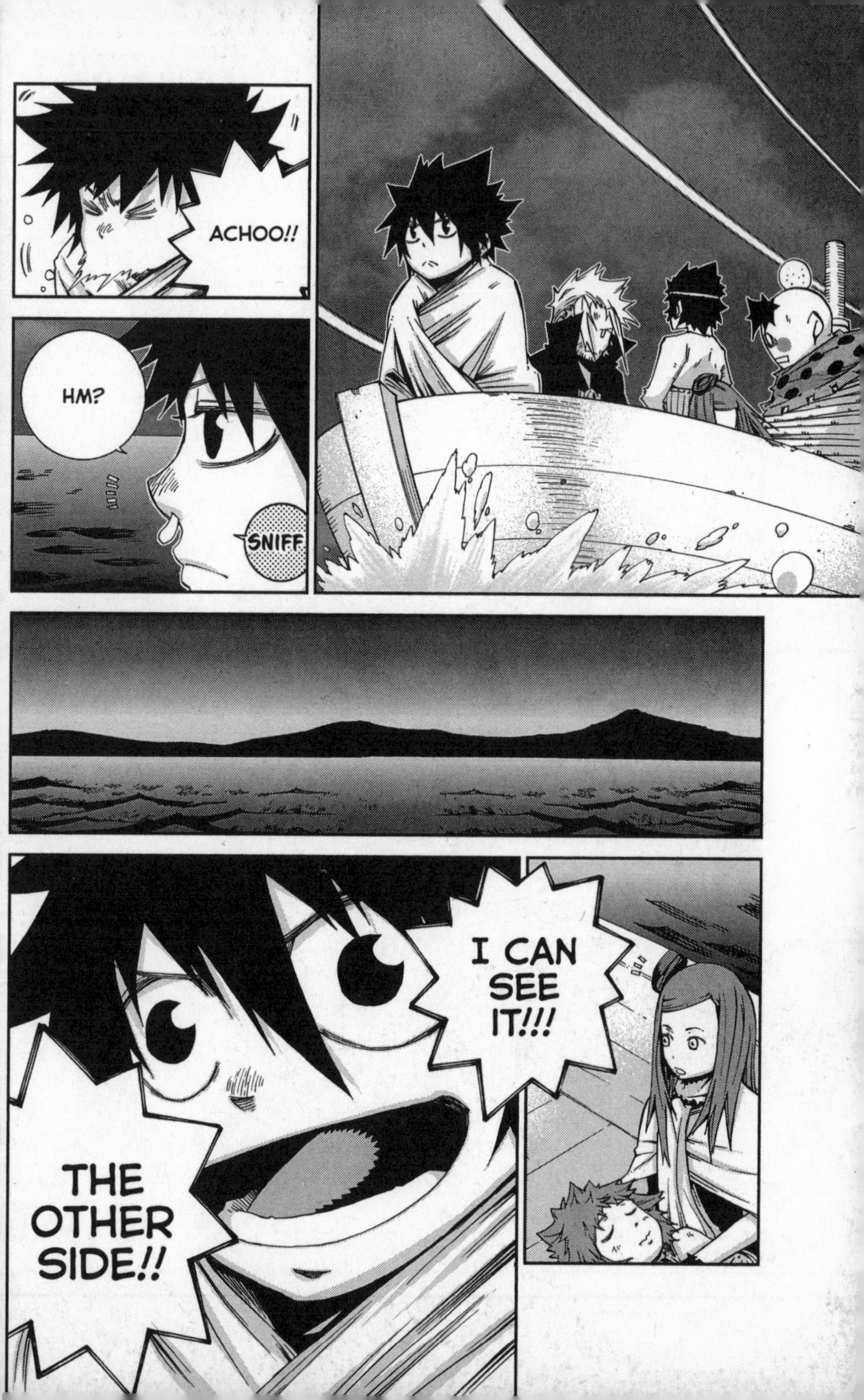
ACHOO!!
HM?
SNIFF
I CAN SEE IT!!!
THE OTHER SIDE!!

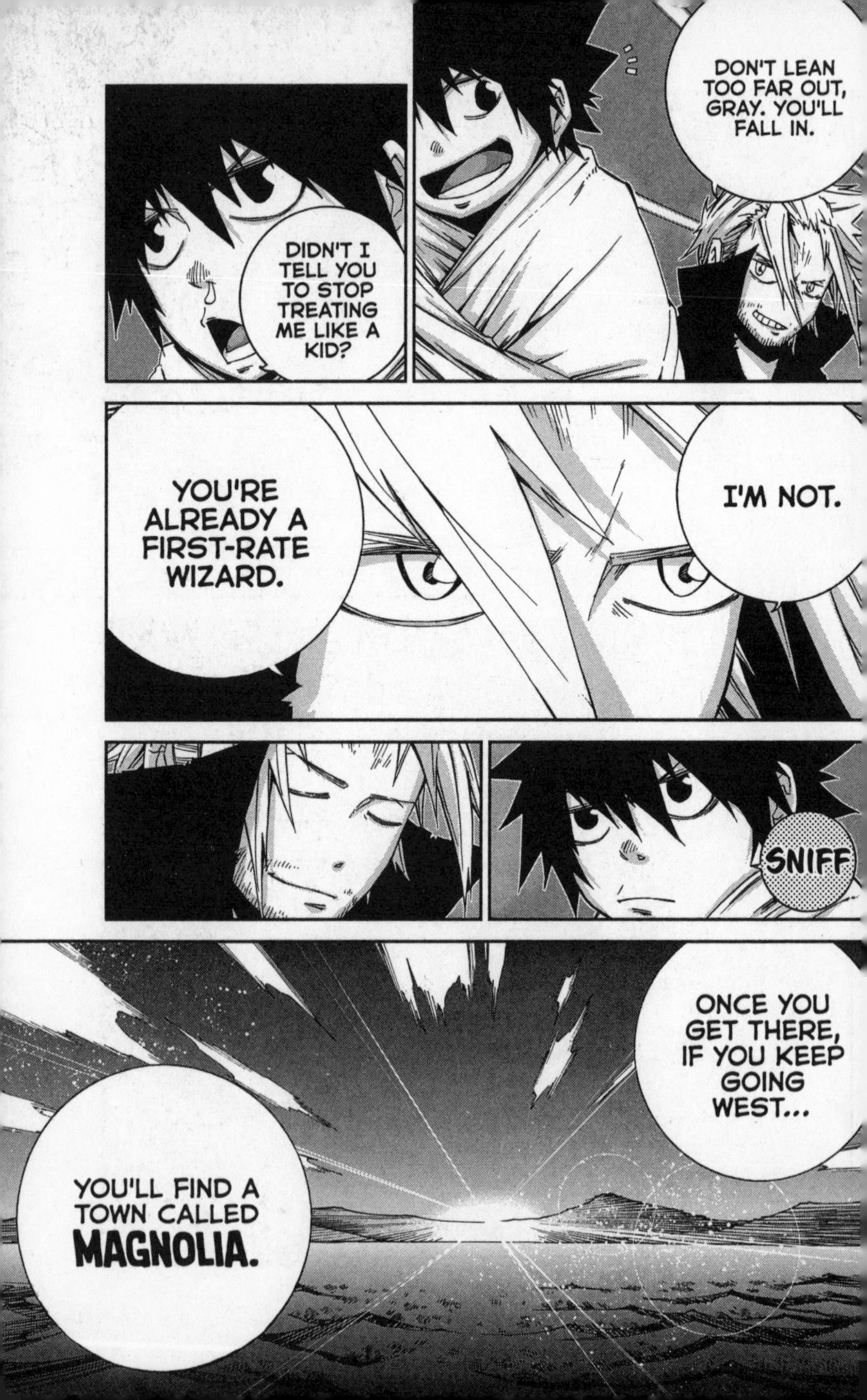
DON'T LEAN TOO FAR OUT, GRAY. YOU'LL FALL IN.
DIDN'T I TELL YOU TO STOP TREATING ME LIKE A KID?
I'M NOT.
YOU'RE ALREADY A FIRST-RATE WIZARD.
SNIFF
ONCE YOU GET THERE, IF YOU KEEP GOING WEST...
YOU'LL FIND A TOWN CALLED MAGNOLIA.

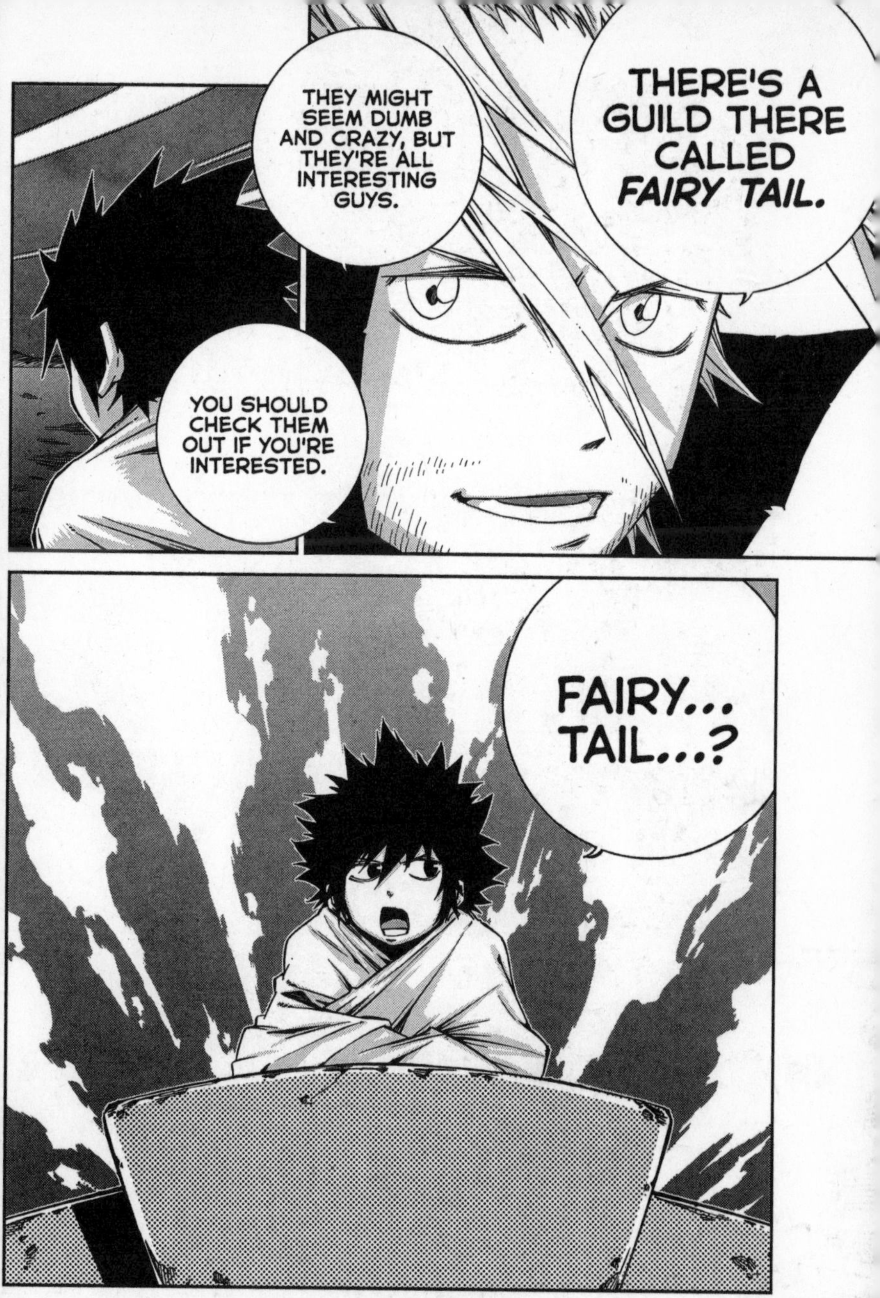
THERE'S A GUILD THERE CALLED *FAIRY TAIL.*
THEY MIGHT SEEM DUMB AND CRAZY, BUT THEY'RE ALL INTERESTING GUYS.
YOU SHOULD CHECK THEM OUT IF YOU'RE INTERESTED.
FAIRY... TAIL...?

TO BE CONTINUED

FAIRY TAIL: ICE TRAIL

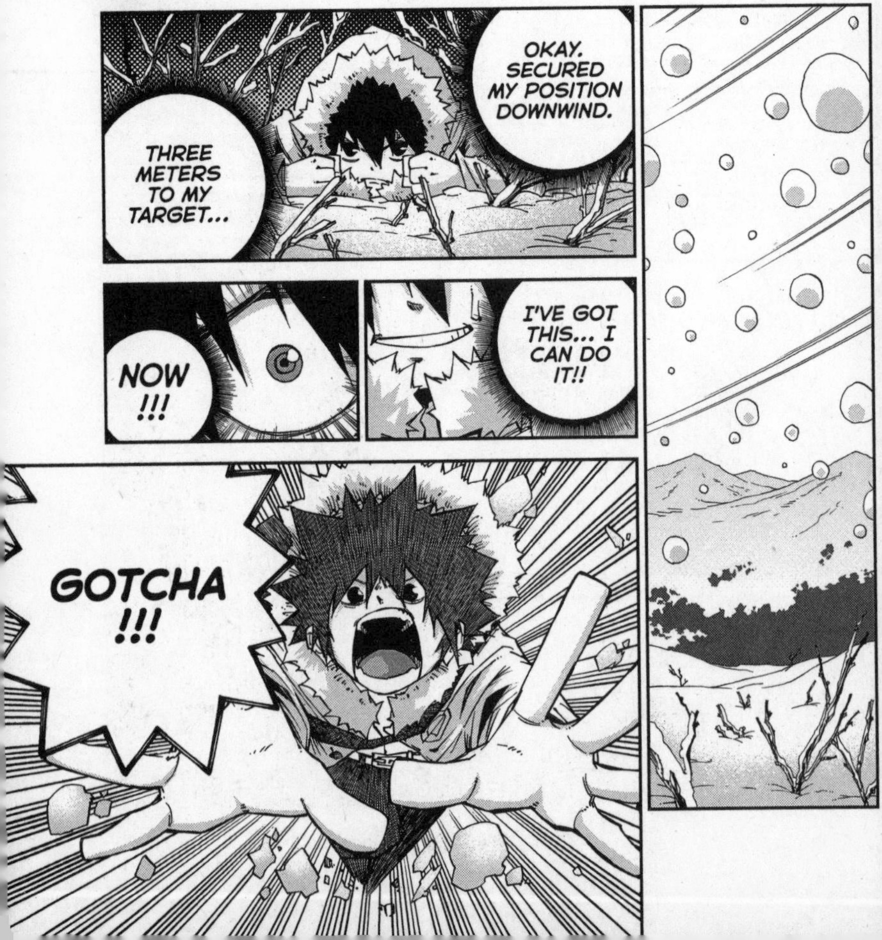
OKAY. SECURED MY POSITION DOWNWIND.
THREE METERS TO MY TARGET...
I'VE GOT THIS... I CAN DO IT!!
NOW !!!
GOTCHA !!!

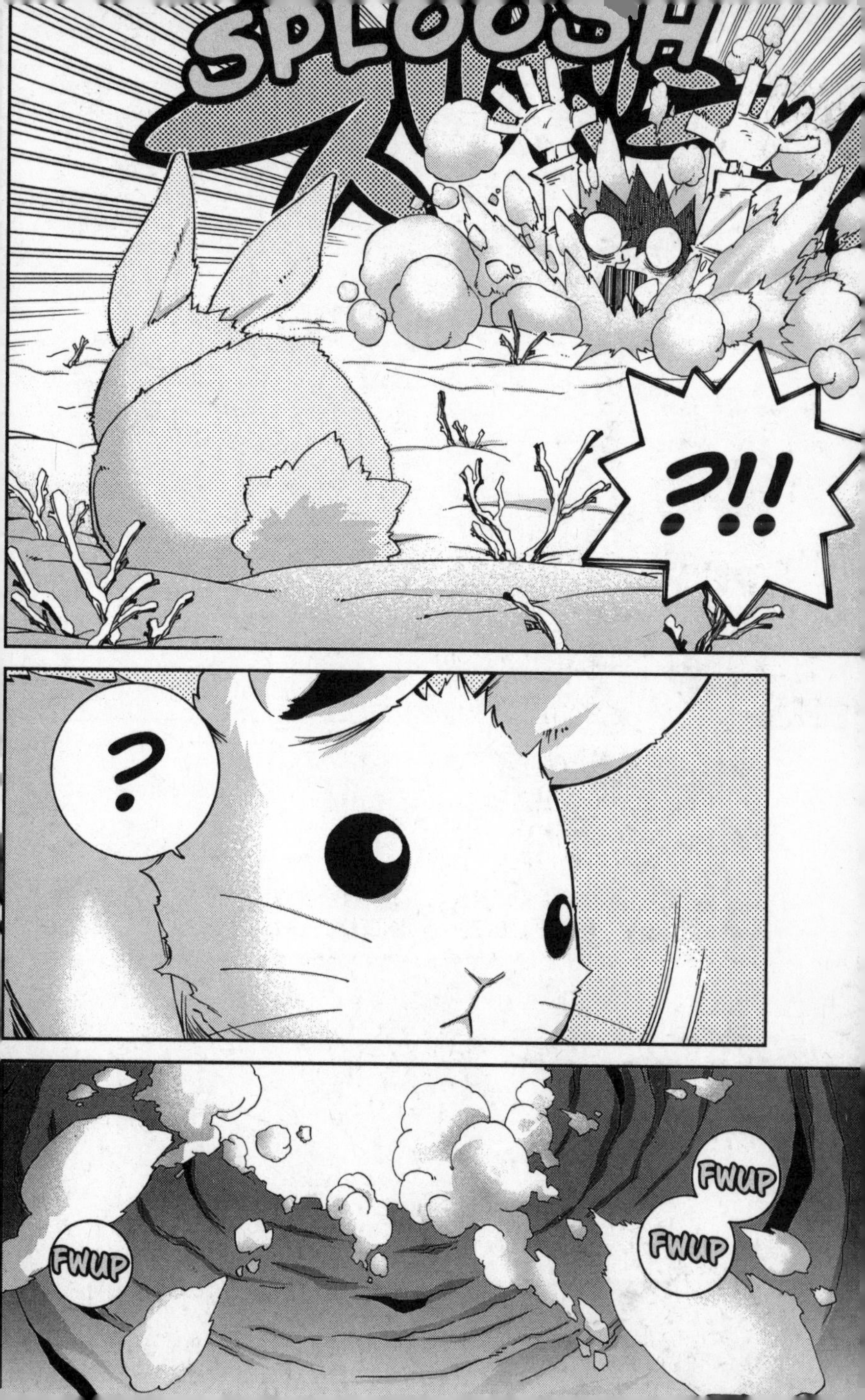
SPLOOSH
?!!
?
FWUP
FWUP
FWUP

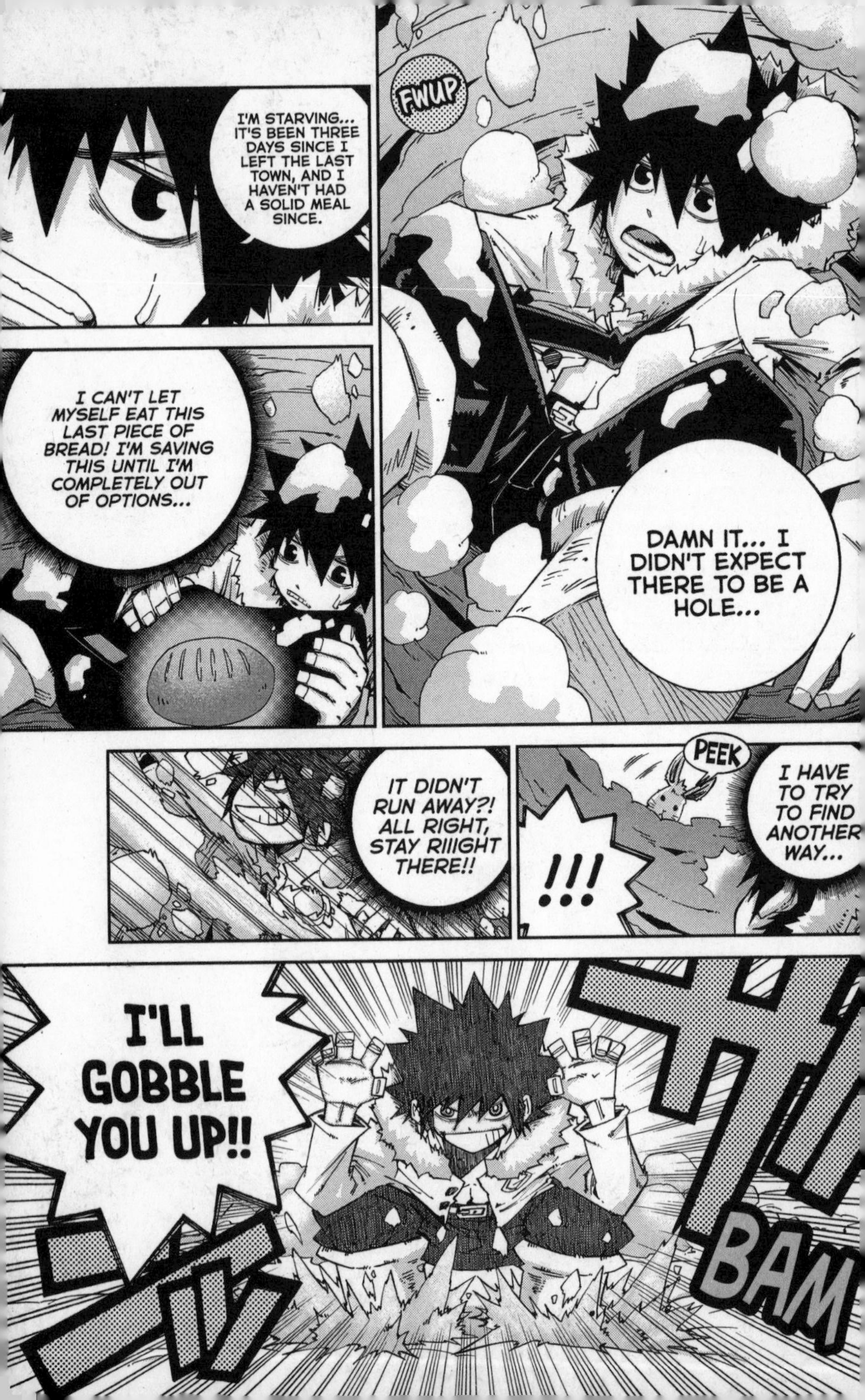
FWUP
DAMN IT... I DIDN'T EXPECT THERE TO BE A HOLE...
I'M STARVING... IT'S BEEN THREE DAYS SINCE I LEFT THE LAST TOWN, AND I HAVEN'T HAD A SOLID MEAL SINCE.
I CAN'T LET MYSELF EAT THIS LAST PIECE OF BREAD! I'M SAVING THIS UNTIL I'M COMPLETELY OUT OF OPTIONS...
I HAVE TO TRY TO FIND ANOTHER WAY...
PEEK
!!!
IT DIDN'T RUN AWAY?! ALL RIGHT, STAY RIIIGHT THERE!!
I'LL GOBBLE YOU UP!!
BAM

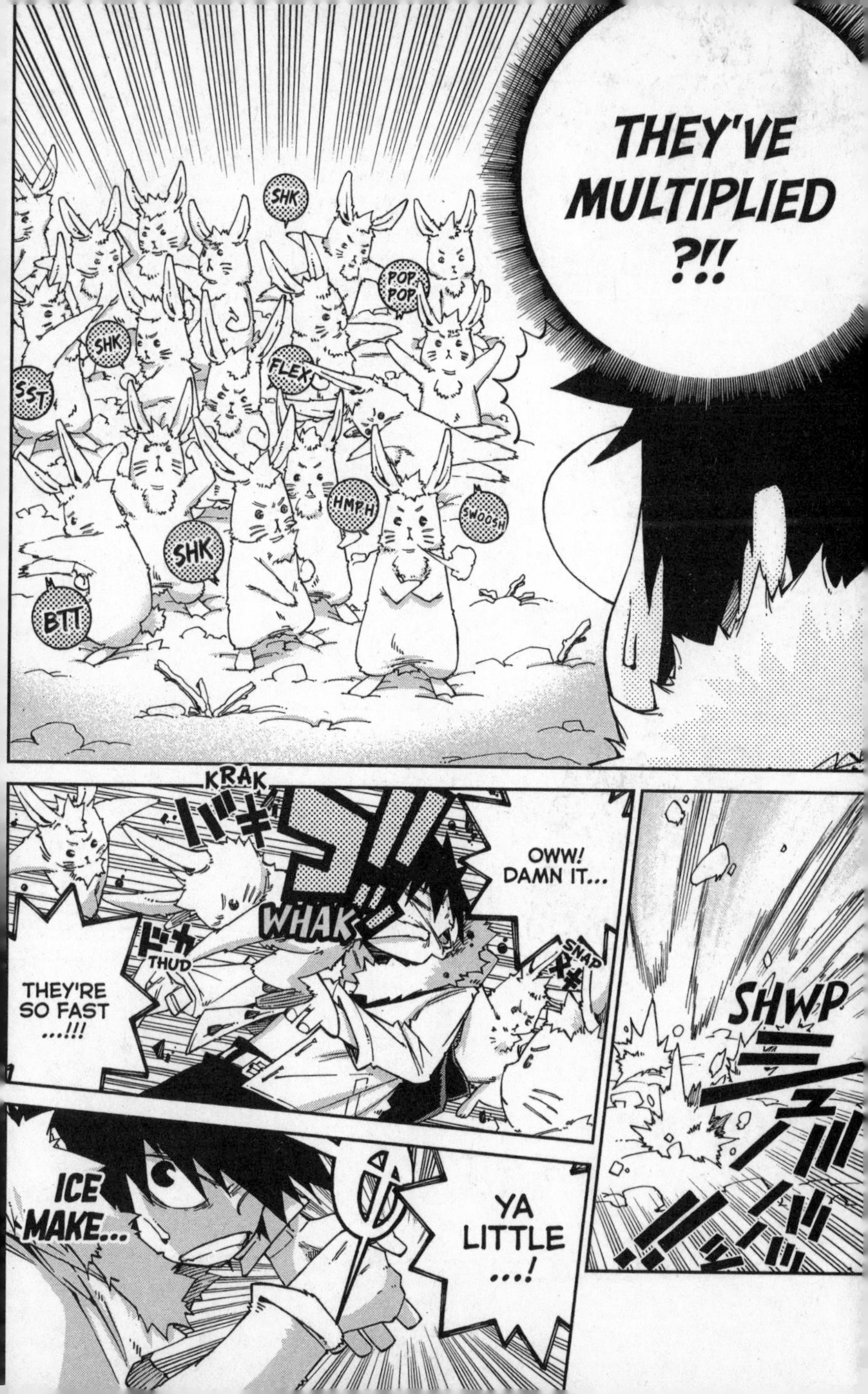
THEY'VE MULTIPLIED ?!!
SHK
POP POP
SWOOSH
HMPH
FLEX
SHK
SHK
SST
BTT
SHWP
OWW! DAMN IT...
KRAK
WHAK
SNAP
THUD
THEY'RE SO FAST ...!!!
YA LITTLE ...!
ICE MAKE...

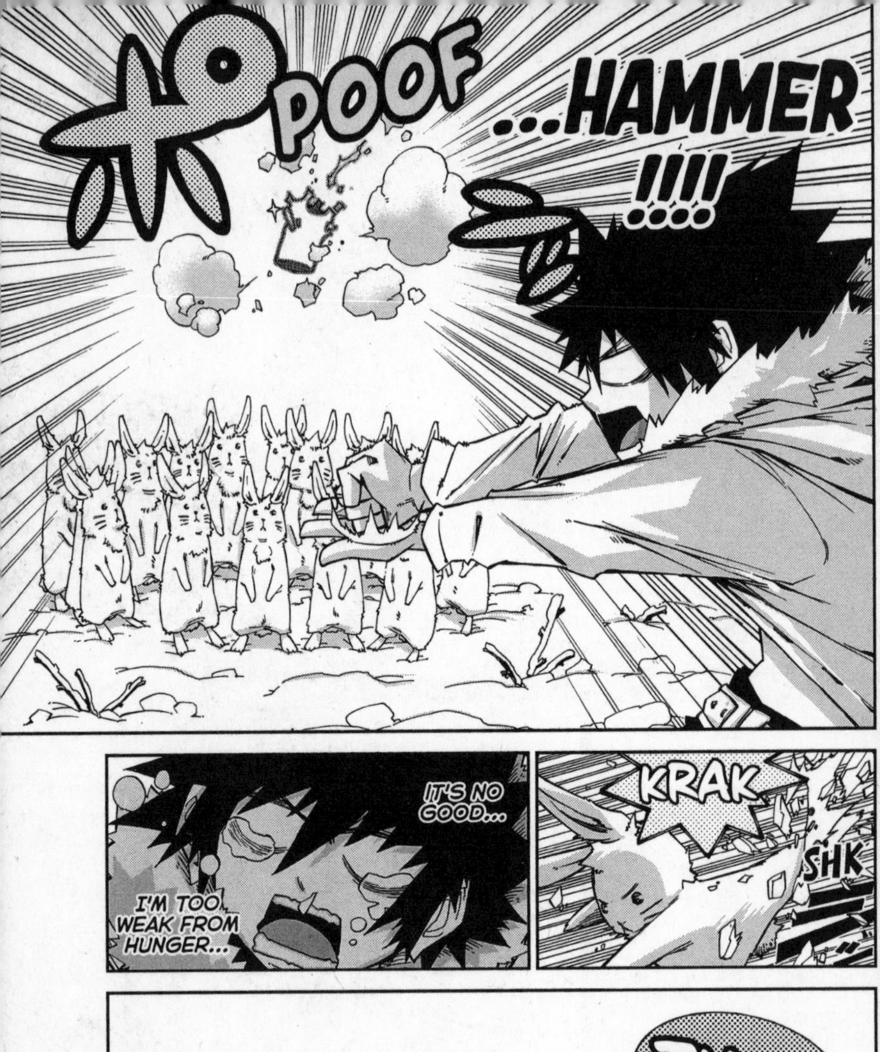
...HAMMER
!!!!
POOF
KRAK
SHK
IT'S NO GOOD...
I'M TOO WEAK FROM HUNGER...
THUD

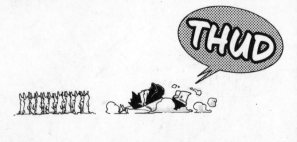

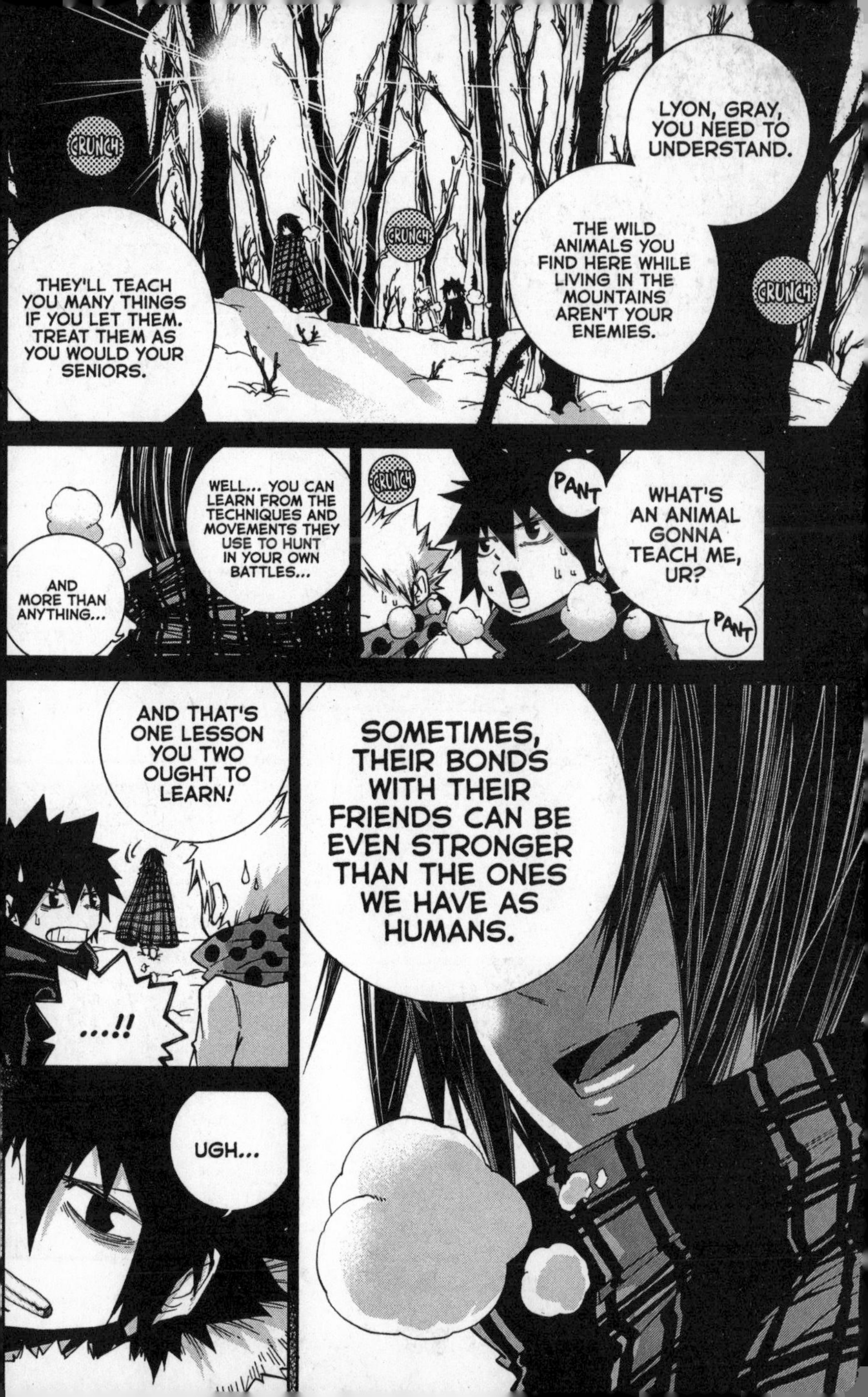
LYON, GRAY, YOU NEED TO UNDERSTAND.
CRUNCH
THE WILD ANIMALS YOU FIND HERE WHILE LIVING IN THE MOUNTAINS AREN'T YOUR ENEMIES.
CRUNCH
CRUNCH
THEY'LL TEACH YOU MANY THINGS IF YOU LET THEM. TREAT THEM AS YOU WOULD YOUR SENIORS.
PANT
WHAT'S AN ANIMAL GONNA TEACH ME, UR?
PANT
CRUNCH
WELL... YOU CAN LEARN FROM THE TECHNIQUES AND MOVEMENTS THEY USE TO HUNT IN YOUR OWN BATTLES...
AND MORE THAN ANYTHING...
SOMETIMES, THEIR BONDS WITH THEIR FRIENDS CAN BE EVEN STRONGER THAN THE ONES WE HAVE AS HUMANS.
AND THAT'S ONE LESSON YOU TWO OUGHT TO LEARN!
...!!
UGH...

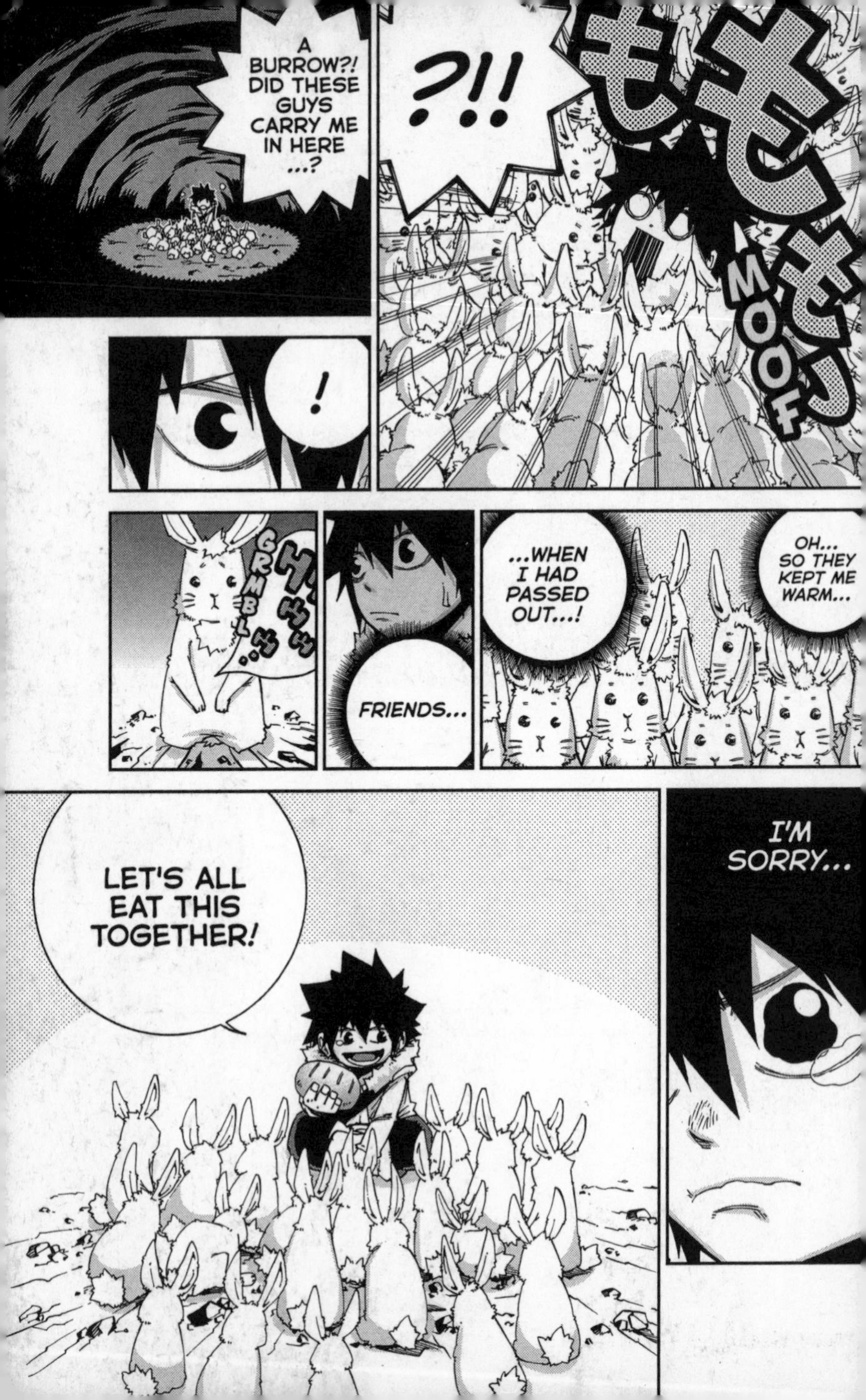
?!!
MOOF
A BURROW?! DID THESE GUYS CARRY ME IN HERE ...?
!
OH... SO THEY KEPT ME WARM...
...WHEN I HAD PASSED OUT...!
FRIENDS...
GRMBL..
I'M SORRY...
LET'S ALL EAT THIS TOGETHER!

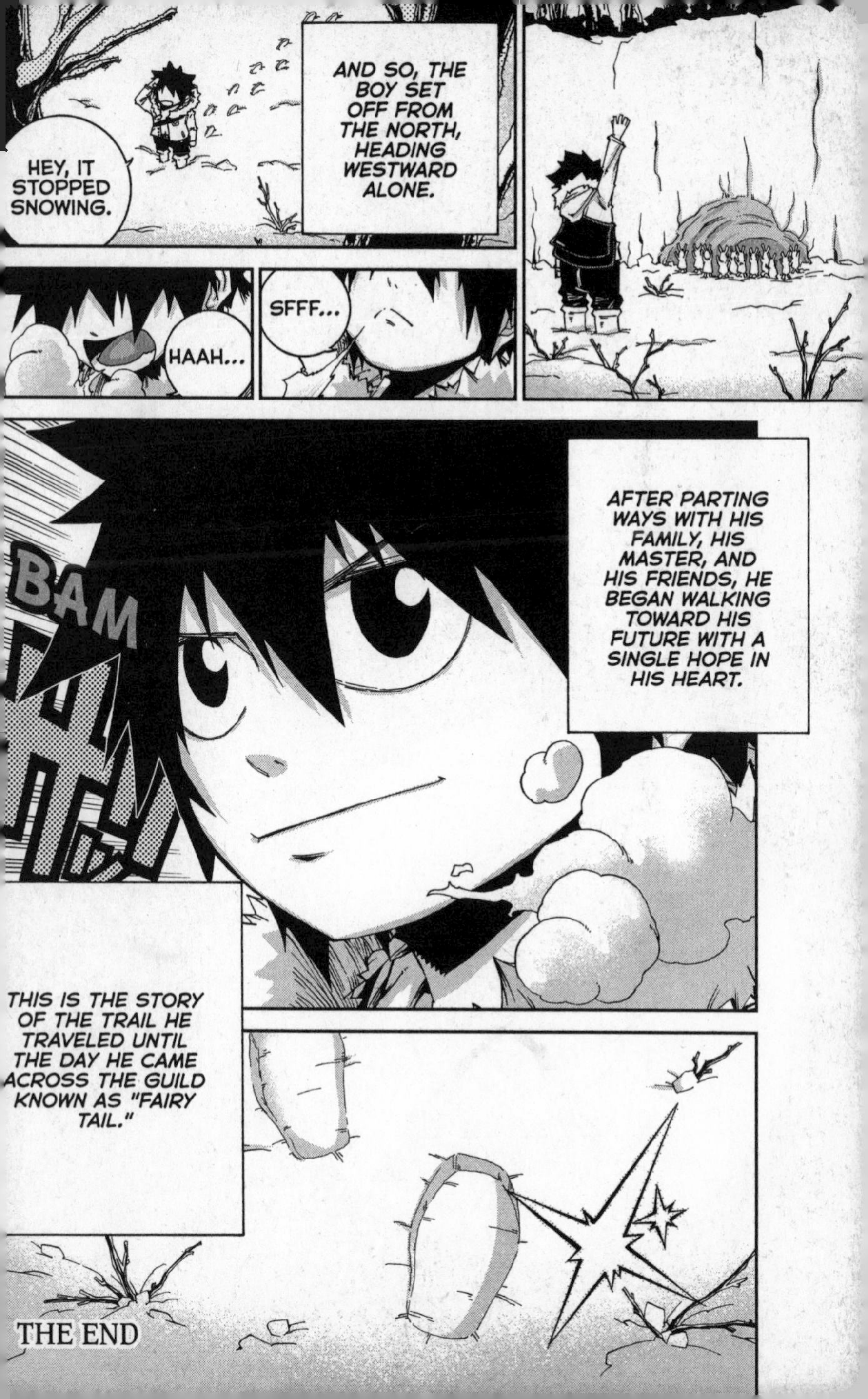

AND SO, THE BOY SET OFF FROM THE NORTH, HEADING WESTWARD ALONE.
HEY, IT STOPPED SNOWING.
SFFF...
HAAH...
AFTER PARTING WAYS WITH HIS FAMILY, HIS MASTER, AND HIS FRIENDS, HE BEGAN WALKING TOWARD HIS FUTURE WITH A SINGLE HOPE IN HIS HEART.
BAM
THIS IS THE STORY OF THE TRAIL HE TRAVELED UNTIL THE DAY HE CAME ACROSS THE GUILD KNOWN AS "FAIRY TAIL."
THE END

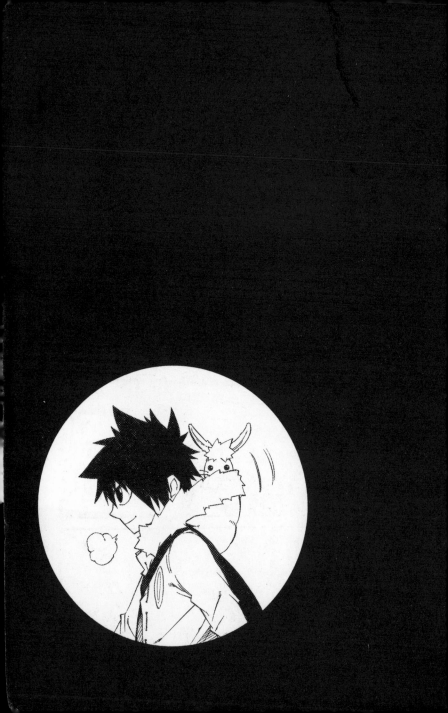

A Kodansha Comics Trade Paperback Original.

Fairy Tail Ice Trail volume 1 copyright © 2015 Hiro Mashima / Yuusuke Shirato
English translation copyright © 2015 Hiro Mashima / Yuusuke Shirato

Published in the United States by Kodansha Comics, an imprint of Kodansha USA Publishing, LLC, New York.

Publication rights for this English edition arranged through Kodansha Ltd., Tokyo.

First published in Japan in 2015 by Kodansha Ltd., Tokyo
ISBN 978-1-63236-283-4

Printed in the United States of America.

www.kodanshacomics.com

9 8 7 6 5 4 3 2 1

Translation: Ko Ransom
Lettering: AndWorld Design
Editing: Ajani Oloye
Kodansha Comics edition cover design by Phil Balsman